PENAL POPULISM, SENTENCING COUNCILS AND SENTENCING POLICY

Editors

Arie Freiberg and Karen Gelb

WILLAN
PUBLISHING

Published in the UK by:
     Willan Publishing
     Culcott House
     Mill Street, Uffculme
     Cullompton, Devon
     EX15 3AT UK
     Tel: + 44(0)1884 840337
     Fax: + 44(0) 1884 840251
     e-mail: info@willanpublishing.co.uk
     website:www.willanpublishing.co.uk

Co-published in Australia by:
     Hawkins Press
     A division of The Federation Press
     PO Box 45, Annandale, NSW, 2038
     71 John St, Leichhardt, NSW, 2040
     Ph (02) 9552 2200 Fax (02) 9552 1681
     E-mail: info@federationpress.com.au
     Website: http://www.federationpress.com.au

First published 2008

Hardback
ISBN 978-1-84392-278-0

Paperback
ISBN 978-1-84392-277-3

British Library Cataloguing-in-Publication Data
A catalogue record for this book is available from the British Library

Text printed on
100% recycled paper

Typeset by The Federation Press, Sydney, NSW, Australia.
   Printed by Ligare Pty Ltd, Sydney, NSW, Australia.

Contents

Contributors   v

Chapter 1
Penal populism, sentencing councils and sentencing policy   1
Arie Freiberg and Karen Gelb

Chapter 2
Sentencing policy and practice: the evolving role of public opinion   15
Julian V Roberts

Chapter 3
Penal scandal in New Zealand   31
John Pratt

Chapter 4
Dealing the public in: challenges for a transparent and
accountable sentencing policy   45
David Indermaur

Chapter 5
Myths and misconceptions: public opinion versus public
judgment about sentencing   68
Karen Gelb

Chapter 6
The Minnesota Sentencing Guidelines   83
Richard S Frase

Chapter 7
The United States Sentencing Commission   103
Judge Nancy Gertner

Chapter 8
English sentencing guidelines in their public and political context   112
Andrew Ashworth

Chapter 9
The New South Wales Sentencing Council   126
The Hon Alan Abadee AM RFD QC

Chapter 10
The Sentencing Commission for Scotland   138
Neil Hutton

Chapter 11
The Victorian Sentencing Advisory Council: incorporating
community views into the sentencing process   148
Arie Freiberg

Chapter 12
A perspective on the work of the Victorian Sentencing Advisory
Council and its potential to promote respect and equality for women   165
Thérèse McCarthy

Chapter 13
Sentencing reform in New Zealand: a proposal to establish a
sentencing council   179
Warren Young

Chapter 14
A sentencing council in South Africa   191
Stephan Terblanche

Chapter 15
A federal sentencing council for Australia   200
Australian Law Reform Commission

Chapter 16
Institutional mechanisms for incorporating the public   205
Neil Hutton

Chapter 17
Does it matter? Reflections on the effectiveness of institutionalised
public participation in the development of sentencing policy   224
Rob Allen and Mike Hough

Index   240

Contributors

Arie Freiberg is the Chair of the Victorian Sentencing Advisory Council. Professor Freiberg is the Dean of Law at Monash University, after spending ten years as the Foundation Chair of Criminology at the University of Melbourne. With degrees in both Law and Criminology, he has focused his academic attention over the years on topics such as sentencing, confiscation of the proceeds of crime, corporate crime, juries, juvenile justice, sanctions and victimology, among other areas of interest. He is Australia's acknowledged expert in the field of sentencing issues and has undertaken extensive research on sentencing theory, policy and practice. In 2002 Professor Freiberg completed a major review of sentencing  for the Victorian Attorney-General, which was published as *Pathways to Justice* (2002). One of the outcomes of this report was the establishment of a Sentencing Advisory Council as an independent statutory body.

Karen Gelb is the Senior Criminologist at the Victorian Sentencing Advisory Council. Dr Gelb obtained her doctorate in Criminology from New York University and is currently the Senior Criminologist for the Sentencing Advisory Council in Victoria, Australia. She spent five years at the National Centre for Crime and Justice Statistics, part of the Australian Bureau of Statistics. Since 2005 Dr Gelb's work at the Sentencing Advisory Council has focused on the issue of public opinion on sentencing, and on developing a suite of methodological tools for the Council's use in measuring public opinion in Victoria. She has also conducted research and policy development work on the issue of detention and supervision of  high-risk offenders. Her publications include *Myths and Misconceptions: Public Opinion versus Public Judgment about Sentencing* (2006) and *Recidivism of Sex Offenders* (2007).

The Hon Alan Abadee AM RFD QC is a former Chair of the New South Wales Sentencing Council and is a retired Judge of the Supreme Court of New South Wales. He was admitted to the Bar in 1964 and appointed one of Her Majesty's Council (QC) in 1984. He was also a Deputy Judge Advocate General of the Australian Defence Force between 1996 and 2000. Mr Abadee was the Chairperson of the Sentencing Council from 2003 until April 2006.

Rob Allen is Director of the International Centre for Prison Studies, King's College, London. Between 2001 and 2005 he was the Director of Rethinking Crime and Punishment, an organisation set up by the Esmeé Fairbairn Foundation to raise the level of debate about prison and alternatives to it. He was previously the Director of Research and Development at the National Association for the Care and Resettlement of Offenders and Head of the Juvenile Offender Policy Unit in the UK Home Office. He was a member of the Youth Justice Board for England and Wales from 1998 to 2006 and has extensive experience of international penal reform work, mainly in the field of juveniles and alternatives to prison. Mr Allen also chairs CLINKS, an umbrella body representing charities working in the criminal justice system in England and Wales.

Andrew Ashworth is the Vinerian Professor of English Law at the University of Oxford. In 1993 Professor Ashworth was elected a Fellow of the British Academy and in 1997 he was appointed a QC *Honoris causa*. In 1999 he was appointed a member of the Sentencing Advisory Panel, and in 2002 he became a member of the Criminal Committee of the Judicial Studies Board. Professor Ashworth has published books on criminal law, sentencing, the criminal process and European human rights law, and pursues a wide range of interests in the field of criminal justice.

The Australian Law Reform Commission (ALRC) is a permanent, independent federal statutory corporation. Established in 1975, the ALRC conducts inquiries into areas of law reform at the request of the Attorney-General of Australia. The ALRC is not under the control of government, giving it the intellectual independence and ability to make research findings and recommendations without fear or favour. ALRC recommendations provide advice to government but do not automatically become law. However, the ALRC has a strong record of having its advice taken up, with nearly 80 per cent of its reports having been either substantially or partially implemented.

Richard Frase is the Benjamin N Berger Professor of Criminal Law at the University of Minnesota Law School where he teaches courses, seminars and clinics in criminal law, criminal procedure, comparative criminal procedure and sentencing. He has also taught several times in exchange programs at French and German law schools. Professor Frase is the author or editor of six books and over 50 articles, essays and chapters on various criminal justice topics. His principal research interests are sentencing reform (especially sentencing guidelines in Minnesota and other States), punishment theory and comparative criminal justice.

Nancy Gertner is a Judge of the United States District Court for the District of Massachusetts. Judge Gertner graduated Barnard College and Yale Law School and received her MA in Political Science at Yale University. She practiced for 23 years as a criminal defence lawyer and a civil rights lawyer. During her career as a practising lawyer, she also taught at Harvard and Boston University. In 1994 she was appointed by President William J Clinton to the United States District Court for the District of Massachusetts. She has continued her teaching at Yale Law School, teaching sentencing for the past six years. In addition, she has taught at Boston College, Northeastern University and University of Iowa. She has been the Charles R Merriam Distinguished Professor at Arizona State Law School and lectured on sentencing throughout the United States. Judge Gertner has been on the faculty of the American Bar Association – Central & Eastern European Law Initiative Advisory Council, and is now on its Advisory Board. She has also lectured on women's rights, human rights and criminal law in China, Vietnam, Cambodia, Turkey and Israel.

Mike Hough is Professor of Criminal Policy at the School of Law, King's College London, and Director of the Institute for Criminal Policy Research. He has published extensively on public attitudes to crime and sentencing and has a long-standing interest in research on policing and police effectiveness. Professor Hough has also written on topics including crime prevention and community safety, anti-social behaviour, probation and drugs. Recent publications include *Surveying Crime in the 21st Century* (with M Maxfield), *Understanding Public Attitudes to Crime* (with J Roberts) and *Mitigation: The Role of Personal Factors in Sentencing* (with J Jacobson).

Neil Hutton is co-Director of the Centre for Sentencing Research at the University of Strathclyde and was a member of the Sentencing Commission for Scotland. Professor Hutton is Dean of the Faculty of Law, Arts and Social Sciences at the University of Strathclyde. He is a leading member of the team that developed the Sentencing Information System for the High Court in Scotland. Recent research projects include a study of public knowledge and attitudes to sentencing and punishment in Scotland, and an examination of social enquiry reports and sentencing funded by the Economic and Social Research Council.

David Indermaur is a Senior Research Fellow at the University of Western Australia Crime Research Centre. Dr Indermaur has a PhD in criminology and has worked in the field of corrections and criminology since 1976, teaching in this field in both Canada and Australia. He has published various articles exploring public perceptions of sentencing since 1987 and was a co-author of *Penal Populism and Public Opinion* published in 2003. His current work is largely centred on the evaluation of therapeutic jurisprudence, offender treatment and crime prevention initiatives.

Thérèse McCarthy is the Deputy Chair of the Victorian Sentencing Advisory Council. Ms McCarthy has a long history of involvement with community organisations such as Centres Against Sexual Assault and other Victorian domestic violence and community legal services. She has worked to enhance the relationship between courts and the community in her role as the inaugural Director, Community Relations, Federal Court of Australia and as the Executive Director of Court Network, a Victorian support organisation. Ms McCarthy was an adviser to the Victim and Witness Unit at the International Criminal Tribunal for the Former Yugoslavia, training support staff in sensitive witness assistance procedures. She has also worked with Amnesty International in Papua New Guinea and, as adviser to the Public Prosecutor there, she assisted in the development and delivery of training programs that implemented new legislation protecting victims in rape trials and improving the understanding of rape law. Ms McCarthy has published in the areas of rape law reform, victim impact statements and "battered woman syndrome".

John Pratt is Professor of Criminology and Reader in Criminology at Victoria University of Wellington, New Zealand. He has published extensively in the field of punishment and corrections, most notably the book *Punishment and Civilization* (2002), and his work has been translated into French and Spanish. Dr Pratt was Editor of the *Australian and New Zealand Journal of Criminology* from 1997 to 2005. His most recent publication is the book *Penal Populism* (2007).

Julian V Roberts is a Professor of Criminology, Faculty of Law, University of Oxford and Assistant Director, Centre for Criminology, University of Oxford. Professor Roberts has explored various empirical and theoretical issues in the area of sentencing and has conducted many original research studies in the field of public opinion, crime and criminal justice. His books include *Punishing Persistent Offenders* (Oxford University Press, forthcoming, 2008); *Understanding Public Attitudes to Criminal Justice* (2005, with M Hough); *The Virtual Prison* (2004); *Public Opinion and Penal Populism* (2003, with M Hough, D Indermaur and L Stalans); *Changing Attitudes to Punishment* (2002, with M Hough) and *Public Opinion, Crime and Criminal Justice* (2001, with L Stalans).

Stephan Terblanche is Professor of Law at the College of Law at the University of South Africa. He was appointed in the Department of Criminal and Procedural Law in 1992, after a career as a magistrate. His research and teaching experience centres on sentencing, with the law of evidence as a secondary interest. Professor Terblanche is the author of the current standard textbook on sentencing in South Africa: *A Guide to Sentencing in South Africa* 2nd edn (2007). His recent articles in South African law journals have focused in detail on the mandatory sentencing scheme that has been in place in South Africa since 1998, as well as the need for sentencing guidelines in that country.

Warren Young is the Deputy President of the New Zealand Law Commission. Dr Young was appointed a full-time Law Commissioner for a term of three years from 3 May 2004. He was appointed Deputy President from 23 May 2005. Prior to that he was Deputy Secretary for Justice for four years, with responsibility for criminal law, criminal justice and crime prevention. From 1980 to 2000, Dr Young was Director of the Institute of Criminology and then a Professor of Law at Victoria University of Wellington. He also served as Assistant Vice Chancellor (Research) for five years. He was a Fulbright Fellow in 1985 and has been a co-author of *Adams on Criminal Law* since 1992.

1

Penal populism,
sentencing councils and sentencing policy

Arie Freiberg and Karen Gelb

Introduction

This book is the product of a conference held in Melbourne, Australia in July 2006 that brought together members of the public, public servants, criminologists, judicial officers and members of sentencing advisory boards, panels, councils or commissions from around the world to discuss the relationship between politics, public opinion and the development of sentencing policy, but with particular reference to the role of these emergent advisory bodies.

A decade ago such a conference would not have taken place. While sentencing commissions have been in existence in the United States since the late 1970s, when the Minnesota Sentencing Guidelines Commission was established (Frase, Chapter 6), their primary rationale was the structuring of sentencing discretion. This need arose following years of criticism of indeterminate and unfettered sentencing and administrative discretion in relation to sentencing and parole release decisions.

There are currently 19 sentencing commissions in the United States at State and federal levels whose primary role is to create, monitor or advise on sentencing guidelines for the courts, though more have been established and not survived. As Frase notes, they vary widely "in their purposes, design, scope, and operation" (Frase, Chapter 6). The creation of similar councils or panels in England in 1998 (Sentencing Advisory Panel; Ashworth, Chapter 8) and 2003 (Sentencing Guidelines Council) and Scotland in 2003 (Sentencing Commission for Scotland; Hutton, Chapter 10) was a major development in these jurisdictions where judicial sentencing discretion has been more constrained than in the United States and where there has been a long tradition of appellate review.

There is an abundance of literature on sentencing commissions, sentencing guidelines and sentencing discretion that traverses significant issues such as the distribution of sentencing authority between the legislature, the judiciary and executive bodies, the scope and nature of discretion, the relationship between sentencing commissions and the legislature, the constitutionality of guidelines and other matters. The purpose of the conference was not to rehearse these issues, important as they are, but to examine these bodies through a different conceptual lens, namely the relationship between "the public", public opinion, and the development of sentencing policy.

Most of the sentencing councils discussed in this book were born out of a paradoxical political and social environment. While the early development of the

Minnesota Sentencing Guidelines Commission presaged the more recent explosion of such bodies, these more recent councils have arisen during a fraught period in our history. The judiciary is coming under increasing attack as the public claims a greater voice in the criminal justice system; politicians feel that elections cannot be won without a tough "law and order" stance; yet, paradoxically, crime rates are decreasing.

As a response to the many crises that inevitably arise within such a complex environment, sentencing councils have been established around the world. As Freiberg (Chapter 11) notes:

> In the sometimes heated political environment in which debates about senten-
> cing policy may take place, the Council can play a useful role in defusing
> issues by taking on contentious matters and considering them in a calmer
> atmosphere and over a longer period when some of the emotion produced by
> the original event has dissipated.

Chapters 6 through 14 of this book introduce us to the key purposes, functions and roles of the various sentencing councils. They were all created with a long-term function of defusing political crises and of attempting to balance the various interests of the judiciary, the public, politicians and the media.

The emergence of sentencing councils

The particular impetus for this conference was the emergence of newer bodies in New South Wales in 2003 and Victoria in 2004 whose purpose was not solely to develop sentencing guidelines, but to deal with sentencing matters more broadly and to involve a wider range of parties in the development of sentencing policy. In particular, the Victorian Sentencing Advisory Council was established following a review that was specifically required to consider whether there were mechanisms that could be adopted to incorporate more adequately community views into the sentencing process (Freiberg, Chapter 11).

The reasons underlying this change of focus in the creation and functions of sentencing advisory bodies are important. As both Hutton and Pratt (Chapter 3; Pratt, 2007) note, the past three decades have seen a shift in the governance of public affairs "away from a directive and paternalistic State to the vision of a State that enables public and private organisations to collaborate" (Hutton, Chapter 16). This is evident in a number of areas of public policy, of which the criminal justice system is only one. It has been driven by many factors including the delegitimi-sation of both the judiciary and "experts" and the rising influence of the media.

David Garland has identified several currents of social change that have affected the development of penal policy and that are relevant to our discussion of penal populism and the role of sentencing councils in the development of senten-cing policy. These broad currents include: the decreased importance of rehabili-tation in penal institutions; the reappearance of retribution as a generalised policy goal; the increased salience of public fear of crime as a characteristic of contem-porary culture; the new and urgent emphasis on protecting the public; the public loss of confidence in criminal justice; and the development of a highly charged political discourse around crime and justice (Garland, 2001, pp 8-20).

Pratt (Chapter 3) identifies a number of underlying causes that he considers to have brought about the dramatic changes to the distribution of penal authority: the decline of deference to authority or establishment figures, including the courts; the decline in trust in politicians and existing political processes; the effect of globalisation, which has weakened "the authority of sovereign states which makes them seem vulnerable to external organizations and forces"; the growth of "ontological insecurity" or general fear and anxiety, possibly fuelled by the increased crime rates between the 1960s and 1980s; the role of the media in misreporting the true nature and levels of crime and punishment; and, finally, the democratisation of news media, which has provided the opportunity for the emotive experiences and opinions of ordinary people to become the framework through which crime and punishment is understood. In his chapter Pratt illustrates these forces in the New Zealand context, showing how the "emotive, ad hoc and volatile forces of populism can now override scientific expertise and the rationalities of penal bureaucracies".

Public opinion

Public opinion, however defined, has clearly become more salient. As Michael Tony has noted, "sentencing matters" (Tonry, 1996). Since Professor Anthony Bottoms coined the term "populist punitiveness" in 1993 (Bottoms, 1995), the discourse concerning the relationship between politicians, the public, public opinion and sentencing policy has been more focused by bringing together the literature on public opinion with that of the development of sentencing policy (Roberts, Chapter 2). "Populist punitiveness" is a phrase that pervaded the conference. Bottoms used the term not to refer to public opinion per se, but rather "the notion of politicians tapping into, and using for their own purposes, what they believe to be the public's generally punitive stance" (Bottoms, 1995, p 40). Populist punitiveness, Bottoms argued, was not only crucial to an understanding of the increasing imprisonment rates characteristic of a number of Western countries, but was embedded in a number of other social changes characterising modernity, one of the most important of which is a widespread sense of insecurity into which politicians feel free to tap.

The impact on sentencing law of public opinion, mediated or unmediated, is clearly evident across the jurisdictions surveyed. In all of them, laws such as sex offender registration and community notification schemes, "three strikes and you're out" provisions, and increased mandatory minimum and maximum sentences have been introduced as legislative responses to a perceived punitive public (Freiberg, Chapter 11).

Most of these initiatives have not come from law reform commissions, parliamentary committees or other governmental advisory bodies; they have come from public pressure expressed sometimes directly on the streets, more often through the print and electronic media, through political pressure directly applied to political parties and indirectly through the ballot box at election time and, in some countries, through propositions placed on ballots and similar citizen-initiated referendum processes (Pratt, Chapter 3). Whereas law reform has traditionally been the province of technical experts and public officials, mediated through the parliamentary political process, over the past few decades the dynamic of law reform has altered and, in the area of sentencing, it appears to have become less technical and more demotic or more democratic.

Some of the changes effected through these means have been large and profound. Some have been short-lived and ineffective. Some have signalled major shifts in sentencing philosophy and practices while others have proved to be counterproductive. In most of these jurisdictions, prison populations have burgeoned, with the attendant burden on the public purse. Bending to the perceived punitive desires of the public may be electorally popular, but it comes with high financial and social costs.

What is the significance of this? Pratt (Chapter 3) suggests that these changes are "symptomatic of a new axis of power which has come into play and which significantly reorganises both the terms of penal debate and who is allowed to contribute to this" – that popular commonsense has become a "privileged driver of policy". There is little value in criticising politicians for being "political" or for listening to their constituents; politicians in a democracy have a duty to be responsive to the public. Public opinion defines the boundaries of what is acceptable (and therefore possible) in public life. As Roberts notes: "There is general agreement that the criminal justice system should be responsive to the community that it was created to protect", a fact also noted by the Halliday review of sentencing in the United Kingdom (Roberts, Chapter 2).

The difficulties in determining the nature and relevance of "public opinion" in relation to sentencing form the first part of this book. The work (over many decades) of Roberts, Doob, Hough, Indermaur and others has explored methodological problems in gauging public opinion and has reported on public attitudes to issues such as the adequacy of sentences, the principles of punishment and other sentencing issues (for a brief overview of this body of work, see Gelb, Chapter 5). Time and again, researchers have emphasised the importance of distinguishing between "the findings of social scientific public opinion research and more volatile impressions of public mood, usually based on newspaper headlines or the like" (Pratt, Chapter 3), between "attitudes" and "judgments" and between hastily formed views and deliberated responses to properly contextualised questions (Indermaur, Chapter 4; Gelb, Chapter 5). In particular, the extensive body of evidence built by these researchers has convincingly shown that people who seem to be punitive when asked for "top-of-the-head" responses to simplistic, abstract questions, become far less punitive when allowed to provide a considered, thoughtful response to more detailed information about a specific case. This is the difference between mass "public opinion" and informed "public judgment".

Even if "public opinion", or preferably "public judgment", can be ascertained in relation to a particular sentencing issue, should it be relevant to court decision-making, to institutional decision-making and to the political process? If so, how? Roberts (Chapter 2) poses two fundamental questions in relation to the courts:

(1) To what extent should courts consider public opinion when imposing sentence?

(2) Are community views a legitimate *general* consideration at sentencing?

Roberts notes the tension present in the relationship between community views and the determination of sentence. On the one hand, courts are expected to impose sentences that are not radically inconsistent with public expectations. On the other hand, public opinion is not a legally recognised factor at sentencing. Reviewing the evidence from the United Kingdom and Canada, he does not find any conclusive evidence that sentencing trends – that is, individual sentencing decisions or aggregate sentencing trends such as prison populations – reflect changes in public opinion. However, at the political or sentencing policy level, he finds stronger evidence that public opinion has influenced the evolution of sentencing policy, particularly following moral panics or extensive media coverage of an emotive issue. In such instances, policy shifts have exhibited a certain asymmetry, moving in a more punitive direction to reflect the views of an allegedly punitive public.

The distinction between individual sentencing decisions (both at first instance and on appeal) and sentencing policy is not necessarily well understood by the public. Individual sentencing involves a decision to allocate a sanction in a specific instance, while sentencing policy relates to issues concerning the relation-ship between legislatures, the courts, the executive and sentencing commissions/councils. In both instances, the public expects a certain degree of responsiveness. Sentencing decisions and sentencing policy that are made outside the framework of community perceptions are seen as being "out of touch". Chief Justice Murray Gleeson of the High Court of Australia addressed this issue in a speech to the Judicial Conference of Australia Colloquium in October 2004. It is particularly useful to consider his comments, as opportunities to hear directly from judges themselves on issues of public opinion are rare.

The Chief Justice begins by accepting that judges are expected to know, and be conspicuously responsive to, community values (Gleeson, 2004, p 1). But he then poses a series of questions that is immediately relevant for our discussion of the role of sentencing councils in the development of sentencing policy:

> How should judges keep in touch? Should they employ experts to undertake regular surveys of public opinion? Should they develop techniques for obtaining feedback from lawyers or litigants? And what kind of opinion should be of concern to them? Any opinion, informed or uninformed? What level of knowledge and understanding of a problem qualifies people to have opinions that ought to influence judicial decision-making? Who exactly is it that judges ought to be in touch with? …Whose values should we know and reflect?

Chief Justice Gleeson's questions reflect the difficult role faced by sentencing councils around the world. Regardless of their specific remit, councils that are obliged to consider community views when developing their guidelines or their policy advice are faced with the precise challenges illustrated by the Chief Justice. Overcoming these challenges is a critical function of sentencing councils, especially in the current climate of low public confidence in both the criminal justice system in general and the courts in particular.

Public confidence

Public attitudes to the courts and the criminal justice system as institutions are crucial to an understanding of the shifts in sentencing power between the legis-lature, the courts and the executive, but particularly away from courts through the use of mandatory and minimum sentences and strict sentencing guidelines. Both Indermaur (Chapter 4) and Pratt (Chapter 3) refer to a crisis of confidence or legitimacy in the courts, but suggest that the problem is chronic rather than acute. Indeed, public confidence in the courts has been consistently lower than levels of confidence in the police, prisons or the criminal justice system as a whole for many decades. The status of judges and the courts has gradually been eroded by constant media polls and reports that the courts are "soft on crime" and therefore failing to protect the community. Roberts (Chapter 2) notes that, in England, some newspapers have published the names and photographs of "soft" judges who are accused of failing their duty to their community. Canadian legislation has introduced the notion of a "judicial registry" that will record sentences imposed and allow people to identify "lenient" judges – those who impose sentences far below the statutory maximum.

The problem of public confidence in the courts is, of course, wider than the problems of sentencing. A conference held in Canberra, Australia in February 2007 on this topic[1] identified other factors that also contribute to what is perceived to be a major issue for the modern judiciary. These included: issues of judicial appointment, demeanour and accountability; perceptions of outcome and process expressed by victims of crime; the role of the media; the adversarial nature of the process; and the ability of courts to explain themselves to the public.

This issue forms the foundation for the work of many of the sentencing councils discussed in this book. Indermaur (Chapter 4) suggests that the primary rationale for formalising public input into sentencing policy remains political: "Where the judgments of the court appear to disregard public sensitivities there is good copy for the media, ammunition for the opposition and trouble for the government". But Roberts (Chapter 2) notes that the desire on the part of legislatures to establish stronger links between the criminal justice system and the community is consistent with a broader movement to make public services more responsive to the communities they serve. In conjunction with greater community consultation comes a need for greater community education about the principles and practices of sentencing. Roberts (Chapter 2) suggests that "the challenge to sentencing commissions and legislatures is clear: to ensure some degree of community engagement in the sentencing process without descending into populist punitiveness".

Recognising that public opinion is influential in the development of sentencing policy, the Victorian government invested the Sentencing Advisory Council with the statutory function of gauging public opinion. Gelb's chapter (Chapter 5) reports on a project by the Council:

> [T]o ascertain and analyse the current state of knowledge about public opinion on sentencing on both a national and international level. The project was designed to examine and critically evaluate both the substantive issues in the area (what we know about public opinion on sentencing) and the methodological issues in this field (how we measure public opinion on sentencing).

The purpose of the project was to create a range of methodological tools that could be used by the Council to gauge public opinion in relation to the various sentencing issues that form the core of its work. The project was significant because of its attempt to collect, summarise, interpret and disseminate a large amount of academic literature to a broader public and professional audience who would not be acquainted with it. The ensuing report (Gelb, 2006) has been well received in Victoria, particularly by judicial officers, who find it useful to validate their own intuitions and understandings and to provide them with information they otherwise would not have time to obtain. The report is one of the most frequently accessed on the Council's website, indicating a broad interest in public perceptions of sentencing.

Public opinion polls and other survey methodologies are only some of the tools used to gauge public views and attitudes. Public opinion can be ascertained through formal consultative mechanisms, law reform bodies, referenda or plebiscites, through jury sentencing and the work of lay magistrates. Over recent years, victims' views have been recognised and institutionalised through representation on parole boards and other release authorities with determinative, rather than advisory, powers alone.

Sentencing advisory bodies

The next step in the process of recognising broader community views has been the establishment of advisory bodies such as sentencing councils and law reform bodies with public membership. Ashworth (2005) and others have argued that because the current system of developing sentencing policy has produced a "democratic deficit" it is necessary to broaden the range of "perspective, expertise and experience that is required for a robust sentencing policy that is acceptable to the community" (cited in Hutton, Chapter 16).

Part 2 of this book examines the role of advisory councils, commissions, panels or boards in the development of sentencing policy with a view to exploring their relationship with the community rather than the courts. It provides an overview of the way in which the public, and public opinion, have been formally incorporated into the development of sentencing policy.

Chapters 6 to 14 provide detailed information on the background and operation of existing bodies (the United States Federal Sentencing Commission and those in Minnesota, England and Wales, New South Wales and Victoria), proposed bodies (in both South Africa and New Zealand) and Scotland's defunct sentencing body. Chapter 15 provides an extract from a report by the Australian Law Reform Commission (2006) which rejected the establishment of a federal sentencing council on the grounds that the work of such a council was already being, or could be carried out, by other existing bodies.

There are similarities among these sentencing councils: all occupy a place somewhere between the legislature, the executive and the judiciary, and all act to some degree as a buffer between public and media calls for punitive responses to crises and a more considered legislative response. But what is striking about these various councils is their heterogeneity, which is not surprising given that they have been developed for different purposes at different times and in different political, cultural and legal contexts. As a result they vary on dimensions such as terms of reference, membership and consultation.

Some of the sentencing bodies discussed in this book are statutory, some administrative, some permanent, some temporary. Bodies that are required to develop guidelines may have an ongoing remit, while others such as the Sentencing Commission for Scotland were designed from the start to have a limited lifespan. Others will likely continue to exist as long as the government of the day finds them politically and socially useful – it is presumed that they will continue to operate until such time as they are no longer deemed necessary.

Some of the bodies are appointed by the executive, some by more formal means. None is democratically elected. There are significant differences in the relationships between commissions and the legislature, particularly in the United States, and between commissions and the courts, both sentencing courts and courts of appeal. Some must report through the executive (such as in New South Wales) while others can report directly to the community (Victoria).

The specified functions of the councils vary according to the degree of delegation of authority accorded them in legislation. Some can initiate references themselves while others can only respond to requests from the executive or the courts.

Terms of reference vary widely between bodies and include:

- issuing or advising on guidelines or standard non-parole periods;
- monitoring of adherence or departure from guidelines;
- considering the cost or effectiveness of sentences;
- considering the relationship between sentencing and prison populations;
- advising governments;
- gauging public opinion;
- educating the public;
- collecting and analysing statistics;
- conducting research generally; and
- consulting with government, the public and interested parties.

Some of these terms of reference have a more pragmatic focus, such as examining the costs of various sentencing options or the impact of sentences on corrective services, while others allow for a broader investigation of sentencing issues via general research and consultation.

Membership of these bodies varies widely in scope and balance. Some are heavily weighted towards judicial members (Sentencing Guidelines Council, United Kingdom), while others have none (Sentencing Advisory Council, Victoria). Non-judicial members include: victims' representatives; community members; people with experience in the criminal justice system (in areas such as risk assessment, reintegration of offenders into society and the impact of the criminal justice system on minorities); prosecution and defence lawyers; academics; corrections personnel; and sometimes legislators. Some members are appointed to be formal representatives of organisations or interest groups, others as individuals who have a particular background. As Hutton notes, membership rarely includes people with no background or experience with the criminal justice system at all, that is, truly a member of the "general public". "Public", in this context, tends to mean "non-legal".

Councils, governments and the public

The relationships between public opinion and governments, and between councils and non-government organisations, are complex. Most sentencing councils have formal or informal mechanisms for consulting with the public. Some recognise that sentencing communication is not a one-way process: if public opinion is to be taken into account in the development of sentencing policy, then it should be "informed". Accordingly, if public opinion is to be valued, then governments, councils, non-government organisations and even academia all have a responsibility to be involved in providing the public with information about the operation of the criminal justice system. This was the primary focus of the *Rethinking Crime and Punishment* project in the United Kingdom that commenced in 2001, which is referred to in Indermaur's chapter (Chapter 4) and is discussed by Allen and Hough (Chapter 17). It is also an important part of the work of the Victorian Sentencing Advisory Council (Freiberg, Chapter 11) and, since 2006, the New South Wales Sentencing Council (Abadee, Chapter 9).

The two American commissions discussed in this volume were designed to deal with the problem of sentence guidance rather than with incorporating the public into the sentencing policy process, though indirectly they were responses to crises in confidence in the sentencing process itself. The authors of the chapters on Minnesota (Frase, Chapter 6) and the United States Sentencing Commission (Gertner, Chapter 7) were asked to reflect on the issue of public involvement rather than on sentencing guidelines per se, and their contributions illustrate the secondary role that this aspect has had on the work of these bodies.

Frase reflects on the desired balance between public and professional dominance of sentencing policy formulation, and concludes that, ultimately, "each jurisdiction must decide, in light of its traditions and current conditions, how to balance democratic values and public participation with fair and rational sentencing policy formulation". Gertner notes that the United States Sentencing Commission was designed "to do what Congress had been unable to do, namely resist public pressure to punish disproportionately whatever the 'crime du jour' happened to be". She goes on to highlight the ironic reality that came to be – that the public "was not remotely as punitive, remotely as vengeful ... as Guideline sentences required".

The English Sentencing Advisory Panel was the first to be established outside the United States (in the English speaking jurisdictions). As Ashworth notes (Chapter 8), its primary purpose was to draft sentencing guidelines, consult widely on them and advise the Court of Appeal. Its work, and that of the Sentencing Guidelines Council, is thus focused on the structuring of sentencing discretion through guidelines. The major issues are not so much the role of such bodies vis á vis the community, but the relationships between the courts, Parliament, the executive and the Council/Panel in relation to the creation of guidelines and determining appeals. In this instance the "democratic deficit" was remedied by giving Parliament a great role in scrutinising draft guidelines, rather than by including more community representatives in their memberships.

Ashworth describes the process of consultation with organisations that the Panel is required to consult, as well as with others who might be particularly interested in the topic of the guideline under consideration. He concludes that:

The English guideline system places a considerable premium on ascertaining the opinions of members of the public. In the first place, three of the members of the Panel are members of the public who have no other connection to the criminal justice system. Secondly, the Panel conducts a wide public consultation on its provisional proposals. Thirdly, the Panel occasionally commissions research on public attitudes to specific kinds of crime. And fourthly, the Council also conducts a public consultation on its draft proposals for guidelines. Whether the frequency of consulting the public translates into greater public influence on the formulation of guidelines and, ultimately, on sentencing practice is difficult to assess. Most of the responses to consultations, and often the most closely reasoned responses, come from legal organisations or from individuals involved in the sentencing process (be it judges, barristers, police officers, probation officers or magistrates). But the consultation and research on rape demonstrates that the attitudes of the public (including victims) can have a significant effect.

The second council to be established outside the United States was that in New South Wales in 2002 and, as its first Chair notes, it "was no mere copy or mimic of any sentencing body, council or commission that had been earlier established overseas" (Abadee, Chapter 9). The Council was created as part of a package of sentencing reforms responding to public disquiet over what were perceived to be inadequate sentences, and its main task was to establish a scheme of standard minimum sentences for a number of serious offences. This form of sentence was a response to calls for mandatory minimum sentences that would have more severely constrained judicial discretion. The involvement of the public in the development of sentencing policy and the expectation that this would bolster public confidence in the sentencing process was another, albeit subsidiary reason for its creation. Abadee concludes that the Council has indeed "contributed to the strengthening of public acceptance and understanding of the sentencing process and the maintenance of confidence in that process".

The third body to be established outside the United States, the Sentencing Commission for Scotland, had limited terms of reference and a limited lifespan, both reflecting Scottish political accommodations at the time (Hutton, Chapter 10). As Hutton observes, the driving force was not the broad purpose of increasing public involvement but the delivery of a series of reports that could fit into the government's legislative program. Its public input was limited and when it completed its reports it quietly went out of existence. Hutton argues that the case of Scotland "shows very well how the work of a sentencing institution can be subject to the pressure of political forces". He concludes that "absolute independence is impossible and the precise contours of independence will depend on local political and cultural conditions". Despite a recommendation for the creation of a new body to promote sentencing reform in Scotland, nothing has eventuated.

The Victorian Sentencing Advisory Council (Freiberg, Chapter 11; McCarthy, Chapter 12) was also the product of a long political process, partly concerned with sentencing discretion and the role of the courts, and partly with political legitimacy and responsiveness to the community. A dominant reason for its establishment was that it would be a mechanism to incorporate community views into the sentencing process: it is probably singular in this respect. Compared to most of the other bodies, its terms of reference are broader and its independence of the courts and the executive greater. Its summary aim – to "bridge the gap between the community, the courts and government by informing, educating and advising on sentencing issues" – encapsulates this unusual role. As Freiberg (Chapter 11) concludes:

> The Council is an experiment in the incorporation and institutionalisation of diverse voices in the development of sentencing policy, both through its constitution and its processes. Though such a body can never be truly representative, its representation is wider than many similar councils and its legitimacy, if it has some, derives from this diversity. It also derives from the perhaps vain attempt to ground sentencing policy in empirical evidence, research, thorough and considered deliberation of options and respectful consideration of professional and community views.

The New Zealand Law Commission had the advantage of reviewing the experiences of all of the other bodies and fashioning one suitable for its polity while addressing the problems of its criminal justice system. Young (Chapter 13) outlines the proposal for a Council in New Zealand that is primarily concerned with sentencing guidelines. The proposed guidelines would be based not on the "grid" systems common in the United States, but instead on the work of the Sentencing Guidelines Council in the United Kingdom, with guidelines being created for specific offence types. The proposal was made against the backdrop of a rapidly increasing prison population, community disenfranchisement and a "perhaps misguided belief that the judiciary who have been responsible for determining sentence severity are out of touch with the public mood". While the Council is not intended to be representative of the community in terms of its membership, it is envisaged that it will undertake extensive public consultation and parliamentary approval processes for each of its draft guidelines. The purpose of such consultation is to achieve the community confidence that derives from a sense of enfranchisement.

The South African Law Reform Commission's proposal for a Sentencing Council for South Africa has never been acted upon (Terblanche, Chapter 14). In form and purpose, it was closest to the United States and English bodies, with a focus on the production of sentencing guidelines. The proposed shifting of sentencing authority from the courts to an independent body was probably too radical a move. As Terblanche notes, the Commission did not address the role of public opinion, rather, it "was happy that public opinion could be expressed through the various institutions that could compel the Council into establishing or revising guidelines, and through the fact that the general public is entitled to approach the Council towards the same purpose". With regard to sentencing commissions and councils more generally, Terblanche concludes that one needs to "remain realistic about the extent to which they can transform sentencing practices". Indeed, as Michael Tonry has observed, "there have been many more failed sentencing commissions than successful ones" (Tonry, 1991, p 314; cited in Terblanche, Chapter 14).

Legitimation, blame shifting or policy buffer?

In his chapter Indermaur argues that the problems of sentencing generally and the legitimacy of the criminal justice system will not be solved by involving the public in the process of developing sentencing policy, especially through sentencing councils. He suggests that the involvement of public members on councils, in addition to processes of public consultation, can only be cynical symbolic exercises in participation without substantive effect, aimed at "defending, embellishing or reinforcing existing power arrangements" (Indermaur, Chapter 4). The term "public education", in his view, is a cipher for bringing the public around to the correct way of thinking, for doing things "to" rather than "with" the public. For Indermaur, sentencing councils are a limited form of interest group pluralism, not genuine public participation.

His argument has a number of elements. First, that public confidence in the criminal justice system can be maintained without public involvement. Secondly, he argues that current methods of public consultation and participation in relation to sentencing are simplistic and inadequate and that the methodologies that have been employed in other areas of public controversy could be employed in this context. Indermaur then outlines those elements of the process that can properly include the public in policy formulation (Indermaur, Chapter 4):

> [A] well thought out consultation strategy; accurate, sensible and comprehensive measures of public preferences; integration of public preferences with existing and proposed sentencing frameworks; and publication of the results in a way that is accessible to all.

Hutton (Chapter 16) argues that sentencing bodies may perform a wider range of functions than merely involving the public or broadening the formal inputs into the development of sentencing policy. These functions include: legitimation (the decisions of a broader body, following an inclusive consultative process are more likely to be accepted than unilateralist, secretive, executive decisions); blame shifting and credit claiming (if it fails it is the fault of the council/commission; if it succeeds, it shows the wisdom of the government); cost containment; and political crisis management. This last function is noted by both Abadee in New South Wales (Chapter 9) and Freiberg in Victoria (Chapter 11). Abadee writes:

> [I]n circumstances where a controversial sentencing issue arises, an opportunity exists for the Council to be utilised to deal with it by the Minister seeking its reports or views. This may have the advantage of neutralising the sensational or emotive issue, allowing time for calm informed consideration of such an issue and avoiding a reactive or potentially unprincipled response to an issue that may be stoked by media reporting.

The concept of sentencing councils acting in this way as "policy buffers" is further discussed below.

McCarthy (Chapter 12), reflecting on her background in working against gender-based violence and her membership of the Victorian Sentencing Advisory Council, discusses the potential for the Council to reduce "sex discrimination in sentencing through accurate understandings of the etiology and nature of gender-based violence" through "open engagement between gender-based violence advocates, the judiciary and the community". By challenging simplistic populist approaches (more punishment and retribution) to the problem of gender-based violence, McCarthy regards the Council's community engagement and education roles as important means to alter both community attitudes and sentencing practices. Adopting a more optimistic approach than Indermaur, her chapter argues that:

> [The establishment of the Council] has created new possibilities for reform and dialogue that presage non-discriminatory, inclusive and relevant sentencing policy that takes account of individuals and the interests of the wider community, formerly excluded, in ways that could not and have not been contemplated in the past.

Allen and Hough (Chapter 17) use the case of the United Kingdom to illustrate how sentencing policy can be swept away in a tide of penal populism in the wake of a moral panic. They suggest that this case can provide some useful lessons on how not to engage with the public on issues relating to penal policy. Although they admit to "moments of deep pessimism" about the ability of sentencing councils to contain the development of sentencing policy based on subscription to penal populism, they believe that is essential that independent councils continue to be used to defuse such political crises. According to Allen and Hough, sentencing councils must "ensure that there is greater public understanding of sentencing" and must work to improve relations among the key players in the criminal justice system.

Sentencing councils and penal populism

In an era of penal populism, a political and social minefield is created when political crisis management results in the clashing of stakeholder interests. The reality for sentencing councils is that they must navigate this minefield in order not only to produce thoughtful recommendations or guidelines, but also to survive. The discussions in this book illustrate the difficulties facing sentencing councils as they act to counter the knee-jerk legislative responses that may be made in the name of penal populism.

Sentencing councils may be seen as "policy buffers" within the complex and inter-woven relationships that exist among the executive, the judiciary, the public and the media. In an era of penal populism, where the vast majority of the public learns about crime and the criminal justice system from the media, a combination of sensationalist reporting practices and populist political responses to moral panics has resulted in widespread myths and misconceptions about sentencing (Gelb, Chapter 5).

Penal populism and its perceptions of a punitive public are of particular concern given the recent world-wide fall in crime rates. The powerful role of the single, sensational case on which such perceptions are founded is illustrated in the case of Minnesota (Frase, Chapter 6), where sentence severity increased despite the State's lack of a tabloid newspaper, despite its progressive political climate and despite its falling crime rates.

Within the context of penal populism, attempts to develop sentencing policy are fraught with danger for sentencing councils that must find a balance between responsive politicians, an entrenched judiciary, an often inflammatory press and an increasingly vocal public that is not always well informed. The sentencing council can defuse the tension existing between quick political responses to public outcries and the careful creation of fair and thoughtful sentencing policy. In this sense, the sentencing council acts as a "policy buffer" to dampen the forces of "blind populism" (Roberts et al, 2003, p 180). Allen and Hough (Chapter 17) suggest that, in fulfilling this role:

> [Sentencing councils] will turn out to be of real value if they prove able to interrupt the way that governments privilege perceived public opinion about the desirability of ever harsher sentences over other considerations including the effect of measures in reducing and preventing crime.

In addition, the sentencing council can respond to, and influence, public opinion via its educative role. While not all the bodies discussed in this book are charged with such a role, the promulgation of accurate and up-to-date information on sentencing policy and practice would seem to be a key function of those bodies designed to promote and disseminate advice and information on sentencing. The recent addition of such a role to the New South Wales Sentencing Council (Abadee, Chapter 9) is clearly indicative of the understanding that education and information can play a major role in improving public perceptions of, and confidence in, the criminal justice system.

In a time when the public is more active, more demanding of a role in the criminal justice system and more interested in holding the judiciary accountable, the sentencing council can create a climate in which people are more interested and more informed in the debate on the development of sentencing policy.

Notes

1   For more information on the issues covered at this conference, see <http://law.anu.edu.au/nissl/courts_prog.pdf>.

References

Ashworth, A (2005). *Sentencing and Criminal Justice*. 4th edn, Cambridge: Cambridge University Press.

Australian Law Reform Commission (2006). *Same Crime, Same Time: Sentencing of Federal Offenders*. Publication No 103. Sydney: Australian Law Reform Commission.

Bottoms, AE (1995). The Philosophy and Politics of Punishment and Sentencing. In C Clark and R Morgan (eds), *The Politics of Sentencing Reform*. Oxford: Clarendon Press.

Garland, D (2001). *The Culture of Control: Crime and Social Order in Contemporary Society*. Oxford: Oxford University Press.

Gelb, K (2006). *Myths and Misconceptions: Public Opinion versus Public Judgment about Sentencing*. Melbourne: Sentencing Advisory Council.

Gleeson, M (2004). *Out of Touch or Out of Reach?* Presentation to Judicial Conference of Australia Colloquium, 2 October, Adelaide.

Pratt, J (2007). *Penal Populism*. London: Routledge.

Roberts, JV, Stalans, LJ, Indermaur, D and Hough, M (2003). *Penal Populism and Public Opinion: Lessons from Five Countries*. Oxford: Oxford University Press.

Tonry, M (1996). *Sentencing Matters*. New York: Oxford University Press.

2

Sentencing policy and practice: the evolving role of public opinion

Julian V Roberts

It is generally agreed that for law to be regarded as good law, it must ... in some sense represent the social consensus ... (Silvey, 1961, p 349)

Introduction

This chapter explores the relationship between public opinion and sentencing policy as well as practice. Recent years have witnessed change in the importance ascribed to views of the public in both areas. The chapter begins by evaluating the evidence that public opinion influences sentencing practices or sentencing policies. It then discusses the increased attention currently paid to public views.

Research on public opinion and sentencing

Impact of public opinion on sentencing practice

Individual sentencing decisions

To what extent should courts consider public opinion when imposing sentence? Shute (1998) reviews the caselaw in England and Wales with respect to the relationship that should exist between public opinion and sentencing. He concludes that, with respect to the law of sentencing, courts should not totally ignore community values; nor, however, should judges of first instance attempt to incorporate public opinion into their sentencing deliberations. In this jurisdiction at least, there is no real clarity with respect to the legal relevance of public attitudes. That said, it is clear that sentencers are sensitive, in varying degrees, to the views of the public. This conclusion is supported by the limited number of surveys of the judiciary. In one Canadian study judges acknowledged considering the likely reaction of the public when imposing certain sentences – in this case a community-based penalty in a case of serious violence. Thus Roberts, Doob and Marinos (2000) found that a significant percentage of judicial respondents stated that they considered the likely reaction from the community before imposing a house arrest sanction[1] on an offender convicted of a serious crime of violence.[2] On a more general level, Indermaur (1990) reports that a significant majority of a sample of Australian judges expressed the view that public opinion should be a consideration at sentencing.

There is some legal justification for judges to consider community views as a legitimate *general* consideration at sentencing. It relates to one of the reasons why appeal courts have always been reluctant to interfere with sentences on appeal. In common law jurisdictions there is a long-standing tradition of deference to the trial court in matters of sentencing. Generally speaking, appellate courts interfere with a sentence under appeal only if the disposition was manifestly unfit or if there has been an error in law. The leading decision from the Supreme Court of Canada notes that "absent an error in principle … a court of appeal should only intervene to vary a sentence imposed at trial if the sentence is demonstrably unfit".[3] The fact that the appellate court would have imposed a different sentence on the same set of facts has long been considered insufficient grounds to reverse a sentence on appeal.

The language of the Canadian Supreme Court echoes that used a century earlier at the inception of sentence reviews by the Court of Criminal Appeal in England and Wales. The Lord Chief Justice noted that:

> The Court would not interfere with a sentence unless it was apparent that the judge at the trial had proceeded upon wrong principles … it was not possible to allow appeals because individual members of the Court might have inflicted a different sentence.[4]

The justification for this deference lies in the questionable assumption that sentencers at the trial court level are closer to the community and therefore better able to know what is likely to prove acceptable. The Canadian Supreme Court has recognised this justification for deference on a number of occasions. Most recently (in *R v Proulx*) the Court noted that "trial judges are closer to their community and know better what would be acceptable to their community".[5] It is a curious justification for deference to the trial court. In reality, sentencers have no better idea of the true nature of public opinion than you or I – indeed they may be less well placed to know what the public thinks as they are unlikely to have the time or training to review systematic research into public attitudes to sentencing. And, unlike you or me, judges are periodically the object of negative media commentary for the sentences they impose, and this may affect even the most thick-skinned and independent sentencer.

To summarise, there is a clear tension present in the relationship between community views and the determination of sentence. Courts are expected to impose sentences that are not radically inconsistent with public expectations. On the other hand, public opinion is not a legally recognised factor at sentencing. Judges should not increase the quantum of punishment if they feel that this will gratify the general public.

Impact of public opinion on sentencing patterns[6]

The second question that needs to be addressed is whether there is any evidence that sentencing trends reflect changes in public opinion. If judges are sensitive in some degree to public views of sentencing, it might be possible to detect the influence of community views on aggregate sentencing patterns. To date, no systematic time-series analysis has been undertaken to determine whether changes in aggregate sentencing patterns are related to shifting public attitudes. There has been no shortage of speculation, however. Let us examine the possibility that some measure of punitiveness – whether the number of prisoners or the custody rate – appears to fluctuate as a function of shifts in public views of sentencing. Two examples are illustrative: the prison population in England and Wales and the custody rate in Canada.

Some researchers attribute the abrupt rise in the prison population in England and Wales during the 1990s to the impact of public opinion. The prison population began to rise shortly after the Bulger murder case[7] and has been attributed to intense public pressure on sentencers. Hough, Jacobson and Millie (2003) identify a more punitive climate as one of four principal explanations for the rise in the prison population in England and Wales. The weakness of the thesis that public opinion drives – or even influences – the imprisonment rate is that changes in the prison population have been dramatic while there has been no change in public attitudes toward sentence severity. In England and Wales the use of custody as a sanction has varied considerably over the past decade yet public attitudes to sentencing severity have remained constant. For example, in 1996 79 per cent of the British public held the view that sentences were too lenient; 10 years later the percentage was almost the same (74 per cent; see Hough and Roberts, 2007). If sentencers have made their sentences harsher to reflect public criticism of lenient sentencing, it is necessary to explain why this started to occur in the mid 1990s, rather than before.

In other jurisdictions the evidence to support the "community impact" hypothesis is equally equivocal. Thus Pfeiffer, Windzio and Kleimann (2005) report a shift towards more punitive sentencing in Germany during the 1990s. Absent any changes in the seriousness of cases appearing before the courts, they argue that the increase in the number of prisoner-years imposed can be traced to media-driven public demands for harsher punishment: "The evidence gives grounds to suspect that the courts are working on the false assumption that they need to take a hard line" (p 279). However, as with England and Wales, there is no hard evidence that this is in fact the case.

Further evidence – although once again correlational in nature – of a link between community values and judicial practice comes from the United States. Bowers and Waltman (1994) report a significant correlation between sentence lengths and conservativism scores using data from 29 States. They conclude that this demonstrates that judges are responsive to public opinion, but other hypotheses are equally plausible. Earlier research by Glick and Pruet (1985) also from the United States found no positive correlations between sentencing and public attitudes. These researchers concluded that their research suggests that "courts ignore or do not know community norms" (p 341). In defence of the "community impact" hypothesis it should be added that these studies are quite old now, and it is possible that the influence of public opinion on sentencing practices only became detectible in recent years.

Impact on sentencing policies

If the evidence for public influence over individual sentencing decisions or aggregate sentencing trends is ambiguous, is the same true with respect to sentencing policy? There is a very substantial literature on the relationship between public opinion and sentencing policies, one which defies summary within a single chapter. However, there does appear to be more evidence that the public has influenced punishment policies in a number of jurisdictions.

History is replete with sentencing policy shifts – at times abrupt – that appear to have been caused by public opinion. More recent experience suggests a certain asymmetry with respect to these policy changes: they usually entail movement in a more punitive direction reflecting a desire on the part of policymakers to move the practice of criminal justice closer to the views of an allegedly punitive public. In addition they usually follow in the wake of protracted media coverage of a "problem" in sentencing – which usually means a statutory provision or criminal justice program which attracts adverse media coverage and political criticism. Matters eventually reach what might be described as a "tipping point" when the force of public or media pressure compels the government to act. Three examples from the jurisdiction with which I am most familiar present themselves; readers may well have examples from their own jurisdictions.

- The federal government in Canada introduced a new youth justice statute in 2003. The *Youth Criminal Justice Act* was introduced in large measure because of intense public criticism of the former statute the *Young Offenders Act*. This public criticism focused on the sentencing provisions which were perceived to be too lenient.[9]

- A controversial provision that permits most life prisoners to apply for a jury review of their parole eligibility date was the subject of a great deal of negative media coverage. If successful in their application prisoners serving life for murder were able to benefit from a reduction in the custodial portion of their sentences by up to 10 years. A number of politicians argued that the provision was contrary to public opinion and therefore should be amended or repealed outright. The pressure on the government to act was considerable. In response the federal government introduced a number of amendments which restricted the number of eligible offenders and reduced the likelihood that applications would succeed[10] (see Roberts and Cole, 1999).

- In 1996 a new community based form of imprisonment was introduced in Canada. Prison-bound offenders perceived to be a low risk were permitted to pass the sentence at home if they complied with a number of conditions such as a curfew (see Roberts, 2004). The sentence is similar to house arrest sanctions in some other jurisdictions. As the sanction has a broad ambit of application, it has been imposed for some of the most serious offences including aggravated assault, aggravated sexual assault and manslaughter. A number of these cases attracted intense media coverage and led to repeated calls by politicians to restrict the use of this sanction to less serious cases. Eventually (in 2006) the newly elected Conservative government introduced legislation to eliminate the use of this community sentence in cases of serious violence (Roberts, 2006).

Besides these examples of specific reforms that have been explicitly tied by policy-makers to public opinion, there are many instances in which policy shifts have been linked to public attitudes. This creates a causality problem for researchers who need to determine whether public opinion has driven policy changes. The difficulty is that it is rare for either a court or a legislature to cite public opinion as having played a determinative role in the genesis of a particular judgment or policy, with the result that the question of causality remains unanswered. Did the decision of the United States Supreme Court in *Roe v Wade* reflect public support for more liberal abortion laws, or did the status of the Court confer additional legitimacy on the pro-abortion position thereby leading to a shift in public opinion? Commentary is divided on the issue. For example, the *Encyclopedia of Crime and Justice* concludes that "one reason for the Court's opinion could have been its awareness of and responsive to public opinion" (Winick, 1971, p 1335).[11]

The paradox of capital punishment

The death penalty is another issue that provides ambiguous or conflicting evidence with respect to the role of public opinion. Legislators in some countries have defied community views regarding capital punishment while in others public opinion appears to have played a determinative role. Capital punishment was abolished in England and Wales in 1965, a decision re-affirmed by Parliament five years later. The last parliamentary motion to restore the death penalty in that jurisdiction was resoundingly defeated, yet public opinion has unwaveringly favoured restoration. Thus a poll conducted in 2003 found over two-thirds of the sample in favour of re-introducing capital punishment (Observer, 2003). A comparable gap between community views and legislation can be seen in other common law jurisdictions such as Canada and Australia.

One of the justifications for retention of the death penalty in Middle Eastern countries is the strong community support for executions. In the United States capital punishment has been abolished or reinstated, and sometimes abolished and then reinstated, as a result of plebiscites. Why some legislatures are subservient to, and others independent of, public opinion regarding this issue remains unclear. If politicians are so eager to placate the public with regards to sentencing, why have we not witnessed more – or more robust – attempts to reintroduce capital punishment in these nations? It seems paradoxical that the issue of greatest interest to the public – the punishment of offenders convicted of murder – is the one on which politicians have been least likely to accede to the wishes of the community. The general point, however, is that no clear pattern emerges with respect to the impact of public opinion on death penalty policy.

Summary

To summarise, the evidence for the direct influence on individual sentencing decisions or aggregate sentencing policies is inconsistent. However, a sufficient number of case histories exists to justify the conclusion that public opinion has contributed to the evolution of sentencing policies in a number of jurisdictions. The discrepancy should not be surprising; punishment policies lie within the jurisdiction of politicians who are responsive to public opinion. Courts, however, have long attempted to insulate themselves from popular pressures. At this point I will discuss the increased attention devoted to the views of the public with respect to the sentencing environment.

The evolving role of public opinion

The quote that began this chapter acknowledges a truth accepted by most commentators, namely that some degree of correspondence should exist between the criminal law and the community to which it applies. More succinctly, as Rod Morgan observed in his discussion about the issue, "congruence is desirable" (2002, p 215). There is general agreement that the criminal justice system should be responsive to the community that it was created to protect. The link between criminal policy and public opinion was articulated 40 years ago when a Presidential Commission on Law Enforcement observed that "what America does about crime depends ultimately on how Americans see crime" (1967, p 49).

Events in England and Wales within the past decade have highlighted two contrasting perspectives on the role that public opinion should play in the sentencing process. The 2001 Home Office Sentencing Review placed public opinion in the forefront of its discussion on the future of sentencing reform in that jurisdiction. The Review cites public views repeatedly (see Home Office, 2001). To its credit the Review conducted a considerable amount of research into the views of the public. In addition, awareness of the importance of public opinion can be discerned in remarks made by the Home Secretary at the time, who noted the importance of putting the sense back into sentencing – which some may interpret as a coded reference to aligning the sentencing process more with community opinion.

In his review of the criminal courts Lord Auld (2001) took a different approach to the relationship between sentencing policy and the views of the public. He argued that a more rational sentencing structure would inspire greater confidence in the courts. According to this view, public opinion should be affected by changes to sentencing policy, and should not be a justification for adopting a specific direction for reform. Lord Auld's view appears to be a minority one; contemporary governments around the world appear to recognise the importance of allowing public views to shape criminal justice policy development. If we apply this logic to the area of sentencing we must accept the position that the sentencing process should reflect community values. But in what ways should public opinion influence sentencing policies or the practice of the courts? Should we privilege sentencing purposes that attract the greatest degree of public support? Should the nature and range of penalties reflect public attitudes? Is it incumbent upon courts to impose sentences that are broadly consistent with public opinion? And even if we respond affirmatively to any or all of these questions we are left with the vexed question of how best to determine the nature of public views. Questions of methodology have been addressed elsewhere (see Green, 2005; Stalans, 2002): this chapter addresses the broader questions pertaining to the role of public opinion.

Traditionally, members of the public have been bystanders with respect to the development of sentencing policy. Until the inception of public opinion polling, community views had to be inferred indirectly. Moreover, no formal mechanism existed by which to incorporate the views of the public. Public sentiment was expressed through the positions taken and speeches made by elected politicians who, it was assumed, were able to divine the attitudes of their constituents. The influence of public opinion was therefore indirect, with community views being filtered through the members of a legislative assembly. With the advent of the era of polling, matters obviously changed. From the 1960s[12] on it has been possible to demonstrate the general position of the public regarding important social issues such as punishment policies – albeit with the important limitations on Gallup-style surveys.

Western nations have witnessed a considerable evolution in the role of public opinion in sentencing policy and practice. Until fairly recently, an effort was made to exclude public views. Legislation was designed to shape public attitudes, and one of the purposes of individual sentencing decisions was to educate the public about offending. This view is encapsulated in the oft-quoted judgment (*R v Sargeant*) wherein it was affirmed that "the main duty of the courts is to lead public opinion".[13] The limited empirical literature on the pedagogical function of sentencing provides no support for the hypothesis. For example, Walker and Marsh (1984) found that the severity of sentences had no effect on public disapproval of specific crimes in Britain. With respect to statutory penalties, the Canadian Sentencing Commission found that changes in the penalty structure had no effect on public perceptions of the seriousness of crimes (Roberts, 1988). This finding is consistent with other tests of the hypothesis in the literature in countries such as Australia (Nesdale, 1980; see also Andenaes, 1971).

Today, most common law jurisdictions pay more and more systematic interest to public attitudes in the area of sentencing policy and practice. The present volume attests to the diversity of ways in which public input into sentencing policy and practice is encouraged. This interest in community views does not go so far as to create a formal consultation mechanism – sentencing legislation is subject to parliamentary review as in the past, and there are few examples of specific policies becoming subject to plebiscite before ratification. However, organisations responsible for developing sentencing policy or issuing guidance to sentencers now undertake considerable consultation and conduct a great deal of research as a way of informing the direction that policy and practice should take. The following examples illustrate this tendency:

Canada

In the mid-1980s the Canadian Sentencing Commission conducted a series of national surveys to explore public knowledge of and attitudes towards sentencing and parole in that country (Roberts, 1988). The federal Department of Justice Research has conducted research into public views of sentencing ever since (see Roberts et al, 2007).

United States

In the 1990s the US Sentencing Guidelines Commission undertook a large national survey to compare the federal guideline ranges with public opinion (Rossi and Berk, 1997). This survey was a direct consequence of the *Sentencing Reform Act* of 2004, which instructed the Commission to consider "the community view of the gravity of the offence".[14]

England and Wales

As noted, the Home Office Sentencing Review (2001) conducted a number of polls to evaluate public attitudes towards sentencing policies. The Sentencing

Advisory Panel has commissioned research into public attitudes towards rape (Clarke, Moran-Ellis and Sleney, 2002), to sentencing in cases of domestic burglary (Russell and Morgan, 2001) and most recently towards driving offences resulting in death. The chairman of the Sentencing Advisory Panel made the relevance of public opinion clear when he wrote that "it is particularly important that the Panel's proposals take proper account of public opinion". The purpose of the research was noted in the following way:

> [T]he Panel decided, before putting a proposal to the Court of Appeal ... to obtain a more in depth picture of the public's views on current sentencing practice for this offence, and on the factors which make one burglary more serious than another. (Wasik, cited in Clarke et al, 2001, p 1)

Scotland

The Scottish Parliament has commissioned a form of "deliberative poll" in an attempt to understand better public views of sentencing (see Hutton, 2005).

New Zealand

In the consultation draft of its proposed reforms to sentencing and parole, the New Zealand Law Commission notes that its recommendations are designed, among other reasons, "to allow community perspectives to be brought to bear on the development of sentencing policy" (New Zealand Law Commission, 2006, p 6).

Australia

One of the statutory functions of the Sentencing Advisory Council in Victoria is "to gauge public opinion on sentencing matters" (*Sentencing (Amendment) Act 2003* (Vic)). The Council has released a research paper to promote better understanding of public attitudes to sentencing (Gelb, 2006). In addition, while it remains for the present a proposal, the New South Wales Law Reform Commission has published a consultation paper on the role of juries in the sentencing process. The paper asks for views on a proposal to allow juries to make sentencing-related recommendations to the trial judge once an offender has been convicted (New South Wales Law Reform Commission, 2006).

In addition to these formal initiatives to evaluate and incorporate public attitudes to sentencing policy and practice, there has been an increase of interest across many jurisdictions in the issue of public confidence in the courts and the justice system. This attention has spawned a number of surveys of public confidence in the court system and in criminal justice professionals (see Hough and Roberts, 2003, for a review). In South Australia, for example, a major initiative of the Courts Administration Authority was entitled "Courts Consulting the Community Conference". This initiative included a survey of the public on a range of issues pertaining to the courts. Similar initiatives have emerged in Belgium, Canada and the United States, among other countries.

Finally, sentencing advisory bodies often include members drawn from the general public in addition to criminal justice professionals such as judges and prosecutors. By appointing community members in this way these councils hope to ensure that the sentencing process is in some way reflective of community views (see discussion in Hutton, this volume).

Explaining the increased importance ascribed to public views

What explanations may be offered to account for the increased attention to the views of the public? First, it is important to be clear about the level of public input, which can take one of two general directions. It may be a result of populist forces, as politicians attempt to ensure that they introduce legislation likely to receive the approbation of the public. This has been variously labelled "penal populism" or "the new punitiveness" and has been the subject of much scholarship in recent years (for example, Bottoms, 1995; Pratt et al, 2005; Pratt, 2007; Roberts et al, 2003). Polls are cited by politicians to bolster specific policies. Mandatory sentencing is the most visible example of this kind of populism. A more reasonable way in which community views may influence sentencing policy and practice is through the kinds of initiatives identified above.

Populist pressures on courts

Traditionally, judges have seen themselves as being insulated from the force of public opinion; judicial independence entails more than simply independence from the executive branch of government. The increasing "media-sation" of criminal justice has generated greater pressure on courts. The most compelling examples of this come from the United Kingdom, where tabloid campaigns to pressure courts are commonplace. In the summer of 2006 the *News of the World* began a "name and shame" campaign to identify judges "guilty" of imposing excessively lenient sentences. But Britain is not the only country in which such pressures exist. In Canada, legislation was introduced in the Ontario legislature to create a "judicial registry". This registry would record every sentence imposed, noting the identity of the judge and, most bizarrely, the statutory maximum penalty for the offence of conviction. Once operational this database would permit people to identify lenient judges – helpfully defined as those who imposed a sentence far below the maximum penalty allowed by law.

The language of these initiatives is interesting: judicial registry echoes sex offender registries, and name and shame campaigns are also directed against sex offenders and individuals on whom anti-social behaviour orders (ASBOs) have been imposed. In this way the tabloid press has attempted to align the courts with offenders. Small wonder therefore that the British Prime Minister's campaign to "re-align" the justice system in favour of the victim has struck a nerve in this country.[15] Implicit in the metaphor of balance is the view that the justice system, and in particular the courts, have drifted towards the offender and assumed a hostile posture against the crime victim and the community from which victims emerge. These messages have not been lost on the public. Although no poll has evaluated the extent to which the justice system is "tilted towards the offender", surveys in a number of countries have revealed that the public sees lenient sentencing as a cause of, as well as a response to, rising crime rates (see Roberts and Hough, 2005).

Insulation or isolation?

Insulating the criminal courts and the machinery of government from public opinion has traditionally been regarded as a virtue. Judges who ignore the views of the populace will be able to act in a disinterested manner and will be able to impose appropriate sentences free from popular pressure. Academics have called for the policy process to be insulated in a similar fashion by means of "policy buffers" – institutions that prevent populist criminal justice initiatives from being rapidly adopted. For example, one of the functions ascribed to a sentencing commission is to serve as a buffer between populist politicians and the sentencing process.

In the absence of such a body, legislative proposals will emerge from government departments that may be excessively responsive to ministerial initiatives. However, this insulation carries a price. Courts that fail to acknowledge the importance of community views or fail to engage with the community in some way will be perceived as increasingly isolationist. Indeed, the central criticism of sentencers today – particularly in Britain – is that they are isolated and are unrepresentative of the community. Similarly, the criticism that the justice system is tilted in favour of the offender at the expense of the victim also implies that it has drifted away from the community.

Public services have become increasingly professionalised over the past century and criminal justice is no exception. This reflects an attempt to achieve more consistent outcomes and to ensure consistency of treatment. But here too there are costs. As criminal justice professions become more professionalised they inevitably suffer in the eyes of the public. Another element of the public critique of criminal justice is that the system is run by professionals concerned with making it work, rather than "doing justice".[16] When judges and prosecutors elect not to explain key decisions to the community this contributes to the perception that they are simply ensuring that the system runs smoothly.

There has been a clear transformation in conceptions of legitimacy. During much of the past century legitimacy was conferred on courts and judges through the authority of the state. Some of this legitimacy derived from the very clear line between judges and the executive. The concept of judicial independence can be seen as a source of legitimacy. Today, judges are more likely to be regarded as public servants who should be held accountable to the community for their sentencing decisions. Deference on the part of appellate courts may still exist, but there is far less deference to members of the judiciary on the part of the public.

Some implications for sentencing policy and practice

This movement towards greater public consultation needs to be considered carefully. It implies first and foremost a shift in the model of sentencing policy, from one in which sentencers are insulated from community views and policy-makers consider those views only periodically, to one in which a continuous and formal consultation is required.

The current relationship between public opinion and sentencing policy would appear to involve two elements. First, there is a clear desire on the part of legislatures and some criminal justice professionals to establish stronger links between the system and the community. This desire is consistent with a broader movement towards making public services more accountable and more responsive to the communities they serve. The criminal justice system, and in particular the judiciary, has a clear need for greater community "outreach"; public attitudes towards sentencers are quite negative in all western nations (see Roberts and Hough, 2005, for a review), and public criticism reflects a perception that sentencers are out of touch and unresponsive. When members of the public criticise specific sentencing decisions for lacking commonsense, the term should possibly be "community sense". Members of the public have a strong intuitive sense of sentencing and are not afraid to express their views about sentences reported in the media.

In conjunction with greater consultation comes a need for greater education. Members of the public hold strong views on criminal justice issues; nowhere is this truer than in the area of sentencing. In their haste to condemn specific sentences members of the public can overlook important elements of the sentencing process such as grounds for mitigation. A number of sentences reported in the British newspapers in the summer of 2006 have provoked public condemnation because the offender received a sentence "discount" for pleading guilty. In this example the system needs to educate the public about the principles of sentencing, not adjust sentencing practices to placate uninformed critics.

The challenge to sentencing commissions and legislatures is clear: to ensure some degree of community engagement in the sentencing process without descending into populist punitiveness. As Arie Freiberg points out in his contribution to this volume (Chapter 11), many punitive initiatives, including "three strikes" laws, community notification schemes and flat time (no parole) sentences of custody have emerged as a result of popular pressure. Achieving the balance is far from easy. Media reports frequently advert to allegedly inappropriate factors taken into account by judges at sentencing which result in a lenient disposition. The first offender and guilty plea "discounts" are good examples of such factors. A populist approach to reform might entail examination of these and other factors with a view to reducing their impact, or possibly eliminating them altogether. Few criminal justice professionals or academics in the area of sentencing would endorse such a reform.

A similar "opportunity" to reconcile sentencing practices with public opinion might exist with respect to early, conditional release from prison. Many people criticise parole for simply being "time off" the sentence and demand flat time (no-parole) sentences of custody. Should we abolish parole on this ground? If not, some may ask the following question: if public opinion has no place in determining the nature and weight of sentencing factors or the custody-community ratio of a sentence of imprisonment, where and in what way are community views to be considered?[17]

Dangers of promising more than can be delivered

There is also a clear danger of creating false expectations. An analogy can be made with victims and the sentencing process. Victim input into sentencing is achieved in most common law jurisdictions through the use of a victim impact statement. Victims are allowed – indeed encouraged – to submit a statement to the court with respect to the impact of the crime. Yet this form of victim input is carefully circumscribed by the adversarial process. Absent exceptional circumstances, victims are prevented from expressing a view on the nature or quantum of punishment that should be imposed.[18] Some victims take exception to this restriction on their input. Research into victim impact statements suggests that some victims become disillusioned with the sentencing process for failing to allow "submissions" with respect to sentencing (see discussion in Roberts, 2003). In this way, an initiative designed to consult the victim and thereby promote victim confidence in the sentencing process may backfire.

A similar situation may arise with respect to public input into the sentencing process. A common way of promoting public input into sentencing is through the use of laypersons on sentencing commissions or councils. Members of the public may be pleased to learn that such bodies include community members. But what happens when the community members take a position that is at odds with a progressive and evidence-based sentencing policy? Either the sentencing council becomes more populist or the individual has to be overruled. Let us return momentarily to the proposal to allow juries to make submissions to the court before sentencing. What will jurors think of the sentencing process if the sentence ultimately imposed is contrary to the jury's desires?

Lay magistrates

Finally, it is worth adding a word about a feature of the sentencing process that may represent part of the solution to the problem of incorporating the public into the sentencing process: the use of lay magistrates. As is well known, the vast majority of sentencing decisions in England and Wales are made by panels of lay magistrates.[19]

It is important to be seen to be listening to the community; one of the common perceptions of sentencing in a number of countries is that the process and the individuals who administer the process are insulated from and out of touch with the public. For example, the 1996 British Crime Survey found that almost half the sample (46 per cent) held the view that judges in England and Wales were "very out of touch" with what ordinary people think (Hough and Roberts, 1998). It is worth noting that magistrates fared significantly better, with only 21 per cent of the sample holding this negative view of the magistracy. Similarly, only 18 per cent of the sample held the view that judges were in touch with the public, compared to 37 per cent who perceived magistrates in this way. The explanation for this discrepancy in public views probably lies in the fact that people have more faith in sentencers drawn from the community rather than appointed to the bench.[20] One way of diffusing public anger towards sentencing decisions or, put more affirmatively, of promoting public confidence in the sentencing process, might therefore be to increase the use of laypersons.

Conclusion

The era when courts imposed sentence without any consideration of community views has long passed. We now live in a time in which the public seeks accountability from all public services, including criminal justice. In the absence of a reliable measure of public attitudes, we have no way of knowing whether the

Victorians had more or less confidence in the courts than the contemporary public. It is clear, however, that promoting public confidence in criminal justice is a major preoccupation of western governments. As sentencing is the stage of the criminal process that attracts the most attention and criticism, it is unsurprising that efforts to promote public confidence have focused on the sentencing system.

These efforts include: conducting public opinion surveys of public attitudes to sentencing; creating sentencing commissions and councils with community representatives in addition to criminal justice professionals; creating judicial "outreach" initiatives in which judges attempt to explain the work of the courts; and creating community liaison officers who attempt to explain individual sentencing decisions to the public and to the news media. More radical ways of harmonising the community and the court system include the increased use of lay magistrates or the limited use of juries in sentencing hearings. Whether these initiatives will result in effecting a rapprochement between courts and communities remains to be seen. It is significant that no jurisdiction has yet devised any strategy for dealing with the primary cause of public disenchantment with sentencing and sentencers: the news media. Until and unless the news media – particularly the tabloid media – provide information to the public in a more balanced way, public perceptions of the courts will continue to be determined by tabloid media values. Clearly, much remains to be done before courts and the communities they represent are, and are perceived, in Silvey's words, to "represent the social consensus" (1961, p 349).

Notes

1   This sanction had provoked a great deal of adverse media coverage and public criticism when it had been imposed for a very serious crime such as manslaughter or sexual assault (see discussion in Roberts, 2004).

2   Some community justice advocates would argue that courts should consider community sentiment when making decisions in individual cases. Sentencing circles represent an example in which the court incorporates the views of community members when determining sentence.

3   *R v M (CA)* [1996] 1 SCR 500 paras 90-2.

4   *R v Sidlow* (1908) 1 Crim App at p 29.

5   *R v Proulx* (2000) 140 CCC (3d) at p 504.

6   It has long been argued, in both Britain and Canada, that parole boards are influenced by public opinion. The assertion is made that parole grant rates drop sharply following public outcry over a highly publicised crime committed by an offender on parole. It is an interesting hypothesis although I have seen no hard supporting evidence. It would not be surprising if parole authorities were more susceptible to public opinion in this way as members of the parole board do not have the same degree of tradition of independence as that associated with the judiciary. Moreover, some parole board members are drawn from the general public and may see reflecting community views as part of their role.

7   The argument appears to be that this horrific crime created a more punitive climate towards offenders. The public was outraged as details of the crime emerged on a daily basis in the national media. Sentencers then responded by becoming more punitive and this occasioned the subsequent rise in the prison population.

8   I am not convinced that it even constitutes circumstantial evidence. Why would public outcry over a most exceptional case of murder by two very young children make judges resort to imprisonment more often and for longer periods when sentencing *adult* offenders. The steep and sudden rise in the prison population would also have required a very high percentage of sentencers to have decided to get tougher.

9   The irony is that, despite a great deal of tough talk with respect to the new Act, the legislation in fact contains a number of provisions that restrict youth courts from imposing a term of custody. The result has been a significant reduction in the number of youth court committals to custody.

10   This was accomplished by introducing judicial pre-screening of cases going before a jury and requiring a unanimous rather than a majority decision from the jury.

11   Determining causality is even more difficult when a longer time-scale is adopted. One of the significant, cross-jurisdictional changes in sentencing practices is clearly the movement away from corporal or corporeal punishments and towards the use of other sanctions. The transition from the infliction of pain to the deprivation of liberty is itself a remarkable change. These transformations are consistent with a change in public attitudes. Few members of the public today would support a return to flogging or other such penalties. But are these changes a consequence of a shift in public consciousness? Is the "civilising process" in penal practices a cause or an effect?

12   Although the American Institute of Public Opinion was founded earlier, in 1935, the widespread use of polls in the United States emerged in the 1960s and was greatly accelerated by the movement towards telephone interviews in the early 1970s.

13   *R v Sargeant* (1974) 60 Cr App R 74 at p 77.

14   28 USC S 994(c)(4).

15   Difficulties of interpretation abound in this field. The current British government has over the past few years attempted to "re-balance" the criminal justice system. By this the government means redressing an imbalance that favours the suspect, defendant or offender at the expense of the interest of the crime victim. This policy direction is part of the Home Office's four-year Strategic Plan (see Home Office, 2003), and was repeatedly promoted by the Prime Minister (see Blair, 2006). The "re-balancing" strategy policy has clear implications for the sentencing process. Although the strategy has proved popular it is hard to know whether public opinion has driven the policy or whether the policy simply reflects popular views.

16   A similar perception is often held about public health care systems that are sometimes seen by the public as being more interested in administrative efficiency than patient welfare.

17   There are clear parallels with the role of the victim at sentencing. Many victims' rights advocates want victims to have input into the sentencing process but do not wish this input to be determinative. Victims should be heard more often we are told, but when what we hear speaks to the sentence that will be imposed, we stop listening. Similarly with members of the public – we wish to engage them more in the sentencing process but we generally stop far short of following their advice in terms of specific reforms.

18   Courts in most common law jurisdictions appear to make an exception if the imposition of a particular sentence (for example, imprisonment) would create undue hardship for the victim or other innocent parties. If this is the case, judges often seek an alternate disposition. In these circumstances the victim is having a degree of influence over the sentence imposed.

19   The critical experiment in which members of the public rate the same sentencing decision described either as having been taken by a professional judge or a lay magistrate has yet to be conducted. If the presence of lay magistrates does confer some additional legitimacy from its closer connection with the community, it would be reasonable to expect more positive evaluations under the condition in which the sentence was imposed in a magistrates' court. Similar research might be conducted in the United States comparing public reaction to appointed versus elected judges. One might predict that the public would regard the sentencing decisions of the latter as more legitimate since they have been elevated to the bench by the community.

20   One reason why the police inspire more public confidence than any other criminal justice professionals is that they are highly visible as a result of their uniforms. Higher levels of contact may also explain the higher levels of public confidence in the police – most people have some contact with a police officer on an annual basis (see discussion in Hough and Roberts, 2003). Members of the public are far more likely to have contact with a magistrate than a professional judge, and this may contribute to the superior public ratings associated with the former.

21   The critical experiment in which members of the public rate the same sentencing decision described either as having been taken by a professional judge or a lay magistrate has yet to be conducted. If the presence of lay magistrates does confer some additional legitimacy from its closer connection with the community, it would be reasonable to expect more positive evaluations under the condition in which the sentence was imposed in a magistrates' court. Similar research

might be conducted in the US comparing public reaction to appointed versus elected judges. One might predict that the public would regard the sentencing decisions of the latter as more legitimate since they have been elevated to the bench by the community.

References

Andenaes, J (1971). The Moral or Educative Influence of Criminal Law. *Journal of Social Issues* 27: 17.

Applegate, B (2001). Penal Austerity: Perceived Utility, Desert, and Public Attitudes toward Prison Amenities. *American Journal of Criminal Justice* 25: 233.

Ashworth, A (2006). The Sentencing Guideline System in England and Wales. *South African Journal of Criminal Justice* 19: 1.

Auld, Lord Justice (2001). *Review of the Courts of England and Wales*. London: Stationery Office.

Blair, T (2006). *Our Nation's Future Criminal Justice System*. Speech given at Bristol, 23 June, <www.number-10.gov.uk>.

Bottoms, A (1995). The Philosophy and Politics of Punishment and Sentencing. In C Clarkson and R Morgan (eds), *The Politics of Sentencing Reform*. Oxford: Clarendon Press.

Bowers, D and Waltman, J (1994). Are Elected Judges More in Tune with Public Opinion? A Look at Sentences for Rape. *International Journal of Applied Criminal Justice* 18: 113.

Clarke, A, Moran-Ellis, J and Sleney, J (2002). *Attitudes to Date Rape and Relationship Rape: A Qualitative Study*. London: Sentencing Advisory Panel.

Gelb, K (2006). *Myths and Misconceptions: Public Opinion versus Public Judgment about Sentencing*. Melbourne: Sentencing Advisory Council.

Glick, H and Pruet, G (1985). Crime, Public Opinion and Trial Courts: An Analysis of Sentencing Policy. *Justice Quarterly* 2: 319.

Gottfredson, S and Taylor, R (1984). Public Policy and Prison Populations: measuring opinions about reform. *Judicature* 68: 190.

Green, D (2005). Public Opinion versus Public Judgment about Crime. *British Journal of Criminology* 46: 131.

Home Office (2001). *Making Punishments Work. Report of a Review of the Sentencing Framework for England and Wales*. London: Home Office.

Home Office (2003). *Confident Communities in a Secure Britain. The Home Office Strategic Plan 2004-2008*. London: Home Office.

Hough, M, Jacobson, J and Millie, A (2003). *The Decision to Imprison: Sentencing and the Prison Population*. London: Prison Reform Trust.

Hough, M and Roberts, JV (1998). *Attitudes to Punishment: Findings from the British Crime Survey*. Home Office Research Study 179. London: Home Office.

Hough, M and Roberts, JV (2004). *Confidence in Justice: An International Review*. London: Home Office, Research, Development and Statistics.

Hough, M and Roberts, JV (2007). Public Opinion, Crime and Criminal Justice: The British Crime Survey and Beyond. In M Hough and M Maxfield (eds), *Surveying Crime in the 21st Century*. Cullompton: Willan.

Hutton, N (2005). Beyond Populist Punitiveness? *Punishment and Society* 7: 243.

Johnson, B and Huff, C (1987). Public Opinion and Criminal Justice Policy Formulation. *Criminal Justice Policy Research* 2: 118.

Maxfield, L, Martin, W and Kitchens, C (1995). *Just Punishment: Public Perceptions and the Federal Sentencing Guidelines*. Washington, DC: US Sentencing Commission.

Morgan, R (2002). Privileging Public Attitudes to Sentencing? In JV Roberts and M Hough (eds), *Changing Attitudes to Punishment*. Cullompton: Willan.

Nesdale, A (1980). The Law and Social Attitudes: Effects of Proposed Changes in Drug Legislation on Attitudes towards Drug Use. *Canadian Journal of Criminology* 22: 176.

New South Wales Law Reform Commission (2006). *Sentencing and Juries*. Issues Paper 27. Sydney: New South Wales Law Reform Commission.

New Zealand Law Commission (2006). *Reforms to the Sentencing and Parole Structure. Consultation Draft*. Wellington: New Zealand Law Commission.

Observer, The (2003). Crime Uncovered. 27 April.

Pfeiffer, C, Windzio, M and Kleimann, M (2005). Media Use and its Impacts on Crime Perception, Sentencing Attitudes and Crime Policy. *European Journal of Criminology* 2: 259.

Pratt, J, Brown, D, Brown, M, Hallsworth, S and Morrison, W (2005). *The New Punitiveness. Trends, Theories, Perspectives*. Cullompton: Willan.

Pratt, J (2007). *Penal Populism*. London: Routledge.

Roberts, JV (1988). *Public Opinion and Sentencing: Surveys by the Canadian Sentencing Commission*. Research Reports of the Canadian Sentencing Commission. Ottawa: Department of Justice Canada.

Roberts, JV (2002). Public Opinion and Sentencing Policy. In S Rex and M Tonry (eds), *Reform and Punishment: The Future of Sentencing*. Cullompton: Willan.

Roberts, JV (2003a). Public Opinion and Mandatory Sentences of Imprisonment: A Review of International Findings. *Criminal Justice and Behaviour* 20: 1.

Roberts, JV (2003b). Victim Impact Statements and the Sentencing Process: Enhancing Communication in the Courtroom. *Criminal Law Quarterly* 47(3): 365.

Roberts, JV (2004). *The Virtual Prison. Community Custody and the Evolution of Imprisonment*. Cambridge: Cambridge University Press.

Roberts, JV and Cole, D (1999). Sentencing and Parole Arrangements for Cases of Murder. In *Making Sense of Sentencing*. Toronto: University of Toronto Press.

Roberts, JV, Crutcher, N and Verbrugge, P (2007). Public Attitudes to Sentencing in Canada: Exploring Recent Findings. *Canadian Journal of Criminology and Criminal Justice* 49: 75.

Roberts, JV, Doob, AN and Marinos, V (2000). *Judicial Attitudes Towards Conditional Sentences of Imprisonment: Results of a National Survey*. Ottawa: Department of Justice Canada.

Roberts, JV and Hough, M (2005). *Understanding Public Attitudes to Criminal Justice*. Maidenhead: Open University Press.

Roberts, JV, Stalans, LS, Indermaur, D and Hough, M (2003). *Penal Populism and Public Opinion. Lessons from Five Countries*. Oxford: Oxford University Press.

Rossi, P and Berk, R (1997). *Just Punishments. Federal Guidelines and Public Views Compared*. New York: Aldine.

Russell, N and Morgan, R (2001). *Sentencing of Domestic Burglary*. Research Report 1. London: Sentencing Advisory Panel, <www.sentencing-advisory-panel.gov.uk/saprr1. htm>.

Shute, S (1998). The Place of Public Opinion in Sentencing Law. *Criminal Law Review*: 465.

Silvey, J (1961). The Criminal Law and Public Opinion. *Criminal Law Review*: 349.

Stalans, L (2002). Measuring Attitudes to Sentencing. In JV Roberts and M Hough (eds), *Changing Attitudes to Punishment*. Cullompton: Willan.

Thomas, C, Cage, R and Foster, S (1970). Public Opinion on Criminal Law and Legal Sanctions: An Examination of Two Conceptual Models. *Journal of Criminal Law and Criminology* 67: 110.

Tomaino, J (1997). Guess Who's Coming to Dinner? A Preliminary Model for the Satisfaction of Public Opinion as a Legitimate Aim in Sentencing. *Crime, Law & Social Change* 27: 109.

Walker, N and Marsh, C (1984). Do Sentences Affect Public Disapproval? *British Journal of Criminology* 24: 27.

Waltman, J and Bowers, D (1993). Do More Conservative States Impose Harsher Felony Sentences? *Criminal Justice Review* 18.

Whitehead, J, Blankenship, M and Wright, J (1999). Elite versus Citizen Attitudes on Capital Punishment: Incongruity between the Public and Policymakers. *Journal of Criminal Justice* 27: 249.

Winick, C (1971). Public Opinion and Crime. In S Kadish (ed), *Encyclopedia of Crime and Justice*. Volume 4. New York: The Free Press.

3

Penal scandal in New Zealand

John Pratt

Introduction

Over the past 15 years or so, increasing attention has been given to what is thought to constitute "public opinion" in relation to the development of sentencing and penal policy. The views and aspirations of the general public are regularly invoked by politicians, usually as a justification for more severe sentencing, or when drawing attention to perceived inadequacies in existing criminal justice and penal systems. For example, Tony Blair has claimed that "there are more prison places, sentences are longer and sentences are tougher but if you look where the public is on this issue, the gap between what they expect and what they get is bigger in this service than anywhere else *and we have got to bridge it*" (*The Guardian* 9 June 2006, p 1, my italics). The clear implications of this and similar speeches that have been made by politicians in many other western countries are that in this area the views of the general public are paramount, and that there is something seriously amiss when public expectations are not being met by those implementing or delivering policy.

This chapter intends to address three aspects of these developments. First, what is it that is meant by the term "public opinion"? This is of considerable importance as there is a large gap between the findings of social scientific public opinion research and more volatile impressions of public mood, usually based on newspaper headlines or the like: it will be argued that it is the latter that politicians usually have in mind when they speak to public expectations in this area. Secondly, what is the sociological significance of all these invocations of the public and exhortations to judges and policy-makers? It will be argued that these are symptomatic of a new axis of power which has come into play and which significantly reorganises both the terms of penal debate and who is allowed to contribute to this. Thirdly, what consequences does this have for understanding policy development and the input of the general public, or at least those who claim to speak on its behalf? By reference to current developments in New Zealand, it will be argued that popular commonsense can now become a privileged driver of policy: but at the same time, in the more emotive context in which penal policy is now decided, strategic use of scandal is one way to undermine its influence. Scandal should not be understood as the exclusive property of the law and order lobby.

Public opinion and punishment

On the face of it, a good deal of opinion poll evidence would seem to confirm the impression that the general public does indeed want longer and harsher prison sentences. For example, an opinion poll published in the British *Sunday Telegraph* (2 July 2006, p 1) found that 86 per cent of the public thought that violent crime was rising, 81 per cent were worried about the level of crime, and 81 per cent thought that prison sentences were too short. There is, though, nothing that is new about such findings, nor are they confined to Britain. In the United States surveys from the late 1970s onwards show that around 85 per cent of Americans consistently express the view that the courts have not been dealing harshly enough with criminals (Savelsberg, 1994). In Canada between 61 and 69 per cent of the public has held this view over the same period (Roberts et al, 2003, p 29). In New Zealand the largest demonstration of public support for tougher sentences occurred in the 1999 election when 92 per cent of the electorate voted for the following referendum: "Should there be a reform of the criminal justice system placing greater emphasis on the needs of victims, providing restitution and compensation for them and imposing minimum sentences and hard labour for all serious violent offences?

However, the fact that much of this polling has taken place in countries where recorded crime has been in decline and where prison sentences have already been increasing is indicative of the gulf that exists between the actualities of crime and punishment in a particular society and the understandings and attitudes of the general public when asked about these matters in abstract or very general terms. In New Zealand, for example, in contrast to the assumptions underlying the referendum, recorded crime has declined by some 25 per cent since 1995, while the rate of imprisonment has increased from 128 to 194 per 100,000 of population from 1995 to 2007. One reason for this disjuncture between crime and punishment realities and public perceptions would seem to be that most people, when asked about law and order at a very general level, will obviously give importance to it. As it is, though, all they are doing is verbalising or enumerating views which in the general course of events will be left unsaid: the importance of law and order is taken for granted. Nonetheless, law and order issues usually poll well behind others in importance – health, education, employment, pensions and so on – when the public is asked to rank them. Law and order tends to figure highly only at particular times – usually of short duration – when prompted by a specific event, usually a heinous crime. In these respects, what proved to be the catalyst for the launch of the New Zealand referendum, was a brutal attack on the elderly mother of Norm Withers, the man who was to become the organiser of the referendum.

But when members of the public are asked to consider specific cases, or are given more detailed information about crime and punishment issues, then their views are usually much more nuanced and reflective, to the point where their judgments are usually in line with the sentences that are actually given in these cases, or are sometimes even less punitive than those of the judges who were dealing with the particular case (Roberts et al, 2003). Equally, when presented with choices about particular policies (and notwithstanding significant bedrock support for severe punishments for violent offenders – see Cullen et al, 2000), the general public again seems much more liberal than would otherwise seem to be the case. In New Zealand, in contrast to the referendum vote, an opinion poll in 2004 showed that there was strong public support for parole with safeguards. Another in 2006 indicated that more people favoured community-based sentencing rather than the building of more prisons (see Pratt, 2006a). What I am suggesting, then, is that all the invocations of public opinion regularly made by politicians, sections of the media, the law and order lobby, talk-back radio hosts and so on, as a justification for more severe sentencing, may in fact be quite misleading. Indeed, if it were actually the case that public opinion poll research evidence was being allowed to drive penal policy and sentencing, then in countries such as New Zealand the course would probably have taken a rather different route from that which has been followed during the past decade. However, these more liberal and quanti-fiable aspects of public opinion provided by social science research seem to have little impact on political discourse on crime and punishment. Instead, the public opinion that is invoked by politicians and others to justify harsher penal sanctions and more intrusive methods of social control is usually more of a commonsense construct, based on nebulous feelings, intuitions and sentiments.

This pandering to public sentiment and mood (not "public opinion" in the social scientific sense of the term), which frequently wins electoral support, repre-sents something more than the machinations of individual politicians or their parties. It is also representative of a new axis through which penal power is now exercised. This revolves much more around relationships between governments and the various organisations, individuals and groups who claim to speak on behalf of "the people", or who seem to represent, in some way or other, the public mood or "public opinion" (as this term is commonsensically understood) than was previously the case. For example, Moriarty (1977, p 128) wrote as follows of the late 1960s juvenile justice reforms in England and Wales:

> [They] clearly owed much to the members of the [advisory] group, of course, but also to the generally available sources of expertise or received wisdom – the penal sources themselves, the legal and academic communities, the various reform bodies and interest groups and a quantity of published official material.

At that time, the views of the public, amidst this range of influences on some of the most important 20th century juvenile justice legislation in that country, did not receive one mention. Now, however, politicians from both left and right of the spectrum have sought electoral success by aligning themselves more closely with such representations of the public mood and have disparaged or distanced them-selves from the values of those establishment elites who had previously been in control of penal debate and knowledge. Thus, in Britain, the *Crime and Disorder Act* 1998 (UK) which introduced anti-social behaviour legislation was described by the Home Secretary as "a triumph for democratic politics – *in truth a victory for local communities over detached metropolitan elites*" (Hansard HOC April 1998, vol 370, my italics).

This has meant that, in those jurisdictions where this new axis has come into effect, populist commonsensical concerns about law and order – concerns that seem to speak to the public mood (although not opinion poll research) – have become much more central to political debate. Indeed, the emotive, ad hoc and volatile forces of populism can now override scientific expertise and the rationalities of penal bureaucracies. The success and influence of the New Zealand referendum is one of the clearest examples of this. The result was taken as a cue by all the main parties that longer and harsher sentences would win favour with the electorate. In the aftermath of a particularly virulent law and order campaign in 2002, the *Sentencing Act* 2002 (NZ), *Parole Act* 2002 (NZ) and *Victims of Crime Act* 2002 (NZ) were passed later that year (Pratt and Clark, 2005). These measures prescribed, inter alia, longer prison terms for some groups of offenders, enhanced the rights of victims to make representations at various points in the criminal justice process and, rather more quietly, cut parole eligibility to one-third of the sentence for most prisoners, as if in anticipation of the blow-out in the prison population that the other measures would produce. As it was, on the passing of the *Sentencing Act* 2002 *(*NZ), the Justice Minister telephoned Withers to congratulate him on the success of the referendum. Furthermore, when addressing this legislation, the Ministry of Justice (2002, p 1, my italics) acknowledged the need to *"respond to the referendum which revealed public concern* over the sentencing of serious violent offenders".

Levels of imprisonment have also significantly increased across many other modern societies where populism has been influential. Leaving aside the exceptionalism of prison rates in the United States which began their rise to the current level of 737 per 100,000 of population in the 1980s, since 1995 imprisonment rates in England have increased from 99 to 145 per 100,000 of population in 2005. Even more spectacularly, the rate in the former icon of liberalism, the Netherlands, has increased from 66 to 127; while there have been increases in the Scandinavian countries as well, even if at a significantly lower rate: in Sweden, for example, from 65 to 78 (see Roberts et al, 2003; van Swaaningen, 2005; and Tham, 2001).

However, the effects and consequences of penal populism extend well beyond rising imprisonment rates. In some jurisdictions, for example, aspects of the punishment of offenders have been turned into a symbolic spectacle of reassurance for the onlooking public, and into one of humiliation and debasement for its recipients. Hence the development of naming and shaming penalties, in various mechanisms, in the United States, Britain and New Zealand. Similarly, crime victims have been repositioned so that they are at the centre of the criminal justice process. Its task then becomes one of determining the extent to which those who have offended against them have to be punished to expiate the harm they have done, rather than how to address any needs or deficiencies of their own that their crime has brought to light.

To further these ends, some long-standing criminal justice rights and processes that are thought to favour criminals at the expense of the law-abiding community have been curtailed or annulled: the rights of the community increasingly supersede the rights of individual criminals. Three strikes laws or derivatives, community notification procedures, sexual predator and dangerous offender laws all change long-standing assumptions about the moral and ethical basis of punishment in modern society – assumptions such as proportionality in sentencing, privacy on completion of a prison term and presumptions against indefinite sentencing or the double jeopardy consequences conjured by the United States sexual predator laws.[1]

Underlying causes

What is it that has brought about these dramatic changes? There would seem to be five underlying causes. The first is the decline of deference – a rejection by much of the general public of the hitherto unquestioned acceptance of authority or establishment figures and the values they represent. Nevitte (1996) argues that this has been the natural consequence of the success of post-war social reforms that raised the living standards of the whole population – to the effect that those in positions of power by virtue of wealth and privilege would no longer be viewed as the social superiors of the rest of society, no longer be allowed to govern, unquestioned, as they had done previously. This has had a significant impact on the rise of penal populism in so far as it can transform the relationship between governments and their civil service, undermining the ability of the latter to keep penal policy within their own exclusive grasp and determination. Instead, weakened by internal restructuring and the competing influences of outside pressure groups, think tanks and the law and order lobby, policy development can be left vulnerable to whatever external influences populist politicians choose to ally themselves with. Furthermore, the authority of criminal justice officials has been diminished. Judges and magistrates, for example, are regularly thought to be "out of touch" or "from another planet" by the public (Hough, 1996). Without the barrier of deference that used to be placed in front of political and populist influences from outside the criminal justice establishment when policy was being developed, commonsense concepts such as "three strikes" and "zero tolerance" have been allowed to become the normative values of sentencing systems (Zimring and Johnson, 2006).

Secondly, there has been substantial evidence in many modern societies of a decline in trust in politicians and existing political processes (Pratt, 2006b). While the venality of particular politicians may have contributed to this, a more general cause is likely to be the perceived inability of politicians and existing political processes to respond to the needs of "ordinary people" – the key constituency from which populism draws its support. For example, in countries such as Britain and New Zealand this disillusionment set in during the 1970s when the inflexibilities of welfare bureaucracies and strategies seemed to block their aspirations (Garland, 2001) while simultaneously favouring such unworthy members of society as "dole bludgers" and "scroungers". The subsequent shifts to a neo-liberal polity in these societies provided a much greater sense of personal freedom and choice but at the same time removed many state-provided safety nets for those who then made the wrong choices – leading to societies that were strong on individualism but weak on social bonds and interdependencies.

Thereafter, the impact of globalisation has further weakened the authority of sovereign states and makes them seem vulnerable to external organisations and forces. The most popular answer to the question in a BBC Radio poll "who runs Britain" was "the EU Commissioner", followed by press baron Rupert Murdoch.[2] Against this backdrop, it should be of no surprise that there is little faith in politicians and in existing democratic processes: "the established political class is no longer able to resolve the most basic problems, [and] politicians generally [seem] too absorbed with themselves to be able to adapt to a rapidly changing world" (Betz, 1994, p 41). It is for these very reasons – at the exact time that governments no longer seem to be in control of events – that a greater citizen involvement in politics itself takes place, but in the form of a new politics that finds expression in single issue pressure groups and more fickle and unpredictable electoral support. This new politics is no longer tied to rigid class hierarchies and party political allegiance determined at birth, but instead is prepared to flirt with politicians of whatever shade and with new parties that are prepared to speak to these matters.

A third cause is ontological insecurity. During the development of modern society, one of the ways in which individuals had been able to guard against "existential anxiety" was by developing "a framework of ontological security of some sort, based on routines of various forms. People handle dangers and the fears associated with them in terms of the emotional and behavioural formulae which have come to be part of their everyday behaviour and thought" (Giddens, 1991, p 44). However, it is clear that many of the conditions necessary for such formulae are no longer in place. Many of the pillars of stability and security that had been built up during the development of modern society have crumbled away: tenured employment has all but disappeared; family life has been shattered by divorce and marriage has given way to more transient cohabiting practices; and there have been declines in church attendance, trade union membership and various other forms of community involvement (Fukuyama, 1995). Furthermore, amid these examples of the general decline in organic community life, the seemingly inexorable rise in recorded crime during the 1980s and 1990s became one of the most obvious indicators that security and stability seemed to be breaking down, and governments, whatever their political colour, seemed to have no control over such events. When social cohesion seems to be unravelling in these ways, the more strident will be the demands for penal severity as a way of restoring the authority of the criminal law and of providing consensus and uniformity (Tyler and Boeckmann, 1999). Under these circumstances many citizens will be more likely to put their trust and support in those populist organisations and political movements which claim to have the solutions to such problems – magical, commonsense solutions usually based on invocations of some golden period in the past when social stability and social order was unquestioned.

A fourth cause is the media. It might seem particularly ironic that, from the mid 1990s, penal populism should become so extensive at exactly the same time that crime began to decline in most western countries. New Zealand again provides a very good demonstration of this pattern. Nonetheless, there is clear survey evidence suggesting that most people still think that crime is increasing even though it has been in decline (see van Kesteren et al, 2000; Ministry of Justice, 2003). This is because, in the changing nature of social relations in the modern world, most people are likely to elicit their knowledge of such events from vicarious rather than direct sources: they will rely primarily on the mass media rather than on their neighbours and family for news of such events. In these respects, the nature of crime reporting in the media confirms commonsense assumptions that crime is out of control, even though all the statistical gauges of it may demonstrate the opposite (Jewkes, 2004). Furthermore, the dimensions of the crime problem are enlarged through the over-emphasis of crime news, making the problem seem one that is acute and requiring drastic action while simultaneously highlighting the apparent leniency of the criminal justice authorities when punishing criminals (Ashworth and Hough, 1996). Changes in the structure of the media, particularly the popular media, have been brought about by the impact of deregulation and new information technology. News reporting and current affairs programs have had the time allocated to them reduced while simultaneously their content has been simplified. For example, in relation to the CBS flagship current affairs program *Sixty Minutes*, Fallows (1997, p 57) found that "of the nearly 500 stories between 1990 and 1994, more than one third were celebrity profiles, entertainment industry stories, or exposes of ... petty scandal. Barely one fifth of the stories concerned economics, the real workings of politics, or any other issue of long-term significance".

In addition, access to the mass media has been democratised. The development of talk-back radio has accelerated moves towards mass participation in news-making and opinion-forming. Such programs are usually hosted by "entertainers" or "personalities" rather than journalists, who nonetheless present their shows as a legitimate forum for serious consideration of political events and issues. But, unlikely to have specialist knowledge or training themselves, they are likely to fall back on commonsense as a way of understanding these matters and by so doing reaffirm the commonsense world views of their listeners. In such ways, the impact of new information technology provides ordinary people with the opportunity to make, report and comment on the news themselves, ensuring that broadcasting elites no longer have exclusive control of knowledge and information about crime and other matters. Law and order lobbyists have grasped such opportunities much more effectively to date than their opponents. They not only always seem to be available for comment, but at the same time, the knowledge they draw on is easily understandable by the general public as it is based on personal experience, common sense rather than social science research, and newspaper headlines rather than detailed analysis of crime patterns. Norm Withers, when campaigning for his referendum, thus claimed that "you read the papers every day, look what's happening. It's time to toughen up so we can deter [criminals] from wanting to go back to prison. These do-gooders and civil libertarians who want to look after the well-being of criminals, it's time they got real and thought about the victims" (*The Dominion* 1 January 1999, p 1). In contrast, civil servants and judges are normally precluded from making any public comments on such matters, while academics have often been disdainful of these opportunities or else present their comments in such a way that they are generally not accessible to the demands of the news media and the public at large (Haggerty, 2004).

Finally, this democratisation of the news media has provided the opportunity for the emotive experiences and opinions of ordinary people rather than detached and objective expert analysis to become the framework through which crime and punishment is understood. In these respects, victimisation has come to be regarded as a particularly authentic expression of this new mode of knowledge. The harm that has been inflicted on victims is seen as harm inflicted on the rest of society, justifying the much greater penal severity that spokespeople for such victims demand. Indeed, victimisation has assumed an iconic status in populist discourse. The way in which particular laws have been named after crime victims ("Megan's Law" is the most obvious example) becomes a way of honouring them and memorialising them through the protection that the legislation they have inspired may now provide for potential victims in the future. At the same time, the victim's voice, *or the voices of those who claim to speak on their behalf*, has been given an authenticity and validity in relation to the development of crime control policies, while the authority and influence of the criminal justice expert has been decried and reduced (Garland, 2001). As such, victims of crime who fight back in defence of their family or property when it seems that the criminal justice authorities cannot provide this assistance, can become popular heroes; they become another emblem of the way in which the interests of such "ordinary people" have been overlooked or dismissed by the criminal justice establishment.

Penal populism in New Zealand

I am not saying that all modern societies will have this exact arrangement of social forces in them at the present time. What seems clear, however, is that in those societies where there is the most acute concentration of them, then the influence of penal populism will be particularly strong. In these respects, New Zealand has enjoyed something of a "full house". Not only is this a society where elites and establishment forces have always enjoyed little deference, for various historico-cultural reasons (Pratt, 2006c), but, in addition, in 1984 it moved almost overnight from being the most regulated western society to the most deregulated. For a decade thereafter governments from both Right and Left insisted that "there was no alternative". Notwithstanding the ways in which such economic restructuring has turned New Zealand into a more market-driven, cosmopolitan and hetero-geneous society, it has also contributed to a collapse of faith in establishment politics amidst the growth of insecurities and anxieties that this dramatic shift in governance has brought about. As a response to this disenchantment, and itself a reflection of the declining authority of the New Zealand central state at that time, in the early 1990s politicians voted to change the electoral system from "first-past-the-post" to proportional representation while simultaneously providing for non-binding citizens' referenda (Pratt and Clark, 2005). In such ways, it was thought that public opinion and sentiment would have more direct influence on government policy and that politicians would be more accountable to the electorate.

Some of the most obvious outlets for these sentiments relate, of course, to crime and punishment issues. Fringe parties having law and order as one of their central issues have been able to gain leverage for it when becoming junior partners in the inevitable coalition governments that this electoral system leads to. At the same time, there have been "bidding wars" (Newburn and Jones, 2005) between Labour and National – the two main parties – as they have tried to prove their respective law and order credentials to the electorate. Indeed, taking a leaf out of New Labour's successes in Britain, the New Zealand Labour Party replicated Tony Blair's "tough on crime, tough on the causes of crime" catchphrase in their election manifestos of 2002 and 2005.

In addition, the deregulation of the news media in this country has facilitated the prominence given to law and order issues while promoting the role played by law and order lobby groups as opinion formers. Since the late 1980s, New Zea-land's national broadcasting company, TVNZ, which had originally followed the BBC model of public service broadcasting, has for all intents and purposes become a commercial channel far more dependent than before on advertising for its revenue source, with attendant consequences for the reporting and analysis of crime news. Cook (2002, pp 140-1) writes in relation to TVNZ that "the average length of a news item has reduced by approximately 20 seconds (90 to 70) between 1984 and 1996". The maximum length of any news item fell from nine minutes in 1984 to four minutes 30 seconds in 1996. Again, from the mid 1990s, fear of crime, despite the largely unremarked fall in recorded crime, was regularly stimulated by the focus in news reporting on idealised victims, those who were completely innocent and defenceless, the personification of all that is good and innocent, but who had been victimised by others who then could only be seen as utterly malevolent and irredeemable. For example:

> Norm Withers tapped a deep well of justified public unease when he launched the petition to hold the referendum. The laws and the justice system seem to many to be too geared to meeting the needs of the criminal and too forgetful of the victim. Mr Withers' own experience is tragic proof of that. His mother Nan was brutally beaten and needed 75 stitches to her face and head. She walks with difficulty, and has lost some speech and sense of taste. Her attacker ... was on parole at the time, even though he had an astonishing 56 previous convictions. His sentence was 10 years, but he will serve far less than that (*The Dominion* 13 October 1999, p 12).

Similarly, the very prominent and influential law and order organisation – the Sensible Sentencing Trust – was formed in 2001 in part as a response to the prosecution of Mark Middleton. When persistently asked by a television news journalist what his reaction was to the news that the murderer of his stepdaughter would soon be applying for parole (which he was never granted), Middleton threatened to kill him. This statement caused Middleton's own arrest and subsequent conviction for threatening behaviour (for which he received a suspended sentence). Both the Withers and Middleton cases confirmed the popular view of criminal justice in New Zealand which was that offenders flourished while victims suffered. Urged on by the Sensible Sentencing Trust, successive governments then tried to close this "justice gap" with support for longer sentences and the like, notwithstanding the fact that the prison population was then beginning to escalate while crime was already in decline (Pratt and Clark, 2005).

The power of scandal

If this represents a dramatic portrayal of the power of penal populism once it takes hold in a particular jurisdiction, what we are now witnessing in New Zealand is an attempt by the Labour-led coalition government to bring a halt to its rampages. As events in some American States have begun to illustrate (Lawson, 2004; Jacobson, 2005), there are likely to be moral and financial limits to the advances that penal populism can make in a given jurisdiction, although such boundary lines of acceptability are very much dependent on local histories and contingencies: there is no set formula that can determine where these might lie. Nonetheless, when penal populism does arrive at these boundaries, then what it has accomplished may suddenly cease to be a sign of political virility but instead becomes one of scandal.

Sparks (2000, p 133) writes of scandal that "particular events, stories and controversies can in their aftermath exercise profound effects, both at the level of popular consciousness and of political, legislative and system level change". In most contemporary penal discourse, scandal has become the almost exclusive property of populists. They make great play of what they see as scandals – prison sentences that seem insufficiently long or prison conditions that seem far too luxurious – in their attempts to undermine the criminal justice establishment. Meanwhile their opponents in the academy or penal reform bodies have not really been able to capture public debate. This is because in the new axis of penal power, rationality – the continuous restating of arguments about prison costs, lack of effectiveness, reconviction rates and so on that was the kernel of policy under the previous axis – will no longer prevail in and of itself. It is exactly this kind of detailed, informed, technocratic knowledge which may be central to the thinking of the criminal justice establishment but which is so difficult to fit within more general modes of public discourse and communication which governments now look to when developing policy. Within the framework of the new axis, the terms of penal debate and those who may participate in it have changed. As Indermaur and Hough (2002, p 210) acknowledge, "the appeal of simplified and tough minded penal policy lies in its ability to resonate with public emotions such as fear and anger ... Anyone who wants to improve public debate about crime needs to be attuned to this emotional dimension".

However, the strategic use of scandal might be one way to make more effective intervention against populism. It is not simply too liberal penal policy that provokes scandal; *penal policy that is too severe* also provokes it. Penal policy that is too severe also contravenes local penal sensibilities (Brown, 2005, p 33). For much of the previous decade, scandal about luxurious prisons and out of touch judges had fuelled the New Zealand populist momentum. In 2004, for example, six prisoners were awarded (modest) damages for ill-treatment they had received for being held in conditions akin to an American supermax prison, for which there was no lawful authority. Amidst great public consternation (that they had success-fully sued, not that they had been ill-treated) the Labour government quickly passed the *Prisoners' and Victims' Claims Act* 2005 (NZ). This allows victims of crime to sue ex-prisoners who offended against them for up to six years after their release for any windfall they have since received (including, as in the above case, damages for unlawful treatment by the Department of Corrections).

However, from late 2005, the convergence of a range of incidents relating to the inhumanity of prison conditions and the consequences of penal severity have had sufficient force to become *scandalous*, attracting the interest of the media, particularly journalists and television reporters working in crucial opinion-forming positions in it. First, the $1 billion cost of four new prisons currently being built (the cost of one might have gone unnoticed), vastly in excess of what was originally budgeted (around $320 million), at a time when public expenditure is under pressure in areas that have more public utility, has become a matter of continuing public debate. Secondly, there have been two authoritative reports, one from the Office of the Ombudsman (2005), the other from the Salvation Army (Smith and Robinson, 2006), that have highlighted the enforced idleness and the absence of work or education for most prisoners in this country. This information undercuts public expectations that prison expenditure should have *some* purpose, whether it be hard labour or rehabilitation: to spend so much money to no effect – *to keep most prisoners doing nothing whatsoever* – generates public agitation. Thirdly, New Zealand's high rate of imprisonment is beginning to become an inscribed feature of political and public debate as it so clearly challenges the reputation for egalitarianism and social justice that is also associated with this country (Pratt, 2006c).

There have also been regular features on prisons and penal policy on leading radio and television current affairs programs and a major and well publicised conference organised by the Prison Reform Trust (*Beyond Retribution: Advancing the Law and Order Debate*) At the same time, particular incidents have high lighted the unsustainability of current policies. Reports in the media, for example, of prisoners having to sleep in a prison van in the street outside the gaol they had been sent to because it was full; of prisoners being taken to rugby clubs to shower because of the strain placed on prison facilities by overcrowding (*The Dominion Post* 26 October 2005, p 3); of young offenders being held in remand in police cells for days on end because there was no prison accommodation for them; and of the brutal murder of a 17 year old, remanded in custody for burglary and for stealing his mother's car, while in transit from court to prison by one of his peers (*The Dominion Post* 28 August 2006, p 1).

In early 2006 the public interest that had already been provoked in these ways encouraged a commercial television station – TV3 – to make and screen a program in prime time that very unfavourably compared the New Zealand prison system with that of Finland, thereby giving the scandal more food and energy.[3] The country's two leading newspapers ran features on the problems of New Zealand's prisons,[4] even if the reporting has been somewhat schizophrenic at times. For example, in the same edition of *The Dominion Post* (28 February 2006), the front page headline was: "Jail lets sex crims out to pick fruit". This event was reported as a scandal that would fuel populism. In reality, sex offenders had been given day release to pick fruit on local farms at a time of acute labour shortages. Meanwhile the editorial (p B4) explained that: "New Zealand has proved itself very good at locking up criminals. It is what is happening after the prison door slams that is an unacceptable failure … society needs to look again at how it deals with its criminals, and look at it more urgently." Now the paper was addressing a different kind of prison scandal – one provoked by the very attitudes and style of reporting displayed on its front page. Inevitably, though, when much of the media is attracted to scandal, its engagement with it is likely to be ad hoc, contingent and unpredictable. Nonetheless, the general convergence of interest around prison issues has helped to rewrite the way in which prison can be "scandalised" in this country. Scandal no longer focuses exclusively on escapes and luxuries – although it still does focus on these when provided with appropriate opportunities – but it also asks what such levels of imprisonment, and what such prison conditions are saying about New Zealand as a society.

As this series of scandals began to unravel, the government made it increasingly clear that it wanted to change policy. New Corrections and Justice Ministers were appointed towards the end of 2005 with seemingly more liberal views than their predecessors, and they made visits to countries such as Finland, famous for dramatically reducing its prison population. High profile seminars were sponsored by the Ministry of Justice. The themes were public attitudes to crime and sentencing, in particular the gulf between general responses to law and order questions and the more considered, reflective opinions that gave very different results when people were asked about specific case studies. In effect, it was as if the government was attempting to position itself closer to the realities of public opinion research rather than to populist impressions of the public mood. The extent of the intended change of course was then revealed in a high profile launch in August 2006 of the Law Commission's (2006) report to government advocating the establishment of a Sentencing Council, which was presided over by the Prime Minister (Young, this volume). The proposal has the support of the government. It is intended that the Council will provide more "truth in sentencing". Parole eligibility will be restricted until two-thirds of the sentence has been served (as it was before the 2002 "get tough" reforms!). In this way, a prison term would bear a closer relation to the sentence pronounced in court. Meanwhile, to reduce the prison population, sentence lengths will be reduced by some 25 per cent with the Sentencing Council establishing appropriate guidelines to bring this about. It is intended that the Council will restrict disproportionate and inconsistent sentencing while relieving some of the political pressures on judges to pass longer sentences. Through its composition, it recognises that sentencing is not the exclusive property of judges and the criminal justice authorities. Its membership of 10 will include four judges, the Chair of the Parole Board (himself a judge) and five others with expertise or understanding of such issues as criminal justice, prisoner reintegration, the welfare of crime victims and community issues affecting the courts and the penal system. As such, there is likely to be some formal presence for those who claim to speak on behalf of the general public in the determination of sentencing policy rather than their being left free to run wild with claims and accusations as at present. At the same time, though, they will clearly not be the only determinants of policy – they will have to share ownership of it.

For the present government, New Zealand's high level of imprisonment – which it played a large part in generating – has become a source of shame. At the launch of the Law Commission's report, the Prime Minister commented that "prison levels are too high ... the goal must be to get the prison rate back to something more consistent with our peers ... the criminal justice system cannot go on as it is [with] an unacceptably high rate of imprisonment". What these changes will lead to remains to be seen. Penal populism has to date been much easier to let loose than to rein in. It does, though, point to the beginning of another chapter in recent penal developments in this country: the government that was so eager to buy into penal populism now seems very keen to disavow it as its chickens come home to roost. That this is happening is testament to the power of scandal and the way it can undermine populism as well as support it.

Notes

1   That is, indefinite confinement in a mental institution for those so judged, after serving a finite term of imprisonment for their crime.

2   *People and Politics,* BBC World Service, 28 January 2006.

3   *Cambell Live,* 7 February 2006.

4   See *New Zealand Herald*, "Our Idle Jails", 25 February 2006 to 4 March 2006; *The Dominion Post*, "Bulging Prisons Spark Rethink", 25 February: A10.

References

Ashworth, A and Hough, M (1996). Sentencing and the Climate of Opinion. *Criminal Law Review*: 776.

Betz, HG (1994). *Radical Right-Wing Populism in Western Europe*. Basingstoke: Macmillan.

Brown, D (2005). Continuity, Rupture or Just more of the "Volatile and Contradictory"?: Glimpses of New South Wales' Penal Practice behind and through the Discursive". In J Pratt, D Brown, S Hallsworth, M Brown and W Morrison (eds), *The New Punitiveness: Theories, Trends, Perspectives*. Cullompton: Willan.

Cook, D (2002). Deregulation and Broadcast News Content: ONE Network News 1984 to 1996. In J Farnsworth and I Hutchinson (eds), *New Zealand Television: A Reader*, Palmerston North, NZ: Dunmore Press.

Cullen, F, Fisher, B and Applegate, B (2000). Public Opinion about Punishment and Corrections. *Law and Society Review* 34: 1.

Fallows, J (1997). *Breaking the News*. New York: Vintage.

Fukuyama, F (1995). *Trust: The Social Virtues and the Creation of Prosperity*. New York: Free Press.

Garland, D (2001). *The Culture of Control*. New York: Oxford University Press.

Giddens, A (1991). *Modernity and Self-Identity*. Cambridge: Polity Press.

Haggerty, K (2004). Displaced Expertise: Three Constraints on the Policy Relevance of Criminological Thought. *Theoretical Criminology* 8: 211.

Hough, M (1996). People Talking about Punishment. *Howard Journal of Criminal Justice* 35: 191.

Indermaur, D and Hough, M (2002). Strategies for Changing Public Attitudes to Punishment. In J Roberts and M Hough (eds), *Changing Attitudes to Punishment: Public Opinion, Crime and Justice*. Cullompton: Willan.

Jacobson, M (2005). *Downsizing Prisons: How to Reduce Crime and End Mass Incarceration*. New York: New York University Press.

Jewkes, Y (2004). *Media and Crime*. London: Sage.

Law Commission (2006). *Sentencing Guidelines and Parole Reform*. Wellington: Law Commission.

Lawson, RG (2004). Difficult Time in Kentucky Corrections – Aftershock of a "Tough on Crime" Philosophy. *Kentucky Law Journal* 93: 305.

Ministry of Justice (2003). *Attitudes to Crime and Punishment: A New Zealand Study*. Wellington: Ministry of Justice.

Moriarty, M (1977). The Policy-making Process: How it is Seen from the Home Office. In N Walker (ed), *Penal Policy-making in England*. Cropwood Conference, Institute of Criminology, Cambridge.

Nevitte, N (1996). *The Decline of Difference: Canadian Value Change in Cross National Perspective*. Peterborough, Ontario: Broadview Press.

Newburn, T and Jones, T (2005). Symbolic Politics and Penal Populism: The Long Shadow of Willie Horton. *Crime, Media, Culture* 1: 72.

Office of the Ombudsman (2005). *Ombudsman's Investigation of the Department of Corrections in Relation to the Detention and Treatment of Prisoners*. Wellington: Office of the Ombudsman.

Pratt, J (2006a). Punishment, Politics and Public Opinion: The Sorcerer's Apprentice Revisited. Conference paper presented at *Beyond Retribution: Advancing the Law and Order Debate*. Prison Reform Trust Conference, May.

Pratt, J (2006b). *Penal Populism*. London: Routledge.

Pratt, J (2006c). The Dark Side of Paradise. *British Journal of Criminology* 46(4): 541.

Pratt, J and Clark, M (2005). Penal Populism in New Zealand. *Punishment and Society* 7: 303.

Roberts, JV, Stalans, L, Indermaur, D and Hough, M (2003). *Penal Populism and Public Opinion.* New York: Oxford University Press.

Savelsberg, J (1994). Knowledge, Domination and Criminal Punishment. *American Journal of Sociology* 99: 911.

Smith, L and Robinson, B (2006). *Beyond the Holding Tank: Pathways to Rehabilitative and Restorative Prison Policy.* Manukau, NZ: The Salvation Army Social Policy and Parliamentary Unit.

Sparks, R (2000). The Media and Penal Politics. *Punishment and Society* 2: 98.

Tham, H (2001). Law and Order as a Leftist Project?: The Case of Sweden. *Punishment and Society* 3: 409.

Tyler, T and Boeckmann, R (1997). Three Strikes and You are Out, but Why? The Psychology of Public Support for Punishing Rule Breakers. *Law and Society Review* 31: 237.

van Kesteren, JN, Mayhew, P and Nieuwbeerta, P (2000). *Criminal Victimisation in Seventeen Industrialised Countries: Key-findings from the 2000 International Crime Victims Survey.* The Hague: Ministry of Justice, WODC.

van Swaaningen, R (2005). Public Safety and the Management of Fear. *Theoretical Criminology* 9: 289.

Zimring, F and Johnson, DT (2006). Public Opinion and Governance of Punishment: Democratic Political Systems. *Democracy, Crime and Justice, Annals of the American Academy of Political and Social Science* 605: 265.

4

Dealing the public in: challenges for a transparent and accountable sentencing policy

David Indermaur

Introduction

Calls for the courts more accurately to reflect public opinion can be seen as one of the signs of a crisis of confidence in the courts. Although it is debatable whether the term "crisis" is appropriate for such a perennial problem, there is little doubt there is a problem to be addressed here at both the political and judicial level. The fundamental problem concerns perceptions, not only that sentencing is out of touch with popular opinion, but that it lacks coherence and is neither transparent nor accountable outside an elite group. The problem has been around for some time and is clearly on the minds of many governments, as indicated by the range of inquires and mechanisms that have been developed in response to the crisis. Various proposals have been developed and applied to address the lack of confidence.[1] Some of the proposed solutions involve "dealing the public into" the process of forming sentencing policy and these comprise the focus of this chapter. The present discussion touches on the role of sentencing advisory bodies.

The chapter begins with an overview of developments designed to accommodate the public into the formation of sentencing policy in England and Wales, Australia and New Zealand. Sentencing advisory bodies in these and similar countries have tried to involve the public in a variety of ways including directly appointing community members and inviting public comments on released documents. It will be argued in the third section of this chapter that these mechanisms are not sufficient to achieve the goal of including the public into the sentencing review or policy-formation process in any meaningful way. When we consider what has been developed elsewhere as suitable frameworks for public participation, the current efforts appear to be at best piecemeal and at worst tokenistic. Most importantly these efforts do not appear to be based on a careful analysis of the nature of public disenchantment with sentencing. In the fourth section it will be argued that the problem of public mistrust of the courts has particular social and political dimensions that need to be addressed in shaping a strategy of public engagement. In the fifth section of the chapter some of the obstacles that must be overcome to enable a genuine process of public participation are outlined. It is concluded that a robust and transparent process of providing for public participation will require an approach and mechanisms that are likely to be beyond the capacity of sentencing advisory bodies as they are currently structured. However, there are other imperatives that may result in sentencing reforms that are responsive to public concerns and thus help build confidence in the courts.

Responding to the crisis of legitimacy

Introduction

Public opinion has always been highly relevant to sentencing and will remain so not least because of the sensitivity of individual sentencers to perceived public opinion. Part of the ultimate benefit of formalising public input into sentencing policy may be to counter the undifferentiated and idiosyncratic interpretation of public opinion by sentencers. But the primary rationale remains political. Where the judgments of the court appear to disregard public sensitivities there is good copy for the media, ammunition for the opposition and trouble for the government.

There has been a range of responses to the crisis of confidence, the best known coming under the umbrella of penal populism (see Roberts et al, 2003; Pratt, 2007). However, there are also several more measured responses that have sought to restore confidence. These include initiatives that seek to engage the public in various ways (see Hough and Roberts, 2004). One of the main responses of governments in England and Wales, Australia and New Zealand has been to establish sentencing advisory bodies that are charged with the responsibility of incorporating input from the public. This section focuses on the way these bodies have emerged and how they are situated within more general responses to the crisis of confidence.

England and Wales

There have been several events that could be considered to be "milestones" in the recent sentencing reform process that seeks to include a public voice in England and Wales, starting with the establishment of the Sentencing Advisory Panel (SAP) in 1999. Following this, 2001 saw the release of the Home Office Review of Sentencing and Auld reports followed by the White Paper *Justice for All*.[2] Subsequently the *Criminal Justice Act* 2003 (UK) retained the SAP and also created a Sentencing Guidelines Council (SGC) to take over the role previously adopted by the Court of Appeal. Both the SAP and the SGC have within their remit the task of considering public opinion in their deliberations, although the responsibility for detailed investigation or consultation is undertaken by the SAP, which then advises the SGC (see Ashworth, this volume). Since its establishment the SAP has commissioned two investigations into public attitudes relevant to sentencing, both published in 2002. The first concerned public attitudes to domestic burglary and the second attitudes to date and relationship rape.

The Halliday report represents an attempt to formulate a comprehensive sentencing policy and situate a public voice within it. The review commissioned a public opinion survey and followed a small sub-group to test out the effect on attitude of providing more information.[3] Halliday recommended both increasing the level of communication about sentencing from the courts to the public and aligning sentencing with community expectations.[4] Apart from government activities from 2001 to 2004 the *Rethinking Crime and Punishment* project[5] funded under the Esmée Fairbairn Foundation provided funding to 57 projects aimed at engendering a "more rational penal policy" through increasing public knowledge and improving the level of public debate (Allen, 2004). One of the projects was an analysis of the results of a deliberative poll on crime and punishment that had been undertaken in 1994 (Hough and Park, 2002).[6]

Since the release of the Halliday report the government has been vigorous in its efforts to structure and direct reforms of criminal justice, including sentencing, to attend to the interests of "the law abiding majority" with a renewed focus on public safety as a primary concern. The need to increase public confidence has been a consistent theme. The government of England and Wales continues to include improvements in public confidence in the criminal justice system as targets within public service agreements. The government also commissioned an international review of public confidence in criminal justice to explore the underlying factors and the remedies that have been adopted (Hough and Roberts, 2004).

In November 2006 the government released a consultation paper, (*Making Sentencing Clearer*), that proposed changes to simplify sentencing and make it more accessible to the public.[7] The paper was released with the statement that "[t]he government wants to initiate a wide-ranging public discussion on the way forward on sentencing".[8] The Home Secretary was clearly concerned with the gap in understanding between the public and the courts. The language of the release was peppered with pleas for public involvement and showed a concern for the lack of transparency and public confidence as well as a desire to increase public understanding of sentencing: "We need to find ways to increase public understanding of how sentences are calculated and the consequences for the offender". Part of the remedy appears be a wide and open public discussion as the report is also prefaced with the following statement from the Home Secretary, Attorney General and Lord Chancellor (*Making Sentencing Clearer*, p 2):

> When we announced our plans to rebalance the Criminal Justice System in favour of the law abiding majority we set out our intention to initiate a wider discussion on a range of sentencing and related issues. This consultation is part of that wider debate.

Despite the fact that the most recent consultation documents came with details about where to send responses and how they would be processed and publicised[9] it was not clear how the government expected to canvass public responses effectively. There was no evidence of a system that could fairly test the perceptions of the general public and it remained unclear how representative of the general public the responses submitted would be. Consider, for example, the following question (one of 16):[10]

> Do you think there should be power for the prison or other authorities to refer a sentence for reconsideration of automatic release if an offender gives serious cause for concern during the custodial part of his sentence and if so who should have the power to refer? If so should this reference be to a High Court judge, or do you have another idea?

Although there may be problems with its methodology, there appears to be little doubt that the government wanted to undertake a direct "discussion" with the public in regard to sentencing reform, raising questions about the role of the sentencing advisory bodies in this regard. These bodies also pay much deference to the notion of public involvement. Consider for example the following statement from the SGC website under the area headed "public consultations":[11]

> As part of the process of formulating sentencing guidelines, we consult widely with all interested parties. One way we do this is by regularly issuing public consultations.
>
> Public consultations are an opportunity for anyone with an interest in guidelines formation to influence our thinking. We welcome responses from all. To take part in a public consultation, read the current open consultations papers and respond in writing to the Secretariat.

However, there is little information available on the degree of importance given to these submissions, what they said, or even how many were received. It would be hard for any individual or group within the public to judge whether it was worth their effort to make a submission. There is nothing stated in the purpose or focus of either the SAP or SGC that obliges them to consider public views, to canvass these views comprehensively, to respond to them in an organised way or indeed include them in their recommendations. There has been no plan or mechanism established to enable anyone to measure the success of these bodies in achieving their stated goal of incorporating public views.[12]

The New Labour government was obviously determined to make sentencing policy more responsive to public demands. However, the key question is how well the government and its sentencing advisory bodies have provided for public input. Ultimately it remains to be seen how much importance the public voice is actually given in developing sentencing policy. Do these advisory bodies simply add extra layers of bureaucracy without changing anything fundamental in regard to the politics of sentencing? Are they useful in assisting the courts to improve their performance in accordance with public interests or wishes? Are they really supposed to be mechanisms to allow genuine public consultation or public input into the formulation of sentencing policy? Perhaps by considering what constitute the essential steps in providing for public participation we may be in a better position to address these questions and assess the efforts of specialist bodies and governments to "deal the public in". Before we do this we will briefly consider the developments in Australia and New Zealand that have reflected, albeit on a much smaller scale, the developments in England and Wales.

Australia and New Zealand

The underlying dynamics of the crisis of confidence are very similar in Australia and New Zealand although they have played out differently. However, the "democracy deficit" is a common concern as Lovegrove (1998, p 294) notes: "the public does not see itself being consulted and has no reason to believe that its views are being taken seriously". Not surprisingly, the dynamics of penal populism are well established leading to the passage of numerous mandatory sentencing laws, truth in sentencing legislation and a general toughening of sentencing and release decisions (Roberts et al, 2003). The problem of penal populism has followed a slightly different path in New Zealand, which has generally been regarded as an exemplar of tolerance and liberal social policy. Penal populism rose very sharply from the late 1990s and has since largely dominated discussions on sentencing. Pratt and Clark (2003) have discussed both the universal as well as some interesting local factors leading to the strong surge in penal populism in New Zealand (see also Pratt, this volume). Not least of these was a widespread feeling in the public that the courts were impervious to public wishes in regard to sentencing.

One major formal positive response to the crisis of confidence in both Australia and New Zealand has been the establishment of sentencing advisory bodies. In their international review Hough and Roberts (2004) also discuss the initiatives taken in South Australia by that State's Courts Administration Authority to increase public confidence.[13] Sentencing advisory councils have been introduced in two Australian States[14] and are viewed by the foundation chair of the New South Wales Council (Abadee, 2006, p 6) as a way to provide for greater community input into sentencing: "It is clear that councils with adequately conferred powers and functions can play a role in educating, informing and enhancing informed public opinion and indeed political opinion as well as engaging such".

The council established in Victoria, unlike New South Wales, has incorporated the aim of gauging public opinion as one of its main goals. The Victorian Sentencing Advisory Council also routinely releases documents for open public consultation and engages in public education.

The proposed establishment of a sentencing council in New Zealand represents one of the most recent developments in attempts to accommodate a wider perspective through establishing a sentencing advisory body (Young, this volume). Up to this point perhaps New Zealand's most notable contribution to ways of including public input came with the referendum question posed to all voters at the 1999 general election.[15] The question was:

> Should there be a reform of the criminal justice system placing greater emphasis on the needs of victims, providing restitution and compensation for them and imposing minimum sentences and hard labour for all serious violent offences?

Voters were given a simple choice of yes or no; not surprisingly 92 per cent of voters responded to the sentiment in the affirmative. Pratt and Clark (2003) argue that the referendum and the political manoeuvrings before and after to accommodate the growing drive for tougher penalties derived from a lack of trust in the courts and a disenchantment with existing democratic processes. Something of the mood of rising public anger and its effect on the government is revealed in the warning of the Justice Minister to judges that "public opinion does not take kindly to being ignored, particularly when there is a suspicion it is being dismissed arrogantly".[16] The mistrust of politicians and political bureaucracy appears to have provided the seed bed for the emergence of a number of single issue lobby groups, including one – the Sensible Sentencing Trust – that galvanised public opinion and made sentencing a central issue in New Zealand politics. The result has been the ascendancy of reform initiatives including a sentencing council that was designed to include representatives from beyond the judiciary and a desire to seek public input into the development of guidelines. The establishment of the council forms one part of the Criminal Justice Reform Bill that was before Parliament in 2007.

The structure of the sentencing council proposed by the New Zealand Law Commission (Young, this volume) shares many similarities with the British model. However, there were recommendations for expanding the sources of influence on sentencing policy partly by establishing the council with a majority of non-judicial members (including the chair) and a concern for transparency. Beyond this there was no specification for public participation or gauging public responses. The general public mainly features as the target of education in the hope that this would increase public confidence in the system. The sixth and final proposed function of the council (New Zealand Law Commission, 2006, p 13) is to "[i]nform the general public about sentencing and parole policies and decision making, and thereby promote public confidence in the criminal justice system".

We thus see in the direction of the Australian and New Zealand sentencing advisory councils no system of providing for public participation in policy development that could be described as routine or representative. The Victorian Sentencing Advisory Council has included mechanisms for gauging public preferences as one of its core aims and New Zealand, like Victoria, has gone to some lengths to ensure that the governance of council is not dominated by the judiciary, but neither of these amounts to a systematic plan for involving the public. The next section considers what such a plan might look like.

Public participation in sentencing reform: ideal and reality

Planning to involve the public

There are several challenges faced by any attempt to involve the public in developing sentencing policy. In general terms these can be seen to be a trade off between depth and breadth and between selective and representative. The kind of open (respond if you want) consultation process described in parts of the previous section does not attempt breadth or representativeness. Easy, but not very helpful. No mechanism is specified by which the public voice can be represented in a fair or meaningful way. At the other extreme we can see a similarly unhelpful approach in the New Zealand referendum question – this time trading depth for breadth.

It is clear that to involve the public in sentencing policy there needs to be a well constructed plan. However, before establishing such a plan it is important that the grounds for public participation be firmly established. Do we really want to involve the public in the development of sentencing policy? Perhaps we really only want to increase public confidence, and reluctantly see public participation as a means to achieve this. The question of how to build confidence is a broader one than how to involve the public. In their review of the crisis of confidence Hough and Roberts (2004) discuss a range of possible responses, most of which do not involve a formal process of public engagement. Thus one may increase confidence without involving the public in any structured way. Similarly it may be possible to involve the public for the purposes of increasing confidence but not have that involvement relate to any changes in sentencing policy. The discussion here is concerned not with these endeavours but with the prospect of involving the public in some structured way so as to inform sentencing policy.

Developing a plan for public involvement in sentencing policy represents a complex challenge. The task is to find ways to integrate the expertise necessary to structure policy with that needed to open it up to public debate.[17] There is now a burgeoning literature on the business of providing for public participation in developing policy, including complex areas of social policy.[18] This experience points to the necessity of a multi-layered strategy where policy questions are carefully formulated before any attempt at formally engaging the public. The engagement stage is followed by stages that integrate the public input and publish the resulting policy. The actual engagement of the public remains the key stage, and this will be examined in some depth later in this section. However, we will begin with an overview of the other stages and the multi-layered strategy in general.

In the preparation stage, components or aspects of sentencing policy, where it is valuable to obtain public input, need to be identified by a suitably qualified group and then questions developed where public preferences or responses are relevant. This initial stage could involve key groups of stakeholders, as has been the practice elsewhere, to help frame relevant questions for the public debate (see Renn et al, 1993). This enables some key groups, such as victims of crime, to have a role at the beginning of the process in identifying key areas to be put to the public.[19] This stage also involves developing a range of policy positions and questions. Policy options need to be formulated and embellished with vital information such as cost benefit analyses and other considerations to allow meaningful and realistic policy options to be posed in an appropriate way to a sample of the public.

Public input is more likely to be useful when focusing on the overarching goals of sentencing and the principles that govern choices to be made in regard to competing aims. Technical details and unusual cases are less relevant and a less useful way of gauging public values. Questions for public debate also need to be staged in an appropriate way – working from the general to the specific. The most important questions should be framed so that the responses can directly inform policy considerations. Careful surveying can ascertain a hierarchy of goals and sentencing principles relevant to those drafting policy. Questions that are either too general or too specific to be of any practical use in formulating policy are signs of process that is either insincere or ill considered.

From the public engagement stage, discussed below, we can arrive at a set of principles and priorities that reflect an informed and considered public view. The penultimate stage in the multi-layered strategy is to synthesise these and integrate them with other inputs (for example, from sentencing scholars, special reviews) and the existing framework. Following the development of a draft policy the final stage comprises the publication and promulgation of the policy. This stage is important to ensure transparency and accountability. Ultimately if one of the aims is to assist in increasing the legitimacy of the sentencing system and engender confidence in the courts this last phase should be emphasised.

To sum up, it is suggested that there are four essential components of a plan to include the public in policy formulation: a well thought out consultation strategy; accurate, sensible and comprehensive measures of public preferences; integration of public preferences with existing and proposed sentencing frameworks; and publication of the results in a way that is accessible to all.[20] In the remainder of this section the focus will be on measuring public preferences. The measurement of public preferences forms the heart of any process seeking to involve the public and would be a valuable contribution even in the absence of other aspects of the multi-layered plan. The measurement of public preferences alone could, for example, reveal that there are not substantial gaps between public preferences and existing policy, thus providing a degree of legitimacy for policy.

Measuring public preferences

Central to the process of involving the public is some reliable way of understanding its position, preferences and concerns. Well designed surveys that incorporate the necessary information and provide opportunities for question and debate are necessary to make a claim that the process has comprehensively canvassed public views. The particular methodology to be adopted in preparing questions for public deliberation and debate and ways then to incorporate the results into sentencing policy also need to be established. If the aim is to consult with "the general public" a random sample of the population is a necessary starting point to ensure equality of selection and to overcome the inherent bias of self-selection or nominations by the government or its agents.

There are several key concepts to clarify before we should endeavour to map public preferences. First, the concept of "attitude" is very different from "judgment". Simple opinion polls construct a situation where the respondent is placed in the role of a customer choosing from a menu. This is not only somewhat patronising but is neither realistic nor helpful for a business where choices must be made between competing alternatives to achieve some stated goal. Placing respondents into a position where they need to weigh up competing goals, sensitivities and constraints and arrive at a responsible decision is more realistic and invites a more considered response. Studies of measures of public attitude have found this to be a crucial shift which informs and colours the outcome significantly.[21]

There is now a mass of evidence that suggests that the thing we call "public opinion" is largely dependent on the context and question asked (Roberts and Stalans, 1997; Cullen et al, 2000). The thoughts and positions adopted by a member of the public in relation to a question are usually pre-primed by media and political discussions which sketch out the contours of the responses along the lines of already established socio-political interests. Even a slight re-wording of questions to include meaningful alternatives can have massive implications as evidenced by the substantially different results that emerge from questions about preferences for the death penalty when the option of "life without parole" is included as an alternative. The inclusion of this alternative has helped reconfigure the view of public attitudes to the death penalty in the United States and has contributed to the growing movement for the abolition of the death penalty in that country.[22] A number of other studies in the field of public attitudes to sentencing have found that members of the public tend to be responsive to reasonable propositions and logical arguments.[23] The public is thus likely to be receptive to reforms that promise more in the way of engaging offenders, preventing crime and reducing re-offending.

Traditional measures usually assume that respondents have all the necessary information and a simple yes/no response to a question, posed as a general proposition, is enough. However, we now know that in most cases these responses are more likely to reflect an individual's presumptions, emotions and values and less their knowledge or considered thought about a particular topic. When given sufficient information and asked what to do in certain scenarios people respond in a more sober fashion and the responses provided thus represent a more relevant and useful guide to public preferences. Studies in this area consistently find that these responses generally begin to approximate the position that could be summarised or derived on the basis of sentencing practice (for example, see Chapman et al, 2002; Indermaur, 1990; St Amand and Zamble, 2001).

The process of not only providing information but also allowing for deliberation through some mechanism of probing and debate is central to serious attempts to ascertain informed views that are relevant to developing sentencing policy. The best known way to do this is to arrange a process whereby information is presented by experts to respondents, who subsequently have an opportunity for questions, debate and deliberation on selected policy issues. This then leads to the possibility of considered choices on a range of specific questions. The deliberative poll (Fishkin et al, 2000; Luskin, Fishkin and Jowell, 2002) uses such a process and is arranged so that the choices are made on an individual basis and there is no need to arrive at a consensus within a small or large group. However, other strategies such as citizen juries and consensus conferences using a similar approach do seek to arrive at an agreed position in the same way as a jury does in a trial.

Active deliberation is essential to forming considered judgment. By considering policy choices, testing assumptions, seeking further information and balancing all this information in relation to proposed actions and their alternatives, members of the public are able to engage seriously with policy relevant questions. In advanced strategies for gauging public judgments such as citizen juries the debating process is necessary to test the robustness of certain views and explore what is essential and what is more peripheral or expendable in regard to public preferences. This process also tests out how public views can respond and change with the addition of information – like the relative costs of certain proposals and some of their unwanted or unanticipated consequences.

The deliberative poll is the best known mechanism of this kind in the field of criminal justice. This is largely attributable to the substantial deliberative poll on crime and justice held in Manchester in 1994 funded by a television channel (Hough and Park, 2002; Luskin, Fishkin and Jowell, 2002). This poll involved an initial face-to-face interview with 869 persons[24] followed by a weekend event in which 301 of these interviewees participated. More recently, Green (2006) has proposed using deliberative polls more widely as a way to break through the "comedy of errors" whereby sentencing policy is adjusted to respond to ill-informed and ill-measured public opinion.[25] However, there are problems with the deliberative poll, in particular the one held in 1994. The problems are largely twofold. First the group that eventually attends the special event could not be seen to be a fair or representative sample of the general population. Despite the best efforts of researchers it takes a particular type of person to give up an hour of their time let alone a weekend. The second problem is probably even more significant. Placed within the context of a "special event" and accepting a range of inducements and privileges the respondent is already somewhat obliged to the organisers. They are then presented with a package of selected information. Most respondents will gain a sense of what the expected or preferred responses are. The process is then completed when the respondent provides the researchers with the desired responses. These "demand characteristics" or "social desirability" effects, as they are labelled in the social psychological literature, present a particular challenge to the validity of focus groups and approaches such as the deliberative poll (Ladd, 1996; Fishkin, 1996). Although these problems need to be recognised they are not insuperable. The most important point to note here is that it is possible to develop procedures to allow policy relevant questions to be examined in depth. However, this in-depth analysis needs to be carefully balanced with a linked survey which poses policy relevant questions to a representative sample of the population. Further, to overcome the demand characteristics of the deliberative poll extra effort needs to be invested to ensure that a balanced presentation of the evidence and options is presented, allowing the public to come to an independent or unencumbered judgment.

Reality

We can see elements of the multi-layered consultative process emerging in some of the initiatives from the United Kingdom discussed earlier. The Home Office (2001) review of sentencing integrated public attitudes although the assessment of public preferences falls well short of what could be described as comprehensive. As noted earlier, the United Kingdom government is producing policy documents on sentencing and issuing them for comment at a considerable pace. The SAP and SGC include representatives from key victim stakeholder groups and the SAP has initiated two intensive public attitude surveys with the level of detail that would be useful in sentencing reform. However, the main weak point in the design of the government consultations or the approach of the sentencing advisory bodies in regard to public input is that they either rely on selected individuals, self-selected public responses or traditional surveys. Further, they have no way of formally sharing the whole process of consultation with the public.

The structure and plans of the sentencing advisory bodies, as noted earlier, have focused less on the value of public participation and more on the value of "public education". However, even here there is little that has been formally provided or evaluated. The focus on public education neatly avoids the issue of incorporating public views and assumes that the problem does not relate to the current system but rather public ignorance. This view is consistent with the notion that sentencing is complex and requires the unique expertise that sentencing authorities possess. However, it does not accommodate some important realities. Sentencing is special because it represents, through action, the will and judgment of the public. In other words, sentencing is not only a technical matter but is also a statement of collective morality.[26] Thus, as discussed in the next section, the crisis of confidence has political and social dimensions that need to be addressed in formulating a plan to involve the public.

Social and political dimensions of the crisis of confidence

The crisis of confidence in the courts can be characterised by rifts between practitioners, governments, the media and the "public". Although many commentators interpret the driving force to be for increased punishment some (for example, Freiberg, 2005) have noted that most of the big sentencing reforms of the past decade or so have mainly been for more transparency, accountability and certainty.

This is reflected in calls for mandatory sentencing, truth in sentencing, determinate sentencing and similar mechanisms.

Whether the call is for increased punishment or greater certainty, it is populism that has dominated most of the political responses to the crisis of confidence. Canovan (1995, p 5) argues that populists claim authority by purporting to speak for the " 'silent majority' of 'ordinary decent people' whose interests and opinions are (they claim) regularly overridden by arrogant elites, corrupt politicians and strident minorities". It is now well understood that there is political mileage in creating an image of taking control of an ineffectual, and/or unaccountable judiciary. In the campaign for the 1996 State election the Western Australian Premier, Richard Court, pledged to "put his foot in the revolving door down at the Children's Court". The Canadian Prime Minister, Stephen Harper, in the campaign that swept him to office early in 2006 used a similar image: "the revolving door of criminal justice of this current government bears significant responsibility for the tide of gun, drug and gang crime plaguing our cities".[27]

Although populists may be content to work with caricatures of public opinion these not only provide a poor guide to sentencing but the punitive responses built on them do not result in a greater degree of public satisfaction with sentencing (Roberts, 2002a). This is largely because they offer no plan for establishing confidence in the system but simply exploit sentiments of discontent and complaint. Although for some the implication of this dilemma is to try to separate policy from expressive politics, another possibility is to engage more vigorously with the public by inviting the public into the debate on the priorities and principles of sentencing. But what, precisely, is the problem we are trying to address and what do we hope to achieve by involving the public? What is the value of consultation or education and how would it resolve the identified problem? Although many liberal reformers see the problem to be public punitiveness there is much evidence that the crisis of confidence in the courts is a function of a general decline in the level of public trust.[28] It is the decline in the level of trust in government, Zimring and Johnson argue (2006, pp 276-7), and not increases in public punitiveness, that explains the increase in imprisonment in the United States:

> Much of the punishment hardware that facilitates leniency depends on trust in government's expertise and benevolence. Citizens are restrained from acting on emotions and "throw away the key" sentiments when they believe that there are principles of punishment – legal proportionality, predictions of dangerousness, responsiveness to treatment – that require governmental expertise. As soon as the claim of expertise is discredited, people on the street (or their state representatives) are every bit as expert as judges, parole boards, or correctional administrators.

> Discretion is an even more obvious derivative of trust in those who exercise it. Trust the judge and discretion makes sense. Distrust the judge and mandatory minimum penalties become a preferred method of ensuring that social enemies are punished.

The courts may attract more than the usual serving of distrust as there is little provided to the sceptic in the way of explanations, justifications and/or proof that the sentencing policy adopted actually makes sense. The system has clearly not been built with public accessibility or accountability in mind and arguably takes public trust for granted. But populism thrives where such trust in elites can no longer be sustained. In this environment the idea of public education needs to be handled carefully. The educating "mission" might have the opposite effect, throwing fuel on the fire of public indignation by attempting to put it out with patronising gestures.

If trust is the central issue, perhaps the main focus of efforts to restore confidence should be on "building bridges" between the courts and the public. One way this could be achieved is to provide regular information about how the system works in ways that are important to the public. This means providing information on topics that are of most interest to the public and in ways that make sense to the layperson. Providing such relevant information in a way that is accessible may help achieve a convincing picture of accountability which in turn could go some way to building confidence in the courts.

As the Home Office (2001) review of sentencing found, the public is largely concerned with utilitarian aims: evidence on the effectiveness of the system in meeting certain goals is thus most relevant to levels of confidence in the courts. Information to match public concerns would thus focus on the impact of sentencing on re-offending rates and the efforts being undertaken to reduce re-offending. Reflecting the point made above by Zimring and Johnson, Doob (2000) reported that while most members of the public in his survey were open to keeping offenders in the community they often favoured imprisonment because they were not confident that community sentences were carried out or adequately enforced by the courts. This belief that many offenders facing the court remain remorseless and largely untouched by the court process is not an unreasonable or unjustified concern based on available statistics.[29] Doob found that members of the public believe that the system should be accomplishing something and should be justified in some sensible manner. Further, although they want to see evidence that the functions of sentencing are being earnestly pursued, it appears that people are not necessarily wedded to the notion that the response of the courts be severe or involve imprisonment.

Whilst the public demand for accountability can be linked to a frustration with the impotence of the courts it is likely that it also reflects a distrust that has deeper roots. When we analyse where public dissatisfaction with the courts is greatest we see that "lower" socioeconomic groups stand out. These groups are also more likely to be tabloid readers and have lower levels of knowledge about the courts (Chapman et al, 2002; Indermaur and Roberts, 2005). It is debatable which of these variables is the more relevant and how they relate to each other. Those who wish to distance the crisis of confidence from its social and political dimensions would naturally focus on the knowledge deficit. Those concerned with the influence of the media might focus on the role of the tabloids. However, political scientists will be more interested in the aspect that is routinely exploited by populists – the experience of exclusion and the split between the "ordinary people" and the "elites". This provides the basis for the kind of distrust that populists are able to capitalise on. It relates to perceptions that the courts are not open and that the business of the courts is directed and guarded by a remote group of elites whose interests are aligned with privileged classes far removed from the insecurities of "ordinary people".

This view is supported by Ryan's (2005) description of how penal policy in the United Kingdom was historically formulated by an elite group comprising top public servants and leading criminologists from Cambridge. Ryan (2005, p 140) argues that this group was mainly concerned about the public voice, not so that it could be "accommodated", but rather so that it could be "circumvented". In noting the direction of changes to political arrangements through the conservative and New Labor eras in the United Kingdom, Ryan (2005, p 143) notes:

> [P]olicy making in many western democracies is far less of an exclusive top down business than it once was. Politicians are required to engage with the public in a manner that a generation ago would have been unheard of in most western democracies. To put the same thing more directly, the wider public refuses to be air brushed out of the policy making equation; the idea that difficult questions – domestic or foreign – can be left to a handful of clever people ... is no longer an option.

However, as discussed in the previous section, there is little evidence of a systematic plan for engaging the public and thus the question arises as to whether there is a genuine will to "deal the public in". If Ryan is right perhaps the current period represents a transitional phase between the old "elite dominated" stage and a period where policy inputs will be more "democratised". There are certainly many observers who are critical of the promises and language of inclusion and point to the credibility gap that is being created in their wake. For example, Johnstone (2004) discussed the problems in the United Kingdom with the Labor government attempts to open up policy to "popular influence". Failing any formal mechanism for bringing the public into the policy-making apparatus, debates have been conducted through the media. This approach favours the expression of simplistic and punitive sentiments. Johnstone concluded that much of the effort in the United Kingdom to include the public in policy-making amounted to little more than empty rituals designed to placate the public whilst conducting business as usual. Thus, what may be emerging is a political strategy of appeasement cloaked by populism. This would allow gestures of public participation to be made without the accompanying commitment to follow through.

This interpretation fits with the course of events in New Zealand. In discussing the effects of penal populism in that country Pratt and Clarke (2003) observed that despite the heavy rhetoric and bold promises that followed the referendum on punishment the system was largely able to survive with little substantial change. It appeared that once the single issue groups were able to win some apparent concessions they no longer had the organisational vigour or purpose to continue and thus their ultimate impact was limited.

Johnstone (2004) argues that only at the levels of participation that involve some degree of power sharing and meaningful partnerships in a process of policy formulation can we claim to have truly provided for citizen involvement. However (as Johnstone acknowledges), such a democratisation of sentencing policy is likely some way off as the obstacles to "dealing the public in" are considerable. These obstacles largely relate to the interests and investments of a range of powerful forces. It is important to develop a clear picture of these, as outlined in the next section, if we are to appreciate the nature of the challenges faced in accommodating the public in anything more than a superficial way into the development of sentencing policy.

The politics of "dealing the public in"

The democratisation of sentencing policy

How should we think about the different levels or forms of "involvement" of the public in developing sentencing policy that are possible? The ideal sketched earlier was for a process of deliberation embedded within a multi-layered consultation process. However, this would not be possible without considering how power over sentencing policy is currently distributed and how this would need to change to provide for the proposed model. Public input will only be given greater value if a distinctly different role for the public is constructed than exists at present. The positions currently imagined for the public can be seen in the responses of populists on the one hand and responses (such as public education) embraced by liberal reformers on the other. In terms of the degree of power or agency afforded to the public these traditional approaches, populist or liberal, reflect a view of a public that is disempowered: a school room of passive subjects waiting to be rescued or educated.

The preference for public education underlies the perception that the current arrangements for guiding sentencing policy are not the problem but public ignorance is. Sentencing authorities thus construct their own position vis á vis the public in a manner that accords with the belief in the legitimacy of elite power. Many of the other suggestions about how to deal with the crisis of confidence can also be seen to be methods, not of producing any fundamental changes or "dealing the public in", but of defending, embellishing or reinforcing existing power arrangements. For example, efforts to change public attitude directly, provide policy buffers or influence the nature of media coverage (Roberts et al, 2003) all construct the problem to be outside of the current policy-formulation process. Similarly populism, even though it appears to deliver power to the people, does not engender any process of public debate or deliberation and effectively deals the public out of a role in policy formulation. As Ryan (2005, pp 139-40) notes in discussing the increasing demands for the inclusion of the public:

> [T]his development should not be confused with populism per se; it represents something more enduring, and arguably more democratic, calling for a more considered outward looking political strategy from those groups campaigning for a progressive penal politics in punitive times.

Responses that begin to engage with the public on a respectful level, as an ally in the reform process, are those that seek to enhance information and make policy more transparent and accountable along with efforts to understand more accurately the nature of public preferences. The end point in this progression towards empowering the public is a formal process of public debate. Table 1 provides an overview of the responses to the crisis of confidence and the problems with these responses. The responses are organised along a continuum according to the degree of power or influence afforded the public in the process of policy development as opposed to elites.

Table 1: Potential solutions to the crisis of confidence in sentencing

Continuum of power/engagement	Solution	Problems
Exploiting the public	Penal populism	Costly solution, little public benefit
Elite power position	Change public attitude	Little evidence of practical effectiveness
	Educate the public	Little evidence of practical effectiveness
	Protect current arrangements better	Denies legitimate concerns
	Inform and influence policy-makers	Experts become political actors
	Change/influence media coverage	Experts become political actors
Privileging the public	Provide more/better information	
	Make policy and practices more transparent	
	Make policy and practices more accountable	
	Better measures of public attitude	
Democratisation of sentencing policy	Formal process of public engagement/debate	

The idea of a hierarchy of responses based on the degree of power afforded to the public is not new. For example, Arnstein (1969) used the metaphor of a ladder of public participation, working up from manipulation at the lowest rung, through consultation and "information giving" to participatory democracy at the highest level. As many have noted (for example, Roberts et al, 2003) penal populism represents a form of exploitation of public sentiments for political advantage and in the process removes a meaningful role for the public in the development of policy. This is why penal populism appears at the most conservative end of Table 1. Shand and Arnberg (1996) also provided a continuum of possible types of public involvement in policy development based on the degree of citizen participation. In their continuum the low end reflected the position of a passive democracy where citizens are not expected to participate and would simply be the recipients of information.[30]

Although the responses listed as reflecting an elite power position in Table 1 do not abuse or exploit the public in the way that populism does they also fail to envisage any value in bringing the public into a position of power in regard to forming policy. The favoured solutions to the crisis of confidence involve "doing things to" the public so that the crisis is resolved without upsetting current power arrangements for elites. The things to be done to the public largely concern either trying to change public attitudes directly or trying to educate the public. The elites concerned should not be thought of simply as the judiciary and sentencing scholars. Sentencing advisory bodies, reflecting traditional pluralist attempts to "open up" policy-making, have invited the involvement of special interest groups.[31] Interest group pluralism has led to a new range of actors being involved in policy formation. However, the individuals involved are likely to be well educated and for personal, social or political reasons will not present an obstacle for established elites, particularly when outnumbered in committee. Indeed, it is these new actors associated with special interest groups whose position is most likely to be threatened by the more direct involvement of the public, as Hendricks (2002, p 64) points out:

> There are inherent tensions between traditional, more pluralist forms of public participation and new deliberative democratic processes ... These innovative processes ... challenge existing roles and power relationships between interest groups and the state. Instead of having key access to the policy stage, interest groups are required to be "bystanders", "information providers" and ultimately "process legitimisers". With such a radical shift in roles and power structure, there are few apparent reasons why interest groups would want to participate in such deliberative processes.

The three other classes of response shown in Table 1 as associated with the position of elite power concern strategic responses to protect sentencing from populist pressure. Much of the concern over the past decade or more in regard to sentencing policy has centred on how to oppose the tide of penal populism. In attempting to achieve this some have sought to insulate policy from populist pressure or to influence policy-makers and the media. However, these individuals or groups are more likely to see themselves as radical or liberal reformers rather than protectors of the status quo. The proposed solutions in this category again start from the position that the public is largely misinformed about the nature of crime and punishment. The concern, however, is that this state of ignorance will be routinely exploited by populists leading to a punitive criminal justice system. In the interests of achieving a better crime policy the solutions proposed amount to out-manoeuvring the populists. These include ways for liberal reformers to find a seat at the table where policy is being formulated in an attempt to wield influence from the inside. Analyses of the ways that penal populism is played out by special interest groups, the media and politicians indicate some potential areas for influence. To play the media, to reshape public debates, in effect to enter the fray and influence the outcome for a more rational sentencing policy, are seen as the most realistic and pragmatic ways to ensure a more humane criminal justice system.

Some of these "strategic" responses show elements of privileging the public rather than ignoring its value. For example, part of this power play is to try and influence the nature and the content of media coverage so that it becomes more informed and more reasonable. Propositions for a "replacement discourse" (Barak, 1994; Henry, 1994) seek not to stifle public debate but to enhance it and shift it to a different level to influence what people are talking about so that it is less likely to lead to simplistic solutions favoured by populists. Although these efforts may result in the public getting better quality information, this remains uncertain as they are more likely to affect discussion in the broadsheets rather than the tabloids. Perhaps, most importantly, they do not address the "democracy deficit". However, these efforts do also signal an essential shift in focus: the public is being seen less as an adversary and more as an ally for progressive change.

Demands for transparency and accountability signal a new relationship with the public. By beginning to place the public in the position of the "owners" of public policy who should be presented with evidence on the performance of sentencing and criminal justice more generally we move to a position of privileging the public. Adopting a posture of respect to the public changes our response to the problem considerably. Information is still the key, but now this is seen as something that should be provided to the public as a matter of course because the public is respected as the ultimate stakeholder. Without accurate information on crime and justice and the success of various policies and strategies how are people able to asses its performance? In the same vein, accessible information on the rationales for sentencing, both generally, and in particular decisions, should be promptly provided. In Table 1 efforts to measure more accurately and to understand public preferences are seen as reflecting a position of privileging the public. This is because documenting public preferences, concerns and sensitivities is fundamental to a system that purports to take the public seriously. By engaging the public in a process of dialogue, deliberation and debate and carefully gauging the responses, we are allowing more input from the public than simple "top of the head" opinions which fundamentally disrespect and disregard the value of public judgment.

The next stage in the progression of distributing power to the public in the formation of policy is to formalise the process of engagement and commit to including adequately deliberated principles into sentencing legislation. This amounts to what might be described as the democratisation of sentencing policy.

Prognosis for public involvement in sentencing policy

It is obvious to anyone associated with the field of sentencing reform that there are strong views about the best way to accommodate the public in regard to sentencing. Many see the public and the media as a threat that needs to be effectively neutralised so as not to drag the system down to a less humane and more punitive regime. Thus some see populism as a necessary response at a political level but if managed properly the damage at the "ground level" can be minimised. It is true that populist rhetoric and promises can have the effect of placating an angry public and buying time. Meanwhile the system is able to adjust slightly, perhaps present a face of public inclusion but essentially preserve the current arrangements with minimal disruption. There is certainly a strong view (for example, espoused in Auld, 2001) that the appropriate way to respond to the crisis of confidence is to ensure that the sentencing system operates with the form, shape and precision that it should and then inform, educate or persuade the public that they have the best system possible.

Lord Auld's view perhaps most succinctly captures the view of the judicial elite. Sentencing is their territory and they see little advantage to "dealing the public in". If this is true then the problem with using sentencing advisory bodies as the main vehicle through which to engage the public is that those in charge of this process actually do not believe in its value. Tonry and Rex (2002, pp 10-11) argue that the problem with putting judges in charge of such bodies is that they tend to protect practices and values they hold dear and will hold out against compromises they see as diminishing the system:

> Judges tend to be less dissatisfied with sentencing than other people and often to be wedded to the belief that they have a unique understanding of sentencing issues. As a result, commissions comprised entirely or mostly of judges tend to attach great importance to preserving judicial discretion and less importance to the achievement of such goals as increased consistency and predictability, reduced disparities, successful implementation of new policies and resources management.

Tonry and Rex (2002, p 11) go further in their criticism of proposals that eventually led to the establishment of the SGC describing them as akin to "asking a fox to provide hen house security". Strong words, but certainly it is valid to ask: why would a group with such strong interests in preserving isolation from the public be placed in the position of organising such participation? Perhaps we should begin further back and ask: what kind of institution or institutional arrangement can best meet the needs of engaging the public? As discussed earlier, such institutions or authorities need to establish a framework, an agenda and parameters for discussion and organise the measurement of public judgment. It is doubtful that the type of sentencing advisory bodies that have emerged so far have the resources for conducting such a project even if they were the enthusiastic supporters of it. Therefore, if public participation is to become part of the process of forming sentencing policy perhaps we need to look for an alternative institutional structure to provide it.

Conclusion

Calls to incorporate the public view into sentencing policy have been a defining feature of the past decade of reform in many countries; however, a meaningful mechanism to achieve this has yet to be established. Apart from philosophical objections, this is likely the result of a range of factors such as the fear of giving up territory or beliefs that sentencing policy is too serious and complex to allow for public input. Such beliefs and postures are quickly coming to be seen as outdated, unwarranted or illegitimate. There is now much accumulated wisdom on how to provide mechanisms for "dealing the public in" to the development of sentencing policy. Most importantly, there is every reason to believe that when properly managed and taken seriously, public input will be responsible and responsive to practical concerns. A sentencing policy that is properly "democratised" will be stronger and more impervious to outlandish and unproductive attacks from populists. The result will be a more reasoned, honest and justifiable sentencing system.

Notes

1   See Hough and Roberts (2004) for a comprehensive and international examination of the crisis of confidence and responses to it.

2   The Home Office Review of Sentencing Report (Home Office, 2001) is commonly referred to as the Halliday report and will be referred to as such throughout the remainder of this chapter. The *Justice for all* White Paper is available at the website set up as part of the recommendations of that policy: <http://www.cjsonline.gov.uk/>.

3   The Home Office subsequently published reports on the effect of providing information (Chapman et al, 2002; Salisbury, 2004), see also Mirrlees-Black (2002).

4   This largely implied redeveloping the sentencing framework so that it had more of a utilitarian focus. Roberts (2002b) argues that this presents some fundamental contradictions for a system that has previously put proportionality or desert as its core organising principle.

5   <http://www.rethinking.org.uk/>.

6   The 1994 event had not previously been documented in the literature, although in the same year as the Hough and Park chapter appeared an article was published by the main proponents of deliberative polling (Luskin, Fishkin and Jowell, 2002).

7   *Making Sentencing Clearer* was supported by another document (*Bringing Offenders to Justice*) released two months later intended to summarise the government's position. Both documents are available at <http://www.cjsonline.gov.uk/>. The release was also supported by Secretary of State for Constitutional Affairs and Lord Chancellor Lord Falconer who said: "This consultation is a useful step ... we need to learn the lessons of the summer. This consultation seeks to do so". The lessons of the summer referred to the furore over the case of Sweeny (*R v Sweeney* 12 June 2006 – see Hutton, this volume) which formed the basis for the discussion on indeterminate sentencing in section three of the consultation paper.

8   The quotes provided here come from the press release available at <http://www.cjsonline.gov.uk/the_cjs/whats_new/news-3473.html> accessed 6 January 2007.

9   As well as six consultation criteria in keeping with the *Cabinet Office Code of Practice on Consultation*. However, the minimum 12-week period specified in the first criterion was reduced to 8 weeks (*Making Sentencing Clearer*, pp 23-6).

10   *Making Sentencing Clearer,* p 14. Similarly unhelpful would be unrepresentative responses to easier questions, like the second one which asks: "Should the way sentences are explained by courts need to be changed so the public can understand them more easily?"

11   See <www.sentencing-guidelines.gov.uk/consultations/index.html> accessed 13 September 2007.

12   Although the relationship with the public might be uncertain there is ample evidence of sensitivity to publicity. For example, in his introduction to the 2005/2006 annual report of the Sentencing Guidelines Council, the Chairman of the Council focused on the responses of the tabloids to his first judgment and the headlines he received. Something of the attitude to the public is conveyed in the following: "Clearly publicity is important – for it helps to assist the public to understand the work the Council is engaged in" (Phillips, 2006, p 1).

13   These included developing a strategic plan, conducting regular surveys, reviewing practices and using the internet to provide public information. Importantly targets were set. These included measurable increases in public confidence so that the effectiveness of the strategy could eventually be evaluated.

14   New South Wales and Victoria. See Abadee, this volume; Freiberg, this volume; and McCarthy, this volume.

15   The referendum was proposed by a crime victim and attained the necessary number of signatures (250,000) to force a referendum under New Zealand law.

16   Reported in *The Press* (26 February 2000, p 1), as cited in Pratt and Clark (2003, p 307).

17   Lovegrove (1998, p 293) put forward four criteria that should be satisfied in any plan to involve the community. These included sufficient accessibility and understanding of policy in the community, a process of debate and a valid mechanism for community involvement.

18   For example, see Catt and Murphy (2003); Goodwin and Dryzek (2006); Ackerman et al (2004); Smith and Wales (2000); Shand and Arnberg (1996); Bishop and Davis (2002); Hendricks (2002); Einsiedel and Eastlick (2000); Pratchett (1999); Fischer (1993); Carpini et al (2004); and Rowe and Frewer (2005).

19   However there are particular challenges here, with various individuals and groups claiming special authority to represent sub-sectors of the general public. The degree to which individuals may actually represent fairly the interests of the sub-group or even be said to be a representative of the group are all subject to question. If representative sub-groups are to be given a special role in the formation of sentencing policy there needs to be an explicit rationale for how the interests of the group are actually articulated, particularly where there is no formal process of election (see Catt and Murphy, 2003).

20   For discussion and examples of multi-layered strategies for involving the public, see Catt and Murphy (2003); Renn et al (1993); or Rowe and Frewer (2005).

21   See for example, Durham, Elrod and Kinkade (1996) who found that support for the death penalty changed substantially when respondents were placed in more of a decision-making role and were presented with a vignette of a case rather than a simple "do you favour …?" question. Similar results were documented by Doob and Roberts (1983) and Indermaur (1987).

22   For example evidence using the reformed public opinion surveys was recently used by the New Jersey Death Penalty Study Commission in its report released on 2 January 2007 to build its case that the death penalty no longer enjoyed public support and should be abolished in that State (<www.njleg.state.nj.us/committees/dpsc_final.pdf>).

23   Indermaur (1987); Doob and Roberts (1983). For example, in one study (Indermaur, 1987) the proposal was put that offenders serving sentences of less than three months in prison not be sent to prison but rather spend the time at an "attendance centre" engaging in programs designed to address their offending behaviour. Most respondents expressed agreement with this proposal.

24   This number represents a response rate of 74 per cent of those approached (Luskin et al, 2002).

25   The quote comes from an article by Allen (2003, p 5) and was cited by Green (2006, p 132) as " 'a comedy of errors' in which policy and practice is not based on a proper understanding of public opinion and that same opinion is not based on a proper understanding of policy and practice".

26   It is precisely this point that Canovan (1999) argues is at the heart of the problem of populism, as democracy naturally requires institutions such as the court play an important "detached" role of administering justice. However, these institutions cannot then satisfy the other aspect of democracy which she describes as "redemptive". This tension, Canovan argues, is an inevitable and perennial dilemma establishing the grounds whereby populism exploits the gap between the "promise" and the "performance" in democracy.

27   In Toronto on 5 January 2006: <http://www.cbc.ca/story/canadavotes2006/national/2006/01/05/elxn-harper-crime.html>.

28   Levels of public punitiveness have changed little in Canada, the US, the United Kingdom or Australia over the past 25 years (Roberts et al, 2003; Indermaur and Roberts, 2005). Hough and Roberts (2004) provide an authoritative international review of the problem of lack of confidence in the criminal justice system and reveal some consistent trends across western nations. For findings on the low level of trust in the courts in Australia, see Bean (2005).

29   For example, Cuppleditch and Evans (2005) found that in the United Kingdom two year re-offending rates exceed 50 per cent for all community-based dispositions apart from community punishment orders which were approximately 40 per cent.

30   Bishop and Davis (2002) provide a description and a critique of models for describing public participation in policy including the ones mentioned here.

31   Part of the problem is that the individuals or groups invited in may or may not be representative of a sub-section of the population. They are only rarely elected in any formal sense. So, even if a pluralist model is considered the best way to integrate some alternative community input, there is no way of assessing whether the identified interests are being fairly represented.

References

Abadee, A (2006). *The Role of Sentencing Advisory Councils.* Paper presented at Sentencing: Principles, Perspectives and Possibilities conference. Australian National Museum. Canberra 10-12 February.

Akkerman, T, Hajer, M and Grin, J (2004). The Interactive State: Democratisation from Above? *Political Studies* 52: 82.

Allen, R (2003). "There Must Be Some Way of Dealing with Kids": Young Offenders, Public Attitudes and Policy Change. *Youth Justice* 2: 3.

Allen, R (2004). *Rethinking Crime and Punishment.* London: Esmée Fairbairn Foundation, <www.rethinking.org.uk/>.

Arnstein, S (1969). A Ladder of Citizen Participation. *Journal of the American Institute of Planners* 35: 216.

Auld Report (2001). *Report of the Review of Criminal Courts of England and Wales.* London: HMSO.

Barak, G (1994). Newsmaking Criminology: Reflections on the Media, Intellectuals and Crime. In G Barak (ed), *Media, Process and the Social Construction of Crime: Studies in Newsmaking Criminology.* New York: Garland.

Bean, C (2003). Is There a Crisis of Trust in Australia? In S Wilson, G Meagher, R Gibson, D Denmark and M Western (eds), *Australian Social Attitudes: The First Report.* Sydney: University of New South Wales Press.

Bishop, P and Davis, G (2002). Mapping Public Participation in Policy Choices, *Australian Journal of Public Administration* 61(1): 14.

Canovan, M (1999). Trust the people! Populism and the Two Faces of Democracy. *Political Studies* 47: 2.

Carpini, M, Cook, F and Jacobs, K (2004). Public Deliberation, Discursive Participation and Citizen Engagement: A Review of the Empirical Literature. *Annual Review of Political Science* 7: 315.

Catt, H and Murphy, M (2003). What Voice for the People? Categorising Methods of Public Consultation. *Australian Journal of Political Science* 38(3): 407.

Chapman, B, Mirrlees-Black, C and Brawn, C (2002). *Improving Public Attitudes to the Criminal Justice System: The Impact of Information.* Home Office Research Study 245. London: Home Office.

Cullen, F, Fisher, B and Applegate, B (2000). Public Opinion about Punishment and Corrections. In M Tonry (ed), *Crime and Justice: A Review of the Research Volume 27.* Chicago: University of Chicago Press.

Cuppleditch, L and Evans, W (2005). *Re-offending of Adults: Results from the 2002 Cohort.* Home Office Statistical Bulletin, 25/05. London: Home Office.

Doob, A (2000). Transforming the Punishment Environment: Understanding Public Views of What Should be Accomplished at Sentencing. *Canadian Journal of Criminology* 42(3): 23.

Doob, A and Roberts, J (1983). *An Analysis of the Public View of Sentencing.* Ottawa: Department of Justice, Canada.

Durham, A, Elrod, H and Kinkade, P (1996). Public Support for the Death Penalty: Beyond Gallup. *Justice Quarterly* 13(4): 705.

Einsiedel, E and Eastlick, D (2000). Consensus Conferences as Deliberative Democracy. *Science Communication* 21: 323.

Fisher, F (1993). Citizen Participation and the Democratisation of Policy Expertise: from Theoretical Inquiry to Practical Cases. *Policy Sciences* 26: 165.

Fishkin, J (1996). Bringing Deliberation to Democracy. *The Public Perspective* 7(1): 1.

Fishkin. J, Luskin, R and Jowell, R (2000). Deliberative Polling and Public Consultation. *Parliamentary Affairs* 52(4): 657.

Freiberg, A (2005). Sentencing. In D Chappell and P Wilson (eds), *Issues in Australian crime and criminal justice.* Sydney: LexisNexis. Butterworths.

Goodwin, R and Dryzek, J (2006). Deliberative Impacts: The Macro-political Uptake of Mini Publics. *Politics and Society* 34(2): 219.

Green, D (2006). Public Opinion Versus Public Judgment about Crime: Correcting the "Comedy of Errors". *British Journal of Criminology* 46: 131.

Hendricks, C (2002). Institutions of Deliberative Democratic Processes and Interest Groups: Roles, Tensions and Incentives. *Australian Journal of Public Administration* 61(1): 64.

Henry, S (1994). Newsmaking Criminology as Replacement Discourse. In G Barak (ed), *Media, Process and the Social Construction of Crime: Studies in Newsmaking Criminology.* New York: Garland.

Home Office (2001). *Making Punishments Work: Report of a Review of the Sentencing Framework for England and Wales* (the Halliday Report). London: Home Office Communications Directorate.

Hough, M and Roberts, J (1998). *Attitudes toward Punishment: Findings from the British Crime Survey.* Home Office Research Study No 179. London: Home Office, Research and Statistics Directorate.

Hough, M and Roberts, J (2004). Confidence in Justice: An International Review. ICPR Research Paper No 3, <www.kcl.ac.uk/icpr/>.

Hough, M and Park, A (2002). How Malleable are Attitudes to Crime and Punishment? Findings from a British Deliberative Poll. In J Roberts and M Hough (eds), *Changing Attitudes to Punishment: Public Opinion, Crime and Justice.* Cullompton: Willan.

Indermaur, D (1987). Public Perceptions of Sentencing in Perth, Western Australia. *Australian and New Zealand Journal of Criminology* 20: 163.

Indermaur, D (1990). *Perceptions of Crime Seriousness and Sentencing: A Comparison of Court Practice and the Perceptions of the Public and Judges.* Report to the Criminology Research Council. Canberra: Australian Institute of Criminology.

Indermaur, D and Hough, M (2003). Changing Attitudes to Punishment. In J Roberts and M Hough (eds), *Changing Attitudes to Punishment: Public Opinion, Crime and Justice.* Cullompton: Willan.

Indermaur, D and Roberts, L (2005). Perceptions of Crime and Justice. In S Wilson, G Meagher, R Gibson, D Denmark and M Western (eds), *Australian Social Attitudes: The First Report.* Sydney: University of New South Wales Press.

Johnstone, G (2000). Penal Policy Making: Elitist, Populist or Participatory? *Punishment and Society* 2: 161.

Ladd, E (1996). Magic town: Jimmy Stewart Demonstrates the "Hawthorne Effect". *The Public Perspective* 7(3): 16.

Lovegrove, A (1998). Judicial Sentencing Policy, Criminological Expertise and Public Opinion. *Australian and New Zealand Journal of Criminology* 31(3): 287.

Luskin, R, Fishkin, J and Jowell, R (2002). Considered Opinions: Deliberative Polling in Britain. *British Journal of Political Science* 32: 455.

Mattinson, J and Mirrilees-Black, C (2000). *Attitudes to Crime and Criminal Justice: Findings from the 1998 British Crime Survey.* Home Office Research Study No 200 London: Home Office.

Mirrlees-Black, C (2002). Improving Public Knowledge about Crime and Punishment. In J Roberts and M Hough (eds), *Changing Attitudes to Punishment: Public Opinion, Crime and Justice.* Cullompton: Willan.

New Zealand Law Commission (2006). *Sentencing Guidelines and Parole Reform* Report No 94. Wellington: New Zealand Law Commission.

Philips (Lord) (2006). *Foreword,* Sentencing Guidelines Council and Sentencing Advisory Panel Annual report 2005/06. London: HMSO, <www.http://www.sentencing-guidelines.gov. uk/docs/Annual-Report-2005-06.pdf>.

Pratchett, L (1999). New Fashions in Public Participation: Towards Greater Democracy? *Parliamentary Affairs* 52: 616.

Pratt, J and Clark, M (2003). Penal Populism in New Zealand, *Punishment and Society* 7(3): 303.

Renn, O, Webler, T, Rakel, H, Dienel, P and Johnson, B (1993). Public Participation in Decision Making. *Policy Sciences* 26(3): 189.

Roberts, J (1992). Public Opinion, Crime and Criminal Justice. In M Tonry (ed), *Crime and Justice: A Review of the Research, Vol 16.* Chicago: University of Chicago Press.

Roberts, J (2002a). Public Opinion and Sentencing Policy. In S Rex and M Tonry (eds), *Reform and Punishment: The Future of Sentencing.* Cullompton: Willan.

Roberts, J (2002b). Alchemy in Sentencing: An Analysis of Sentencing Reform Proposals in England and Wales. *Punishment and Society* 4(4): 425.

Roberts, J and Stalans, L (1997). *Public Opinion, Crime and Criminal Justice.* Boulder, CO: Westview Press.

Roberts, J, Stalans, L, Indermaur, D and Hough, M (2003). *Penal Populism and Public Opinion: Lessons from Five Countries.* New York, NY: Oxford University Press.

Rowe, G and Frewer, L (2005). A Typology of Public Engagement Mechanisms. *Science, Technology and Human Values* 30(2): 251.

Ryan, M (2005). Engaging with Punitive Attitudes Towards Crime and Punishment: Some Strategic Lessons from England and Wales. In J Pratt, D Brown, M Brown, S Hallsworth and W Morrison (eds), *The New Punitiveness: Trends, Theories, Perspectives.* Cullompton: Willan.

Salisbury, H (2004). *Public Attitudes to the Criminal Justice System: The Impact of Providing Information to British Crime Survey Respondents.* Home Office On-line Report 64/04, <www.homeoffice.gov.uk/rds/pdfs04/rdsolr6404.pdf>.

Shand, D and Arnberg, M (1996). *Responsive Government,* OECD Background Paper. Paris: OECD.

Smith, G and Wales, C (2000). Citizens Juries and Deliberative Democracy. *Political Studies* 48: 51.

St Amand, M and Zamble, E (2001). Impact of Information about Sentencing Decisions on Public Attitudes toward the Criminal Justice System. *Law and Human Behavior* 25(5): 515.

Tonry, M and Rex, S (2002). Reconsidering Sentencing and Punishment in England and Wales. In S Rex and M Tonry (eds), *Reform and Punishment: The Future of Sentencing.* Cullompton: Willan.

UK Government (2007). *Making Sentencing Clearer Consultation,* A consultation and a report of a review by the Home Secretary, Lord Chancellor and Attorney-General <www.noms.homeoffice.gov.uk/news-publications-events/publications/consultations/Making_sentencing_clearer_consul>.

Zimring, F and Johnson, D (2006). Public Opinion and the Governance of Punishment in Democratic Political Systems. *Annals of the American Academy* 605: 266.

5

Myths and misconceptions: public opinion versus public judgment about sentencing

Karen Gelb

Introduction

The Victorian Sentencing Advisory Council (Freiberg, this volume; McCarthy, this volume) has, as one of its statutory functions, the gauging of public opinion (*Sentencing Act* 2001 (Vic) s 108(1)(d)). In 2005, soon after its establishment and pursuant to this mandate, the Council initiated a year-long project to ascertain and analyse the current state of knowledge about public opinion on sentencing on both a national and international level. The project was designed to examine and criti-cally evaluate both the substantive issues in the area (what we know about public opinion on sentencing) and the methodological issues in this field (how we mea-sure public opinion on sentencing). The ultimate goal of the project was the creation of a suite of methodological tools that could be used to gauge public opinion on the wide range of issues that form the work of the Council.

This chapter presents the findings of this project (Gelb, 2006). In particular, analyses of both the substantive and methodological issues in the field are presented, with a discussion of ways to progress the capacity of the Council to gauge public opinion on sentencing in Victoria.

The role of the public in the development of sentencing policy

The rise of the public

The 1960s saw the rise of the victims' movement and the development of the victim as a third party (along with the offender and the state) in the criminal justice process. In the ensuing three decades this movement became more coherent and organised, leading to the institutionalisation of victims' views in the criminal justice system via formal mechanisms such as victim impact statements and victim representation on parole boards (Freiberg, 2003).

The importance given by governments to the voice of the public is evidenced by the recent institutionalisation of public participation in the criminal justice system through formal mechanisms such as public representation on parole boards. The most obvious mechanism for public representation is the development of bodies such as the Sentencing Advisory Council and its counterparts in other Aust-ralian States and around the world. In the United Kingdom the Sentencing Advisory Panel and the Sentencing Guidelines Council both have community members and a mandate to incorporate public opinion in their advice (Ashworth, this volume). The Scottish Sentencing Commission and similar commissions at both a State and federal level in the United States are also formal mechanisms for incorporating public opinion into the criminal justice process (Hutton, this volume; Frase, this volume). With this institutionalisation, the public has been transformed from an observer to a participant in the criminal justice system (Freiberg, 2003).

In order to ascertain public views on sentencing, over the past 40 years there has been a dramatic increase in the use of public opinion polling both by the press and by political leaders along all parts of the political spectrum. Public opinion – a concern with rising crime rates and dissatisfaction with sentencing – has been used by western governments over the past two decades as justification of a hard-line approach and "tough-on-crime" political rhetoric (Casey and Mohr, 2005).

Penal populism and the development of sentencing policy

Most western governments now routinely conduct public opinion polls about attitudes to important issues in criminal justice. To some degree, this heightened sensitivity to the views of the public reflects an element of penal populism. Anthony Bottoms coined the phrase "populist punitiveness" to describe "the notion of politicians tapping into, and using for their own purposes, what they believe to be the public's generally punitive stance" (Bottoms, 1995, p 40). Policies are populist if they are used for winning votes without regard for their effectiveness in reducing crime or promoting justice – allowing the electoral advantage of a policy to take precedence over its penal effectiveness (Roberts et al, 2003, p 5).

The central tool of penal populism is imprisonment. Penal populism provides a framework within which to understand increasing imprisonment rates around the world as well as the proliferation of punitive sentencing policies. Justification for policies such as three-strikes legislation, mandatory minimum sentences and sex offender notification laws is found in this framework of penal populism, which describes a punitive public fed up with crime and with the perceived leniency of the criminal justice system.

Belief in a punitive public is driven primarily by the results of decades of opinion polls that show that the public believes the criminal justice system, and courts in particular, to be overly lenient. But while governments and the mass media continue to place high credence in the basic opinion poll question of whether sentencing is "too harsh, about right or too lenient" as a way to justify calls for punitive penal policy, academic researchers have repeatedly shown that public opinion on crime and justice issues, and on sentencing in particular, is far more nuanced and complex than such surveys show.

The measurement of public opinion

How is public opinion measured?

There have been several approaches to the measurement of public opinion on crime and justice issues. The primary methods are:

1. media polls;
2. representative surveys;

3. focus groups; and
4. deliberative polls.

Each of these methods has its advantages and disadvantages. The approach chosen for any particular study depends on the aim of the research, the issues to be addressed and the proposed use of the findings.

Media polls

The most basic way to measure public opinion is the viewer or reader poll. This type of poll asks a single directed question about a specific issue (for example, "Should suspended sentences be abolished?"). As this is designed to capture a snapshot of current public opinion on an issue, no further explanatory or classificatory questions are asked.

While this method allows for a potentially very large sample to be accessed quickly, easily and cheaply, there are severe limitations to the generalisability of the findings due to the self-selected nature of the sample. There is no opportunity for follow-up questions that might help explain respondents' answers to the primary question. As there is no collection of further information about the respondents, the sample has unmeasured demographic characteristics and so bears an unknown relationship to the broader community.

Media polls tend to be linked with the presentation of a specific controversial news item. Through this linking, the media are creating a contextual priming of respondents such that reported attitudes may represent momentary responses rather than enduring and transferable beliefs (Casey and Mohr, 2005). Given these limitations, researchers tend to avoid this approach in favour of more robust survey methods.

Representative surveys

The representative survey has been the most common method of measuring public opinion over the past 40 years. Using representative samples of the public, researchers have asked a range of questions to ascertain public opinion on a wide variety of criminal justice issues, including many issues in the area of sentencing policy.

The representative survey has the potential to be a powerful tool for gauging public opinion on a wide variety of issues. A sufficiently large sample, spread across categories of demographic characteristics (such as gender, age, education and income), can accurately represent the broader population from which the sample was drawn. This allows the findings of the research to be generalised to the broader community, making the representative survey a far more useful policy tool than the media poll. While representative surveys have great potential for gathering detailed information from respondents, each additional question on a survey adds to the time and costs involved. In order to reduce costs, surveys often try to maximise the amount of information they can gather from a minimal number of questions. As a result, not all surveys are equally meaningful – a single abstract question cannot provide as much information to the researcher as a detailed set of questions when attempting to explain complex and emotive issues such as sentencing.

Opinion surveys are most useful when they provide information on various publics; are at least to some extent open-ended; track people's opinions over time;

link people's opinions on specific issues to their general views of the world; and link people's opinions to their level of knowledge and understanding of the issues.

A third methodological approach tips the scales in favour of gathering extensive and detailed information from respondents.

Focus groups

In order to gather detailed, in-depth information from respondents, a few researchers have made use of the focus group approach. This methodology involves gathering small groups of participants to discuss a particular issue. Discussion is usually led in order to ensure that all aspects of the issue to be examined are actually addressed, but the structure of the discussion tends to be open and to follow lines of thought as they arise. Respondents' opinions are expressed in open-ended form, without the need for respondents to classify their opinions into pre-existing response categories.

The primary advantage of the focus group is that it is able to elicit far more detailed, thoughtful and insightful responses from participants than the traditional survey method. During the course of the focus group itself participants are able to discuss their views, clarify their responses and ask the researchers for explanations of difficult concepts. The great richness of the qualitative data gathered from focus groups is a useful source of information that is not available from large-scale quantitative surveys. They are particularly useful when assessing opinions on a specific issue of a particular group of people, such as victims' representatives, judges or offenders.

Unfortunately, the qualitative nature of focus group research means that it is difficult to generalise results to the broader community. Very small samples are used due to the difficulty of gathering discussion groups, and the open-ended nature of the questions means that it is difficult to replicate the findings. The costs involved with speaking at length with these small groups (sessions often last around 90 minutes) mean that this approach is impractical for those wishing to assess broad community opinions on an issue. But while external validity is a concern with this method (the extent to which findings can be generalised to the broader population), it is a valuable adjunct to large-scale representative surveys.

In order to improve the generalisability of results from focus groups, while at the same time maintaining the richness of data they provide, a fourth method has evolved that is a hybrid of the qualitative focus group and the quantitative representative survey.

Deliberative polls

To achieve a greater depth of insight into public opinion, a handful of researchers have attempted a much more ambitious methodological approach – the deliberative poll.

Deliberative polls are based on the conclusion, from much previous research in the field, that the general public has very little knowledge about crime and justice issues. According to this premise, people can only have an *informed* opinion if they are first given information about the issues to be studied. It is anchored to the notion of public deliberation – the open and informed dialogue between equals critical to the generation of durable and informed preferences – and goes further towards achieving the ideal of public judgment than any other approach.

Deliberative polls use a pre-test – post-test approach: they measure people's opinions before they are provided with information on the subject, then provide detailed information, then measure their opinions again afterward. This methodology both facilitates and measures informed public opinion. It is generally used for measuring opinion on specific issues such as public attitudes to community-based penalties.

This approach has the advantage of being able to elicit detailed, extensive information from respondents about their informed opinion. Respondents have the opportunity to discuss the issues with other respondents and with the researchers, allowing them to deliberate and form a considered opinion. It has been suggested that changes in respondents' opinions over the course of the focus group can be enduring, making this approach a useful tool for educating the public about crime and justice facts.

Although deliberative polls have the potential for collecting extremely rich data, very few have been conducted. The resources involved in such an approach – the cost and time involved in gathering experts to participate in discussion sessions with respondents – have made the deliberative poll prohibitive for widespread use. As they necessarily focus on a detailed examination of a particular issue, deliberative polls are also limited in the scope of issues that can be covered in a single study. This limits the breadth of information that can be collected for researchers who want to understand correlates of opinion.

Each of these methodological approaches has its own set of advantages and disadvantages. Roberts and Stalans (1997) suggest that a comprehensive picture of public knowledge can only be obtained by a multi-method approach: representative opinion polls can be used to set the approximate bounds on public attitudes while focus groups are needed to evaluate the depth of a particular opinion. Together these various methodological approaches have been part of a large body of knowledge around the world about public opinion on crime and justice.

What do we know about public opinion internationally?

Most of the research in this field has been conducted in the United States, the United Kingdom and Canada. Despite this variation in countries, and despite the use of the various methodological approaches discussed above, the research on public opinion on crime and justice has reached a number of consistent conclusions.

In the abstract, the public thinks that sentences are too lenient

Roberts and Hough note that "one of the leitmotifs of public attitudes to criminal justice is the desire for a harsher response to crime" (Roberts and Hough, 2005b, p 13). This perception has persisted despite substantial variation in actual crime rates and reform to the criminal justice system itself.

When representative surveys first came into widespread use, the most common way of measuring public opinion on sentencing was to use the general question of whether sentences are "too harsh, about right or too lenient". This question, in some variant or another, has been used in opinion polls across the world for the past 40 years.

Responses to this question have been remarkably consistent both over time (from the 1970s to current research) and across countries (from North America and Australia to the United Kingdom and Europe): over the past three decades about 70 to 80 per cent of respondents in these countries reported that sentences are too lenient, with slightly lower rates in Canada in recent years (60 to 70 per cent) and slightly higher rates in the United States (up to 85 per cent) (Roberts et al, 2003, pp 27-9). When asked about juvenile offenders, slightly higher proportions of respondents felt that sentences are too lenient: ranging from 71 per cent in a 2003 Office of National Statistics Omnibus Survey in the United Kingdom (Roberts and Hough, 2005a) to 88 per cent of respondents in a 1997 Canadian survey (Doob et al, 1998).

On the basis of these survey findings alone, politicians, policy-makers and the media have concluded that the public is substantially punitive and would therefore support increasingly punitive penal policies.

In more recent years, however, this conclusion has been called into question. In particular, researchers have hypothesised that the finding of a highly punitive public is merely a methodological artefact – a result of the way in which public opinion has been measured.

Since the 1980s researchers have attempted to go beyond the single question poll to include further questions in representative surveys that can clarify and further explain the apparent harshness of public attitudes. In this way the research has attempted to address the methodological limitations of using a single abstract question to measure complex and nuanced public attitudes.

People have very little accurate knowledge of crime and the criminal justice system

Looking at large-scale surveys of public opinion about crime and punishment in the United States, United Kingdom, Canada, Australia and New Zealand, Roberts et al (2003) conclude that the public has very little accurate knowledge about the criminal justice system. Of particular relevance to attitudes to sentencing are findings that show that people have extensive misperceptions about the nature and extent of crime, about court outcomes and about the use of imprisonment and parole. Consistent results from many of the studies in this field (see, for example, Hough and Roberts, 2004; Mattinson and Mirrlees-Black, 2000; Hough and Roberts, 1998; Doob and Roberts, 1988; Roberts and Stalans, 1997; Sprott, 1996; Indermaur, 1987) show that people tend to:

- perceive crime to be constantly increasing, particularly crimes of violence;
- over-estimate the proportion of recorded crime that involves violence;
- over-estimate the proportion of juvenile crime that involves violence;
- over-estimate the percentage of offenders who re-offend;
- under-estimate the severity of maximum penalties;
- under-estimate the severity of sentencing practices (for example, the incarceration rate); and
- know little about sentencing alternatives and focus instead on imprisonment.

It is evident from the research that this lack of knowledge about crime and the criminal justice system is a significant factor in perpetuating public misperceptions and misunderstanding.

The mass media is the primary source of information on crime and justice issues

Most people do not have direct access to first-hand information about the criminal justice system, either through personal experience or from the experience of family and friends. Instead, people tend to learn about crime and the criminal justice system through the mass media, in particular via newspapers. Given the ubiquity and popularity of the mass media (tabloid newspapers in particular), they play an integral role in the construction of both public opinion and the public "reality" of crime.

Newspaper portrayals of crime stories do not provide a complete and accurate picture of the issue. Papers report selectively, choosing stories, and aspects of stories, with the aim of entertaining more than informing. They tend to focus on unusual, dramatic and violent crime stories, in the process painting a picture of crime for the community that overestimates the prevalence of crime in general and of violent crime in particular. Thus public concerns about crime typically reflect crime as depicted in the media, rather than trends in the actual crime rate (Roberts et al, 2003, p 78).

Media reporting plays a critical role in the development of public opinion on sentencing, as it presents an inaccurate and incomplete picture of sentencing practice, thus contributing significantly to a misinformed public. The media do not do this in a conscious way, but, according to Indermaur (2000), it is the combination of media reporting practices with populist politics that results in these misperceptions.

Indermaur (2000, p 3) suggests that:

> The continuing disparity between the media-constructed reality of crime and justice and the non-media reality of crime and justice results in the public receiving an unnecessarily distorted image that supports only one anti-crime policy approach, an expanded and enhanced punitive criminal justice system – an approach lacking evidence of success.

When people are given more information, their levels of punitiveness drop dramatically

There is substantial evidence that the public's lack of knowledge about crime and justice is related to the high levels of punitiveness reported as a response to a general, abstract question about sentencing. Based upon the conclusion that increasing the provision of information will decrease levels of punitiveness, many researchers have moved from traditional survey questions to those which provide much more information to people before asking for a response. The crime vignette approach in a representative survey is a way in which to provide more information about the offence, the offender and the impact on the victim.

By providing the opportunity to ascertain a more informed public opinion, crime vignettes address one of the disadvantages of the traditional survey question

– that such questions cannot adequately uncover the nuances of public opinion on the complex issues of crime and justice.

In their groundbreaking work, Doob and Roberts (1983) conducted a series of 13 studies for the Canadian Department of Justice in order to determine the effect of providing more information on respondents' attitudes.

In a small study of 116 randomly selected respondents (one of a large series of studies), Doob and Roberts contrasted the response given to brief descriptions of unusual sentences (only offence and sentence information) to those given to more complete descriptions of the same cases (including a case summary). Respondents were initially asked a general question about their perceptions of court sentencing practice. In the abstract, over 90 per cent of the total group reported that in general the courts are too lenient.

Respondents were then randomly assigned to one of two groups, one to receive a brief description of a manslaughter case (akin to the type of information provided in media accounts) and one to receive a more detailed description with information on incident and offender characteristics.

Most of the respondents provided with a short description of the case felt that the sentence was too lenient (80 per cent), while only 7 per cent felt that the sentence was about right. For those given a longer description of the case, 15 per cent felt that the sentence was too lenient and 30 per cent felt that the sentence was about right. It is interesting to note that fully 45 per cent of this group described the sentence as too harsh (Doob and Roberts, 1983, p 6).

Doob and Roberts conclude that, were the public to form opinions from court-based information instead of through the lens of the mass media, there would be fewer instances of calls for harsher sentences.

Despite apparent punitiveness, public sentencing preferences are actually very similar to those expressed by the judiciary or actually used by the courts

To test the hypothesis that the public is more punitive than judges, Roberts and Doob (1989) looked at a 1986 representative survey conducted by Gallup for the Canadian Sentencing Commission. The survey asked respondents what proportion of offenders should be incarcerated for various crimes. These preferences were then compared to the proportion of convictions for this offence that actually resulted in custody in the Canadian courts. No significant difference was found between the two groups: average incarceration rates across 10 offences (both violent and property offences) were 66 per cent for the public and 67 per cent for the courts (Roberts and Doob, 1989, p 510).

A similar approach was adopted by Diamond and Stalans in their 1989 comparison of lay and judicial responses to case study vignettes in Illinois, in which respondents were asked to impose sentences on the same four moderately severe cases in which prison was a possible, but not inevitable, sentencing outcome.

Respondents were presented with detailed information about each of the four cases, including a presentence report (including information on the nature of the offence and on the offender's background) and a video of the sentencing hearing. Respondents were told the range of possible sentencing options legally available for that case and then completed a questionnaire indicating sentencing preferences.

The non-judicial respondents were also told that offenders sentenced to prison would typically serve about half of their prison terms.

Diamond and Stalans found that there was no evidence in any of the four cases that judicial sentences were more lenient than the sentences of the lay respondents. Judges' sentences in this study were as severe or more severe than those of lay respondents. They conclude that the perception that judges are more lenient than the public is simply a myth.

What do we know about public opinion in Australia?

Despite (or perhaps because of) the proliferation of research in countries similar to Australia, there has been little work done in Australia to ascertain informed public opinion on sentencing. Over the past 20 years there have been but a handful of studies that are drawn from a national sample and that focus on public opinion within Australia. The most relevant to this work are the Australian Institute of Criminology's research in the late 1980s and the recent Australian Survey of Social Attitudes.

How the public sees sentencing: an Australian survey

The Australian Institute of Criminology surveyed a representative, multi-stage probability sample of 2555 Australians aged 14 years and over. Respondents were asked to rank the seriousness of 13 crimes and, for each, to act as a judge in allocating their preferred punishment. Respondents were given a list of the available forms of punishment, including "no penalty" and capital punishment (even though this has not been available in any Australian jurisdiction since 1984). They were asked to specify both the form and the severity of the sentence (amount of fine, length of imprisonment).

The average response was broadly in line with typical court decisions including a tendency to punish violent offenders with prison and property offenders with non-custodial penalties, especially fines (Walker, Collins and Wilson, 1987, p 3).

Significant numbers of Australians were willing to accept non-custodial alternatives to imprisonment: fines, probation and community service orders. The authors conclude that, despite media headlines suggesting the opposite, punitiveness is not a characteristic of Australians, and that people acknowledge the complexity of the sentencing process and are quite sophisticated in their attitudes.

The Australian Survey of Social Attitudes

In analysing the most recent study of public attitudes in Australia, Indermaur and Roberts (2005) explored Australian perceptions of crime and criminal justice from questions in the *Australian Survey of Social Attitudes 2003* (AuSSA). This survey asked 4123 respondents if they believed that crime had increased or decreased or stayed the same over the past two years in order to test the accuracy of public knowledge about crime trends. The results are consistent with previous research both in Australia and overseas: more than two-thirds of all survey respondents (70 per cent) believed that crime had increased over the past two years with more than a third overall (39 per cent) responding that it had increased "a lot". In

Victoria, where 1065 people were surveyed, 26 per cent felt that crime had increased a lot; 29 per cent felt it had increased a little; 29 per cent felt it had stayed the same; and 11 per cent felt it had decreased to some degree. The proportion of Victorian respondents who felt that crime had increased was smaller than in any other State (Indermaur and Roberts, 2005, p 143).

Looking at actual crime trends from 2001 to 2003, it is apparent that the majority of Australians hold inaccurate perceptions of crime in their communities. Overall, only 5 per cent of all Australian respondents reported correctly that crime had decreased, with respondents in Victoria being slightly more knowledgeable (with 11 per cent reporting accurately) (Indermaur and Roberts, 2005, p 143).

While this survey included over one thousand respondents from Victoria, the focus of the research was not specifically on that State. In addition, only three questions were asked about public attitudes to sentencing. Thus while the survey allows for comparisons with other States, it does not allow an in-depth analysis of the finer aspects of Victorian attitudes toward sentencing.

What do we know about public opinion in Victoria?

There is a real dearth of information about public opinion on sentencing specifically in Victoria, with only a single study looking closely at the Victorian community in any detail. This study was part of a review of sentencing initiated in 1996, and included an extensive public consultation process using both submissions and a focus group methodology.

The Victorian Community Council Against Violence

As part of a 1996 review of the *Sentencing Act* 1991 (Vic), the Victorian Community Council Against Violence (VCCAV) was asked to provide mechanisms for members of the public to express their views about sentencing and the nature of sentences imposed in Victoria.

The VCCAV determined that public opinion would be more useful if a level of accurate information was provided before the consultation process. An Information Paper was developed that contained information on current sentencing practices, and it included a set of questions to guide submissions.

Sixteen focus groups were convened with community members, prisoners and representatives of victims' groups. Community hearings were also held and almost 150 submissions were received in response to the discussion paper.

In the report of the consultations, "most" refers to 80-99 per cent of participants; "many" refers to 60-79 per cent; "several" refers to 30-59 per cent; and "few" refers to less than 30 per cent of participants.

Community knowledge of sentencing

The vast majority of people making submissions felt that sentencing information in Victoria was either unavailable or was extremely difficult to access (VCCAV, 1997, p 10). Many acknowledged that their knowledge of sentencing was thus limited to very general information, primarily based on media reporting. Those who used the media as their main source of information acknowledged that the picture the media provide is not necessarily an accurate one. Indeed, some participants noted that the media's emphasis on sensationalism and controversial or violent cases can lead to a distorted view of risk of crime victimisation and the level of crime in the community, thus raising community levels of fear (VCCAV, 1997, p 14).

Perceptions of the purposes of sentencing

Participants who emphasised punishment as the primary purpose of sentencing were more likely to be unhappy with the current system and sentencing practice (VCCAV, 1997, p 24). In submissions, many people appreciated that rehabilitation must be accompanied by social condemnation of the offending behaviour via a severe penalty. But a view was also expressed by many, particularly those who argued for tougher sentences, that rehabilitation is either not possible or has not worked. This was especially the view for sexual offenders (VCCAV, 1997, p 28).

For more serious crimes and repeat offenders, the most important purposes of sentencing were deterrence, community protection and punishment. Participants felt that only in extremely violent offences should punishment and protection be the only purposes of sentencing; for others, these are secondary and most meaningful if coupled with rehabilitation (VCCAV, 1997, pp 32, 69).

Perceptions of imprisonment

A number of people felt that the proportion of offenders receiving a sentence of imprisonment was too small, especially in the case of serious crimes such as murder and sexual assault. Others suggested that life in prison was too easy, with too many facilities, and therefore was more expensive than it should be.

On the other hand, other submissions suggested that imprisonment should be used very selectively as the social and economic costs are so high. They also suggested that more opportunity should be provided to offenders to access treatment programs to prevent violence and assist in preparing for work (VCCAV, 1997, pp 44-5).

Focus group participants felt that imprisonment should be a sentence of last resort, most appropriate for serious violent offenders and for those with prior convictions who were beyond rehabilitation (VCCAV, 1997, p 70).

Aggravating and mitigating factors

A number of those who made submissions suggested that mitigating factors unduly affect the leniency of a sentence. In particular, it was felt that the offender's character should not be held as a mitigating factor. When mitigating factors are given too much weight in a case, the offender seems to be given more rights than does the victim (VCCAV, 1997, p 50).

Focus group participants considered a case study and nominated the factors they thought should be aggravating or mitigating. Aggravating factors were prior convictions and significant victim impact. Mitigating factors were offender age (young), home life (disrupted), employment history (unemployed but actively looking) and early guilty plea (VCCAV, 1997, p 74).

Sentence discounts

A number of people who made submissions were concerned that offenders receive lenient sentences when they have pleaded guilty to a lesser charge or to a smaller number of charges than may have been warranted. Concerns were also expressed both by focus group participants and in submissions about concurrent sentences in that they effectively offer a discount to offenders (VCCAV, 1997, p 55).

The VCCAV concluded that, while clear generalisations cannot be made from the consultations due to the range of responses received, the community has high expectations about sentencing that are frequently not being achieved in current practice.

The approach of the Sentencing Advisory Council

As a result of this research the Council concluded that it is necessary to understand the nature of *informed* public opinion in Victoria in terms of both general perceptions and in relation to specific sentencing options for specific offences. What is needed is a combination of large-scale representative surveys with well-considered questions (using both the more simple question and the more complex crime vignette) combined with the qualitative aspects of the deliberative focus group that will provide a richness of detail on specific issues. By triangulating our methodology, the Council should be able to create a more complete, nuanced and sophisticated picture of the complexities of public opinion on sentencing in Victoria, thereby counteracting populist perceptions of a punitive public.

The Council believes that there is no "silver bullet" to the methodological issues raised in the research literature. Rather, a suite of methodologies is required that allows the research questions to determine the most appropriate method by which to gather the community's opinions. Thus there should be a different methodological model used for different research questions.

The Council's approach to seeking input on its work differentiates between the expert advice afforded by a targeted consultation process and the more general opinion that may be gathered via traditional survey and focus group techniques.

Seeking expert advice

For some of its projects, the Council believes it is appropriate and desirable to garner the advice of people who are acknowledged experts in the field under investigation. In particular, legal professionals, judges and magistrates, and victim support workers are able to provide the Council with detailed and nuanced insight into the issues surrounding particular topics. Consultations with such groups are conducted in the form of roundtable discussions (akin to focus group discussions), bilateral meetings (akin to personal interviews) or via written submissions in response to specific discussion questions (akin to a written version of a personal interview).

Roundtable/focus group discussions

The Council has employed this method extensively in its work on issues such as reform of suspended sentences and post-sentence detention of high-risk offenders. Using this approach, separate discussions are organised for people whose expertise provides a particular perspective on the issues at hand. For example, the Council has convened roundtables for legal professionals; for forensic clinicians; for victims' advocates; for mental health support workers; for youth support workers; and for those working with drug- and alcohol-addicted offenders. This approach has been invaluable, as it has allowed the Council to gather expert advice and opinion on its work from a range of perspectives. It will continue to be a critical part of the Council's consultation strategy in future projects.

Bilateral meetings/personal interviews

The Council has employed this approach in a number of its projects. It is of particular use when there are specific individuals who are acknowledged experts in a field, or when material of a more sensitive nature is to be discussed. For example, the Council's work examining the advantages and disadvantages of a sentence indication and sentence discount scheme for Victoria involved the use of both an expert Advisory Group to identify the broader issues for discussion, as well as individual meetings with acknowledged experts in the field. This approach has allowed the Council access to the detailed, nuanced advice of key individuals in a field; it will continue as a cornerstone of the Council's consultation strategy.

Submissions/responses to discussion questions

For several of its projects, the Council has released to the general public discussion papers with specific questions for consultation. This approach is useful in reaching a wide audience of potential respondents and it allows people with an interest in the issues to participate in the consultation process. By providing a discussion paper from which people may form their opinions, the Council is facilitating the development of *informed* public opinion. This approach will continue to be employed in appropriate Council projects in the future.

The Council's approach to seeking expert advice has been employed success-fully in several projects to date. For future work, the Council plans to continue to refine its strategy to ensure that appropriate groups and individuals have sufficient opportunities to participate in the consultation process.

The Council has also developed its consultation strategy for a specific part of the community that is particularly affected by sentencing laws and practices: offender populations. For some projects, such as the Council's investigation of the possible use and form of a sentence indication scheme in Victoria, the opinions of offenders are critical in understanding the practical implications, advantages and disadvantages of reform.

In order to consult with offenders, the Council works closely with the Victorian Association for the Care and Resettlement of Offenders (VACRO) to refine its suite of methodologies for gauging the opinions of offenders. The approach involves working closely with VACRO staff to conduct surveys, focus groups and personal interviews with both offenders in prison and those who are in the community. This approach gives the Council an inside view of the impact of the criminal justice system on Victorian offenders.

Gauging public opinion

For some projects, the Council seeks to gather broader input from the community at large. Qualitative focus groups allow the Council to delve more deeply into the complexities of people's opinions on particular issues. This approach has been employed in several projects, most recently in the Council's work on sentence indication and on post-sentence detention of high-risk offenders. Providing community members with the opportunity to enter into an informed debate and discussion, and to learn about the complexity of the issues at hand through presentations by experts, allows the Council to unearth the nuances of public opinion. In our experience, rarely are members of the public as punitive as might be thought; indeed, these focus groups have illustrated for us that community views on sentencing issues are varied and subtle, and that people are far more accepting and tolerant of alternatives to punitive sentencing than populist sentiments would have us believe.

This kind of session provides the Council with a measure of *informed* public opinion by giving people some factual foundation upon which to build their opinions. This approach will continue to be a major part of the Council's consultation strategy.

One other methodology – the deliberative poll that combines both quantitative survey and qualitative focus group approaches – has been applied in the context of the Council's "You be the Judge" seminar series. Participants are asked to complete a survey on perceptions of sentencing before the seminar begins. The session then provides participants with information about sentencing practices and policy in order to illustrate the difficulties that sentencers face in arriving at an appropriate sentence and to allow for discussion and debate about the issues. Finally, participants once again complete the same survey.

The Council plans to develop further this deliberative poll methodology for use in future "You be the Judge" seminars. The methodology can also be adapted for use when examining specific issues, such as the advantages and disadvantages of continuing detention orders. The Council also hopes to develop, test and implement a large-scale, representative survey on sentencing issues for use with the general community, as well as surveys that focus on specific topics of interest that arise during the course of its project work.

Conclusion

While there is now a considerable body of research around the world in relation to public opinion on sentencing, there is clearly much work that remains to be done to understand informed public opinion in Victoria. But coming to public judgment, as David Green suggests, is hard, time-consuming work – people cannot achieve informed public judgment unassisted. It requires partnerships between experts and the public that provide for dialogue and debate about current knowledge in the field and about the likely consequences of potential reform.

In entering such partnerships and attempting to understand the complexities of public opinion on sentencing, the Sentencing Advisory Council is playing its part in incorporating the public into the development of sentencing policy. And by ensuring that members of the public have the opportunity to become *informed* about sentencing issues before providing their opinion, the Council is acting as a "policy buffer", countering the forces of penal populism and challenging prevailing presumptions about a punitive public.

References

Bottoms, AE (1995). The Philosophy and Politics of Punishment and Sentencing. In C Clark and R Morgan (eds). *The Politics of Sentencing Reform*. Oxford: Clarendon Press.

Casey, S and Mohr, P (2005). Law-and-Order Politics, Public-Opinion Polls and the Media (Australia). *Psychiatry, Psychology and Law* 12(1): 141.

Diamond, SS and Stalans, L (1989). The Myth of Judicial Leniency in Sentencing. *Behavioral Sciences & the Law* 7(1): 73.

Doob, A and Roberts, JV (1983). *Sentencing: An Analysis of the Public's View of Sentencing*. Ottawa: Department of Justice Canada.

Doob, A, Sprott, J, Marinos, V and Varma, K (1998) *An Exploration of Ontario Centre of Criminology*, University of Toronto.

Doob, A and Roberts, JV (1988). Public Punitiveness and Public Knowledge of the Facts: Some Canadian Surveys. In N Walker and M Hough (eds) *Public Attitudes to Sentencing: Surveys from Five Countries*. Aldershot, England: Gower.

Freiberg, A (2003). The Four Pillars of Justice: A Review Essay. *Australian and New Zealand Journal of Criminology* 36(2): 223.

Gelb, K (2006). *Myths and Misconceptions: Public Opinion versus Public Judgment about Sentencing*. Melbourne: Sentencing Advisory Council.

Green, DA (2006). Public Opinion versus Public Judgment about Crime. *British Journal of Criminology* 46: 131-154.

Hough, M. and Roberts, J.V. (1998). *Attitudes to Punishment: Findings from the British Crime Survey*. Home Office Research Study No. 179. London: Research and Statistics Directorate, Home Office.

Hough, M and Roberts, JV (2004). *Confidence in Justice: An International Review*. London: Institute of Criminal Policy Research.

Indermaur, D (2000). *Voodoo Politics in the Era of the TV Game Show: Public Opinion, the Media and Political Decision Making*. Presentation to the Centre for Criminology at the University of Hong Kong and the Hong Kong Criminology Society.

Indermaur, D and Roberts, L (2005). Perceptions of Crime and Justice. In S Wilson et al (eds) *Australian Social Attitudes: The First Report*. Sydney: University of New South Wales Press.

Mattinson, J and Mirrlees-Black, C (2000). *Attitudes to Crime and Criminal Justice: Findings from the 1998 British Crime Survey*. Home Office Research Study No 200. London: Research, Development and Statistics Directorate, Home Office.

Roberts, JV and Doob, A. (1989). Sentencing and Public Opinion: Taking False Shadows for True Substances. *Osgoode Hall Law Journal* 27(3): 491.

Roberts, JV and Hough, M (2005a). Sentencing Young Offenders: Public Opinion in England and Wales. *Criminal Justice* 5(3): 211.

Roberts, JV and Hough, M (2005b). *Understanding Public Attitudes to Criminal Justice*. Berkshire, UK: Open University Press.

Roberts, JV and Stalans, L ((1997). *Public Opinion, Crime and Criminal Justice*. Boulder, CO: Westview Press.

Roberts, JV, Stalans, LJ, Indermaur, D and Hough, M (2003). *Penal Populism and Public Opinion: Lessons from Five Countries*, Oxford. Oxford University Press.

Sprott, J (1996). Understanding Public Views of Youth Crime and the Youth Justice System. *Canadian Journal of Criminology* 38(3): 271.

Victorian Community Council Against Violence (1997). *Community Knowledge and Perceptions of Sentencing in Victoria: A Report on the Findings of the Consultations*. Melbourne: Victorian Community Council Against Violence.

Walker, J, Collins, M and Wilson, P (1987). How the Public Sees Sentencing: An Australian Survey. *Trends and Issues in Criminal Justice* No 4. Canberra: Australian Institute of Criminology.

6

The Minnesota
Sentencing Guidelines

Richard S Frase

Introduction

Public opinion and direct public participation have played only a limited role in the development and implementation of Minnesota's Sentencing Guidelines. To some extent this was by design – independent sentencing commissions are valued not only for their expertise and research capacity but also because they promote a long-term, fiscally responsible perspective and help to insulate sentencing policy development from short-term political pressures driven by sudden shifts in public opinion.

However, the Legislature and the Guidelines Commission in Minnesota have taken steps to ensure that the public is informed of the Commission's work and that public input and perspectives are taken into account. Several seats on the Minnesota Sentencing Guidelines Commission are reserved for members of the public; some of these members have played influential roles. When the Commission was designing and implementing the original version of the Guidelines it adopted an open process, inviting public attendance at the Commission's discussions and holding meetings in various locations around the State. Since the Guidelines went into effect in 1980, the Commission's regular monthly meetings have continued to be open to and attended by the public, and the Commission has recently adopted a policy of inviting public comment at each meeting. At least once a year a public hearing is held to receive comments on proposed Guidelines changes.

Although public attendance at the Commission's meetings and hearings has been light in recent years, and the Commission has never surveyed the public's opinions or knowledge of sentencing issues, there is reason to believe that informed members of the public are aware of the existence and nature of the Guidelines.

The Commission regularly disseminates information about its work and the operation of the Guidelines: through annual reports to the Legislature; by annual summaries of sentencing data and periodic reports evaluating Guidelines implementation or special issues; by making detailed sentencing data freely available to interested outside researchers; and, in recent years, by maintaining a website containing a wide range of sentencing data, reports and other useful information about the operation of the Guidelines and the Commission. Furthermore, the Guidelines and the Commission are frequently mentioned in newspaper articles. This press coverage facilitates a two-way dialogue through which the public learns about current and proposed sentencing policy and the Commission learns about particular public concerns relating to existing policy or desired changes in policy.

The remainder of this chapter is organised as follows. The first part introduces the Minnesota Guidelines system by briefly describing the State's political and social climate and the current scope and operation of the Guidelines and other sentencing laws. The second part summarises the origins and evolution of the Minnesota Guidelines since passage of the enabling legislation in 1978, drawing attention to the ways in which public opinion and participation have occasionally shaped the design and modification of sentencing policy. The third part examines the nature and frequency of public input into sentencing policy formulation in recent years, and the ways in which the Commission publicises its work. Finally, the fourth part analyses media reporting on the Guidelines and the Commission's work in an effort to estimate, first, what the public knows or could know about these matters and, secondly, what kinds of public concerns are reflected in these stories (and thus are known or knowable by the Commission). One highly publicised recent case is presented as an example of how intense media attention is translated into legislative and Commission action, producing substantially changed State sentencing law and policy. The conclusion reflects on the balance Minnesota has struck between public versus professional and expert dominance of sentencing policy formulation.

Two preliminary points need to be addressed. First, as this chapter was prepared for an international conference at which the only United States jurisdictions represented were Minnesota and the federal government, it must be stressed that Minnesota's experience is not necessarily typical of other jurisdictions in the United States, even States with sentencing guidelines. A recent survey (Frase, 2005c) found operating guidelines systems in 18 States and the federal capital city (Washington, DC), but these systems varied widely in their purposes, design, scope, and operation.[1]

A second preliminary task is to define what is meant in this chapter by members of the "public". As judges, attorneys, legislators, executive branch officials, and other public officials and criminal justice actors have direct power over sentencing policy and/or case outcomes, it will be assumed in this chapter that the interest in "public" participation and opinion relates to members of the general public (including news reporters) who are not affiliated with any policy-making political body or criminal justice agency involved in law enforcement, prosecution, adjudication or sentencing. As will be seen, however, the definition of a "public member" of the Minnesota Sentencing Guidelines Commission has been interpreted fairly broadly to include, for example, the Director of a private, chemical dependency treatment centre to whom offenders are often sent from criminal court or in lieu of prosecution.

Introduction to Minnesota Guidelines sentencing

This part of the chapter introduces Minnesota and its Guidelines system by explaining the political and social climate of the State, the overall structure of Minnesota's sentencing laws, and the scope and operation of the Guidelines.

The political and social context

Since the 1970s Minnesota has generally been a politically liberal State, consistently voting Democratic in Presidential elections, but it has become considerably more moderate in recent years (for example, the three Governors elected since 1990 have all been Republicans or Independents). In the late 1970s, when the Guidelines were formulated and implemented, the State's political culture was described as one in which "citizens tended to view government as a means to achieve a good community through positive political action" (Martin, 1984, p 28). The consensus needed to achieve major sentencing reform was facilitated by Minnesota's relatively small population (about four million in 1970), its substantial degree of ethnic and cultural homogeneity (98 per cent of the State population in 1970 was White, mostly of northern European ancestry) and its "tradition of citizen participation in government, including the involvement of interest groups in policymaking" (Martin, 1984, pp 28-9). Reform consensus – and in particular, the decision to delegate guidelines formulation to an independent sentencing commission – was further encouraged by the Legislature's tradition (up to that time, at least) of non-partisanship with respect to criminal justice policy issues (Martin, 1984, p 61 n 180). Political and public consensus may also have been facilitated by the moderate tone of the State's principal news media. Neither of the two papers with State-wide circulation can be characterised as a "tabloid" although these papers do occasionally publish sensational crime stories and features.[2]

Sentencing reform consensus and moderation have also been encouraged by the generally non-partisan nature of Minnesota's judicial system. Judges serve six-year terms and run for election or re-election without political party endorsement (Martin, 1984, p 30). In practice, most judges are initially appointed by the Governor to fill an unexpired term and then are routinely re-elected in uncontested elections;[3] they usually retire during their terms so that their successors can likewise be appointed. Chief prosecutors in each county are also chosen in non-partisan elections, but (unlike judges and public defenders) they are "a well-organised and active political force" (Martin, 1984, p 30).

Although Minnesota's population remains quite homogeneous in comparison to others in the United States, the State has become much more ethnically diverse since the 1970s. Minnesota's Black population more than tripled from 1980 to 2000 (Frase, 2005b, p 201) and there have also been major increases in the State's Asian population, due primarily to an influx of Hmong refugees after the end of the Vietnam war. The State has relatively few Hispanic residents (less than 4 per cent in 2005, compared to over 14 per cent for the nation: Frase, 2006b). The growing diversity of Minnesota's population is reflected in the State's criminal case loads: from 1981 to 2005 the proportion of non-Hispanic Whites among convicted felons declined from 82 per cent to 62 per cent, and there were substantial increases in all non-White categories except American Indians – Blacks increased from 11 per cent in 1981 to 24 per cent in 2005; Hispanics went from 1.6 to 5.5 per cent; and Asians went from 0.2 to 2.0 per cent (Minnesota Sentencing Guidelines Commission, 2006c, p 10).

Minnesota was a low-incarceration State in the 1970s and remains so today. In 1978, when the Guidelines enabling statute was enacted, Minnesota's State prison incarceration rate was 49 per 100,000 State residents; Massachusetts had the same rate, and only two States had lower rates (Bureau of Justice Statistics, 1980, p 4). By 2005 Minnesota's prison rate had risen to 180 per 100,000, but the State still had the second lowest rate in the country (Bureau of Justice Statistics, 2006b, p 4). Minnesota's low prison incarceration rate is due in part to its relatively low rate of violent crime and also to the State's heavy use of local jail sentences. However, even when jail inmates are included, Minnesota's total incarceration rate (300 per 100,000 residents) is still the second lowest in the nation (Bureau of Justice Statistics, 2006a, p 9).

Overview of Minnesota sentencing laws

There have been many changes in Minnesota's Guidelines and other sentencing laws since 1980, but the general features of the sentencing system have remained the same. The following overview is therefore focused on the current Guidelines (Minnesota Sentencing Guidelines Commission, 2006a) and laws to provide a framework for the historical and contemporary material presented in later parts of this chapter.

The Guidelines apply to all felonies except those punishable with life in prison (the most serious murder and rape offences). For lesser crimes (misdemeanours and gross misdemeanours, punishable with maximum terms of 90 days and one year, respectively), there are no guidelines, and judges retain full sentencing discretion.[4]

As to felonies (all of which are punishable by statute with State prison sentences of more than one year), the Guidelines specify the recommended sentences that are presumed to be correct for most cases. These recommendations include both the duration of imprisonment and the "disposition" – whether the prison term should be executed (immediately carried out) or stayed (suspended); in the latter case the offender is normally placed on probation under various conditions, which may include confinement in a local jail or workhouse for up to one year. The Guidelines provide some general, non-binding policies but no specific guidelines concerning the conditions of a stayed sentence or subsequent decisions to revoke the stay.

Except for life sentences, there is no parole release discretion and prison terms may be reduced only by earned good time (up to a one-third reduction of the prison term). Some life sentences are without possibility of parole. For parole-eligible offenders, release is decided by the Department of Corrections (Minnesota Statutes Chapters 243, 244), not a separate parole board, and there is no public membership on the decision-making body. The Department holds hearings on parole release issues that the victim (or if deceased, the victim's spouse or next of kin) may attend. Parole-eligible murderers may not be released until the offender has served 30 years; the minimum terms for life sentences in rape cases are determined by the Guidelines (prison term, less earned good time) and a few mandatory minimum statutes. Subject to these limits, parole release is discretionary and there are no guidelines for these decisions. However, the paroling authorities are directed to consider community sentiments toward the inmate at the time of offence and of proposed release (Minnesota Statutes Section 244.05 Subdivision 5(b)).

How the Guidelines work

Recommended Guidelines sentences are based primarily on two factors: the severity of the offender's most serious current offence and the number and type of prior convictions. The specific recommendations are contained in two grids, one for sex offenders and one for all other felons. Offence severity (the vertical axis, with 11 severity levels on the main grid) is based on the Commission's own rank-order assessments of crime seriousness. The defendant's criminal history score (the horizontal axis, with seven columns on the main grid) consists primarily of previous felony convictions which are weighted by their severity levels (for example, two points for each prior conviction at level nine or higher; half a point each for convictions at levels one and two); limited additional points are added for prior misdemeanour convictions, juvenile delinquency adjudications, and "custody status" (whether the offender was in custody or on some form of conditional release at the time of the current offence).

The Guidelines specify the sentence that is presumed to be correct for each combination of offence severity and criminal history. Judges may "depart" from the presumptive sentence only if they cite "substantial and compelling circumstances". Offenders with low to medium criminal history scores convicted of lower severity offences presumptively receive a stayed (suspended) prison term of a specified number of months; for more serious offences or criminal history scores, the presumptive sentence is an executed prison term within a specified range. Defendants with executed prison terms serve their entire term, less a credit of up to one-third for good conduct in prison. The boundary between presumptive stayed and presumptive executed prison terms is shown on the grid by a heavy black line (the "disposition line"). Cases in the shaded area below the line have presumptive stayed sentences (except for a few cases – mostly involving recidivists or the use of a dangerous weapon – that are subject to mandatory minimum prison terms provided in State statutes).

Additional rules specify permissible and impermissible bases for departure from presumptive disposition and durational rules. In extreme cases, upward durational departures may go all the way up to the statutory maximum prison term for the offence. The prosecution and defence each have the right to appeal the sentence, on the grounds that the departure (or refusal to depart) was improper. Finally, the Guidelines suggest a wide variety of possible conditions of stayed prison sentences, which judges may select in their discretion: up to one year of confinement in a local jail or workhouse; treatment (residential or out-patient); home detention (with or without electronic monitoring); probation (with "intensive", regular or no supervision); fines; restitution; victim-offender mediation; and community service. In felony cases the duration of the stay (that is, the length of probation) may be any period up to the maximum prison term that could have been imposed, or four years, whichever is longer.

History: the origins, purposes and evolution of the Guidelines

Origins

Under pre-Guidelines sentencing law judges had complete discretion in choosing between a prison term or probation, for most felony crimes.[5] If an offender was sent to prison the parole board could grant release at any time, and usually did so substantially before the maximum had been served (Martin, 1984, p 29). Parole guidelines were implemented in May 1976 (Martin, 1984, p 31) and the two-dimensional matrix used in these guidelines (offence severity by offender risk score) probably led the Guidelines Commission to adopt a similar matrix.

The 1978 guidelines enabling statute (1978 Minnesota Laws, Chapter 723) created the Minnesota Sentencing Guidelines Commission[6] and directed the Commission to formulate, implement and monitor guidelines for all felony sentences other than life sentences. The statute specified that the guidelines were to govern both the decision to impose State imprisonment and the duration of such imprisonment, and were to be based on "reasonable offence and offender characteristics". The Commission was also instructed to take into "substantial consideration" two factors: "current sentencing and releasing practices" and "correctional resources, including but not limited to the capacities of local and state correctional facilities". The Commission was also permitted (but was not required) to develop guidelines regulating the conditions of non-prison sentences.

The enabling statute abolished parole release discretion, and substituted a limited reduction (up to one-third off the pronounced sentence) for good behaviour in prison. This earned "good-time" reduction then constitutes a period of parole-type post-release supervision (the Supervised Release Term; longer conditional release terms apply to certain offenders). The statute also implied that denial of good time reductions could only be based on disciplinary violations, not failure to participate in or cooperate with in-prison treatment programs (as all such programs were to become voluntary).[7] Finally, the statute requires sentencing judges to provide written reasons when they depart from the Guidelines, and both defendants and the prosecution are given the right to appeal any sentence (whether or not it is a departure).

Legislative purposes

It seems clear that a major purpose of the statute was to reduce sentencing and prison-release discretion, thus promoting greater uniformity of sentences, but what broader purposes did the Legislature want sentences to serve? The Commission's later reports indicate that it chose to base its guidelines on a hybrid theory it called "modified just deserts". As I have argued in previous writings (Frase, 1991; 1995; 1997; 2005b), the Commission's just deserts approach was actually quite "modified" right from the start and has become steadily more so over time as a result of subsequent Commission modifications, legislative action, interpretative caselaw, and the actual practice of judges, attorneys and probation officers. Moreover, this hybrid approach appears to be what the Legislature intended. The Guidelines, as written and especially as they exist today, are quite consistent with the "limiting retributivism" theory suggested in the writings of Professor Norval Morris (Morris, 1974, pp 73-6; Morris, 1982, p 199; see also Frase, 1997; 2004; 2005a; 2005c). For most defendants, considerations of desert set only upper limits on sentencing severity, while the lower limits that exist are quite flexible. Within these upper and lower limits courts are expected to continue to pursue utilitarian purposes of punishment, especially rehabilitation, and are guided by a general principle of restraint and economy Morris called "parsimony" – sanctions "should be the least restrictive necessary to achieve the purposes of the sentence" (Morris, 1974, pp 59-62; Minnesota Sentencing Guidelines Commission, 2006a, Section I(4)).

The enabling statute's direction to the Commission, to give "substantial consideration" to existing sentencing and release practices, suggested both limited change in such practices and substantial continued emphasis on utilitarian goals. The predictions of dangerousness inherent in parole release were rejected, but not necessarily all predictions of dangerousness. And although prison treatment programs were made voluntary and not tied to release, treatment in the community – even mandated treatment[8] – was not necessarily rejected.

Nor does the legislative history of the enabling statute evince an intent to emphasise retribution, abandon utilitarian goals, or dramatically change any existing sentencing practices. The 1978 Act was the culmination of several years of legislative ferment over the sentencing reform issue, reflecting increasing dissatisfaction with indeterminate sentencing, but disagreement over what to do about it (Clark, 1979; Parent, 1988, pp 21-7; Martin, 1984). Sentencing purposes were rarely debated as such, nor was there much discussion of the need to change the sentencing of any particular offences or offenders. What consensus there was seemed to focus on abolishing the parole board and increasing the uniformity of sentences, without producing any overall increase in sentencing severity or prison populations.[9] It is also worth noting that the 1978 Legislature did not delete the references to utilitarian goals, contained in the State's criminal code.[10] Moreover, the same Bill that created the Guidelines Commission also changed the statute governing pre-sentence investigations to make them mandatory in felony cases, but did not delete or amend references to rehabilitation contained in the same subdivision of that statute (Minnesota Statutes Section 609.115, Subdivision 1).

Thus the most probable legislative purposes in enacting the 1978 enabling statute were: first, to limit sharply judicial and parole discretion in pursuing all of the traditional purposes of punishment, without abandoning any of them or clearly emphasizing some over others; secondly, to emphasise that State prison sentences are imposed primarily to achieve retribution, deterrence and incapacitation, and are not imposed to achieve forced rehabilitation – rehabilitation is to be pursued, if at all, outside of prison; thirdly, to consider other changes in sentencing policy without departing too much from existing practices; and finally to recognise, while pursuing the above goals, that punishment, especially by confinement, is expensive and that overcrowding of facilities and other resources must be avoided.

The public's role at the outset

What was the role of the public and public opinion at the earliest stage of guidelines development? It is fair to assume that the Legislature's increased focus on sentencing policy in the mid-1970s, and its dissatisfaction with key aspects of the indeterminate sentencing system, probably reflected to some extent the views of some constituents, in particular crime victims (who complained about discretion to be lenient) and to a lesser extent, convicted offenders and their supporters (who complained about discretion to be severe and the uncertainties of indeterminacy) (Clark, 1979, pp 4-6; Frase, 1993, p 8; Martin, 1984, pp 26-7; Parent, 1988, p 30). But none of the historical accounts of this early period has stated or implied that public pressure played a particularly strong role. It therefore seems likely that the impetus for sentencing reform in Minnesota came as much or more from within the criminal justice system and from academics. Nor did the Legislature's mandate to the Commission strongly emphasise public opinion or public input. The initial nine-person Commission was to include two "public members appointed by the governor",[11] but the Commission was not instructed to survey public opinion, hold public hearings or otherwise seek and take into account the public's views. This limited statutory provision for public input, and the structure of the Commission itself, is consistent with an intent to insulate the Commission from public opinion and direct electoral accountability, which has often been cited as a major advantage of having a sentencing commission (Frase, 1991, pp 729-30; Tonry, 1996, p 32). The only elected officials on the original commission were the prosecutor and the three judges (and, as noted above, Minnesota judges at that time rarely faced contested elections).

The Commission's early work

In carrying out its statutory mandate, the Minnesota Sentencing Guidelines Commission made several critical policy decisions. One of the earliest decisions was to adopt a "prescriptive" rather than a "descriptive" approach to guidelines development (Minnesota Sentencing Guidelines Commission, 1980, pp 2-3; 1984, pp v, 8-14) – the Guidelines were not designed simply to model past judicial and parole decisions (or the average of those decisions). Although prior practices were studied and taken into account as required by the enabling statute, the Commission made a number of independent decisions about which offenders ought to go to prison and for how long, and what the primary purposes of punishment ought to be. The Commission's most important prescriptive changes in pre-existing sentencing policy related to the following issues:

1. Identification and prioritising of permissible sentencing purposes under the Commission's "modified just deserts" theory (Minnesota Sentencing Guidelines Commission, 1980, p 9) – sentencing was to be proportional to both offence severity and the seriousness of the offender's prior conviction record.

2. Rejection of "real-offence" sentencing. Recommended prison commitment and duration rules, and suggested departure criteria, were based almost entirely on elements of the crime or crimes of conviction and the offender's prior conviction record (Parent & Frase, 2005, pp 13-14).

3. Rank-ordering of offence severity based on the Commission's own sense of the seriousness of each crime (Minnesota Sentencing Guidelines Commission, 1980, pp 6-7).

4. Definition and weighting of criminal history. In particular, the Commission gave limited weight to prior juvenile felony-level adjudications and to prior adult misdemeanour and gross misdemeanour convictions (Minnesota Sentencing Guidelines Commission, 1980, p 7).

5. Recognition of the goal of socio-economic as well as racial and gender neutrality. The Commission explicitly prohibited consideration of the defendant's education, marital status, and employment status at the time of the offence or at sentencing (Minnesota Sentencing Guidelines

Commission, 2006a, Section I(1)), even though employment at sentencing had been a significant factor in prior court decisions when choosing whether to impose prison or probation (referred to in Minnesota as "dispositional" decisions) (Minnesota Sentencing Guidelines Commission, 1980, p 5).

6. Explicit prioritising of prison use – in particular, sending more low-criminal history "person" offenders to prison and fewer recidivist property offenders (Minnesota Sentencing Guidelines Commission, 1980, pp 9-10, 15; 1984, pp 10-14, 21).

7. Matching sentencing severity with prison capacity. The Commission gave great weight to the statutory directive to take existing correctional resources into substantial consideration; accordingly, the Guidelines were designed to produce State prison populations that remained well within (no more than 95 per cent of) current and projected (fully funded) prison capacity. A detailed, computerised projection model was developed and used throughout the drafting process to test the expected prison population that would result from each proposed guidelines rule or procedure. The Commission's "capacity constraint" and its prison population projections forced members of the Commission, as well as outside constituencies and interest groups, to confront the reality of limited prison resources and the need to set priorities in the use of those resources; any member, constituency or interest group that proposed greater severity for one group of offenders was asked to identify other offenders who could receive correspondingly reduced severity (Martin, 1984, pp 46, 54 n 150, 101, 104; Parent, 1988, pp 6-7, 40-5, 92-3). Minnesota was the first jurisdiction to use this approach, which became feasible due to the greater predictability of guidelines sentencing. This policy has helped Minnesota to avoid the problems of prison overcrowding that have plagued most other jurisdictions in the United States in the past several decades. Resource-matching policies were subsequently adopted in some form by almost all State guidelines systems, and the capacity to implement such a policy has become one of the most important reasons leading States to adopt guidelines sentencing (Frase, 1995, p 175).

8. Preference for guidelines rules that are simple to apply and narrow in scope. The Commission recognised that highly complex sentencing rules are difficult for the public and offenders to understand, more costly and time-consuming for practitioners to apply and likely to produce error and new forms of disparity (Frase, 2005b, pp 132, 206). The Commission also chose not to exercise its option to develop guidelines for non-prison sentences (although it did make a number of non-binding recommendations as to such sentences), and it also did not develop, or request a mandate to develop, guidelines for probation revocation, charging and plea bargaining, and misdemeanour sentencing (Frase, 2005b, pp 209-10).

The public's role in the early years

Members of the public played an important part in the initial drafting of the Guidelines, notwithstanding the limited roles assigned to them in the makeup and statutory mandate of the Commission. One of the two public members of the Commission, Jan Smaby, was appointed as initial Chair of the Commission and served in that capacity from 1978 until 1982 (the two years before and after the Guidelines went into effect).[12] (Although some State guidelines enabling statutes specify that the chair shall be a judge, the Minnesota statute permits the Governor to appoint any member of the Commission as Chair). Ms Smaby came from a politically prominent family; she also had considerable experience as a legislative lobbyist and in criminal justice and correctional planning, and she proved to be a very active and effective leader of the new Commission (Frase, 1991, p 730; Parent, 1988, pp 31, 45-7, 136). Considering the number, complexity and novelty of the policy-making, drafting and implementation tasks assigned to and successfully completed by the Commission, which it was given very little time to accomplish,[13] the role of the initial chair was a critical one. However, the success of the Commission under Smaby was probably due as much to her experience, political connections and personality as to her status, per se, as a member of the public (Martin, 1984, p 103).

One of the most important procedural decisions made by the Commission under Smaby's leadership was to apply an "aggressively open political process" to the tasks of guidelines development (Minnesota Sentencing Guidelines Commission, 1984, pp v, 15). This involved two components. First, the Commission reached out to and sought to involve in the drafting process all of the key interested constituencies of sentencing – corrections, defence, prosecution, courts, the Legislature, local government (responsible for most non-prison sentences) and key public interest groups, particularly Blacks, Native Americans and women (Martin, 1983, pp 49-50; Parent, 1988, pp 46-7, 139). Commission members representing these constituencies acted as liaisons, communicating to the Commission the perspective of their group (and, indirectly, the perspectives of the general public that had been conveyed to group members) and explaining to the group the goals, views and policies of the Commission. Commission meetings were well-attended by members of these groups (with typically 20 to 40 people in the audience) and chair Jan Smaby maintained an informal and collaborative meeting style that permitted audience members to participate at any time and at any length (Parent, 1988, p 47).

A second outreach component involved holding numerous public hearings and speaking engagements around the State to explain the Commission's work and solicit public comment and concerns. Hearings were held during the development process and again after the Guidelines had been put into effect, to get input into how they were working. The Commission found this input helpful in modifying the Guidelines and disseminating the Commission's data on sentencing practices under the Guidelines (Minnesota Sentencing Guidelines Commission, 1984, p 15). In the two years leading up to the effective date of the Guidelines, Commission members and staff spoke at more than 100 meetings of professional, business, community and religious groups around the State; the Commission also regularly briefed the media on the Commission's work and worked closely with reporters specialising in sentencing and corrections issues (Martin, 1984, pp 49, 105-6; Parent, 1988, pp 47-8, 137-8).

The evolution of the guidelines

Since their inception in 1980 there have been many changes in the Minnesota Guidelines and related sentencing laws, although the basic structure and operation of the Guidelines remain the same. As I have discussed at greater length in prior writings (Frase, 1997; 2005b), the mix of purposes under Minnesota's hybrid, "modified just deserts" approach has shifted somewhat; greater emphasis is now being given to crime-control purposes and individualised assessments of risk and amenability to treatment, with a corresponding decrease in emphasis on retributive and uniformity goals. The Guidelines and related laws have become more complex, but remain fairly easy to apply. The goal of matching sentencing policy to available correctional resources is still given substantial weight; Guidelines sentencing remains sufficiently predictable to permit accurate forecasts of resource impacts, and the Commission and the Legislature take these forecasts seriously and tailor their proposals to limit State and local resource impacts. As a result, the State's prison population, although growing rapidly, has grown more slowly than in many other States over the past 26 years and has almost always remained within rated capacity.

The public's role today

The public's role in Guidelines policy formulation appears to be more limited and less direct today than it was in the early years of Guidelines development and implementation. There is less attendance at hearings and meetings, and the public members of the Commission have generally played less active roles than Jan Smaby did. The Commission continues to rely on these public sessions and on its public members to learn about the public's views and concerns; as in the early years, the Commission has not sought to gauge public opinion by means of surveys or other research efforts. On the other hand, changes in the Guidelines enabling statute have somewhat increased the importance of the public's perspective, and the Commission has taken steps to publicise and explain its work and to ensure that critical information about the operation of the Guidelines is readily available to news media and the general public.

Changes in the enabling statute reflecting and increasing public input

A 1987 amendment specified that one of the public members must be a felony crime victim and in 1988 (effective in 1990) the Commission was expanded to include a third public member. The increased attention given to crime control, noted above (including a 1989 change in the enabling statute, specifying that public safety should thenceforth be the Commission's "primary goal"), reflected the public's perennial concern about crime and victimisation. In 1996 the enabling statute was again amended, directing the Commission also to take into account "the long-term negative impact of crime on the community" (Frase, 2005b, p 162).

Formal roles of the public members

Since the early years a public member has only once been chair of the Commission – Dan Cain, the Executive Director of a private drug treatment program, was chair from 1987 to 1991. Like all of the later chairs, he was not as active and influential as Jan Smaby and his work as chair seemed to be informed more by his background in drug treatment than by his status, per se as a public member. Indeed, as his treatment program regularly received clients from the criminal courts, he was in some ways as much a criminal justice system "insider" as the non-"public" members of the Commission.

Another prominent public member in recent years has been Connie Larson. She is the mother of a young woman who was abducted, raped and murdered in a very highly publicised case in 1991 (one of two such cases that year, which led to further increases in sentencing severity for sex offenders: Frase, 2005b, p 163). Mrs Larson has served as chair of a subcommittee examining sex offender sentencing and has been an active and thoughtful contributor in public meetings of the Commission (see further discussion below).

The public's role as reflected in Commission meeting and hearing records

To provide a more concrete sense of the nature and extent of public participation in the work of the Commission, the author reviewed the minutes of Commission meetings and public hearings held in calendar years 2000 to 2006 (most of which are posted on the Commission's website: Minnesota Sentencing Guidelines Commission, 2006d). The Commission normally meets once a month and its meetings are open for anyone to attend. Public hearings are usually held once or twice a year, in connection with proposed changes in the Guidelines. These hearings provide a forum for individual members of the public, community and other groups, as well as public officials and criminal justice practitioners to express their opinions concerning the proposed changes. Attendance at the public hearings and monthly meetings by members of the general public is limited; usually no more than two or three such persons attend and sometimes there is none at all.

The minutes reflect not only attendance but the identity of persons requesting to speak or submitting a letter or other written statement. Interest groups often send representatives to the public hearings to promote the group's position. For example, Mothers Against Drunk Driving (MADD) sent representatives to promote adoption of more severe drunk driving penalties; Jewish and African-American community leaders sent representatives to support adoption of racial and ethnic bias as a justification for departure from the Guidelines. Community members also send letters on issues of concern to them. Overall, the Commission seems to be quite responsive to the views of these different public groups and individuals. Often the Commission takes time to discuss the comments made in public hearings or via letters sent to the commission. From time to time the Commission also invites researchers, community leaders or other members of the public to address the Commission on specific topics.

The meeting minutes further reflect the identity of Commission members who spoke at that meeting or who have been active in various aspects of the Commission's current work. Some public members of the Commission have been particularly active as speakers and/or members of important subcommittees. For example, in the 2000-06 period examined, one public member (an attorney employed in the General Counsel's office of the University of Minnesota and subsequently appointed to the State Supreme Court) spoke at many of the meetings; two other public members served as chair and co-chair of important subcommittees studying sex offender sentencing and legislative matters. Indeed, a public member was on almost every subcommittee mentioned in the minutes.[14] The Commission has often involved members of the community and interest groups in these subcommittees.

In September 2006 the Commission decided to encourage additional public input at its monthly meetings by setting aside a time for audience comment, with each speaker allowed to speak for up to three minutes (20 September 2006 meeting minutes, posted on Minnesota Sentencing Guidelines Commission, 2006d).

The Commission's efforts to publicise its work

Each January the Commission submits an annual report to the Legislature. These reports seek to educate or remind legislators about the goals of the Guidelines and the Commission's role, while also reporting highlights of the most recent data on sentencing practices. The annual reports also summarise recent Guidelines changes implemented or proposed and report on any special projects the Commission has been working on at the Legislature's request or on its own initiative. More detailed sentencing data are collected and published in the form of annual summaries and occasional in-depth studies of particular crimes or sentencing policy issues.

The Commission's ongoing monitoring system includes the collection of detailed data on every defendant sentenced under the Guidelines; this information is assembled in annual (calendar-year) data sets that are formatted and easily analysed on a personal computer using SPSS (Statistical Package for the Social Sciences). These data sets have always been made available at no cost to researchers, members of the media and others who request copies.

In recent years the Commission's website (Minnesota Sentencing Guidelines Commission, 2006d) has provided the public and other interested parties with a wealth of information about the Guidelines and the Commission, including brief explanations of the history and operation of the Guidelines; down-loadable copies of the Guidelines, research studies and reports to the Legislature; notices of upcoming Commission meetings; and copies of past meeting and hearing minutes.

Public knowledge and concerns about sentencing policy

As the Commission has never conducted any surveys of public opinion, and few members of the public attend the Commission's meetings and hearings, submit letters or otherwise communicate directly with the Commission, we must resort to indirect measures of public knowledge and concerns about sentencing policy. The first section below examines media depictions of sentencing laws and guidelines and the work of the Guidelines Commission, in an effort to assess what the public "knows" (or could know) about sentencing policy, and what particular public concerns are made known to the Commission through media reports. As radio and television broadcasting leaves few researchable traces, only newspaper stories will be analysed. The second section then examines one particularly well-publicised recent case, showing how the intense media attention generated by such cases is translated into legislative and Commission action, producing substantial changes in State sentencing law and policy.

Media coverage of the Guidelines and the Sentencing Commission

The Sentencing Guidelines and the Guidelines Commission are frequently mentioned in newspaper articles. In the three-year period ending on 30 June 2006, the two main State-wide papers each published over 100 stories mentioning the Guidelines in connection with specific cases. In dozens of other stories (over 50 in the *Minneapolis Star Tribune*; over 100 in the *St Paul Pioneer Press*) there was mention of guidelines in other jurisdictions and/or recent Supreme Court cases significantly affecting guidelines sentencing. This substantial press coverage permits the newspaper-reading public to learn about current and proposed sentencing policy. The issues raised by reporters and by the people they interview also give newspaper-reading Commission members and staff valuable information about the nature and urgency of current public opinions on sentencing law and policy.

Stories on sex crimes and sex offenders, often discussing sentencing laws and sometimes mentioning the Guidelines, have been particularly frequent in the past several years. This heavy coverage resulted from a single, highly publicised case involving the abduction, rape and murder of a college student, Dru Sjodin, and the arrest and charging of a recently released sex offender. The abduction occurred on 22 November 2003 in Grand Forks North Dakota, just west of the Minnesota State line. In the next two and a half years the two main newspapers with State-wide circulation and the two principal papers in the region where the crime occurred, published an average of 304 articles per paper on this case, plus another 302 articles per paper, addressing sex offenders without mentioning the Sjodin case. By comparison, in the three years preceding the abduction, articles mentioning sex offenders appeared with much less frequency in all four of these papers. As shown in the table below, the average number of sex offender articles in these papers was three times higher in 2003-06 than it was in 2000-03 (or four times higher, when articles only mentioning Dru Sjodin are also included).

Table 1: Newspaper articles on sex offenders, 2000-06

	23 November 2003–30 June 2006[15]				2000-03
	"Sex offender" (only)	"Sex offender" + Dru Sjodin	Dru Sjodin (only)	2003-06 total articles	"Sex offender" articles
Minneapolis Star Tribune	189	95	94	378	130
St Paul Pioneer Press	359	183	98	640	183
Grand Forks Herald	365	232	265	862	108
Fargo-Moorhead Forum	294	124	122	540	208
4-paper averages	*302*	*159*	*145*	*605*	*157*
Overall "sex offender" average	**461** [302+159] (2003-06)				**157** (2000-03)

The Dru Sjodin case

This case provides a useful case study of the way in which public concern and intense media coverage, generated by a single high-profile crime, can produce major changes in sentencing statutes and guidelines. As I have described in previous writings, a similar process has occurred several times before.[16]

The crime[17]

Dru Sjodin, a Minnesota resident studying in North Dakota, was abducted from a Grand Forks shopping mall parking lot on 22 November 2003. As she was not promptly located and searchers found one of her shoes it was soon feared that she had been killed (her body was found five months later, in Minnesota). The principal suspect, Alphonso Rodriguez, was arrested on 1 December 2003. He had been seen at the mall, and court documents unsealed a week later revealed forensic evidence linking him to the crime. He was also from Minnesota, and had been released from prison earlier in 2003 after serving 23 years for rape; he was classified as a Level III sex offender (the highest risk category). He was eventually prosecuted in a federal court, in part to permit application of federal death penalty provisions. At his trial, which began in mid-July of 2006, he was convicted and sentenced to death.

The political, legislative and Commission responses

Within a few weeks of Sjodin's disappearance Minnesota governor Tim Pawlenty proposed restoration of capital punishment (last used in Minnesota in 1911), including for some sex offences not resulting in death. Legislators from both major parties, as well as public opinion polls, expressed opposition to the death penalty, but legislators embraced many other harsh proposals for sex offenders.

Bills introduced in the 2004 legislative session included provisions for more severe prison terms, increased or even lifetime supervision, extended civil commitment, life without parole and a return to indeterminate sentencing for some or all sex offenders (Frase, 2005b, p 212). However, none of these legislative proposals was enacted in 2004, due to preoccupation with the State budget and other matters. Another cause of the Legislature's inaction may have been the estimated cost of the severe new sex offender proposals. For example, one of the Bills included mandatory life terms for most first-degree Criminal Sexual Conduct offenders; for this provision alone the projected long-term bed impact was an additional 4,393 beds – a more than 50 per cent increase in Minnesota's prison population at the time (Minnesota Executive Budget Office, 2004).

In its January 2005 Report to the Legislature (Minnesota Sentencing Guidelines Commission, 2005), the Commission suggested a new approach to the sentencing of sex offenders in light of the 2004 legislative proposals, applicable statutory maxima and minima and data on the frequency of upward durational departures given to these offenders. The Commission proposed to create a separate sentencing grid for sex offences (all Guidelines sentences had previously been incorporated into a single grid), with more severe recommended sentences and a revised criminal history formula giving greater weight to prior sex crimes and sex crimes committed while under supervision. The report also included an "off-grid", indeterminate life-imprisonment sentencing option for recidivists and certain other sex offenders. The Commission's fiscal impact assessment projected a need for 580 additional prison beds per year, after a 20-year phase-in period.

The legislative response was included in the Omnibus Crime Bill (House File 1, 2005 Minnesota Laws, Chapter 136), approved in May of 2005. In lieu of the Commission's recommendations for revised sex offender sentencing that remained mostly within the Guidelines framework, the Legislature enacted more severe statutory penalties for sex crimes and sex-related crimes. Mandatory life-without-parole was imposed on certain first- and second-degree criminal sexual conduct offences (including some committed by first offenders); mandatory life-with-parole accompanied by a mandatory minimum term was provided for certain other first- and second-degree offenders (including first offenders) and for certain repeat offenders convicted of first- through fourth-degree criminal sexual conduct or other sex-related violent crimes ("criminal sexual predatory conduct"). The law also increased post-prison supervised release requirements (in some cases, requiring life-time supervision) and expanded provisions dealing with sex offender registration, community notification, tracking of sex offenders from other States and procedures for civil commitment of "sexually dangerous persons". Finally, the Legislature directed the Commission to revise its proposed separate grid for sex offenders, to focus on those not subject to the new statutory provisions.

Accordingly, the Commission's January 2006 Report to the Legislature (Minnesota Sentencing Guidelines Commission, 2006b) proposed a revised separate grid and revised criminal history formula for sex offenders. The Commission estimated that these Guidelines changes would require an additional 380 prison beds per year after a 20-year phase-in period; when added to the impact of the more severe penalties contained in the 2005 crime Bill, the projected long-term increase in required prison capacity was 598 beds per year.

Additional increases in sex offender sentencing severity were enacted in the 2006 Omnibus Crime Bill (House File 2656, 2006 Minnesota Laws, Chapter 260). Mandatory sentences of imprisonment for double the recommended Guidelines duration were provided for persons convicted of first- through fourth-degree criminal sexual conduct or criminal sexual predatory conduct, upon a further finding that the offender is a "danger to public safety" and that his or her "criminal sexual behaviour is so engrained that the risk of reoffending is great without intensive psychotherapeutic intervention or other long-term treatment or super-vision extending beyond the [Guidelines] presumptive term of imprisonment and supervised release" (Minnesota Statutes, Section 609.3455, Subdivision 3a). The Legislature also enacted increased periods of post-prison supervised release for certain sex offenders. Finally, the 2006 crime Bill rejected some of the recom-mended sentences in the Commission's proposed sex offender sentencing grid and requested the Commission to increase the severity ranking of these crimes. The Commission did so in the Guidelines modifications and separate sex-crimes grid, which became effective as of 1 August 2006 (Minnesota Sentencing Guidelines Commission, 2006a).

The 2006 legislative and guidelines changes, combined with previous changes, have resulted in substantially increased sex offender sentencing severity. For first-degree criminal sexual conduct committed by an offender with zero criminal history, the recommended Guidelines sentence was 43 months in 1988; the sentence was increased to 86 months in 1989 and to 144 months in 2000. For a first-degree offender with four criminal history points,[18] the recommended sentence was increased from 95 months (1988) to 134 months (1989) and then to 234 months (2006).

Conclusion

Minnesota's experience over the past quarter century shows that legally binding sentencing guidelines implemented by an independent sentencing commission can achieve many important policy goals (Frase, 2005b) – reducing unwarranted sentencing disparities without greatly complicating sentencing hearings or unduly confining the judge's ability to consider case-specific facts; controlling prison population growth and avoiding overcrowding; setting priorities in the use of limited prison capacity; using appellate review to create a common law of sentencing that assists the Commission and the Legislature in developing sentencing policy; and promoting "truth in sentencing" (limits on prison-release discretion ensure that the amount of time actually served in prison is not dramatically less than the prison term imposed by the court at sentencing). The role of the Minnesota Guidelines in promoting public safety is more difficult to assess, but the similarity between crime trends in Minnesota and the rest of the United States in the past three decades suggests at least that the Guidelines have not seriously interfered with crime control efforts.

The role of the public and public opinion in achieving these results has been limited, and that appears to have been intentional. The decision to create an independent appointed sentencing commission to study and recommend sentencing policy changes was consistent with the State's traditions and so was the makeup of Minnesota's Commission. Unlike some other jurisdictions in the United States, Minnesota has no tradition of direct public participation in law-making via ballot initiatives and referenda. An independent sentencing commission was also consistent with Minnesota's "good government" traditions and its frequent use of specialised administrative agencies. Such agencies are created and given delegated legislative, executive and/or adjudicative power for many of the same reasons that sentencing commissions are created – to apply subject-matter expertise, research and planning capacity, institutional continuity and a long-term perspective to complex public policy issues, while partially insulating controversial issues from direct electoral pressures and short-term swings in public opinion.

The makeup of the Minnesota Commission, including public members and representatives of all major criminal justice agencies and parties, but no legislators, was consistent with the State's traditions of active citizen and interest group participation in government and policy-making (Martin, 1984, pp 40 n 88, 43). But only two of the original nine Commissioners were public members and the Commission was not required to survey public opinion or encourage public input into its policy decisions; those matters were left for the Commission to determine. In the early years, when the Guidelines were being written and put into effect, the Commission decided to seek public input aggressively, by means of open meetings and hearings held around the State. That decision may have reflected, in part, the key role played by one of the public members, Commission

Chair Jan Smaby. But the Commission did not collect or study public opinion data on sentencing policy issues at that time, nor has it done so more recently. And after the Guidelines went into effect the Commission did little to encourage public input, nor have public members on the Commission played key roles.

Perhaps the public could have been given a greater role in the post-implementation period, without sacrificing any of the benefits achieved under the Guidelines. Indeed, it is possible that a greater public role might have lessened the punitive effects of periodic outbursts that have occurred in public concern about sentencing issues, particularly regarding sex offenders. But too great a public role might have threatened the Commission's independence. In the end, each jurisdiction must decide, in light of its traditions and current conditions, how to balance democratic values and public participation with fair and rational sentencing policy formulation.

Notes

1   Most State sentencing commissions belong to the National Association of Sentencing Commissions. For a list of contacts in each State, see National Association of Sentencing Commissions, 2006.

2   For example, in 1991 the *Minneapolis Star Tribune* published a four-part series entitled "Free To Rape", arguing that sex offender penalties were much too lenient (Frase, 2005b, p 163).

3   Contested judicial elections remain rare, but have become somewhat more frequent. Moreover, recent court decisions have invalidated judicial ethics standards that prevented judges from expressing political views or accepting political endorsement, see, for example, *Republican Party of Minnesota v White*, 536 US 765 (2002). But judges and many attorneys have resisted these decisions, and it remains to be seen whether the decisions will have much effect on judicial selection and retention decisions.

4   In all Minnesota felony and misdemeanour cases trial juries only decide issues of guilt or innocence, and make no sentencing recommendations. However, as in other United States jurisdictions with legally binding guidelines, recent Supreme Court decisions have expanded the jury's indirect role in sentencing by requiring that juries find, beyond a reasonable doubt, any contested fact which raises either the statutory maximum sentence or the recommended Guidelines sentence, see, for example, *Blakely v Washington*, 542 US 296 (2004). But these decisions have not thus far had a major impact on Minnesota sentencing procedures and outcomes (Frase, 2006a).

5   However, the 1973 Community Corrections Act discouraged prison terms for less serious crimes by granting participating counties a subsidy to support community corrections and by reducing that subsidy when minor offenders were sent to State prison (Martin, 1984, p 30).

6   The Commission is an administrative agency subject to legislative oversight. The enabling statute provided that the Commission's recommended guidelines would become effective on 1 May 1980 unless the Legislature provided otherwise (which it did not). Subsequent Guidelines changes are proposed by the Commission in January and, unless overruled or modified by the Legislature (which is rare), go into effect the following August.

7   Since 1992, inmates may lose good-time credits if they refuse to work or participate in treatment programs (Frase, 2005b, p 164).

8   Compare with Goodstein (1983), p 494, noting early emergence of the practice of setting mandatory treatment conditions of release.

9   All of the key actors in the 1970s Minnesota sentencing reform movement agreed that there should be no increase in the overall size of the State's prison population (Martin, 1984, p 39, n 85, 43, 100-1, 111).

10   Minnesota Statutes Section 609.01, Subdivision 1 (purposes of Code include deterrence, rehabilitation, incapacitation, fair notice, sentences reasonably related to conduct and character of accused, and fair procedures).

11   The initial Commission's other seven members included: the Chief Justice of the State Supreme Court or his or her designee; two felony trial court judges appointed by the Chief Justice; a public defender appointed by the Governor upon the recommendation of the State Public Defender; a county attorney appointed by the Governor on the recommendation of the County Attorneys Council; the Commissioner of Corrections (in charge of State prisons) or his or her designee; and the chair of the Corrections (parole) Board or his or her designee. The Commission was later expanded to 11 members, including a third public member, a community corrections (probation) officer, a judge of the new intermediate appellate court (replacing one of the trial court judges), and a law enforcement officer (replacing the Corrections Board member). Minnesota Statutes Section 244.09, Subdivision 2.

12   The other public member on the Commission in these early years was Barbara Andrus, who had experience working in minority and community programs (Parent, 1988, p 31).

13   The Commission was not fully staffed and functioning until 1 January, 1979, and its report and recommended guidelines were due by the following 1 January (Parent, 1988, p 210). The enabling statute also specified that the Guidelines would become effective on 1 May 1980 (for crimes committed on or after that date), unless the Legislature rejected or modified them, so the Commission only had a few months to convince the Legislature to accept its recommendations, and only a few more months (before Guidelines-eligible cases reached the charging and sentencing stages) to train judges, attorneys, and probation officers in the use of the new rules.

14   In addition to the sex offender and legislative subcommittees mentioned above, other subcommittees were working on drug policy and intermediate sanctions.

15   This cut-off date was chosen to avoid including the large number of articles that began to appear in early July 2006, covering the Alphonso Rodriguez trial held later that month.

16   See Frase (2005b), pp 159-64, describing high profile rape murders that occurred in 1988 and 1991, and the significant increases in sanction severity that resulted. See also Frase (2005b), pp 165-6, noting further increases in rape penalties in 2000 and 2002.

17   For a useful summary and time line of this case, see *St Paul Pioneer Press* (2004). Details of the case and reactions to it are also discussed in Frase (2005b), pp 211-12.

18   Increases in the weight given to more serious prior convictions and to prior sex crimes, adopted in 1989 and 2006, have substantially increased some offenders' criminal history scores. These changes also mean that a 2006 offender with a given number of criminal history points may have fewer prior convictions than a 1988 offender with the same number of points.

References

Bureau of Justice Statistics (1980). *Prisoners in State and Federal Institutions on December 31, 1978*. Washington, DC: United States Department of Justice.

Bureau of Justice Statistics (2006a) *Prison and Jail Inmates at Midyear 2005*. Washington, DC: United States Department of Justice.

Bureau of Justice Statistics (2006b). *Prisoners in 2005*. Washington, DC: United States Department of Justice.

Clark, S (1979). *An Historical Overview of Sentencing Reform Legislation: 1975–1978*. Unpublished report prepared for the Minnesota Sentencing Guidelines Commission.

Frase, RS (1991). Sentencing Reform in Minnesota, Ten Years After: Reflections on Dale G Parent's Structuring Criminal Sentences: the Evolution of Minnesota's Sentencing Guidelines. *Minnesota Law Review* 75: 727.

Frase, RS (1993). The Uncertain Future of Sentencing Guidelines. *Law & Inequality: A Journal of Theory and Practice* 12: 1.

Frase, RS (1995). Sentencing Guidelines in Minnesota and Other American States: A Progress Report. In R Morgan and C Clarkson (eds), *The Politics of Sentencing Reform*. Oxford: Clarendon Press.

Frase, RS (1997). Sentencing Principles in Theory and Practice. In M Tonry (ed), *Crime and Justice: A Review of Research*, vol 22. Chicago: University of Chicago Press.

Frase, RS (2004). Limiting Retributivism. In M Tonry (ed), *The Future of Imprisonment*. New York: Oxford University Press.

Frase, RS (2005a). Punishment Purposes. *Stanford Law Review* 58: 67.

Frase, RS (2005b). Sentencing Guidelines in Minnesota: 1978-2003. In M Tonry (ed), *Crime and Justice: A Review of Research*, vol 32. Chicago: University of Chicago Press.

Frase, RS (2005c). State Sentencing Guidelines: Diversity, Consensus, and Unresolved Policy Issues. *Columbia Law Review* 105: 1190.

Frase, RS (2006a). *Blakely* in Minnesota, Two Years Out: Guidelines Sentencing is Alive and Well. *Ohio State Journal of Criminal Law* 4: 73.

Frase, RS (2006b). *What Factors Explain Persistent Racial Disparities in Minnesota's Prison and Jail Populations?* Paper presented at the 2006 Annual Meeting of the American Society of Criminology, Los Angeles, California.

Goodstein, L (1983). Sentencing Reform and the Correctional System. *Law and Policy Quarterly* 5: 478.

Martin, S (1984). Interests and Politics in Sentencing Reform: The Development of Sentencing Guidelines in Minnesota and Pennsylvania. *Villanova Law Review* 29: 21.

Minnesota Executive Budget Office (2004). *Consolidated Fiscal Note, 2003-04 Session, Bill No H. 2308.* (March 10).

Minnesota Sentencing Guidelines Commission (1980). *Report to the Legislature, January 1, 1980.* St Paul: Minnesota Sentencing Guidelines Commission.

Minnesota Sentencing Guidelines Commission (1984). *The Impact of the Minnesota Sentencing Guidelines: Three Year Evaluation.* St Paul: Minnesota Sentencing Guidelines Commission.

Minnesota Sentencing Guidelines Commission (2005). *Report to the Legislature, January, 2005.* St Paul: Minnesota Sentencing Guidelines Commission.

Minnesota Sentencing Guidelines Commission (2006a). *Minnesota Sentencing Guidelines and Commentary.* St Paul: Minnesota Sentencing Guidelines Commission.

Minnesota Sentencing Guidelines Commission (2006b). *Report to the Legislature, January, 2006.* St Paul: Minnesota Sentencing Guidelines Commission.

Minnesota Sentencing Guidelines Commission (2006c). *Sentencing Practices: Annual Summary Statistics for Felony Offenders Sentenced in 2005.* St Paul: Minnesota Sentencing Guidelines Commission.

Minnesota Sentencing Guidelines Commission (2006d). <http://www.msgc.state.mn.us>.

Morris, N (1974). *The Future of Imprisonment.* Chicago: University of Chicago Press.

Morris, N (1982). *Madness and the Criminal Law.* Chicago: University of Chicago Press.

National Association of Sentencing Commissions. (2006). NASC Contact List, <http://www. ussc.gov/states/nascaddr.htm>.

Parent, DG (1988). *Structuring Criminal Sentences: The Evolution of Minnesota's Sentencing Guidelines.* Stoneham, Mass: Butterworth.

Parent, DG and Frase, RS (2005). Why Minnesota Will Weather *Blakely*'s Blast. *Federal Sentencing Reporter* 18: 12.

St Paul Pioneer Press (2004). Timeline of Events in Sjodin Disappearance. 18 April, p A10.

Tonry, M (1996). *Sentencing Matters.* New York: Oxford University Press.

7

The United States Sentencing Commission

Judge Nancy Gertner

Introduction

The United States Sentencing Commission was created as part of the *Sentencing Reform Act* of 1984.[1] It was supposed to bring order to federal sentencing by enacting national standards – guidelines – that were designed to eliminate "unwarranted disparity" among similarly situated defendants across the country, as well as to achieve other purposes of sentencing.[2] Significantly, increasing public participation in the criminal justice system was *not* a goal of the legislation. The public's punitive sensibilities were readily – some might say, too readily – reflected in the existing law.

Rather, the idea of reformers was that the Commission would be insulated from politics. It would be able to do what Congress had been unable to do, namely resist public pressure to punish disproportionately whatever the "crime du jour" happened to be. Its work would be accepted by all of the sentencing players – public, Congress, judges – precisely because of its independence from the political process and the extent to which it had an expertise that the other players lacked (Stith and Cabranes, 1998, p 48).

The reality was entirely different. In retrospect, the hopes of the reformers seemed almost naïve: the Commission was not insulated from politics. It became, in the words of the Supreme Court, a "junior varsity" legislature.[3] With a few exceptions, it was captive to the Congress and frequently to the federal prosecutor and the Department of Justice. Nor did its work reflect a unique sentencing expertise not otherwise found in the political process. Ironically, although it was extremely responsive to the people's representatives in Congress, it did not really reflect the public's will. The public was not remotely as punitive, remotely as vengeful – especially in *individual* cases – as Guideline sentences required.

For over 20 years the Commission has been widely criticised. Most recently, the Federal Sentencing Guidelines have been subject to a stark constitutional challenge.[4] When scholars from the American Law Institute, an esteemed American law reform organisation, sought to establish model sentencing laws, the message was clear: avoid the Federal Sentencing Guidelines regime at all costs (American Law Institute, 2004, p 2).

The purpose of this chapter is to attempt to explain why. For other jurisdictions seeking to implement sentencing reform through a sentencing commission, it is a cautionary tale.

To be sure, some of the failures of the United States Sentencing Commission reflect the unique weaknesses of sentencing institutions in the United States (Gertner, 2005, pp 571-3). Before the *Sentencing Reform Act*, the American judiciary had largely resisted all efforts to cabin its sentencing discretion, notably opposing appellate review of sentences, which has long existed in other common law countries.[5] Without appellate review, there was no incentive to write decisions, to articulate standards or to create a common law of sentencing. When the political debate focused on supposedly widespread sentencing disparity in the 1980s, American judges had little with which to counter the charges. In short order, judges were seen as the problem, unable or unwilling to reflect society's values, and even turning a deaf ear to the public outcry about crime.[6] That atmosphere, among factors described elsewhere (Gertner, 2007) undermined the judiciary's voice at all levels – not only in its potential role in setting national standards, but even its historic role in sentencing individuals.

The American Congress was also not without responsibility for sentencing problems. It had been unable to create a rational federal criminal law (Gertner, 2005, pp 571-3). Sentencing guidelines were juxtaposed on top of a chaotic and ill-conceived substantive federal law. While many States had enacted the American Law Institute's Model Penal Code, which provided narrowly defined and graded offences, the federal government, after a decade of effort, had been unable to do so. With the electoral process more and more affected by "law and order" sloganeering, it was no surprise that national legislation was more about sound bites than real reform. In fact, the ink was barely dry on the *Sentencing Reform Act* when Congress passed a number of mandatory minimum sentencing statutes, wholly at odds with the Act's rationale.

But some of the failures of the Commission reflect weaknesses in the *Sentencing Reform Act* itself, as well as in the decisions of that first Commission – and that is the cautionary tale. The structure of the Commission facilitated its politicisation from the outset. Its members did not have the kind of criminal justice experience that the reformers anticipated and on which its legitimacy and influence may well have depended. The Commission's Guidelines were not allowed to be subject to the kind of administrative review to which other agencies were subject, a process that might have strengthened the Guidelines while making its work more accessible to the public and to interested groups. While the Act called on the Commission to implement all of the purposes of sentencing, including rehabilitation and deterrence, the first Commission, to the extent that it considered sentencing purposes at all, focused only on retribution (Gertner, 2005, pp 574-6; Gertner, 2007). That purpose, unlike promoting rehabilitation or deterring crime, was uniquely vulnerable to "popular punitiveness". As the Commission lacked legitimacy on many fronts, Congress had no compunction about aggressively intervening in its work, ordering the Commission to increase sentences in given areas, rejecting Commission staff reports and continuing to pass mandatory minimum statutes reflecting the "crime du jour".

Far from being insulated from politics, the Commission was constantly buffeted by it. And far from reflecting public opinion, it simply mirrored political rhetoric.

The idea of a federal Sentencing Commission

Sentencing in the late 20th and early 21st centuries moved from a world in which "judicial and expert decisions received almost no scrutiny at all" (Barkow, 2005, p 745), during the period of discretionary, indeterminate sentencing, to a world in which sentencing was the contested territory of politicians, on the one hand, and late night talk show hosts on the other. In this atmosphere the influence of a sentencing commission arguably derives from the extent to which it can add value to the political process by contributing something that the other players in the sentencing system cannot. A commission can arguably add value in one of three ways: (1) by its independence from the traditional political process; (2) by its specialised expertise; or (3) by its ability to mediate effectively between the political process and the public at large in a way that traditional political institutions cannot.

Some reformers believed that the Commission would have influence in direct proportion to its political insulation. Senator Edward Kennedy, one of the architects of the *Sentencing Reform Act*, argued that it was necessary to have a commission rather than Congress take the lead in sentencing reform because it is not "likely that Congress could avoid politicizing the entire sentencing issue" (Kennedy, 1979).[7] Alternatively, the commission would have influence because it added something that no other institutional player could add, a specialised sentencing expertise (Gertner, 2005, pp 573-4; Freed, 1992, p 1690). The *Sentencing Reform Act*, for example, required the Commission to develop guidelines not simply based on its study of past sentencing practice, which any government statistician could do, or its analysis of the purposes of sentencing, which, as a normative process, the political actors were well equipped to do, but also its consideration of "advance[s] in [the] knowledge of human behavior as it relates to the criminal justice process",[8] adding criminal justice expertise to the process of generating guidelines. And while it was not the rationale for its existence, the *Sentencing Reform Act* required the Commission to consider public opinion in setting offence levels.[9]

The Commission failed on all fronts.

Makeup of the Commission

The United States Sentencing Commission was to consist of seven members, at least three of whom were judges, with the Attorney General of the United States an ex officio, non-voting member.[10] No more than four of the seven could be members of the same political party [11] and all had to be confirmed by the Senate.[12] Once appointed, they were to serve a set term of six years.[13] While one version of the statute required the President to choose from a list promulgated by the administrative arm of the federal judiciary, the Judicial Conference of the United States, the final version did not. The President only had to "consider" these names.[14]

Significantly, the first members of the commission were "men and women of quality and high regard in their respective professions, but not leaders in the lengthy effort for sentencing reform" (Freed, 1992, p 1741). They were three judges, a correctional official and three professors – an economist, a sociologist and a criminal law scholar. Remarkably, no one had experience in sentencing offenders in a high-volume court, or was a United States Attorney or federal defender with recent criminal justice experience. Nor was there a private defence lawyer or a probation officer. No Commissioner had expertise in criminology or penology.

The Commission's membership tilted almost immediately in favour of prosecution interests (Barkow, 2005, p 764). During the life of the Commission, 13 of the 23 Commissioners were former prosecutors, including the ex-officio members appointed by the Attorney General (Barkow, 2005, p 764). Indeed, as Michael Tonry describes, while "most proponents of guidelines have seen its one-step-removed-from-politics character as a great strength ... the US commission, by contrast, made no effort to insulate its policies from law-and-order politics and short term emotions" (Tonry, 1996, p 63).

The Guidelines as initially drafted

Although the *Sentencing Reform Act* directed that the Guidelines were to reflect all of the purposes of sentencing, they did not. From the outset the Commission conceded that it would not discuss sentencing purposes at all, much less indicate how the Guidelines promoted them. To the extent that the Commission focused on purposes at all, it was one – limited retribution or just deserts (Gertner, 2005, p 574). In a sense, that decision undermined the Commission's mission still more. When the sentencing debate shifts from instrumental goals to retribution, it begins to occupy the terrain of politics, rather than the terrain of criminal justice expertise (Zimring, 1996, p 254). Why defer to an "expert" agency on questions like "just deserts" when the political actors, and more significantly the public, feel well qualified to address the subject (Whitman, 2003, p 94)?

In effect the first Commission sought legitimacy for its work by simply being a codifier of existing sentencing practices. They announced an empirical approach, a study of existing sentencing practices that the initial Guidelines would reflect. The problem is that the Guidelines did not really reflect pre-Guidelines practice (Stith and Cabranes, 1998, pp 38-9). To be sure, the Commission reviewed the average length of sentences in the United States, but it did not look at the factors judges were actually relying on or the standards judges actually used in calculating sentences. The Commission simply compared gross sentencing outcomes before the Guidelines and then decided what factors it believed to be significant. Regardless of the existing lengths of sentences, in many cases the Commission simply increased them (Gertner, 2005, p 575).

The Commission did not conduct deterrence studies, evaluate recidivism, consider the efficacy of particular treatment programs[15] or evaluate the Guidelines' impact on crime control. It did not test the Guidelines over time by reviewing the efficacy of sentencing alternatives. One did not need a well-funded, national expert agency with a substantial staff simply to collect sentencing statistics, to police disparity or to effect political compromises. Even at a time when sentencing theory is fragmented (Tonry, 2002) and when other instrumental theories have not recovered from their precipitous decline (Zimring, 1996, p 254), there are still unique and important contributions that an expert criminal justice agency could have made.[16]

Impact on judges

The participation of judges on the Commission was seen by the reformers as particularly important. They were the quintessentially independent voices, helpful in promoting the Commission's insulation from the political process. After all, before the changes of the 1980s judges had been the acknowledged experts in sentencing.

In time, however, even the independent voices of judges were effectively silenced – not just as participants in the national dialogue about sentencing, but in individual cases. Judges on the Sentencing Commission and in the Judicial Conference ceased acting like judges. Time and again they agreed to guideline provisions that would narrow their own discretion to sentence and would limit their ability to vary from the script. While large numbers of judges had opposed the Guidelines (many holding the *Sentencing Reform Act* unconstitutional), they soon began to enforce the Guidelines with a rigour not at all necessary. Indeed, now, 20 years after enactment of the Guidelines, many federal judges believe that they lack the competence to sentence at all without explicit directives from an "expert" agency (Gertner, 2007).

Public participation – or its lack

While the Commission was charged with "considering" public opinion in setting offence levels, that "consideration" was perfunctory. Most agency rule-making is subject to the *Administrative Procedure Act*. The Act provides for judicial review of agency rules for their fealty to the legislation creating the agency. But the Sentencing Commission was exempt from the judicial review provisions of the *Administrative Procedure Act*.[17] That meant that the Commission did not have to justify a given Guideline in court or build a factual record as to why it made a given choice, much less fully explain what it had done. Only the "notice" and "comment" provisions of the Act applied, which meant that the Commission only had to "give notice" of proposed rules and consult various parties in the criminal justice system. The Act, for example, required that the Commission consult with specific stakeholders in the federal criminal justice system, notably the United States Probation System, the Bureau of Prisons, the Judicial Conference of the United States, the Department of Justice Criminal Division and a representative from the Federal Public Defenders, all of whom were to submit annual reports.[18] Once promulgated, Congressional review of potential guidelines was hardly searching. The Commission was to submit Guidelines to the Congress that would take effect no earlier than 180 days after being submitted (or November of the calendar year that the amendment is submitted) if Congress did not act.[19]

As far as the public was concerned, beyond consulting its stakeholders the Commission did little in terms of meaningfully soliciting views. It rarely justified its guidelines in a way that would be accessible to the general public, instead making decisions that were "off-the-record". Unlike the guidelines of State sentencing agencies, the Federal Guidelines are so complex that they could hardly be meaningfully debated by the general public. Nor has the Commission ever given enough time for the public to absorb the changes it was making. The first Guidelines – an enormously complex grid, with wholly new sentencing concepts – were promulgated in a year. While the chair of the Minnesota Sentencing Commission devised an "open process" to address the divergent interests in sentencing, even deferring implementation of decisions to address political divisions, the Federal Sentencing Guidelines were, quite literally, rushed through (Freed, 1996, pp 1741-2).

Admittedly, a public opinion poll was commissioned in the first few years of the Sentencing Commission, ostensibly to satisfy the statutory dictates. The problem is that in key respects the Commission did not follow the findings of the poll (Rossi & Berk, 1995, pp 82-6). The public did not support harsh treatment of non-violent drug offences, differential sentencing between offenders convicted of distributing crack rather than powder cocaine, increases in the punishment for environmental crimes, violations of civil rights and certain bribery and extortion claims. As to individual sentences – as opposed to aggregate data – there was only a "modest amount" of agreement as between sentences given by the respondents and the Guidelines (Rossi & Berk, 1995, p 208). Finally, the Commission did not test the public's consideration of the kinds of trade-offs that are necessary to support high levels of incarceration, such as the cost of incarceration and the social disruption to communities of incarcerating large numbers of minorities.[20] Notwithstanding what the data suggested about public opinion, each year the Guideline sentences increased for a host of non-violent offences.

The result

Though the Congress had been unable to promulgate a comprehensive criminal code, when the Commission promulgated its Guidelines Congress had no problem intervening in the Commission's final product. Over and over again, Congress passed legislation directing that this or that sentencing range be increased, that this departure ground be narrowed. Even after the Commission recommended an adjustment in the differential sentencing between individuals convicted of crack and powder cocaine offences, buttressed by substantial staff work and research, Congress rejected it. So much for deference to the Commission's expertise.

In 2003 Congress went so far as to enact fundamental reforms to the *Sentencing Reform Act* in order to eliminate departures from the Guidelines in sex offender cases and to reduce them substantially in others, to limit judicial participation on the Commission to a minority position – no more than three judges – and to make the appellate standard of departure review more strict.[21] The Act even required reporting judges to Congress who were too departure-prone – a blow to judicial independence. The reforms were slipped onto the House of Representative's version of a child protection Bill by a little known junior representative from Florida. There had been no public hearings; stunningly, the Commission had not even been consulted.[22]

In the final analysis, the Commission had not "added value" to the sentencing process. It lacked independent expertise in criminal justice matters. It offered no reason why its view of "just deserts" should trump that of Congress or the public. It could not pretend to independence from the political forces swirling around it. Indeed the Commission's acts in increasing sentences over and over again "seem to reflect an agency finely attuned to the political preferences of its overseers" the Congress (Barkow, 2005, p 767).

It surely did not meaningfully include public participation in the process, either reflecting that opinion accurately or explaining its own mission. Perhaps if it had, there would be more of a constituency calling for a robust sentencing commission. Perhaps if it had, the Commission would not have been so easily ignored.

Notes

1   18 USC § 3551-3559, 3561-3566, 3571-3574, 3581-3586 and 28 USC § 991-998.

2   18 USC § 3553 (a)(6).

3   *Mistretta v United States*, 488 US 361, 427 (1989) (Scalia J, dissenting).

4   In *Booker v United States*, 543 US 220 (2005), the Supreme Court held that the mandatory Federal Sentencing Guidelines were unconstitutional. Under the Guidelines, judges were obliged to find facts that had determinate consequences, consequences that were pre-ordained by the United States Sentencing Commission. The judge's role mirrored the jury's role. The only difference – and it was a significant one – was that judicial sentencing in a mandatory system lacked the constitutional protections of a jury trial. The remedy to that constitutional violation, according to the Court, was to make the Guidelines "advisory", to enable judges to exercise judgment again.

5   There were a few exceptions. Some courts adopted benchmarks or guidelines; a few State jurisdictions even had Sentencing Commissions (Freed, 1992, pp 1693-4).

6   The Reagan administration explained that "the judge, while trained in the law, has no special competence in imposing a sentence that will reflect society's values" (*Congressional Digest* 1984, 182, cited in Stith and Cabranes, 1998, p 44).

7   While Barkow suggests that independence from political pressures was the reformer's goal, she points out that in the United States the most successful State commissions are those which have gone in the opposite direction – with "well-connected" and "politically savvy" members who can make the Commission's administrative suggestions politically palatable and publicly acceptable (Barkow, 2005, p 720). State commissions, however, are different from the United States Sentencing Commission. They have leverage that the Federal Commission does not have. Guidelines that increase State incarceration rates put pressure on already straitened State budgets. State commissions can make a unique contribution to the political debate by evaluating the impact of criminal justice policy on State budgets. In contrast, prisons are a very small part of the federal budget. Federal sentencing issues can more easily be debated on a symbolic level, regardless of their impact on cost, much less on crime rates.

8   28 USC § 991(b)(1)(c).

9   28 USC § 994(c)(4)-(5).

10   28 USC § 991(a) (1984). The "three judges" provision was then amended in 2003, Pub L 108-21, Title IV, § 401 (n)(1) (30 April 2003, 117 Stat 676).

11   Id.

12   Id.

13   Id.

14   Id.

15   Barkow notes that it is not clear what the relevant expertise should have been for the new Sentencing Commission. When the model was indeterminate, the relevant expertise was clear – experts in individuation, rehabilitation and so on. With a just deserts model, expertise could be anything from law enforcement to criminology to systems management (Barkow, 2005, p 744).

16   For example, 15 years into its operation, the Commission announced the results of a study of the relationship between recidivism and its criminal history categories (United States Sentencing Commission, 2004).

17   28 USC § 994(x); see 5 USC §§ 701-706.

18   28 USC § 994(o).

19   28 USC § 994(p).

20 In a sense, Rossi and Berk's results were not materially different from existing studies of American attitudes. The more exposure the public has to the facts, the less punitive it is (Barkow, 2005, pp 750-1).

21 Prosecutorial Remedies and Tools Against the Exploitation of Children Today (PROTECT) Act of 2003, Pub L No 108-21, 117 Stat 650 (codified as amended in scattered sections of 18 USC, 28 USC, and 42 USC).

22 United States Sentencing Commission, Report to Congress: Cocaine and Federal Sentencing Policy 91 (2002) (hereinafter 2002 Report to Congress), <www.ussc.gov/r_congress/02crack/ 2002crackrpt.htm>. See also United States Sentencing Commission: Special Report to the Congress: Cocaine and Federal Sentencing Policy (1997), <www.ussc.gov/r_congress/NEW CRACK.PDF>; United States Sentencing Commission, Special Report to Congress: Cocaine and Federal Sentencing Policy (1995), <www.ussc.gov/crack/execsum.pdf>.

References

American Law Institute (2003). *Model Penal Code: Sentencing – 2003 Report*.

American Law Institute (2004). *Model Penal Code: Sentencing, Preliminary Draft No 3*.

Barkow, R (2005). Administering Crime. *UCLA Law Review* 52: 715.

Barkow, RE and O'Neill, KM (2006). Delegating Punitive Power: The Political Economy of Sentencing Commission and Guideline Formation. New York University School of Law. New York University Public Law and Legal Theory Working Papers. Paper 24. <http://lsr.nellco.org/nyu/plltwp/papers/24>.

Frankel, ME (1972). *Criminal Sentences: Law Without Order*: 49.

Freed, D (1992). Federal Sentencing in the Wake of the Guidelines: Unacceptable Limits on the Discretion of Sentencers. *Yale Law Journal* 101: 1681.

Gertner, N (1999). Circumventing Juries, Undermining Justice: Lessons from Criminal Trials and Sentencing. *Suffolk University Law Review* 32: 419.

Gertner, N (2005). Distinguished Jurist in Residence, Sentencing Reform: When Everyone Behaves Badly. *Maine Law Review* 57: 569.

Gertner, N (2006). *What* Yogi Berra Teaches about Post-Booker Sentencing. *Pocket Part, a Companion to the Yale Law Journal*, <http://thepocketpart.org/2006/07/gertner.html>, 3 July 2006.

Gertner, N (2007). From Omnipotence to Impotence: American Judges and Sentencing. *Ohio State Journal of Criminal Law* 4.

Kennedy, E (1979). Toward a New System of Criminal Sentencing: Law with Order. *American Criminal Law Review* 16: 353.

Roberts, JV and Hough, M (eds) (2002). *Changing Attitudes to Punishment: Public Opinion, Crime & Justice*. Cullompton: Willan.

Rossi, PH and Berk, RA (1995). *Public Opinion on Sentencing Federal Crimes*. Report Submitted to the United States Sentencing Commission.

Stith, K and Cabranes, J (1998). *Fear of Judging: Sentencing Guidelines in the Federal Courts*. Chicago: University of Chicago Press.

Tonry, M (1996). *Sentencing Matters*. New York: Oxford University Press.

Tonry, M (2006). Purpose and Function of Sentencing. *Crime & Justice* 34: 1.

United States Sentencing Commission (1995). *Special Report to Congress: Cocaine and Federal Sentencing Policy*, <www.ussc.gov/crack/execsum.pdf>.

United States Sentencing Commission (1997). *Special Report to the Congress: Cocaine and Federal Sentencing Policy*, <www.ussc.gov/r_congress/NEW CRACK.PDF>.

United States Sentencing Commission (2002). *Report to Congress: Cocaine and Federal Sentencing Policy 91* <www.ussc.gov/r_congress/02crack/ 2002crackrpt.htm>.

United States Sentencing Commission (2004). *Fifteen Years of Guidelines Sentencing: An Assessment of How Well the Federal Criminal Justice System is Achieving the Goals of Sentencing Reform*.

Whitman, JQ (2003). Symposium: Model Penal Code: Sentencing: A Plea Against Retributivism. *Buffalo Criminal Law Review* 7: 85.

Zimring, FE (1996) Populism, Democratic Government, and the Decline of Expert Authority: Some Reflections on "Three Strikes" in California. *Pacific Law Journal* 28: 243.

8

English sentencing guidelines in their public and political context

Andrew Ashworth[1]

Introduction

The English approach to sentencing guidelines has changed markedly in the past decade. Since the early 1980s the Court of Appeal had occasionally issued guideline judgments, laying down sentence levels and other guidance (see Ashworth, 2005), but the coverage of these judgments was limited and they were entirely judge-made. This chapter deals with the major developments since then and with their implications. The first section discusses the introduction of the Sentencing Advisory Panel in 1998 and the second charts the creation of the Sentencing Guidelines Council in 2003. In the third section the involvement of the public and of public opinion in the process of creating sentencing guidelines is assessed, while the fourth explores the broader political context of the English developments.

The Sentencing Advisory Panel and the 1998 Act

With ss 80-81 of the *Crime and Disorder Act* 1998 (UK) two major innovations were introduced: first, a Sentencing Advisory Panel was created to draft guidelines, consult widely on them and then advise the Court of Appeal about the form that they should take; and, secondly, the power of the Court of Appeal to give guideline judgments was restricted to offences on which it had received advice from the Sentencing Advisory Panel. In other words, the Court of Appeal lost its power to create guidelines of its own and always had to await advice from the Panel, although it was not bound to accept the Panel's advice.

The Sentencing Advisory Panel, chaired by Professor Martin Wasik, was constituted in July 1999 with 11 members, and three further members were added subsequently. Four of the members are sentencers (judges or magistrates), three are academics, four others have recent or current experience of the criminal justice system and the remaining three are laypeople with no previous connection with the criminal justice system. The Panel meets every three or four weeks, usually for one day and occasionally for two days.

When the Panel was originally established, there were three different ways in which the subject-matter of the Panel's work might be chosen: the Home Secretary (since 2007, Minister of Justice) had the power to refer an offence to the Panel, the Court of Appeal was bound to refer an offence if it held that there was a need for guidelines and the Panel could decide for itself.[2] In practice the last approach was the most frequent. The Panel's method of working is to review the applicable law and statistics and any relevant research, to formulate a consultation paper, and then to seek responses from its statutory consultees and from members of the public. The normal consultation period is three months, after which it considers the responses and any further information before formulating its advice. The whole process takes several months from start to finish, not least because the Panel will normally be running three, four or more separate topics at the same time.

In its first five years of operation the Panel produced draft guidelines on about a dozen offences,[3] which were submitted as advice to the Court of Appeal. New guideline judgments were issued on racially aggravated offences and on child pornography, for example, and a revised guideline judgment on rape was issued.[4] The Court acted on all but one of the Panel's advices: it would wait for an appropriate appeal to be heard and then issue the guidelines as part of the judgment in that case.

In 2000 the government appointed John Halliday, a former senior civil servant in the Home Office then recently retired, with a group of advisers, to conduct a review of the sentencing framework. In the course of this review the arrangements for sentencing guidelines were re-assessed, and Chapter 8 of the Halliday Report argued that steps must be taken towards the formulation of comprehensive sentencing guidelines and that a new machinery should be considered. Halliday set out three alternative approaches (Home Office, 2001, hereinafter referred to as the Halliday Report, paras 8.11–8.22) and the government decided in favour of the creation of a Council "responsible for setting guidelines for the full range of criminal offences" (Home Office, 2002, para 5.15). The Council's remit (and that of the Panel) would also extend to "allocation guidelines", replacing the Mode of Trial Guidelines as a means of deciding which cases in the intermediate category ("triable either way") should be tried in the magistrates' courts and which should be sent up to the Crown Court. The Panel was to continue in operation, so as to carry out the preliminary work and to conduct its wide consultations, but the Council was to take ultimate responsibility for the form of the guidelines.

The Council, the Panel and the 2003 Act

The *Criminal Justice Act* 2003 (UK) changed the guideline system in major ways. The Sentencing Advisory Panel remains in existence (s 171) and continues to devise draft guidelines, to consult members of the public and its statutory consultees about them and then to prepare its advice. However, that advice goes not to the Court of Appeal but to a new body, the Sentencing Guidelines Council, which has the power to issue guidelines (s 170).

The reasons for the change lay in perceived problems with the previous machinery – the Panel only had the power to propose guidelines relating to a "particular category of offence", whereas there is a need for guidelines on types of sentence and matters of general principle; and the Court of Appeal could only issue guidelines as part of the judgment on an appeal before it, so it had to wait for an appropriate case to come along. These problems could easily have been cured by minor legislative amendments. In its White Paper *Justice for All* the government put forward two further reasons for creating the Council – the need for comprehensive guidelines, and the importance of giving Parliament a role in "considering and scrutinizing" draft guidelines (Constitutional Office, 2002, para 5.17).[5] Neither reason actually necessitated the creation of a further body, as the Panel and its procedure could easily have been adapted to allow for this, but it was surely right in principle to separate the function of creating guidelines from the Court of Appeal's function of deciding individual appeals.[6] This separation also makes it easier for guidelines to be laid down on general principles of sentencing and on new sentencing regimes such as the new forms of sentence introduced into English law by the *Criminal Justice Act* 2003 (UK) – types of guidance that would not have fitted well into an appellate judgment.

The new procedure is that the Council may only issue guidelines after receiving an advice from the Panel. The Panel may propose guidelines of its own motion, or after receiving a notification from the Council or the Minister of Justice that guidelines on a particular subject are required.[7] The Panel itself must follow its procedure of preparing a consultation paper,[8] having regard to such matters as sentencing practice, the cost and effectiveness of various forms of sentence and public confidence; and then reviewing the responses and producing an advice for the Council. The Council must then consider framing guidelines and, if it decides to do so, it must first publish them as draft guidelines (having considered the matters enumerated in s 170(5), such as cost and effectiveness, consistency and so on) and then consult the Minister of Justice and the House of Commons Justice Committee about them.[9] Having made any amendment to the draft that it considers appropriate, the Council "may issue the guidelines as definitive guidelines" (s 170(9)). Courts are placed under a duty to "have regard to any guidelines which are relevant" to a particular case (s 172(1)) and to give reasons for passing a sentence outside the range indicated by any guidelines (s 174(2)(a)).

We have noted that the government's purposes in creating the Council included not only making provision for Parliament to have a voice in the creation of guidelines, but also divorcing the function of creating guidelines from that of deciding individual appeals (thereby taking the function of creating guidelines away from the Court of Appeal). It was initially assumed that for this latter purpose an entirely judicial body was needed and so the Panel (with its diverse membership) would not be appropriate; instead a Council composed entirely of judicial members would be introduced, fully recognising "the importance of an independent judiciary" (Home Office, 2001, para 5.15). Thus the Criminal Justice Bill presented to Parliament in 2002 provided for a Council consisting of seven members – the Lord Chief Justice, two Lords Justice of Appeal, a High Court judge, a Circuit judge, a District Judge (Magistrates' Courts) and a lay magistrate.

Then, as the Bill was progressing through Parliament, the Court of Appeal received an advice from the Panel on the sentencing of domestic burglars (Sentencing Advisory Panel, 2002). Lord Woolf CJ in the Court of Appeal gave a guideline judgment which accepted most of the Panel's advice but significantly lowered the starting points for first-time and second-time offenders who committed medium level burglaries, proposing community sentences for them.[10] Although Lord Woolf took care to justify these changes by reference to various government policy statements, the popular press and subsequently the Minister of Justice denounced the judgment as inappropriately lenient. The ensuing furore attracted media attention for some time and the Minister of Justice seems to have decided that an entirely judicial body could not be trusted with this important social function. The government brought forward amendments to the Bill that would add five non-judicial members to the Council – persons experienced in policing, criminal prosecution, criminal defence, the promotion of the welfare of victims of crime and the administration of sentences. It was believed that the person with experience of the administration of sentences would be a civil servant from the Home Office, and objections were taken to this in the House of Lords. To expand the Council from an entirely judicial body to a body with wider membership was one thing; but to extend its membership so as to include a serving civil servant, a member of the Executive who would be bound to put forward departmental views, was quite another thing. The House of Lords Select Committee on the Constitution took advice on the matter and, concluding that such an appointee might not appear independent, expressed its "concern at the proposal that a serving civil servant should act as a member of the Sentencing Guidelines Council" (House of Lords Select Committee on the Constitution, 2003). This part of the amendment was therefore dropped, although a senior civil servant (at present, the Director of the National Offender Management Service) is allowed to attend and speak at Council meetings (*Criminal Justice Act* 2003 s 167(9)).

The original assumption that the membership of the Council should be entirely judicial was presumably either based on the belief that the creation of sentencing guidelines is a judicial function, or was a political compromise to ensure that the judiciary remained supportive of the new arrangements. The former reasoning cannot be sustained now, as we have a Council with a diverse membership (albeit with a judicial majority). So, two reasons for creating the Council remain – the need to divorce the creation of guidelines from the function of determining appeals, and the importance of providing an opportunity for parliamentary input into the process of creating guidelines. However, neither reason tells in favour of creating an additional body, when the Panel already existed. The Panel does not have a judicial majority, although it does have four sentencers and, if chaired by the Lord Chief Justice or another senior judge, its membership would surely not be inappropriate for such a body. Moreover, it has three lay members; and there is no reason why it should not have been required to consult Parliament in the same way that the Council is now obliged to do. As, however, Parliament has decided to create a new, additional body rather than to alter the membership of the Panel so as to fit it for the role of promulgating guidelines, it is certainly beneficial that the Council should have a mixed membership. It has long been argued (see, for example, Ashworth, 1983) that it is desirable to have a body with diverse experience in broad matters of penal policy, not merely because many judges have a tendency to support existing arrangements rather than to favour change,[11] but also because other perspectives have a legitimate place in the deliberations.

Another reason for changing the system for creating guidelines was that the government felt that there was a "democratic deficit" in the pre-2003 arrangements and this is why it was decided to give Parliament and the Minister of Justice a role in "considering and scrutinizing" draft guidelines (Home Office, 2001, para 5.17).[12] In principle, there is no constitutional reason why Parliament should not pass detailed legislation on sentencing matters and from the same standpoint there is no strong constitutional argument against the involvement of parliamentarians in proposing amendments to guidelines (Ashworth, 2005, ch 2.1). At a political level, however, there is obviously a danger that politicians will be looking to either vote-winning or progress within the party rather than trying to take a considered and rounded view of the subject. It remains to be seen whether these new powers are used sensibly or for party political reasons. For the present, some comfort can be taken from the checks and balances in the 2003 Act: the Council is obliged to consult the Minister of Justice and the House of Commons Justice Committee, but it is not obliged to accept their comments and it has the final decision on the form of the guidelines it issues. Thus the first three Council guidelines were issued as drafts, following the statutory procedure, and were then examined by the Justice Committee and commented upon by the Minister of Justice (House of Commons, 2004). Various changes were made as a result of those reviews.

The last point brings the guideline back to the words of the 2003 Act, and it must be recalled that the objective of this guideline is to ensure that courts interpret the new legislation, and their new powers, in a consistent and principled manner.

The process of formulating guidelines and the role of the public

Under the English system, with its two bodies (the Panel and the Council), the process of formulating guidelines is an intensive and lengthy one. It involves several stages and several sources of influence, but for present purposes we may fruitfully discuss six key aspects of the process – sentencing statistics, the existing sentencing principles, the role of empirical research, sub-dividing topics, assessing the responses and seeking a simple and balanced formulation. It will be evident that the public has a role at several stages of this process.

The Panel usually begins its inquiry into a particular topic by calling for the relevant sentencing statistics. These are important in enabling the Panel to identify the effective sentence ranges for a particular offence. Often these ranges are lower than those indicated by any relevant Court of Appeal judgments, but that may be explained on the basis that appeals tend to be brought in relatively extreme cases, often with unusually high sentences, and on the basis that the statistics reflect the "net" sentence, after allowance has been made for mitigating factors such as a plea of guilty.

Also at this early stage the Panel's secretariat will gather together the relevant Court of Appeal decisions and the relevant legislation on the topic. Sometimes, as in the work on offensive weapons offences, there is relatively little to be found. On other occasions, as in the work on reduction of sentence for a plea of guilty, there are many Court of Appeal decisions as well as relevant legislation. The Panel is, of course, bound to apply the legislative provisions as it finds them: thus, where Parliament has provided a prescribed minimum sentence, this must be incorporated faithfully into the guideline (see *McInerney and Keating*, 2003). The Panel and Council are not, however, bound by previous Court of Appeal decisions. What the Panel does is to scrutinise the principles and distinctions that are to be found in the leading decisions, and to form its opinion on whether they are sound. An example of this might be taken from the Panel's work on reduction of sentence for a guilty plea. There was Court of

Appeal authority to the effect that no reduction should be given to an offender who had been caught "red-handed", that is, who had been caught in a compromising position in which there was no realistic defence to the charge. After discussing this, the Panel thought that this was not a good reason for withholding the reduction: any defendant can plead not guilty and the main purpose of the sentence reduction is to encourage guilty people to save the time of the courts and the anxiety of witnesses by pleading guilty at the earliest opportunity. So the Panel took a different view from the Court of Appeal and, in the event, the majority of consultees agreed with this, as did the Council subsequently.[13] However, sentencers and the Court of Appeal have been uneasy about the change and the Panel is now consulting on possible changes to this guideline (Sentencing Advisory Panel, 2006).

On a few occasions the Panel has exercised its power to commission empirical research to assist its deliberations. It has a modest budget for this purpose and, where speed is not of the essence (because empirical research takes some months to commission and to complete), it has taken this step. Research was commissioned on domestic burglary in order to examine public evaluations of the seriousness of different types of burglary. It was, essentially, a kind of public opinion survey focussed on the factors thought to aggravate and mitigate domestic burglary, and also on the factors that should incline courts towards a custodial sentence or towards a community sentence (Russell and Morgan, 2001). Although on one level the research confirmed that members of the public are not well informed about sentencing practice, it also yielded some useful observations on relative seriousness, and enabled the Panel to generate the idea of a "typical burglary", which was then used to differentiate other varieties that are more or less serious.

The Panel has also commissioned research on the relative seriousness of different rapes, which was carried out by means of discussion groups and interviews with members of the public, including 25 victims of rape (17 female, 8 male) (Clarke et al, 2002). One of the outcomes of this research was a strong view among those involved that no distinction should be made, in terms of seriousness, between male and female rapes or between stranger rapes and relationship rapes – a point carried over, after some discussion, into the guidelines. In giving the ensuing guideline judgment, the Court of Appeal explained:

> This does not mean that the sentence will be the same for each of these different classes of rape … Where, for example, the offender is the husband of the victim there can, but not necessarily, be mitigating features that clearly cannot apply to a rape by a stranger. On the other hand, as the advice from the Panel points out, as is confirmed by the research commissioned by the Panel, because of the existence of a relationship the victim can feel particularly bitter about an offence of rape, regarding it as a breach of trust.[14]

This shows how the empirical research fed into the whole process of formulating the guideline. A third piece of empirical research, into sentencing for thefts from shops, was commissioned by the Panel to assist with its examination of that topic; and a fourth project, on public attitudes to offences causing death on the roads, has commenced.

Having formulated draft guidelines and issued them for consultation, the next stage in the work of the Panel is to examine all the responses at the end of the three-month consultation period. Most of the responses will be from "statutory consultees", that is, the organisations that the Panel is obliged to consult,[15] but others will be from organisations or individuals concerned with the particular topic of the guidelines, and some will be from members of the public who read the consultation paper on the website and who respond by e-mail. Every member of the Panel is given a copy of all responses and the secretariat also prepares a summary which notes every response to each question posed in the consultation paper. The Panel works through the responses at a meeting and this may lead to points being re-argued, approaches being changed, new exceptions being added and so on. One issue that looms large at this stage is that the guidelines must be treated only as guidelines: while they seek to shape and to structure the reasoning of sentencers, they leave open the possibility that a court might decide that the facts of a case are so unusual that a departure from the guideline is justified. On some occasions consultees respond as if the guidelines will remove all elements of judgment from individual cases, whereas in fact they require considerable judgment to apply and may be departed from for good reason. The Panel has to strive for a formulation that gives sufficient structure without being overly detailed.

The Panel finally works on the text of its advice, usually going through two or three further drafts, before transmitting it to the Council. The Council then considers the Panel's advice with a view to formulating a draft of the definitive guideline. In this task the Council will bring to bear the experience of its members, particularly the senior judges. Some points will be re-argued and may be altered, and the Council will also strive for simplicity of presentation. The Council will publish a draft guideline, which will not only go to the Justice Committee of the House of Commons and to the Minister of Justice for their comments,[16] but will also be placed on the website for general consultation. The Council will then consider comments from the House of Commons and the Minister of Justice, as well as any further comments from other bodies and individuals, and may reconsider its approach (as it did in relation to the appropriate reduction for a plea of guilty to the crime of murder, which has a mandatory penalty).[17] The Council is not bound to adopt any of the suggestions or comments made by its consultees, and it alone has the responsibility for issuing a definitive guideline.

It is evident from this lengthy process that the English guideline system places a considerable premium on ascertaining the opinions of members of the public. In the first place, three of the members of the Panel are members of the public who have no other connection to the criminal justice system. Secondly, the Panel conducts a wide public consultation on its provisional proposals. Thirdly, the Panel occasionally commissions research on public attitudes to specific kinds of crime. And fourthly, the Council also conducts a public consultation on its draft proposals for guidelines. Whether the frequency of consulting the public translates into greater public influence on the formulation of guidelines and, ultimately, on sentencing practice is difficult to assess. Most of the responses to consultations, and often the most closely reasoned responses, come from legal organisations or from individuals involved in the sentencing process (be it judges, barristers, police officers, probation officers or magistrates). But the consultation and research on rape demonstrates that the attitudes of the public (including victims) can have a significant effect.

The political context of the English guideline system

In the 1990s there were some major public conflicts in England and Wales between the senior judiciary and the government over sentencing policy (see Dunbar and Langdon, 1998; Ashworth, 2001). Although sentence levels (notably the use of imprisonment) increased markedly from 1993 onwards, a fading Conservative government insisted on introducing mandatory minimum sentences – against strong judicial opposition – and the Labour government which took office in 1997 implemented the Conservative legislation and, through various Ministers of Justice, has continued to call for tougher sentences. In this context the introduction of a sentencing guideline system has gained support from the usual arguments – importing rule-of-law values into sentencing and thereby increasing consistency, and broadening the range of input into the details of sentencing policy – but may also have created the conditions for a kind of dialogue between judiciary and government. The senior judiciary is heavily involved in the Sentencing Guidelines Council, which is chaired by the Lord Chief Justice, and that Council is required to consult the Minister of Justice (among others) on any proposed guidelines. However, even though the Council has the last word in that particular dialogue, in the sense that it does not have to adopt the opinions of the Minister of Justice and has the final say on the form of the definitive guidelines, the framework for the dialogue is set by legislation – for it is Parliament that introduces new minimum sentences, higher maximum penalties, new forms of sentence, and so on – and of course Parliament generally adopts the proposals of the government.

Three particular aspects of the political context of the English guideline system merit further discussion – the position of the judiciary, the influence of the press and the role of the House of Commons Justice Committee.

The position of the judiciary

The English movement towards sentencing guidelines was developed by appellate judges, and the early attempts at providing guidelines are to be found in Court of Appeal judgments.[18] However, one foundation stone of the proposal that eventually gave rise to the creation of the Sentencing Advisory Panel (and subsequently the Sentencing Guidelines Council) was that, as sentencing guidelines play a major part in determining sentencing policy (which is an important branch of public policy), they should not be the exclusive preserve of the judiciary but should be formulated after discussions with others who have relevant experience and knowledge – for example, in relation to prison and probation services, prosecutions, policing, victims' services, and research and teaching. In the original proposal, however, it was argued that substantial judicial representation was important in order to ensure the practicality and authority of the guidelines and that it was fitting for the Lord Chief Justice to chair the body charged with the creation of guidelines (Ashworth, 1983, ch 13). As the English system now stands, there are two bodies (the Panel and the Council) with mixed judicial and non-judicial membership. One consequence of the high-level judicial representation on the Council is that the guidelines can be said to be fashioned *for* judges *by* bodies that well know what judges want and respond to.[19]

The American academic commentator Michel Tonry has argued, on the basis of his examination of the various guideline systems at State and federal level in the United States, that any system that has judicial leadership or even a majority of judicial members is doomed.[20] The innate conservatism of judges, he argues, is likely to stand in the way of the kind of innovative approach that a successful guideline system requires. Whether this proves to be a valid criticism of the English system is too early to tell, but there are material differences between the United States and England that may have an influence. Appellate judges in England are experienced at creating guidelines, and sentencers are accustomed to handling guidelines. Moreover, the kind of narrative guideline developed in England is a far cry from the starker, grid-style American guideline. It may be true that an attempt could be made to reduce the former to the latter, by producing a kind of grid that represents English guidelines; but any attempt to achieve that would demonstrate that the English guidelines are also more detailed and nuanced. Tonry's argument about judicial conservatism may suggest that the English system will never succeed in changing English sentencing policy, but that opens up the question of the aim of guidelines. They are a means, and not an end in themselves. The English guideline system does not take sentencing policy away from the legislature. Guidelines could be successful in making sentencing consistently harsh or consistently sparing in the use of imprisonment, for example. The consistency sought by the existing English system is consistency in the application of sentencing laws – and they are more tightly drawn as the years go by and place considerable emphasis on the use of custody for serious, dangerous and persistent offenders. In this context, it may be debated whether judicial conservatism is a good or bad thing.

Two other aspects of the interaction between the guidelines and the judiciary warrant mention. One is whether the guidelines are effective in changing sentencing practice and on this there is no hard evidence available. It is true that, for many years, the Court of Appeal has used guideline judgments as a frame of reference when deciding appeals and from that it can be inferred that most judges broadly follow any applicable guidelines.[21] But we have no detailed evidence on the way in which, or extent to which, judges respond to guideline judgments in their sentencing. Interviews with a group of judges generated the suggestion that the guidelines have produced greater severity in sentencing, bringing lenient sentencers up to the norm but not curbing harsher sentencers (Hough, Jacobson and Millie, 2003, p 25), but that is purely anecdotal. If the influence of guidelines is to be researched, this will require the "shadowing" of judges and a judicial willingness to talk through their reasoning processes in actual cases.[22]

Last, how does the Court of Appeal respond to the guidelines when adjudicating on appeals? Not surprisingly, as senior judges sit on the Council, the Court has supported the guidelines and has insisted that other judges must follow the guidelines loyally even if they disagree with an aspect of them.[23] But it has also emphasised that sentencing should not be viewed as a mathematical exercise and that there is no expectation of "robotic adherence" to guidelines[24] – considerations that are valid, up to a point. The Court of Appeal has also taken it upon itself to issue guidelines of its own on matters that the Panel and Council have not yet had time to consider – from guidelines on theft from shops, which the Court thought were needed urgently,[25] to preliminary non-prescriptive guidance on new provisions in the *Sexual Offences Act* 2003 (UK), which were brought into force before the Council guidelines were prepared.[26] In view of the lengthy process for creating a new guideline in the English system, the Court of Appeal may have further opportunities to adopt this approach.

The influence of the press

The press, and the media generally, have maintained a close watch over the guideline system since the creation of the Panel in 1998. In the first five years, both Consultation Papers and the Advice given by the Panel to the Court of Appeal attracted frequent scrutiny from sections of the press. Even if the Panel was recognised as a body independent of the courts and of the government, some of its publications were met with strong criticism, whereas others passed without much comment at all. The Panel's 2003 Consultation Paper on robbery was criticised in some newspapers for undue leniency, despite the Panel's attempt to differentiate between offences committed by adults and those committed by young people. The Panel's 2002 Advice on burglary attracted some adverse publicity, although that was insignificant compared with the public opprobrium poured on the Lord Chief Justice, Lord Woolf, by the media and by the government when the Court of Appeal went on to issue guidelines that were considerably lower than those proposed by the Panel (Davies and Tyrer, 2003). Since the creation of the Council, the level of media scrutiny has not declined. For example, when the Panel issued a Consultation Paper on sentencing for theft from shops, much of the press reaction was adverse to the point of ridiculing some of the suggestions in the Paper, without placing them in context.[27]

In a democratic country one should, in principle, welcome scrutiny of public policy by the media. To suppress it would be a fetter on freedom of speech. The difficulty is that some of the media coverage is unbalanced, taking one element from an integrated package of guideline proposals and portraying it out of context. The Panel and the Council have the responsibility of working towards a *system* of sentencing guidelines, whereas the press have no duty to place news items in context and indeed can, by juxtaposing one aspect of a proposed guideline with, say, a quotation from a crime victim, convey a less than faithful impression of what is being proposed. It might be said that the English system invites this kind of sniping because it proceeds by proposing individual guidelines whereas, for example, the approach envisaged in New Zealand (New Zealand Law Commission, 2006) and adopted in several United States jurisdictions, is to devise a whole network of guidelines at once so that those who pass comment must inevitably engage with relativities between offences and consider the package as a whole.

The role of the House of Commons Justice Committee

It will be recalled that one of the changes introduced into the English system in 2003 was to give this Committee a role in commenting on draft guidelines issued by the Council. This was an attempt to address the perceived "democratic deficit" in the creation of sentencing guidelines. Even though – as described earlier – members of the public play a part in the process of creating guidelines, it was thought that elected members of Parliament should have an input too. This is an all-party committee with a small secretariat and it has delivered thoughtful comments on the various drafts produced by the Council – sometimes very critical, as in relation to the guilty plea discount in murder cases, and sometimes raising further issues for the Council's consideration.[28] The same may be said of the responses from the Minister of Justice.

However, there remains a question of whether there is a "democratic deficit" that justifies these particular consultations. Should it not be sufficient for Parliament to set the parameters for sentencing by means of maximum penalties and new forms of sentences and then to leave the details to be worked out independently? Or can it be argued that in sentencing policy as in so many other spheres "the devil is in the detail" – that to leave democratic institutions out of the guideline process would be an improper curtailment of their influence?

Conclusions

The English approach to creating sentencing guidelines is, by comparison with most others, a system that is complex (with its two bodies, the Panel and the Council) and slow (with its requirements for public consultation and its piecemeal offence-by-offence approach). One advantage, however, is the emphasis it places on consulting members of the public and various public organisations and on taking those responses or research findings seriously. However, we have seen that the intrusion of politics – whether in the shape of media comments on proposed guidelines, or in the shape of formal responses from the Minister of Justice and House of Commons Justice Committee – cannot be avoided. This is hardly surprising when there is such a public interest in sentencing and when criminal justice policy is thought to be an area of potential danger for governments (in terms of popularity). Thus one of the reasons given for creating some of the early sentencing commissions in the United States was to take sentencing policy away from party politics and place it in independent hands; since then, however, sentencing has become increasingly politicised in many jurisdictions. In the United States the spread of legislation on mandatory and mandatory minimum sentences demonstrates that politics now dominates sentencing.

In England and Wales it is true that both the Panel and the Council are independent and that, even after all the statutory consultations have been carried out, the Council is not bound to give way to the criticisms of consultees when issuing a definitive guideline. However, the Council can only issue guidelines within the legislative framework of sentencing established by Parliament; major parameters such as maximum sentences, minimum sentences, sentences for "dangerous offenders" and new forms of sentence are matters for legislation and not for the Council. The Lord Chief Justice may voice criticisms of aspects of sentencing legislation in extra-judicial speeches,[29] but as chairman of the Council he is obliged to apply the law as he finds it. That means giving effect to a bifurcated sentencing framework, characterised by increasing severity for serious, "dangerous" and persistent offenders and yet also by an innovative range of community orders and what may be termed "semi-custodial" sentences for less serious offenders.[30]

122

Sentencing guidelines, as stated earlier, are merely a means and not an end in themselves (save for the important task of bringing the rule of law further into sentencing practice). In the modern day, sentencing is inextricably entwined with politics in most jurisdictions and it therefore follows that any sentencing guideline system is likely to be drawn into the political arena. Protestations that the Panel or the Council is "only doing its job" are unlikely to prevent media criticism and political comment, even on occasions where it is simply guiding courts on the practical application of legislation for which it is not responsible.

Notes

1   Professor Ashworth has been a member of the Sentencing Advisory Panel since its inception in 1999. This article is written in a personal capacity and does not purport to represent the views of the Panel or the Council.

2   Since the advent of the Sentencing Guidelines Council in 2003, the Council has taken the place of the Court of Appeal and is able to request the production of guidelines on particular topics.

3   Up to 2004, draft guidelines were produced on the following: alcohol and tobacco smuggling offences; causing death by dangerous driving; child pornography offences; domestic burglary; environmental offences; handling stolen goods; importation and possession of opium; manslaughter by reason of provocation; minimum terms in murder cases; possessing an offensive weapon; racially aggravated offences; rape; and robbery. Since 2004 the Sentencing Advisory Panel has offered advice to the Sentencing Guidelines Council on the following: overarching principles of sentencing; new sentences under the *Criminal Justice Act* 2003 (UK); sentencing for breach of protective orders; and offences under the *Sexual Offences Act* 2003 (UK). These are draft guidelines that are awaiting approval.

4   Guideline decisions of the Court of Appeal during the period 1999-2003 included: *Celaire and Poulton* [2003] 1 Cr App R (S) 116 on offensive weapons offences; *Mashaollahi* [2001] 1 Cr App R (S) 96 on importation of opium; *Kelly and Donnelly* [2001] 2 Cr App R (S) 341 on racially aggravated offences; *Webbe* [2002] 1 Cr App R (S) 22 on handling stolen goods; *McInerney and Keating* [2003] 2 Cr App R (S) 39 on domestic burglary; *Milberry et al* [2003] 2 Cr App R (S) 142 on rape; *Oliver, Hartrey and Baldwin* [2003] 2 Cr App R (S) 64 on child pornography offences; *Cooksley* [2004] 1 Cr App R (S) 1 on causing death by dangerous driving; and *Czyzewski* [2004] 1 Cr App R (S) 49 on alcohol and tobacco smuggling.

5   The proposal built on the examination of the issues and options in chapter 8 of the Halliday Report (Home Office, 2001), which argued that "a clear code of sentencing guidelines" must be the aim if consistency is to be achieved (para 8.7). For discussion of developments until the end of 2002, see Wasik (2003).

6   Strangely Schedule 37 to the *Criminal Justice Act* 2003 removes the restriction on the Court of Appeal issuing its own guidelines that had been in introduced in 1998 when the SAP was created.

7   The Council may decide thus to notify the Panel of its own motion or after receiving a proposal from the Minister of Justice: ss 170(2) and 171(1).

8   The consultation period is normally three months; consequently the whole process of formulating an advice takes the Panel several months. However, s 171(4) empowers the Council to notify the Panel that, because of "the urgency of the case", it may dispense with its normal consultations.

9   The terms of s 170(8) allow for other consultations too, as either the Lord Chancellor or the Council itself thinks appropriate.

10   *McInerney and Keating* [2003] 2 Cr App R (S) 240; see further Davies and Tyrer (2003).

11   This is the principal counter-argument of Tonry (2004), ch 5.

12   The proposal built on the examination of the issues and options in chapter 8 of the Halliday Report.

13   The Council's guideline on *Reduction in Sentence for a Guilty Plea* (2004) may be found, as may all other guidelines and Consultation Papers from both the Council and the Panel, on the website at <www.sentencing-guidelines.gov.uk>.

14   *Millberry* [2003] 2 Cr App R (S) 31 at 148.

15   The Panel is required by the Act to obtain and consider the views of bodies approved by the Lord Chancellor, after consultation with the Minister of Justice and the Lord Chief Justice. The current list of 28 consultees includes the Association of Chief Officers of Probation; the Association of Chief Police Officers; the Association of Directors of Social Services; The Centre for Crime & Justice Studies; The Chief Metropolitan Stipendiary Magistrate; the Commission for Racial Equality; The Council of HM Circuit Judges; General Council of the Bar; HM Prison Service; The Howard League for Penal Reform; Justice; Justices' Clerks' Society; Law Society; Liberty; Local Government Association; Magistrates' Association; National Association for the Care and Resettlement of Offenders; National Association of Parole Officers; Parole Board; Police Federation of England and Wales; Police Superintendent's Association; Prison Governor's Association; Prison Officers' Association; Prison Reform Trust; Probation Managers' Association; The Society of Stipendiary Magistrates for England and Wales; Victim Support and the Youth Justice Board for England and Wales.

16   This procedure was first invoked in autumn 2004. The resulting observations are to be found in House of Commons Justice Committee (2004) and in House of Commons Justice Committee (2005).

17   See previous note. The revised approach is set out in Sentencing Guidelines Council (2004).

18   The first guideline judgment from a Lord Chief Justice was *Aramah* [1982] 4 Cr App R (S) 407, but Lawton LJ had started to develop the format in the previous decade – for example, in *Willis* (1974) 60 Cr App R 146 (buggery of boys) and in *Taylor et al* [1977] 64 Cr App R 182 (unlawful sexual intercourse with girls). A different kind of sentencing guidelines was developed by the Magistrates' Association, first for sentencing road traffic offences (from 1966) and later for sentencing other offences in the magistrates' courts (from 1989): for the somewhat turbulent history of these guidelines, see Ashworth (2003).

19   In so far as guidelines laid down by the Court of Appeal continue to be prominent in the English system, this point is even stronger.

20   For selected writings, see Tonry (1996), ch 2 and Tonry (2004), ch 5.

21   Occasional cases in which a judge has declined to follow a guideline judgment have drawn a sharp rebuke from the Court of Appeal: see *Johnson* (1994) 15 Cr App R (S) 827, and *Attorney General's References Nos 37, 38 and others of 2003* [2004] 1 Cr App R (S) 499 at 503 per Kay LJ.

22   See Ashworth (2003) for references to previous efforts in this direction.

23   The leading case is now *Oosthuizen* [2005] Crim LR 979; see also *Bowering* [2005] EWCA Crim 3215 at [12]-[13].

24   For example, *Martin* [2006] EWCA Crim 1035, and *Matthews* [2005] EWCA Crim 2768.

25   *Page* [2005] 2 Cr App R (S) 221.

26   *Corran* [2005] 2 Cr App R (S) 453; the reference to 'preliminary non-prescriptive guidance' comes from *Jones* [2005] EWCA Crim 3414.

27   See, for example, the *Daily Telegraph* and the *Daily Express* for 25 August 2006.

28   See Clarke et al (2002), and *Millberry* [2003] 2 Cr App R (S) 31.

29   An example is Lord Woolf's lecture, 'Making Sense of Sentencing' (12 May 2005), <www.dca. gov.uk>.

30   For further explanation of the new forms of sentence introduced by the *Criminal Justice Act 2003*, see Sentencing Guidelines Council, *New Sentences: Criminal Justice Act 2003* (2004), discussed in Ashworth (2005), chs 9 and 10.

References

Ashworth, A (1983). *Sentencing and Penal Policy*. London: Weidenfeld and Nicolson.

Ashworth, A (2001). The Decline of English Sentencing and Other Stories. In M Tonry and R Frase (eds), *Sentencing and Sanctions in Western Systems*. New York: Oxford University Press.

Ashworth, A (2003). Sentencing and Sensitivity. In L Zedner and A Ashworth (eds), *The Criminological Foundations of Penal Policy: Essays in Honour of Roger Hood*. Oxford: Oxford University Press.

Ashworth, A (2005). *Sentencing and Criminal Justice*. 4th ed, Cambridge: Cambridge University Press.

Clarke, A, Moran-Ellis, J and Sleney, J (2002). *Attitudes to Date Rape and Relationship Rape: A Qualitative Study*. Sentencing Advisory Panel Research Report 2.

Davies, M and Tyrer, J (2003). Filling in the Gaps – a Study of Judicial Culture. *Criminal Law Review*: 243.

Dunbar, I and Langdon, A (1998). *Tough Justice: Sentencing and Penal Policies in the 1990s*. London: Blackstone.

Home Office (2001). *Making Punishments Work: Review of the Sentencing Framework for England and Wales*. London: Home Office.

Home Office (2002). *Justice for All*. London: The Stationery Office.

Hough, M, Jacobson, J and Millie, A (2003). *The Decision to Imprison*. London: Prison Reform Trust.

House of Commons Justice Committee (2004). *Draft Sentencing Guidelines 1 and 2* (5th Report of Session 2003-04). London: The Stationery Office.

House of Commons Justice Committee (2005). *Draft Sentencing Guidelines 1 and 2: Government Response to the Committee's Fifth Report of Session 2003-04* (1st Special Report of Session 2004-05, HC 371. London: The Stationery Office.

House of Lords Select Committee on the Constitution (2003). *Criminal Justice Bill*. London: The Stationery Office.

New Zealand Law Commission (2006). Report 94, *Sentencing Guidelines and Parole Reform*. Wellington: Law Commission.

Russell, N and Morgan, R (2001). *Survey on Public Attitudes to Domestic Burglary*. Sentencing Advisory Panel Research Report 1.

Sentencing Advisory Panel (2002). *Advice to the Court of Appeal – 8: Domestic Burglary*.

Sentencing Advisory Panel (2006). *Revised Guideline: Reduction in Sentence for a Guilty Plea*.

Sentencing Guidelines Council (2004). *Reduction in Sentence for a Guilty Plea*.

Sentencing Guidelines Council (2004b). *New Sentences: Criminal Justice Act 2003*.

Tonry, M (1996). *Sentencing Matters*. New York: Oxford University Press.

Tonry, M (2004). *Punishment and Politics*. Cullompton: Willan.

Wasik, M (2003). Sentencing Guidelines: Past, Present and Future. *Current Legal Problems* 239.

9

The New South Wales Sentencing Council[1]

The Hon Alan Abadee AM RFD QC[2]

Introduction

The constitutions and functions of sentencing councils vary greatly, both overseas and in Australia. There are different understandings as to the appropriate structures and functions of sentencing councils or commissions. Much may depend on whether the body is to be given delegated rule-making power, for example the fixing of sentencing guidelines, or even whether the council is to have mixed functions including rule making functions. Different factors, not merely cultural or traditional, are also involved. Social, economic and political factors may all play a part. Further, the existence of other bodies or agencies participating in sentencing concerns may also be a relevant consideration. It is not surprising that the recent Australian Law Reform Commission's (ALRC) Report 103, *Same Crime, Same Time: Sentencing Federal Offenders* stated: "A significant number of stakeholders supported the establishment of a federal sentencing council. There was some disagreement about the tasks such a body should perform" (ALRC, 2006, para 19.29). One might also observe that there is a relationship between functions and funding as the proper discharge of the Council's functions is dependent on proper resourcing and resources depend on functions.

There is no transportable model for sentencing councils or commissions based on experiences or situations elsewhere. Thus in relation to the establishment of the New South Wales Sentencing Council in 2002, its constitution and statutory functions followed no other model. It was no mere copy or mimic of any sentencing body, council or commission that had been earlier established overseas.

As to the need for State sentencing councils, I would note the very recent observation of the ALRC (2006, para 19.33):

> State sentencing councils in Australia are to be commended. Better sentencing decisions and sound evidence-based policies can be promoted by disseminating sentencing statistics, analysing sentencing trends and conducting broad community consultation.

The New South Wales Sentencing Council is constituted under Part 8B of the *Crimes (Sentencing Procedure) Act* 1999 (the Act), as amended by the *Crimes (Sentencing Procedure) Amendment (Standard Minimum Sentencing) Act* 2002. Its establishment came amidst a number of substantive amendments to the Act. The explanatory note to the Bill stated that the principal objects of the Act were to:

> (a) Establish a scheme of standard minimum sentencing for a number of serious offences; and

(b) To establish a New South Wales Sentencing Council to advise the Attorney General in connection with sentencing matters.

The establishment of both were the first of their kind in Australia.

The Second Reading Speech of the Attorney General provides some guidance as to the rationale and reason for the establishment of the Sentencing Council. The Attorney General said: "The government is confident that this new Sentencing Council will provide an invaluable opportunity for the wider community to make a major contribution to the development of sentencing law and practice in New South Wales".[3] Later, in July 2003, the Attorney General hoped (Debus, 2003):

> The Sentencing Council's collective experience, expertise, independence and ability to consult with others will contribute to the strengthening of public acceptance and understanding of the sentencing process and the maintenance of confidence in that process.

The rationale for the establishment of the Sentencing Council is somewhat different in terms of the measures referred to in the ALRC Report 103: being that the establishment of a sentencing commission or council to advise on matters relating to sentencing "may promote better sentencing decisions" (ALRC, 2006, para 19.33).

At the time of the establishment of the Council there were in New South Wales several bodies already playing a role in relation to advising on sentencing issues. Such bodies include:

- the Judicial Commission of New South Wales;
- the New South Wales Bureau of Crime Statistics and Research (BOCSAR);
- the New South Wales Law Reform Commission;
- the New South Wales Crown Advocate; and
- the Criminal Law Review Division of the Attorney General's Department.

It might reasonably be thought that, by establishing the Council, Parliament considered the Council should be a discrete, "expert" special purpose body that would advise and consult with the Attorney General on sentencing matters falling within its statutory functions, whilst acknowledging at the same time the existence of other bodies or agencies that may also have an involvement or responsibility for sentencing issues or aspects of these. Nevertheless, even allowing for the roles of such bodies or agencies the Council's statutory functions are (and have been shown by experience) to be of a restrictive nature.

It is for the Attorney General to decide whether to consult or seek advice from one or more of these bodies or agencies on one or more sentencing matters. Despite being a discrete special body, the Council has no special status or standing among those other advisory bodies or agencies that have involvement or respon-sibilities regarding sentencing issues. That said, the Council continues a working relationship with each of the above agencies, which is maintained by regular meetings and thus, among other things, avoids duplication and overlap. In this connection there should be noted the provision of s 100J(4) of the Act which permits the Council, in the exercise of its functions, to consult with, receive and consider information from the Judicial Commission and BOCSAR. This the

Council regularly does at the same time as not treating the statutory consultation right as being "exclusive" of a right to consult others. In particular in relation to the exercise of its stated functions to prepare reports at the request of the Attorney pursuant to s 100J(1)(d), the Council not only relies on its own wealth and breadth of knowledge and experience, but also obtains and considers views of interested persons and bodies as it may determine and select.

Membership

A characteristic of the New South Wales Sentencing Council that perhaps sets it apart from other bodies and agencies in New South Wales is its diverse membership. The constitution and structure of the Council very much reflect the stated rationale and reasons for its establishment. Its members are chosen from specified fields with different backgrounds in accordance with the statutory requirements. Section 100I(2) constitutes the Council:

The Sentencing Council is to consist of 13 members appointed by the Minister, of whom:

(a) one is to be a retired judicial officer;

(b) one is to have expertise or experience in law enforcement;

(c) three are to have expertise or experience in criminal law or sentencing (of whom one is to have expertise or experience in the area of prosecution and one is to have expertise or experience in the area of defence);

(d) one is to be a person who has expertise or experience in Aboriginal justice matters, and four are to be persons representing the general community, of whom two are to have expertise or experience in matters associated with victims of crime;

(f) one is to have expertise or experience in corrective services;

(g) one is to have expertise or experience in juvenile justice; and

(h) one is to be a representative of the Attorney General's Department.[4]

Each of the members is appointed in and serves in a personal capacity. The members do not act as representatives of any particular profession, voluntary or special interest group or viewpoint. For example, while the Director of Public Prosecutions (DPP) is a member of the Council he is in fact a member by reason of having expertise or experience in the area of prosecution.

One of the Council's great strengths is its constitution and actual membership. Many of the members have expertise and experience in the criminal law area (for example, the DPP, the Senior Public Defender and former judicial officers) as well as actual experience of the criminal justice system as informed members of the general community. Its actual membership is diverse and reflects a cross-section of different views from within the community and the criminal justice system. Such representation can justifiably give rise to general public confidence in the Council and the quality of its views and advice.

Indeed, the Council is not merely a participant in the criminal justice system but also an ally of it. The Council is an independent and impartial body. It has no direct dealings with Parliament or the courts. The Attorney General may seek a report or advice from it on a sentencing issue, which may be more readily accepted, by policy-makers and indeed by the public, because it emanates from a Council constituted and structured so as to reflect community views, opinions, standards and legitimate expectations. Thus in circumstances where a controversial sentencing issue arises, an opportunity exists for the Council to be utilised to deal with it by the Minister seeking its reports or views. This may have the advantage of neutralising the sensational or emotive issue, allowing time for calm informed consideration of such an issue and avoiding a reactive or potentially unprincipled response to an issue that may be stoked by media reporting.

Despite the diverse and varied backgrounds, experiences and expertise of the Council members, the Council has been able to achieve a shared common and general outlook in relation to sentencing issues. This has been a notable feature of its existence and is a matter of some significance. The Council has achieved a high level of consensus in respect of most of its advice and views. Indeed, it might be thought that the very existence of such a body (with its significant community-based membership coupled with criminal justice policy professionals) would not only enhance public confidence in its role and function but also provide a vehicle for Parliament to refer controversial sentencing issues for consideration. The past three years have seen the Council shaped into a well-functioning, cohesive and well-informed body providing valuable contributions to the development of sentencing law and practice in New South Wales and to the strengthening of public acceptance and understanding of the sentencing process.

It should also not be overlooked that Council members inform and educate each other by participating in robust debate on sentencing issues. Indeed, Council membership also assists in keeping abreast of contemporary issues and the like not only through its members but also through the acceptance of invitations to address the Council by distinguished guests. Each member becomes better informed with the corresponding expression of not merely informed views and opinions but also the conveyance of more informed views of the criminal justice system in their own private capacity to their own constituencies and the public. Members have access to the resources associated with their specific fields and different backgrounds.

Although the right balance of membership has been well achieved, nevertheless it was the Council's view that an additional valuable member for the Council could be a person with expertise or experience in corrective services. Until the *Crimes and Courts Legislation Amendment Act* 2006 (NSW) there was no such institutional representative on the New South Wales Council but this Act increased the Council's membership from 10 to 13, adding, respectively, members with expertise or experience in corrective services, juvenile justice and a representative of the Attorney General's Department.[5]

Functions and operation

Section 100J sets forth the functions of the NSW Sentencing Council:

(a) to advise and consult with the Minister in relation to offences suitable for standard non-parole periods and their proposed length;

(b) to advise and consult with the Minister in relation to
   (i) matters suitable for guideline judgements and
   (ii) submissions to the CCA made by the Attorney General in guideline proceedings;

(c)   to monitor, and to report annually to the Minister on, sentencing trends and practices, including the operation of standard non-parole periods and guideline judgments;

(d)   at the request of the Minister, prepare research papers or reports on particular subjects in connection with sentencing; and

(e)   to educate the public about sentencing matters.[6]

Section 100J makes clear that the NSW Sentencing Council advises and consults directly with the Attorney General and not otherwise. It has no direct dealings or contact with the court itself even with respect to guideline judgments. It has no direct dealings with the Parliament.

Nowadays Parliament has a large input into sentencing not only by way of penalties it prescribes as maximum penalties but also by detailed legislative prescription as to principles of sentencing to be applied (Gleeson, 2004). That said, the Council is not normally asked to express views as to maximum penalties; Parliament provides these as it thinks fit for offences it creates or offences already created.

As has been said, but is perhaps worth repeating, a stated aim for establishing the Council by the Attorney General was "to provide an invaluable opportunity for the wider community to make a major contribution to the development of sentencing law and practice in New South Wales". The advisory nature of the Council and its function of offering wider community contribution to sentencing law are reflected in the composition of the Council. Indeed, four of its members are drawn from the community, with three in fact pre-eminent in victims of crime interests.

The statutory functions of the Council are of a limited kind. To what extent, if at all, the functions will remain the same or will change may be influenced by outstanding reviews of the Act pursuant to ss 105 and 106,[7] which presumably will also address the matter of the Council's role and functions. One may also note that the Act itself provides for the possibility of change by way of s 100J(3).

The New South Wales Sentencing Council does not have a right to initiate advice to the Attorney General on sentencing matters generally. With respect to the Sentencing Council's independence under s 100J(1)(a) and (b), the Sentencing Council furnishes its advice to the Attorney General and then the Attorney decides and determines to what extent, if at all, that advice will be adopted, accepted and implemented. In this sense one can postulate that in the discharge of its functions the Sentencing Council may have regard to, and bring into account, the Attorney General's known or "advanced" indications, views and intentions, even though they will neither be decisive nor conclusive on the Sentencing Council in formulating its advice. There may be occasions when the Sentencing Council in discharging its statutory remit will furnish controversial advice and put forward controversial proposals. Indeed, at its launch the Attorney General even acknowledged that the Council was perhaps bound to come up with ideas that are "controversial or out of left field". The Council has, from time to time, produced ideas meeting such description.

It is also appropriate to mention that in discharging its functions the Council may express views in principle, properly recognising that cost benefits and resourcing are matters for others. Nevertheless, the Council recognises that its advice may impact on the whole of government and may have budgetary consequences. So also does it recognise that many of its recommendations are significant, even if not immediately implemented, because they may facilitate, particularly if published, informed public discussion and the formation of informed public opinion. Indeed, such recommendations may also assist and educate the lawmakers themselves and be relevant to informed political debate in relation to them.

Until the 2006 amendments, the Council's functions did not include any educative role in relation to sentencing matters or gauging public opinion on sentencing matters, although its actual representation perhaps is reflective of a capacity to give effect to informed views on these matters. However, the *Crimes and Courts Legislation Amendment Act* 2006 (NSW) expanded the Council's functions to allow it to "educate the public about sentencing matters", thus foreshadowing a more proactive role in disseminating sentencing information to the general public (s 100J(1)(e)). Its functions do not include conducting independent research and disseminating information to interested persons or bodies, including Parliamentary committees, sentence makers or to bodies other than the Attorney General.

In discharging its functions the Council has furnished two different classes of reports to the Attorney General. The first is a report falling within s 100J(1)(c) of the Act prepared annually on "sentencing trends and practices", including the operation of standard non-parole periods and guideline judgments. This report is prepared by the Council in accordance with the Act, absent any request from the Attorney.

The second class of reports includes those prepared at the Attorney's request on particular subjects in connection with sentencing.[8] The published major reports are as follows:

- abolishing prison sentences of six months or less;
- how best to promote consistency in sentencing in the Local Court;
- whether "attempt" and "accessorial" offences should be included in the standard non-parole sentencing scheme;
- whether further firearm offences should be included in the standard non-parole sentencing scheme; and
- seeking a guideline judgment on suspended sentences.

At present the Council is reporting on the effectiveness of fines as a sentencing option, paying particular attention to the relationship between driving licence sanctions for fine default and subsequent imprisonment.[9]

The Sentencing Council may, with the approval of the Attorney, establish committees to assist in connection with the exercise of any of its functions. It has done this on one occasion when it established a committee in respect of its major project relating to the abolition of prison sentences of six months or less. The committee, under the Chair of the Sentencing Council, consisted of senior representatives of relevant government departments and agencies together with individuals and bodies considered to have particular expertise or knowledge valuable to consideration of the issue.

In the past the Council has received submission requests from various Parliamentary Committees. The Council has declined to accept these, considering that its statutory functions did not extend to putting "submissions" to such bodies. Indeed, the statutory provisions restrict the promotion of the Council's role with other persons or bodies. Nevertheless, the Council's published reports have been accessible to all who are interested in reading and considering them (the public, the media, Parliament and other interested persons or bodies).

The Council accepts that, in relation to its report recommendations and to assist with implementation, there is a consultative process to permit a whole of government response as well as necessary time for this to take place. It also accepts that, whilst its recommendations on some or all may not be accepted, the reports will nevertheless aid and assist in informed debate.

The Council understands that there may be delay in publication of its reports for good and valid reasons. Nevertheless, in order for its reports to be available for public or parliamentary consideration, timely publication is of importance so that informed consideration of the issues can be taken into account. Non-publication of reports or non-timely publication may carry the consequence of denying relevant information to law-makers, courts and informed public discussion and debate.

There are some examples of the relevance and influence of the Council's reports in relation to the formation of public opinion and debate. The Legislative Council Standing Committee on Law and Justice in its Final Report, *Inquiry into Community Based Sentencing Options for Rural and Remote Areas and Disadvantaged Populations* (March 2006), referred frequently to the Council's reports on *Abolishing Prison Sentences of Six Months or Less* (August 2004) and *How Best to Promote Consistency in Sentencing* (June 2004).

In relation to the "six month sentence" report, the Standing Committee expressed support for the Council's particular recommendations to make all community-based sentencing options available uniformly throughout New South Wales, without the need for dealing with its primary recommendation that abolition of short prison sentences should be considered, but not until a number of issues had been addressed. Thus, through its published reports the Council is able to contribute to the knowledge and education of the legislators, and indeed to the community, by facilitating and contributing to informed public discussion.

So also does the publication of reports add to the Sentencing Council's profile, status and standing with legislators and the public. Inclusion on the Council's website permits knowledge to be available even internationally. For example, the Scottish Sentencing Commission has advised that the Sentencing Council's Report on *How Best to Promote Consistency in Sentencing in the Local Court* was of particular relevance and interest.

I believe also that it is important that sentencing councils, particularly those with significant community representation, be advised or informed of proposals (if any) to implement their advices and recommendations. I consider that this is relevant to maintaining the ongoing interest of members in Council participation, which for many is a form of community service. Members should be made to feel that they are making a worthwhile and effective contribution to the administration of the criminal justice system. Under-utilisation of the Council carries with it its own consequences.

Some observations on measuring the performance of the Council's functions should be noted. As already mentioned, the Council, when established, had conferred on it limited and specific statutory functions. So also was it accepted that in respect of sentencing issues it would share an advisory and consulting role with other statutory bodies and agencies.

Several summary points may be made about its advising and consulting role in relation to guideline judgments. First, for good and valid reasons (Abadee, 2006), in the time of the Council's existence there have been no numerical or quantitative guideline judgment proceedings instituted. The Council, with or without the Attorney's request, may give advice in relation to matters suitable for a guideline judgment.

The difficulties in the path of instituting numerical guideline judgments do not need repeating. The point to be made is that one potential function of the Council in fact has not been performed. With regard to what I might refer to as "qualitative" or "in principle" sentencing guideline judgments, the one guideline judgment sought was instituted by the Attorney General, namely the *Attorney General's Application No 3 of 2002* [2004] NSWCCA 303 before the Council's establishment; the Council was not involved. The Council has reported and has given advice in respect of one other guideline judgment matter concerning criteria for suspended sentences, and for reasons stated advised against the institution of proceedings primarily on the basis that, despite the substantive merits, any application could be faced with threshold discretionary problems in the path of success.[10]

A further area of work in which the Council was given a foundation function to provide advice to the Attorney General is in relation to offences suitable for standard non-parole periods and their proposed length. In relation to such matters, advice may also be given to the Attorney General with or without his request. The Council has furnished a report to the Attorney in relation to, inter alia, whether further firearm offences should be included in the standard non-parole scheme. No further offences have been added to the scheme since its inception.

Without going into explanations one may note that the failed special leave application in *R v Way*[11] has left open issues concerning the interpretation of the words "middle of the range of objective seriousness". As pointed out in Abadee (2006) there may be problems for the Council in giving advice with respect to newly created offences where there is no middle of the range or other relevant information. Also to be noted is the outstanding and pending review of the standard parole scheme under s 106 of the Act. The Attorney is reviewing its operation presently. The point to be made is that again in a de facto sense there has been a limited function or role for the Council to play in relation to the standard non-parole scheme.

As to both guideline judgments and the standard non-parole scheme, it may also be noted there are no empirical studies as to the impact on public opinion or public confidence of the guideline judgment or standard non-parole scheme in New South Wales.

The history of the Council's operation of its functions has been very much related to its limited role to prepare, at the request of the Attorney, research papers or reports on particular subjects in connection with sentencing under s 100J(1)(d) and its annual reports under s 100J(1)(c). Again, the work on subjects in connection with sentencing is shared with other agencies or bodies, with the Attorney retaining the full right to determine when and with whom, if at all, he chooses to consult.

The functions and operation of the Council not only reflect those legislatively described above but also the stated views of the Attorney General in his Second Reading Speech[12] when he spoke of the Council providing an invaluable opportunity for the wider community to make a contribution to the development of sentencing law and practice in New South Wales. In my earlier paper I said:

> As to the matter of the Council being established to provide an invaluable contribution to the development of sentencing law and practice (and the participation in doing so) the importance of doing so cannot be underestimated.

As Chief Justice Spigelman observed (Spigelman, 2005):

> The participation by members of the public in the process of the administration of justice whether as parties, witnesses or jurors constitutes a crucial mechanism for ensuring that trust in the administration of justice remains at a high level.

One can perhaps add to this participation list, participation through membership of the Sentencing Council! Indeed, that participatory view is and has also been reflected in not only the composition of membership of the Council but also in part in the discharge by Council of those limited statutory functions conferred. However, when looking at the so called participatory role of jurors one can see historically this role declining as a significant contribution in the process of the administration of criminal justice. The Council establishment coincides with evidence of the reduced use of the jury.

Chief Justice Gleeson observed that (Gleeson, 2004):

> The best way of seeing that the public are informed about the working of the criminal justice system is through the jury system ... The maintenance of the jury system for the trial of serious crimes, and especially crimes of violence, is a vital means of keeping the public and criminal justice in touch.

However, the figures would tend to suggest that the role of the jury is diminishing, effectively eliminating through the jury system a way of informing the public about the working of the criminal justice system. As the New South Wales Law Reform Commission has observed in its recent Report 111, *Majority Verdicts* (2006), the great majority of all criminal cases finalised in 2003 were dealt with in the Local Court with very few criminal cases being prosecuted before a jury. Just 2.68 per cent of matters were finalised in the superior courts, with 0.5 per cent of cases overall proceeding to a defended hearing either before a judge or jury.

Indeed, one might think that a body such as the New South Wales Sentencing Council, constituted with a significant cross-section of the community as members, is well placed to provide to the public some of the information referred to. With adequate functions, the Council could perhaps help fill the vacuum left by the diminishing use of the jury as a forum for keeping the public in touch with the administration of the criminal justice system.

The Council's relationship with the courts

The Council has no direct statutory relationship with the courts. There is no provision for the Council's written views to be sought by the court in relation to the exercise of its guideline judgment jurisdiction or corresponding function of the Council to furnish such a guideline.

In the relatively brief period of its existence to date there has been no citation by the courts' judgments of published reports of the Sentencing Council. Presumably it is but a matter of time before the Council's published reports (like those of the Law Reform Commission for example) will be cited. Nevertheless the Council's role with the courts is perhaps a more indirect one in the sense that its reports and operations will impact and play a role in terms of influencing public debate, creation of informed public opinion and the reflection of legitimate community expectations, standards and values. As was observed by McHugh J in *Markarian v The Queen:*

> Public responses to sentencing, although not entitled to influence any particular case, have a legitimate impact on the democratic legislative process. Judges are aware that, if they consistently impose sentences that are too lenient or too severe, they risk undermining public confidence in the administration of justice and invite legislative interference in the exercise of judicial discretion. For the sake of criminal justice generally, judges attempt to impose sentences that accord with legitimate community expectations.[13]

The Council's published reports can perhaps be utilised to assist on the matter of legitimate community expectations, standards and values.

Indeed, to the extent that the Council plays a role in enhancing public confidence, the Council has a further role with the courts. As has been said by Sir Anthony Mason, modern courts are more concerned to take account of public confidence as an element of judicial decision-making than the courts were in the past (Mason, 2002). Further, as Sir Anthony has also observed, because the courts are concerned with maintaining public confidence in the administration of justice, judges cannot dismiss public opinion as having no relevance in the work of the courts. A difficulty is that in relation to public opinion, as Justice Kirby has observed, a court is not well placed to estimate with precision the impact of any particular legislation on public opinion.[14]

As Chief Justice Gleeson has also observed in his *Out of Touch or Out of Reach* speech in 2004, whilst public opinion is a deceptively simple concept there is no generally shared public opinion in respect of most of the day-to-day work in the courts. Indeed, with respect to courts from time to time referring to "community values" they may create an impression that such values are clear and discernible. Sometimes a judge might be attributing his or her personal values to the community with little empirical justification for a belief that those values are widely shared.[15] The point sought to be made is that in the ascertainment of public opinion on a particular subject-matter falling within the subject of sentencing, the Sentencing Council, with its important spectrum of representation including widely informed community-based representation, has an indirect role in assisting the court by reflecting, among other things, informed public opinion. The same observation may be made in relation to community values as well. Indeed the views reflected through its reports may likewise also assist the law-makers.

Conclusion

The New South Wales Sentencing Council has been in existence for over three years. When established it was the first of its kind in Australia with its own particular constitution and stated functions. Its existing functions have perhaps limited the Council's full potential consistent with its established aims. It is not surprising that operational experience and practice have identified issues, particularly as to functions, that could usefully be visited and further addressed to permit the Council to perform and discharge the purposes and reasons for which it was established even better, and to enhance further the opportunity of the wider community to make a major contribution to the development of sentencing law and practice in New South Wales.

There are some identifiable issues that might be considered of value to address such as whether the Council should have:

- such powers to initiate projects and to advise the Attorney General on sentencing matters generally and of its own motion;

- powers in relation to reporting and publication and for tabling of its reports;

- powers to provide information on sentencing matters to "other interested persons";

- powers to gauge public opinion on sentencing matters;

- the same relationship with Parliament and Parliamentary Committees;

- wider powers of consultation; and

- a direct relationship with the court itself in relation to the court's responsibility for framing and revising guidelines and indeed issues in connection with the court's discretionary power to decline a guideline judgment.

It is not appropriate for me to express views on these matters at this time.

Three years after its establishment, the Council has been shaped from an initial body of 10 members from diverse backgrounds into a well functioning and informed cohesive body that has through its works and reports provided, so far as its functions permit, timely advice and service to the Attorney General, the community and the criminal justice system. It has contributed to the strengthening of public acceptance and understanding of the sentencing process and the maintenance of confidence in that process.

Notes

1   This chapter incorporates and reflects legislative changes made before its publication but subsequent to its delivery at the Victorian Sentencing Advisory Council conference in June 2006.

2   Foundation Chairperson of the New South Wales Sentencing Council from March 2003 to April 2006 and retired Judge of the Supreme Court of New South Wales. The views expressed in this paper are endorsed by the New South Wales Sentencing Council.

3   The Hon Bob Debus, *Hansard*, New South Wales Legislative Assembly, Second Reading 23 October 2002.

4   The Council's membership expanded by virtue of the *Crimes and Courts Legislation Amendment Act* 2006 (NSW), which came into effect on 23 February 2007.

5   Section 100I(2)(f)-(h) of the *Crimes (Sentencing Procedure) Act* 1999 (NSW).

6   Included by virtue of the *Crimes and Courts Legislation Amendment Act* 2006 (NSW), which came into effect on 23 February 2007.

7   Section 106 is confined to the review of the standard non-parole period provisions of the Act.

8   See s 100J(1)(d).

9   The Council's interim report "The Effectiveness of Fines as a Sentencing Option: Court-imposed fines and penalty notices" and a monograph "Judicial Perceptions of Fines: A Survey of NSW magistrates" were published in August 2007.

10   For further discussion, see an earlier paper of the author: 'The Role of Sentencing Councils' presented at the National Judicial College of Australia Conference: *Sentencing – Principles, Perspectives and Possibilities*, Canberra, February 2006, pp 12-14. This paper is available at <http://www.lawlink.nsw.gov.au/sentencingcouncil>.

11   [2004] NSWCCA 131.

12   The Hon Bob Debus, *Hansard*, New South Wales Legislative Assembly, Second Reading 23 October 2002.

13   (2005) 215 ALR 213 at 236.

14   *Baker v The Queen* (2004) 210 ALR 1 at 23 per Kirby J.

15   *Neindorf v Junkovic* (2005) 80 ALJR 341 at 345 per Gleeson CJ.

References

Abadee, A (2006). *The Role of Sentencing Advisory Councils*. Paper delivered at the National Judicial College of Australia's National Sentencing Conference, Canberra.

ALRC (Australian Law Reform Commission) (2006). Report No 103: *Same Crime, Same Time: Sentencing Federal Offenders*.

Debus, B (2003). The NSW Sentencing Council – Its Role and Functions. *Judicial Officers Bulletin* 15(6): 45.

Gleeson, M (2004). *Out of Touch or Out of Reach*. Paper delivered at Judicial Conference of Australia Colloquium, Adelaide.

Mason, A (2007). The Courts and Public Opinion. In G Lindell (ed) *The Mason Papers*. Sydney: The Federation Press.

Spigelman, J (2005). 'Free, strong societies arise from participatory legal systems'. *Sydney Morning Herald*, 16 May.

10

The Sentencing Commission for Scotland

Neil Hutton

Introduction

The Sentencing Commission for Scotland was an independent, judicially led body that was set up by the Scottish Executive under its policy statement "A Partnership For A Better Scotland" in November 2003. It had a specific remit and a limited lifespan; it was dissolved in November 2006. Unlike most other Sentencing Commissions, it was never intended to be a permanent body.

The Commission was comprised of eight lawyers, including two High Court judges, two senior sheriffs, the Deputy Crown Agent (prosecution service – who was appointed as a sheriff in 2006), a solicitor advocate subsequently appointed an advocate depute, the Vice-Dean of the Faculty of Advocates and a professor of law. Of the remaining members of the Commission, most had experience of the criminal justice system: a Chief Constable, the chief executive of Victim Support in Scotland, the chief executive of a major criminal justice non-government organisation, a Prison Governor, a Director of Social Work, a representative from the elected members of Scottish local government with a special interest in criminal justice and a professor with experience of sentencing research (the author of this chapter). The other two members of the Commission had no criminal justice experience: one is a senior figure in the voluntary sector and the other a professor with particular expertise in the political sociology of Scotland.

Almost all of the "lay members" had extensive experience in criminal justice practice and policy, and the two other members had considerable experience of public sector governance in Scotland. In that sense, while the Commission contained significant representation from the "lay" (that is, non-legal) public, it was very much a Commission of experts.

The members of the Commission were all appointed by the Minister for Justice and were not appointed using the standard public appointment process. This is significant because there is a limit on the time that members can serve on a public body without a proper public appointments system being followed; hence the Commission, from its inception, had a limited life span.

With two exceptions, the membership of the Commission was constant. The original chair of the Commission, a senior member of the judiciary, stood down in April 2005 to take up another appointment. He was replaced by another senior judge. In April 2005, one of the academic members resigned from the Commission for business reasons.

The remit

The Commission was given the remit to review and to make recommendations to the Scottish Executive on:

- the use of bail and remand;
- the basis on which fines are determined;
- the effectiveness of sentences in reducing re-offending;
- the scope to improve consistency of sentencing; and
- the arrangements for early release from prison, and supervision of prisoners on their release.

To those familiar with the work of sentencing institutions, this remit might appear unusual. Two of the issues, consistency and effectiveness, are broad and raise more general questions about the principles and purposes of sentencing and punishment. The other three issues are much narrower and more "technical". It might be argued that bail and remand and early release are not, strictly speaking, sentencing issues but rather issues of criminal procedure and corrections, respectively. It would appear that the Commission was established to fulfil some desired political objectives in the broad area of criminal justice policy. The remit was the product of an arrangement between the two parties that formed a coalition government in the first Scottish Parliament in 1999 – Scottish Labour and the Liberal Democrats – and reflected elements from the election manifestos of both parties. So, although the body was called the "Sentencing Commission for Scotland", the remit went well beyond what would be regarded as sentencing policy in most jurisdictions.

The Scottish Executive invited the Commission to give immediate priority to two items: the use of bail and remand and the arrangements for early release from prison, and supervision of prisoners on their release. These had been identified by the Minister as issues of immediate political concern. The Executive further explained in May 2004 that the effectiveness of sentences should be a pervasive theme rather than a separate strand. In early meetings the Commission had debated the remit and the scope that existed for it to be interpreted. The remit did not, on the face of it, offer an opportunity to produce an overall view of sentencing policy and practice. Although a paper on the principles and purposes of sentencing was drafted and discussed at an early meeting of the Commission, it was decided that work on this had to take second place to the work on bail and remand and on early release, which had been prioritised by the Executive. This caused a certain amount of tension in the Commission with several members arguing that it was difficult to make recommendations about how decisions about bail, remand, parole and early release should be taken without a prior debate about the principles and purposes of sentencing more generally.

Working practices

Under the first chair, the Commission met for one half-day each month. The Commission met for the first time on 26 November 2003 and met 18 times. Following the appointment of a new chair in April 2005, it was decided that the

Commission's work could be more effectively progressed by the establishment of sub-groups to take forward the (then) outstanding items on the remit. These would report to the full Commission at suitable junctures. These sub-groups were established in May 2005. An additional group was set up to examine the principles and purposes of sentencing.

Reports

The Commission produced reports on each of the four sections of the remit:

1. The Use of Bail and Remand (published April 2005).
2. Early Release from Prison and Supervision of Prisoners on their Release (published January 2006).
3. Basis on which Fines are Determined (published May 2006).
4. The Scope to Improve Consistency in Sentencing (published September 2006).

In the following sections, the main recommendations of the Commission are summarised. Where legislation has been proposed on areas covered by the work of the Commission, this has been compared with the recommendations actually made by it.

Report 1: The Use of Bail and Remand

The impetus for the review of bail and remand stemmed from several general concerns: about the number of offences being committed by those granted bail; about the time spent on bail awaiting trial; about the inefficiencies caused to the administration of justice by the failure to appear in court of significant numbers of accused persons who have been granted bail; and, finally, about the growth in the prison population caused by increases in the numbers of accused persons remanded in custody. The chair of the Commission noted in the foreword to the report that there was a difficult balance to be struck between protecting the presumed innocence of the accused person and recognising the interests of public protection. The objectives of the Commission were to seek to achieve reductions in offending by those who are granted bail, in the numbers of individuals released on bail who fail to appear in court when required to do so, and in the remand population – all without compromising the safety of the public.

The Commission made 38 recommendations. Some of these were addressed to the judiciary, some to the Lord Advocate (as head of the Crown Office and Procurator Fiscal Service) and some to the Scottish Executive. None of these recommendations proposed radical changes to the status quo; many were concerned with minor amendments to existing practices. There were recommendations that further evidence about the effectiveness of bail supervision, bail information and electronic monitoring should be considered before making changes involving these programs.

In September 2005 the Scottish Executive published a report outlining plans for the reform of bail and remand. These went beyond the recommendations of the Sentencing Commission, and provisions were included in the Criminal Proceedings

Etc (Reform) (Scotland) Bill[1] to restrict the granting of bail for serious repeat offenders and to introduce the option of drug testing and treatment as a condition of bail. The Bill also proposes inserting three new sections into the 1995 *Criminal Procedure (Scotland) Act* which stipulated in legislation the factors currently set out in caselaw to which courts must have regard when considering whether or not to grant bail. This follows a recommendation of the Sentencing Commission.

The Commission recommended formalising in statute the existing practice of courts granting bail where it is not opposed by the Crown. The Executive rejected this recommendation and preferred to emphasise the discretion of the court. The Bill also increases the maximum penalties available for those who breach bail. The Commission report made no recommendations on this point.

Report 2: Early Release from Prison and Supervision of Prisoners on their Release

The Commission took the view that the existing law governing early release was complex and widely misunderstood. The Commission sought to make proposals that brought greater clarity, simplicity and transparency to the law. During the course of the Commission's work, the Scottish Parliament passed the *Management of Offenders (Scotland) Act* 2005[2] which, among other provisions, introduced licence conditions and the possibility of supervision for short-term sex offenders released at the half-way point of their sentence. The Commission was also aware that Scottish Ministers had made public statements to the effect that automatic, unconditional early release must end.

Briefly, the existing law is that short-term prisoners (those serving less than four years in custody) are released automatically and without conditions at the half-way point of their sentence. Long-term prisoners (those serving four years and over) become eligible for early release by the Parole Board at the half-way point of their sentence and are automatically released on licence on reaching the two-thirds point of their sentence. There are separate arrangements for extended sentences and for life sentences, but as no changes to these were proposed by either the Commission or the later Bill, they will not be discussed further here.

Commission recommendations

The Commission recommended that prisoners serving less than 12 months should serve their sentence in full. These prisoners would, however, be eligible for release under a Home Detention Curfew at the half-way point of their sentence. Where the prisoner serving a sentence of less than 12 months "presents a substantial risk of re-offending and causing harm to the public", the Commission recommended that the Scottish Ministers should be given the power to retain the prisoner in custody until the end of his or her sentence.

For prisoners sentenced to 12 months and over, the sentence would be split into a custody part, which is defined as the minimum custodial period required for punishment, deterrence and public protection, and a community part, which should normally represent a fixed proportion of the custody part (the exact amount was not specified). The Commission further recommended that the court should be given the power to order a shorter community part or no community part.

Custodial Sentences and Weapons Bill

This Bill proposes that all custodial sentences of less than 15 days should be served in full. Sentences of 15 days and over should be in two parts, a custody part and a community part. The custody part is intended to satisfy the requirements for retribution and deterrence, but explicitly not the protection of the public: "In specifying a custody part, the court must ignore any period of confinement which may be necessary for the protection of the public".

The custody part must be 50 per cent, unless the seriousness of the offence, previous convictions, and the nature and timing of the guilty plea require a greater proportion of the sentence to be spent in custody (and in this case cannot be more than 75 per cent).[3] During the custody part, the Minister and the Local Authority must establish whether the prisoner, on release from the custody part, "would be likely to cause serious harm to members of the public". If the prisoner is held not to present such a risk, the prisoner must be released on community licence. If the prisoner is held to present such a risk, the case must be referred to the Parole Board.

Potential impact on the prison population

The Commission was explicitly instructed by the Scottish Executive not to take resource implications into account when making its recommendations. However, the Commission did not intend its recommendations to lead to any general increase in the length of prison sentences, only an increase where this was necessary to protect the public from serious harm. Under the existing sentencing regime, there was uncertainty about whether judges take into account the provisions for early release when passing sentence. Did judges sentence an offender to two years, in the knowledge that this would mean an effective period in prison of 12 months and that this was the "right" sentence for the case, or did judges sentence an offender to two years because 24 months in custody was the "right" sanction for the case? The Commission was not able to find evidence to answer this dilemma. The Commission therefore recommended that Parliament legislate to require judges to "recalibrate" their sentencing so as to take account of the entitlement of offenders to early release under the current system. This recommendation does not appear in the Bill.

There are significant potential implications arising from this omission. Under the current system, an offender who is sentenced to two years will be released after 12 months. Under the proposed regime, the offender might receive a sentence of 12 months' custody plus 12 months on licence in the community. Alternatively, the offender might receive a sentence of two years' custody plus two years in the community; that is, double the previous sentence. As there have been no steps taken to identify the "correct" approach, there is likely to be considerable variation in practice. This seems unlikely to contribute either to clarity in sentencing or to public confidence.

Every prisoner serving more than 15 days has to be assessed to establish whether they are a risk of serious harm to the public. This imposes an immense burden of work on local authority services. Evidence to the Justice 2 Committee from the Risk Management Authority expresses concern that it will not be feasible to conduct tests on all eligible prisoners and that the proposals may result in resources being too thinly spread. This in turn might cause a diminution of public safety. Tata (2007) argues that the Executive has quietly accepted that no assessment will be possible for prisoners sentenced to custodial periods of six months or less and comments that, where such offenders commit offences after release, this may result in further loss of public confidence in community sentences.

If the assessment is positive, the case is referred to the Parole Board. This has to be done before the expiry of the custodial part of the sentence (in fact it should be done before the three-quarter point of the sentence). This will also place a considerable burden of new work on the Parole Board and those who service its work.

If the Parole Board determines that the prisoner presents a risk of serious harm to the public, the prisoner will be retained in custody with interim review dates depending on the total length of sentence, up to the end of the total custody and community sentence passed by the court.

This brief comparison of the main proposals in the Bill and the recommendations from the Sentencing Commission show that the Executive paid scant attention to the Commission's recommendations. Most of the submissions received by the Justice 2 Committee of the Scottish Parliament during their consideration of this Bill have been critical of the draft legislation.[4]

Report 3: Basis on which Fines are Determined

This report noted that the proportionate use of the fine had declined in Scotland from 71 per cent of all disposals in 1999 to 64 per cent of all disposals in 2003 (the gap being taken up by custodial sentences at 3 per cent and community sanctions at 4 per cent), but did not see much scope for increasing the use of the fine. The Commission recommended that fines should not be imposed on offenders who can demonstrate by way of verifiable information that they have an extremely low level of income, and on whom the imposition of a fine would create an unreasonable burden (the Commission did not attempt to define either "extremely low level of income" or "unreasonable burden"). For these cases, the Commission recommended that a Supervised Attendance Order (SAO) should be imposed. SAOs should also be imposed as an alternative to prison on those in default of a fine up to the value of £5000. Imprisonment, to a maximum of three months, should be imposed by the court for breach of an SAO where the court considers that imprisonment is the proportionate sanction. The Commission also took the view that guidelines would be of use to sentencers in deciding whether to impose a fine and, if so, what fine to impose.

Report 4: The Scope to Improve Consistency in Sentencing

The Commission accepted that, while there was limited empirical evidence demonstrating the existence of inconsistency in sentencing in Scotland, there was significant anecdotal evidence of inconsistency and a widespread perception among the public of inconsistency. This had led to a lack of public confidence in sentencing. The Commission thus took the view that there was a need for a framework of sentencing guidelines that would promote greater consistency in sentencing.

The Court of Appeal has long had the power to pass guideline judgments, but has not used this power. The Commission recommended that guideline judgments should continue to be issued by the Court of Appeal, but that the Court should be assisted by the establishment of a new body, the Advisory Panel on Sentencing in Scotland (APSS). The APSS should have around 10 members drawn from the judiciary, the legal profession and those with wider expertise in criminal justice. An official from the Scottish Executive should attend meetings of the APSS as an observer. The APSS should draft guidelines for the Appeal Court, which would have the power to approve or reject the guidelines. The guidelines would be voluntary, but the Commission recommended that judges be required to have regard to the guidelines and to state at the time of sentencing their reasons for any departure from the guidelines. The Commission also recommended that the APSS should give priority to guidelines on those offences that normally result in the imposition of a custodial sentence and to areas of criminal conduct in which it is considered that there is a particular need for sentencing guidelines. The APSS should, at the outset, promote sentencing guidelines focusing on the seriousness of offences.

These recommendations leave power over the sentencing decision firmly in the hands of the judiciary, as the Court of Appeal has the final say over any guidelines proposed by the APSS. The Court has shown no interest in developing guidelines, but the establishment of this new institution does provide another source of input into the development of sentencing guidelines.

The Commission also recommended that the Scottish Executive, in consultation with the Lord Justice General, should determine the future for the High Court Sentencing Information System (SIS). This system, which provides judges with access to previous sentencing decisions of the High Court, was introduced into the High Court in 2002 after a lengthy process of research and development (Tata and Hutton, 2003). Since 2002 it has been difficult to gain access to the system and to find out how it is being used. The Sentencing Commission was able to conduct some research, the detailed results of which are not in the public domain. These findings suggested that the post-2002 data in the High Court SIS were not completely reliable and that judges were not making regular use of the database.

What sort of institution was the Sentencing Commission for Scotland?

This section is a personal reflection on the way in which the Commission operated, based on my own experiences and conversations with other members of the Commission.

From the outset, it was not clear to many members of the Commission what sort of body the Commission would be or what sort of work it would produce. Some thought that the remit could be interpreted fairly broadly and that the Commission had an opportunity to conduct a general overview of sentencing policy in Scotland and to make potentially radical recommendations for reform. Others were more focused on the specific detail of the remit.

What did the Commission produce? Of the four reports that the Commission published, two made modest recommendations for relatively minor reforms. The report on bail and remand was used to inform legislative proposals, although most of the proposals in the Bill were not recommendations from the Commission. The fines report also made modest recommendations, although no legislative proposals have yet emerged. The recommendations from the early release report were more or less ignored by the Executive. The proposals in the Custodial Sentences Bill are more radical and significantly different from the recommendations in the Commission report. The consistency report recommends the development of a new institution to promote sentencing reform in Scotland. No legislative proposals have emerged from this.

All of the reports were focused on existing legislation and made detailed recommendations, many of which had direct legislative implications. To this extent, the Commission operated like a law reform institution. Recent examples of such bodies in Scottish criminal justice include the Bonomy[5] and McInnes[6] reports, both produced by bodies chaired by senior judicial officers. This suggests that there was a core driving force behind the Commission dedicated to delivering a set of reports that could fit into the legislative program of the executive. This raises the issue of the independence of the Commission. In theory, the Commission was entirely independent; in practice, the agenda was subtly influenced to meet the needs of the Executive. Most members of the Commission became aware of the existence of an agenda, although few knew much about the substantive content of this agenda well before the end of the Commission's work. The issue of the independence of the Commission was debated frequently and vigorously in early meetings and the topic was revisited on many occasions. A discussion of how the agenda was influenced and constructed is beyond the scope of this chapter.

Communication between the executive branch and an independent sentencing institution is an issue in a number of jurisdictions (Hutton, this volume). Barkow and O'Neill argue that communication is not necessarily a bad thing. Sentencing is a highly politicised area of policy. It would be impossible for a Sentencing Commission to avoid political issues. If a government did not like the recommendations of a Commission, there would be little political cost in ignoring these recommendations (Barkow and O'Neill, 2006). The New Zealand proposals for a Sentencing Council recommend that a representative from the executive branch attend the Commission as an observer. The same arrangement operates in England and Wales (Hutton, this volume).

The experience of the Scottish Commission illustrates this point very neatly. Left to its own devices, it is unlikely that the Commission would have produced the same body of work. The subtle influence exerted by the Executive ensured that the report on early release was produced to fit the timetable of the executive. The content of the recommendations was, however, clearly not to the executive's liking, at least on the evidence of the reforms proposed in the Custodial Sentences and Weapons Bill. This case study shows very well how the work of a sentencing institution can be subject to the pressure of political forces. In this case, the executive needed a "tough" piece of sentencing legislation in the run-up to an election in which they decided they could not afford to be outflanked on law and order. As a result, the recommendations of the Commission, which were in themselves not exactly "liberal", were effectively ignored. Sentencing institutions are always susceptible to political influence but they can also exercise a degree of independence. Absolute independence is impossible and the precise contours of independence will depend on local political and cultural conditions.

Impact of the Commission

The report on early release had the greatest public impact, measured in terms of media coverage. The local tabloid press in Scotland was very positive about the report. The *Daily Record*, in an editorial (24 January 2006), described the report as "a breath of fresh air" because it introduced increased transparency in sentencing. The *Scottish Sun*, the main rival to the *Daily Record*, also welcomed the report: "At last the Executive is listening to the moral majority. Plans to make jail sentences mean what they say are long overdue" (24 January 2006). The *Herald*, one of the two national broadsheets, also supported the report but expressed concerns over the role of Ministers in making decisions about release from custody based on risk assessment, as well as concerns that there would be inadequate social work resources to provide increased supervision requirements (24 January 2006). Both opposition parties, the Scottish National Party and the Conservatives, welcomed the proposals in the report as did other commentators, including a former Chief Inspector of Prisons. The reporting in general focused on the idea that, with the end of automatic unconditional early release, sentences would "mean what they said". In fact the recommendations in the report were more complex. It is at least possible to argue that the Commission's recommendations still left considerable uncertainty over the actual time that would be served for most sentences of imprisonment. Of course, the legislative proposals to reform early release and parole, which appeared in the Custodial sentences and Weapons Bill, were rather different from the recommendations in this report of the Commission. The other Commission reports attracted very little media comment or debate.

Conclusion

It is too early to assess the impact of the work of the Commission. The experience has demonstrated that it is possible to build such an institution in Scotland. It has highlighted the issue of independence and provides a reminder that any future institution will have to keep a close watch on its relationship with the executive branch. The Scottish National Party formed a new minority government after the elections in May 2007. It remains to be seen whether the new government will implement the Commission's recommendation for a Sentencing Advisory Panel for Scotland.

Notes

1   For a useful summary of the response by the Executive to the Sentencing Commission's report, see <www.scottish.parliament.uk/business/research/briefings-06/SB06-25.pdf>.

2   See <http://www.opsi.gov.uk/legislation/scotland/acts2005/20050014.htm>.

3   These three criteria are also those which should be taken into account when the sentencer is selecting the overall sentence. It is not clear why the Bill proposes that sentencers should make the same assessment twice. For further discussion, see Tata (2006).

4   See in particular evidence from the Sheriffs Association, the Risk Management Authority and the
    Parole Board, <http://www.scottish.parliament.uk/business/committees/justice2/ inquiries/csw/j2-
    csb-evid.htm>.
5   <http://www.scotcourts.gov.uk/bonomy/reportHTML/index.asp>.
6   <http://www.scotland.gov.uk/Publications/2004/03/19042/34176>.

References

Barkow, RE and O'Neill, KM (2006). Delegating Punitive Power: The Political Economy
    of Sentencing Commission and Guideline Formation. *Texas Law Review.* 84 (7):1973.
The Hon Lord Bonomy (2002). *Improving Practice: The 2002 Review of the Practices and
    Procedure of the High Court of Justiciary.* Edinburgh: Scottish Executive.
Sheriff Principal McInnes (2004). *Report of the Summary Justice Review Committee.*
    Edinburgh: Scottish Executive.
Tata, C and Hutton, N (2003). Beyond the Technology of Quick Fixes: Will the Judiciary
    Act to Protect Itself and Shore Up Judicial Independence? Recent Experience from
    Scotland. *Federal Sentencing Reporter* 16(1): 1.
Tata, C (2006). Custodial Sentences Bill Lost in a Fog of Contradictions. *Scotsman.* 21
    November 2006.

11

The Victorian Sentencing Advisory Council: incorporating community views into the sentencing process

Arie Freiberg[1]

Introduction

Sentencing is as much about politics as it is about law or criminology. It is as much about the emotional, affective and symbolic elements of crime, order and safety as it is about the rational, effective and instrumental aspects of law-making, judging and the disposition of offenders (Pratt, 2000; Freiberg, 2001). Sentencing has a cathartic as well as a utilitarian function (Stannard, 2002) and it is a process that is played out not only in the courts but in the broader arena of public opinion.

The transformation of the criminal justice system from a bi-polar to a multi-lateral process has been evident for over four decades. Until the 1960s, the traditional adversarial paradigm of criminal justice primarily involved two parties, the state and the offender. The rise of the victims' movement in that decade thrust the hitherto "forgotten party" in crime into the justice arena through the provision of support services to victims of crime, such as state-funded financial compensation, restitution and counselling services. Later, as the movement became more organised and conceptually coherent, victims' views became institutionalised through mechanisms such as victim impact statements, victim representation on parole boards and other release authorities and victim/public registration and notification schemes such as Megan's law. Eventually, the justice paradigm itself has evolved to centre the victim in the process through the development of restorative justice forums such as family group conferences, sentencing circles and victim/offender mediation schemes (Freiberg, 2003).

At the same time, the voices of those indirectly affected by crime, the observers, the readers of newspapers and consumers of electronic media, were increasing in volume as the increasing crime rates of the 1960s, 1970s and 1980s were unsettling their lives and appeared to be unresponsive to rehabilitatively oriented government interventions. Pratt (2002) has argued that the detachment of penal bureaucracies from public opinion exposed politicians to criticism from broader and vocal constituencies who could mobilise the media and possibly influence election outcomes. He referred to the growing and powerful symbiosis between the public and politicians as a "new axis of penal power" (Pratt, 2002, p 181) and he has illustrated the force of that power by developments in sentencing law in New Zealand (Pratt, this volume).

The face of sentencing has changed significantly over recent years. Law reform initiatives have been as much the product of quick political responses to moral panics as they have of the traditional sources of law reform commissions, parliamentary committees or other government advisory bodies. Public pressure for change is manifested sometimes directly on the streets, more often through the print and electronic media, indirectly through the ballot box at election time and, in some countries, directly through propositions placed on ballots and similar citizen-initiated referendum processes.

Examples of governmental responses to what has been perceived to be a more punitive public opinion – populist, or popular, provisions – include: Megan's law, Sarah's law and other sex offender notification and registration schemes; sexual offender orders; sexual offender restraining orders; sexual offences prevention orders; three strikes laws; mandatory, and mandatory minimum, sentences; standard non-parole periods; boot camps; anti-social behaviour orders; increased maximum penalties; political disenfranchisement of offenders; transfers of juveniles to adult jurisdictions; indefinite sentences and continued detention provisions; and matrix and grid sentencing.

The historical role of the Victorian public in the policy process

The Victorian community has never been excluded from the policy-making process. In general, the community is directly involved in policy-making through the traditional approach taken by standing and ad hoc commissions and inquiries that invite public comment and that consult widely. In addition, "community attitudes" are indirectly taken into account in sentencing via the roles of parliamentary representatives, as the maximum penalties that they set for offences are intended both to reflect the level of communal abhorrence of these offences and to act as directives to sentencers about how to weigh the gravity of offending in the cases before them.

In Victoria in the late 1970s and early 1980s, State government inquiries into the sanction of community service and the system of parole and remissions sought the community's views on new sentencing initiatives. In the mid-1980s, a Sentencing Committee chaired by a retired Supreme Court judge, Sir John Starke QC, was established to review sentencing policy and practice (Victorian Sentencing Committee, 1986). That Committee sat for three years and undertook an extensive series of public consultations eventually leading to the enactment of the *Sentencing Act* 1991 (Vic).

In its 1988 Report, the Sentencing Committee strongly recommended that a Judicial Studies Board be established in Victoria, arguing that its major benefit would be to provide a structured method of learning and keeping abreast of changes in the sentencing process. Its recommendations were accepted by the government; the *Judicial Studies Board Act* 1990 (Vic) came into operation on 20 November 1990. The functions of the Board were (*Judicial Studies Board Act* 1990 (Vic) s 5):

(a) to conduct seminars for judges and magistrates on sentencing matters;

(b) to conduct research into sentencing matters;

(c) to prepare sentencing guidelines and circulate them among judges and others;

(d) to develop and maintain a computerised statistical sentencing database for use by the courts;

(e) to provide sentencing statistics to judges, magistrates and lawyers;

(f) to monitor present trends, and initiate future developments, in sentencing;

(g) to assist the courts to give effect to the principles contained in the *Sentencing Act* 1991 (Vic);

(h) to consult with the public, government departments and other interested people, bodies or associations on sentencing matters; and

(i) to advise the Attorney-General on sentencing matters.

The Board was not intended to be inclusive of the public, but was comprised of seven members appointed by the Governor-in-Council and included: the Chief Justice of the Supreme Court or another judge of that court nominated by the Chief Justice, who was the chairperson; another judge of the Supreme Court appointed by the Chief Justice; the Chief Judge of the County Court or nominee; the Chief Magistrate or nominee; and two people nominated by the Attorney-General of whom at least one had to be, or had to have been, employed by a tertiary institution as a member of the academic staff at a level not lower than senior lecturer. The Board had the power to appoint as many research officers as were necessary for its proper functioning. However, term of reference (h) required it to "consult with the public". Despite its legislative and governmental support, the Board never became fully operational and was abolished in 1996. It was an idea whose time had not yet come.

Other efforts have been made to include the Victorian public in the policy-making process. In the mid-1990s, the (conservative) Liberal/National Party government conducted a newspaper survey in an attempt to gauge public opinion on the appropriate sentence for a range of serious offences. In 1996 the Victorian Community Council Against Violence (VCCAV) was asked by the government to inquire into community knowledge and views in relation to sentencing. It was asked to give particular consideration to identifying the community's level of knowledge of sentencing, how the community gains its knowledge of sentencing, community perceptions of the purpose of sentencing, and community expectations, concerns and suggestions in relation to sentencing (VCCAV, 1997).

The 2002 Victorian Sentencing Review

Between 1992 and October 1999 Victoria was governed by a radically conservative government that was elected on, and implemented, a strong "law and order" agenda (Fox, 1993). It introduced laws for indefinite sentences and required community protection to be placed ahead of proportionality in the sentencing of certain groups of recidivist sexual and violent offenders (*Sentencing Amendment Act* 1993 (Vic)). In 1994 it legislated to allow for the receipt of victim impact statements and to require consideration of victims' interests as part of the statutory sentencing guidelines (*Sentencing (Victim Impact Statement) Act* 1994 (Vic)). In 1996 it abolished the non-functioning Judicial Studies Board and in 1997 it expanded the serious offender provisions by adding serious drug offenders and serious arson offenders and generally increased statutory maximum sentences for a range of offences (Fox and Freiberg, 1999, pp 6-7). By the end of its term nearly half its prison population was housed in private prisons.

In style, the government tended to be unilateralist rather than consultative. Where it did consult on sentencing matters, it listened to victim advocacy groups rather than prisoners' rights organisations, civil liberties groups and academic commentators who had had a greater voice in the development of criminal justice policy under the previous Labor government. In addition the Liberal/National government had abolished the Victorian Law Reform Commission soon after it came into office. It had little time for institutionalised law reform that it regarded as being captive to the legal profession and other entrenched defenders of the status quo.

The election of a Labor government in late 1999, partly on a platform of being more responsive to community concerns, was followed a year later by the commissioning of a review of sentencing laws addressing six broad terms of reference relating to maximum penalties for the offence of child stealing, sentencing for drug offences and drug-related offences, sentencing options, sentence indication and spent convictions (Freiberg, 2002). The fourth Term of Reference contained three parts, requiring the reviewer to determine:

1. whether any mechanism could be adopted to incorporate community views into the sentencing process more adequately;

2. whether superior courts in Victoria should adopt a practice of publishing guideline judgments on various categories of offences; and

3. the extent to which a proposed judicial studies institute should be responsible for the collection, analysis and publication of sentencing statistics and other sentencing information for the assistance of magistrates and judges.

In 2000, as seems always, there was great public concern over sentencing and strong pressure on governments to increase maximum penalties and to deal more harshly with offenders. The new government saw the sentencing review as a mechanism through which it could develop a public dialogue on an issue that was politically sensitive and on which non-conservative parties could be seen as vulnerable. Being regarded as "soft on crime" was not regarded as electorally advantageous.

After extensive consultation following the publication of two Discussion Papers, the final report of the review was submitted in 2002. The consultation process produced the predictable public concerns with sentencing: the purposes of sentencing; the length of prison sentences; early release schemes; the role of victims; and the adverse effects of the criminal justice system on mentally disordered and intellectually disabled offenders. It highlighted the need for an ongoing mechanism of feedback and review of sentencing that could replace episodic and reactive reviews, usually born out of a penal crisis or moral panic.

Recommending a Victorian Sentencing Advisory Council

In relation to institutional arrangements, the 2002 Sentencing Review was aware of the failed experiment with the Judicial Studies Board in Victoria just a few years earlier, and of developments in other jurisdictions, particularly the United States Sentencing Commission (Gertner, this volume) and State sentencing commissions whose primary function was to draft sentencing guidelines for the courts (Frase, this volume). Public representation on, and input into, those bodies was limited and their tasks relatively narrow. The Review found that a better model for a Victorian body was the United Kingdom's Sentencing Advisory Panel, established in 1999. Although it was set up to provide advice and information to the Court of Appeal in respect of guideline judgments, its membership was broader than that of the United States Commissions and its consultation requirements were very wide, partly in order to democratise the decision-making process (Ashworth, this volume).

For a number of reasons, the context for the introduction of a Council in Victoria was very different from the environment of just a few years earlier and from overseas or interstate experiences. First, there appeared to be a strong imperative for an ongoing body that would have members of the public on it and that would have public consultation, and the gauging of public opinion, as part of its remit. However, the Review was concerned that "public opinion" be properly ascertained, rather than being guessed at through the obvious, but misleading sources of the daily press.

Secondly, the Review found that Victorian sentencing statistics were in a very poor condition and that the State lacked an independent bureau of crime statistics and research such as existed in New South Wales (Bureau of Crime Statistics and Research), South Australia (Office of Crime Statistics and Research) and Western Australia (Crime Research Centre). Absent such a body, a sentencing council could fill that void at least in relation to sentencing data.

The Sentencing Review, released in March 2002, recommended the establishment of a Council of 12-15 members drawn from diverse sources: the judiciary; ex-judicial officers; the Bar, solicitors, prosecution and legal bodies; corrections; police; victims' groups, persons or bodies; academics; and persons involved in social policy or social services. A wide range of tasks was envisaged for the Council, such as (Freiberg, 2002, p 198):

- conducting research into sentencing matters;
- undertaking and disseminating research about rehabilitation and treatment programs;
- providing information and feedback, especially to the judiciary, on the effectiveness of different sentencing options;
- providing information about recidivism rates, program completion and breach rates in relation to conditional orders;
- conducting analyses of different sentencing reform scenarios, including the impact on sentencing patterns and changes to sentencing options;
- providing information about the costs of sentencing;

- providing sentencing statistics to judges, magistrates and lawyers and others, including information regarding current sentencing practice as required by *Sentencing Act* 1991 (Vic) s 5(2)(b);

- assisting the courts to give effect to the principles contained in the *Sentencing Act* 1991;

- monitoring present trends in sentencing, locally, nationally and internationally and suggesting future developments;

- monitoring imprisonment rates and regularly reviewing the direct and underlying causes of changes in the prison population;

- undertaking studies of whether and, if so, how sentencing practices differ in different levels of courts and geographically;

- consulting with the public, government departments and other interested people, bodies or associations on sentencing matters;

- gauging public opinion on sentencing;

- advising the Attorney-General on sentencing matters generally and responding to particular matters which may be referred to it relating to sentencing law and practice; and

- monitoring the implementation of sentencing reform.

The creation of the Sentencing Advisory Council

Statutory functions

In a ministerial statement entitled *A Fair, Accessible and Understandable Justice System* (Victoria, *Hansard*, 18 April 2002, p 993) the Attorney-General accepted a number of the recommendations of the review including the establishment of the Sentencing Advisory Council. A Bill was introduced into the Legislative Assembly in September 2002 (Sentencing (Further Amendment) Bill 2002) but lapsed because of the election held later that year. Two of the primary reasons put forward by the Attorney for the creation of the Council were that it would "allow properly ascertained and informed public opinion to be taken into account in the criminal justice system on a permanent and formal basis" and it would "promote greater transparency and accountability in the criminal justice system and stimulate balanced public debate on sentencing issues" (Victoria, *Hansard*, 12 September 2002, p 206).

Following the re-election of the Labor party in November 2002, the Bill was re-introduced in March 2003 as the *Sentencing (Amendment) Act* 2003 establishing the Council as an independent statutory authority with the following functions (*Sentencing Act* 1991 (Vic) s 108C):

   (a)   to state in writing to the Court of Appeal its views in relation to the giving, or review, of a guideline judgment;

   (b)   to provide statistical information on sentencing, including information on current sentencing practices, to members of the judiciary and other interested persons;

   (c)   to conduct research, and disseminate information to members of the judiciary and other interested persons, on sentencing matters;

(d)   to gauge public opinion on sentencing matters;

(e)   to consult, on sentencing matters, with government departments and other interested persons and bodies as well as the general public; and

(f)   to advise the Attorney-General on sentencing matters.

In the debate on the Bill, the major concerns that were expressed related to the paucity of sentencing statistics in Victoria and the role of the Council in producing them, and the need for guideline judgments and the role of the Court of Appeal in their formulation. The National Party, in opposition, was particularly concerned over the separation of powers: specifically, whether having a non-judicial body such as the Council with a legislative mandate to be involved in the formulation of a judgment would breach the doctrine of the separation of powers. Despite these reservations, the legislation was supported in principle by the Opposition parties and formally came into operation on 1 July 2004.

Membership

The Council is comprised of up to 12 members, appointed by the Governor-in-Council on the recommendation of the Attorney-General: two with broad experience in community issues affecting courts; one with experience as a senior member of the academic staff of a tertiary institution; one who is a member of a victim of crime support or advocacy group; at least one highly experienced prosecution lawyer and one highly experienced defence lawyer; and the remainder are people who have experience in the operation of the criminal justice system (*Sentencing Act* 1991 (Vic) s 108F(1) and (2)). The Council was structured in such a way as to facilitate broad community input and a balance of views. Members are appointed for terms of three years and the inaugural council was selected following an open advertisement calling for applications. The Council was never intended to be partly or totally judicial and has no existing or past judicial officers on it, although the criteria would allow it to do so under the rubric of "experience in the operation of the criminal justice system".

The announcement of appointments to the Council in August 2004 was greeted by criticism from victims of crime groups who protested that the Council was not sufficiently representative of victims of crime (Ross, 2004). The announcements took place at a time of great public anger over the perceived leniency of a recently imposed suspended prison sentence on a person convicted of rape (Strong, 2004; McCarthy, this volume). The major tabloid newspaper in Victoria, the *Herald Sun*, ran a series of articles highly critical of both the Council and the sentence. The Attorney-General's response was that the Council was a *sentencing* advisory council, not a *victims'* advisory council (Houlihan and Ross, 2004), but he nonetheless referred the matter of suspended sentences to the Council for consideration and advice (this is further discussed below). Later that month, the resignation of one of the inaugural appointees due to her appointment to another body allowed the Attorney to appoint the widow of a murdered policeman to the Council, an appointment that was welcomed by victims' groups (Silvester, 2004). Notwithstanding this appointment, victims of crime set up a "rebel" sentencing advisory group, called the "People's Sentencing Advisory Council", comprised of the families of murdered victims and other victims of crime (Wilkinson, 2004). The group did not survive long beyond its initial public statements.

The Council meets monthly and is supported by a Secretariat of 12 staff of various disciplinary backgrounds: law, social science, statistics and criminology.[2] Its work reflects the view that sentencing is more than a legal issue. The Council is required to report to Parliament annually (Sentencing Advisory Council, 2005c; 2006b).

Early in its life the Council agreed to a summary statement of its aim, as being "to bridge the gap between the community, the courts and government by informing, educating and advising on sentencing issues" (Sentencing Advisory Council, 2006b, p 6). It also agreed to a set of guiding principles, which are:

- demonstrating integrity through evidence-based information and advice;
- adopting an inclusive, consultative, and open approach to [its] work;
- maintaining independence in the process of building a bridge between government, the judiciary and the community;
- being responsive to the needs of stakeholders; and
- supporting and developing staff.

Discharging its functions

The principles of independence, inclusiveness and evidence-based policy have underpinned all the work of the Council as it discharges its various functions.[3]

Guideline judgments

Although widely used and accepted in other jurisdictions, particularly in the United Kingdom (Ashworth, this volume), guideline judgments are highly contentious in Victoria, where the "intuitive" or "instinctive" synthesis approach to sentencing has prevailed. The Victorian Sentencing Committee's Report in 1988 had recommended in favour of guideline judgments and a 1990 Bill contained provisions that empowered the Full Court to hand down such judgments, but it was opposed by a majority of Supreme Court judges and did not make its way into the 1991 Act.[4] The High Court has been similarly antipathetic to this more structured approach to sentencing.[5] The Court of Appeal reaffirmed its opposition to guideline judgments and was supported by the influential Criminal Bar Association (Freiberg, 2002, pp 210-11).

Despite this opposition, and the 2002 Sentencing Review's recommendation not to proceed until there was more support from the legal community, the Attorney included provisions for guideline judgments on the grounds that it would promote greater consistency of approach in sentencing, provide "an opportunity for appeal judges to share their collective experience with primary judges and articulate unifying principles to guide the exercise of judicial discretion" (Victoria, *Hansard*, Legislative Assembly, 2003, p 479).

The *Sentencing Act* 1991 (Vic) allows the Court of Appeal, on its own initiative or on an application made by a party to the appeal, to give or review a guideline judgment, even if it is not necessary for the determination of the appeal (s 6AB).

A guideline judgment may set out the criteria to be applied in selecting among various sentencing alternatives, the weight to be given to the various purposes of sentencing, the criteria by which a court may determine the gravity of the offence, the criteria that may be used to reduce the sentence for an offence and the weighting that is to be given to relevant criteria (s 6AC). Omitted from the list of what might be considered by the Court of Appeal, that was suggested by the Sentencing Review, was that which referred to "the appropriate level or range of sentences for a particular offence or class of offence" (Freiberg, 2002, p 216). This considerably restricts the scope of guideline judgments in Victoria and significantly distinguishes the possible work of the court from what is being done in other jurisdictions.

Under the statutory scheme, the Sentencing Advisory Council plays a major role in the development of a guideline judgment. The Act provides that if the Court of Appeal decides to give or review a guideline judgment it must notify the Council and consider any views stated in writing by the Council. It must also give the Director of Public Prosecutions (or its representative) and Victoria Legal Aid (or its representative) an opportunity to appear and make a submission on the matter (s 6AD). The Court is then required to have regard to these views (s 6AE(c)).

Community input into the sentencing process in this respect can occur through the membership of the Council itself as well as through the Council's consultative process. To date, the Court of Appeal has not yet decided to give a guideline judgment.

Statistical information

The sorry state of Victoria's statistical framework has already been suggested. For some years the Department of Justice had issued sentencing data for the Supreme and County Courts and the Magistrates' Court, but this series ended in 1996 with the cessation of the Department's Case Flow Analysis section. It was not until 2001 that a Court Services Branch was established and in 2003 two publications were produced that provided Supreme and County Court and Magistrates' Court data for the years 1996 to 2002. Two further reports were published in 2004. These publications provided descriptive data only, with little analysis.

In 2003 a Courts Statistical Services Unit was created to provide statistical data and information about courts, including sentencing statistics, to a wide range of consumers. The data provided by the Courts Statistical Services Unit often form the foundation of the Council's own publications and research; the Council is thus reliant on the comprehensiveness and accuracy of the data provided by the Unit. The Council's function is not to produce statistical sentencing data but to provide sentencing information. This aspect of the Council's work is intended to:

1. inform the public and others about what is happening in sentencing;
2. inform its own research into sentencing trends and issues;
3. provide greater transparency of the judicial and correctional process; and
4. provide a basis for sociological critique or research into potential law reform.[6]

One of the Council's first tasks was to work with the Courts Statistical Services Unit in the Department of Justice to obtain sentencing data and to ensure their reliability – a task that turned out to be far larger and more complex than anticipated. It absorbed a great deal of staff time in both organisations.

Having satisfied itself that it had reliable data, the Council has produced a series of *Sentencing Snapshots*, whose purpose is to provide information about sentencing trends for specific offences. Section 5(2)(b) of the *Sentencing Act* 1991 (Vic) requires a court to have regard to "current sentencing practices" in sentencing, but little such information has been available. At the time of writing, 30 snapshots have been produced covering the most serious and common offences in the higher (Supreme and County) courts. They provide information for a five-year period on: the number of people sentenced; sentence types and trends; the age and gender of people sentenced; sentence types by gender and age; principal and total effective sentences; and the length of non-parole periods. These are updated periodically on the Council's website and are distributed in hard copy to the courts and the legislature and to other interested parties.

Although the Victorian courts have found reference to other cases to be of limited assistance in considering whether there is error in the exercise of the sentencing discretion, they have started to refer to the *Snapshots* for the purpose of determining whether a particular form of sentence (for example, custodial or non-custodial) is appropriate, or at least not to be considered manifestly adequate or inadequate.[7]

The sentencing monitoring section of the Council's website also provides a major contribution to public knowledge of the operations of the criminal justice system. These data, presented in graphical and tabular form, provide historical and comparative data about the flow of people through Victoria's criminal courts, as well as sentencing trends for the higher courts, the Magistrates' Court and the Children's Court, and trends in the composition of the State's prisoner and youth detainee populations and community corrections populations.[8]

The Council has also undertaken substantial statistical analysis for a number of specific projects arising from, or referred to it by, other reviews, reports or agencies. For example, arising from the Victorian Law Reform Commission's (VLRC) *Defences to Homicide: Final Report* (VLRC, 2004) and from a request from the Attorney-General, the Council has undertaken to determine the feasibility of establishing a comprehensive database on homicide incidents and sentencing in Victoria over the past 10 years. This database is intended to contain information relating to the characteristics of homicide incidents, perpetrators and victims, as well as sentencing and appeal outcomes.

Conducting research

Unlike other law reform bodies, such as the Victorian Law Reform Commission, the Council is able to undertake projects that it determines to be valuable. Ideas for projects to date have come primarily from Council members and staff and from the courts. The Council has made it a practice to meet regularly with the heads of jurisdiction of the Victorian courts to seek their views on the types of projects that they consider to be the most critical.

The first completed project of this kind emerged from concerns expressed by the Magistrates' Court over the perceived inadequacy of maximum penalties for repeat drink drivers. This resulted in a Report released in September 2005

(Sentencing Advisory Council, 2005a) recommending an increase in statutory maximum penalties, although the Council noted that these measures were only part of a response to the larger social problem of drink-driving. The Council's recommendations were accepted by the government and were enacted in the *Road Legislation (Projects and Road Safety) Act* 2006 (Vic).

Following the recommendations of the Victorian Law Reform Commission (VLRC, 2004), the *Crimes (Homicide) Act* 2005 (Vic) abolished the partial defence of provocation for homicides committed after 22 November 2005. Defendants charged with a murder committed after that date have lost the right to raise the partial defence of provocation, which previously would have reduced a conviction of murder to manslaughter. Judges now have to consider the relevance of any provocative conduct on the part of the deceased in determining an appropriate sentence for the crime of murder, which is a more serious offence. One of the Council's projects examines how provocation has featured in sentencing decisions for non-fatal offences in Victoria and for homicide in jurisdictions where the substantive defence of provocation has been abolished, and looks at interstate and international authorities to extract the sentencing principles that have been applied in such instances.

Gauging public opinion

One of the Attorney-General's terms of reference to the Sentencing Review queried whether there were mechanisms that could more adequately incorporate "community views" into the sentencing process. The relationship between politics, public opinion and the development of sentencing policy is problematic and intriguing.

The 2002 Sentencing Review noted (Freiberg, 2002, p 188):

> Accurately determining the "community's views" on any issue, let alone sentencing, is a difficult task and there are many professional organisations whose job it is to ascertain it. Whether for political parties, commercial organisations, lobby groups or others, it is understood that good policy and successful marketing strategies must be founded on sound, scientific methods. These require both quantitative and qualitative data, an understanding of the nature of the sampling process and accepted tools of analysis.

> Public opinion polls often fail these simple requirements. Simplistic, unscientific surveys can result in spurious or inaccurate conclusions regarding the community's views, but these are often used by the media and others to demonstrate support for their particular policies. It is not difficult to manipulate public opinion by the use of poorly framed questions, simplistic scenarios and unrepresentative samples.

The Review suggested that the development of sentencing policy required a system that permitted "properly informed" and "properly ascertained" public opinion to be taken into account. "Properly informed" meant that respondents should be aware of the reality of crime and punishment, and "properly ascertained" required the use of some scientific methodology (Freiberg, 2002, p 190).

Section 108C(1)(d) of the *Sentencing Act* 1991 (Vic) requires the Council to gauge public opinion. One of the Council's first projects in this area was to undertake research that aimed to describe the current state of knowledge about public opinion on sentencing and to identify the methods by which public opinion could be measured (Sentencing Advisory Council, 2006b, p 21). This resulted in the publication entitled *Myths and Misconceptions: Public Opinion versus Public Judgment about Sentencing* (Gelb, 2006; Gelb, this volume). The paper was circulated to all members of the Victorian judiciary and all members of Parliament. The research has been presented at a number of conferences and the research paper has proved very popular in both print and electronic versions.

In undertaking almost every one of its references, the Council engages with the public generally, with victims' groups and with professional groups, and through these processes obtains feedback on a range of general and specific issues. In this way, the views of segments of the public can be ascertained and, over time, these can be aggregated into a broader and more nuanced understanding of the range and complexity of community views on a variety of sentencing issues.

The Council regards the measurement of "community attitudes" or "public opinion" as a reciprocal and ongoing exercise. As noted above, public opinion that is useful for the development of public policy should be properly informed. The Council thus sees public education as a critical aspect of its work. It aims to achieve this goal in a number of ways.

The Council's website is the major mechanism by which it disseminates information. The site provides information about sentencing in Victoria in a simple, structured and accessible manner as well as providing its publications free of charge. The information provided relates to the principles of sentencing, sentencing factors, the range of sentencing options, the court system, guideline judgments, the sex offenders register, the parole system, victims of crime and sentencing, and sentencing statistics for the higher courts, the Magistrates' Court and the Children's Court. It also provides responses to frequently asked questions and provides links to other similar organisations, services for victims of crime and relevant publications. The website has proved popular and in 2005-06 over 17,000 individual visits had been made (Sentencing Advisory Council, 2006b, p 24).

The Council has created an interactive exercise entitled "You be the Judge" that is aimed at improving participants' understanding of the sentencing process and its complexities. The session takes the form of the presentation of a brief vignette, based on a real case in the courts, to which the audience is invited to respond by imposing a sentence and indicating briefly the reasons behind their decision. The Socratic discussion that follows, supported by written materials and a Powerpoint presentation, examines the factors that a judge must consider when imposing sentence and the difficulties in reconciling the various needs of the state, the defendant and the victim, not to mention the various aims of sentencing (Sentencing Advisory Council, 2006b, p 23). This exercise has been presented in schools, for community groups, for victim and offender support services, for teachers and for the general public during events such as Law Week in Victoria, which is a community legal education program that is conducted every year.

As the reach of this personal exercise is, of necessity, limited, the Council has explored with professional organisations how the session could be developed and incorporated into high school curricula. Ideally, the session could be run online and interactively.

Consulting on sentencing matters

Unlike the United Kingdom Sentencing Advisory Panel, which is required by law to obtain and consider the views of bodies approved by the Lord Chancellor after consultation with the Home Secretary and the Lord Chief Justice (*Criminal Justice Act* 2003 (UK) s 171(3)(a)), the Council is not statutorily required to consult with any persons or bodies. However, the Council's consultative processes have been developed over the three years of its operation to ensure that it obtains a wide range of views on its work.

As would be expected in a relatively small jurisdiction, where the "usual suspects" of those who work in the criminal justice system are relatively well known to each other, the Council has established strong links with a range of organisations that are regularly consulted. These include: the Criminal Bar Association; the Law Institute of Victoria; Victoria Police; Victoria Legal Aid; the Director of Public Prosecutions; the Federation of Community Legal Centres; Youthlaw; various community legal services; the Mental Health Legal Service; victims of crime organisations; Victorian Centres Against Sexual Assault; drug and alcohol services and many others. The Council also consults with other government organisations involved in sentencing, particularly Corrections Victoria, and with judicial officers, both formally and informally. Consultees' views are usually extensively reflected in the Council's reports, even if their specific recommendations have not been adopted.

One group that has not been extensively consulted is offenders, past and present, which is surprising, given that sentencing is ultimately concerned with the disposition of offenders. In its reference on sentence indication schemes and sentence discounts, the Council has surveyed offenders on their experiences with, and attitudes to, these issues and has formalised its links with the Victorian Association for the Care and Resettlement of Offenders, which works with, though does not represent, offenders.

The process undertaken in relation to the contentious suspended sentence reference well illustrates the Council's approach to consultation. The Council first released a preliminary Information Paper, followed by a Discussion Paper that invited public comment. This took the form of several community fora around the State, as well as a series of specialist round tables that focused on issues such as offenders with a mental illness or intellectual disability, offenders with drug and alcohol problems, young offenders and sex offenders. In addition, focus groups were held with victims of crime and with representatives of victims, and there were also individual meetings with interested people. The Council's website also contains the facility for people to make either general comments or specific submissions on a particular project.

The Council employs a full-time Community Engagement Officer whose role is to ensure that all of these consultation activities are effective, innovative and reach as broadly as possible to all interested groups. As well, the Community Engagement Officer is responsible for the Council's public education programs, making sure that, wherever possible, the opinions it gleans through consultations are well informed. It is also conscious of the vast gap that can exist between the often obscure language of the law and public understanding of the criminal justice system. To ameliorate this difficulty, the Council tries to ensure that its documentation is both accessible and comprehensible to a non-legal audience. This often entails publication of different versions of documents with different levels of detail.

Advising the Attorney-General

The Attorney-General may seek advice from the Council on matters relating to sentencing but he cannot compel the Council to provide it. The Council has proved to be a useful addition to the array of advisory bodies available to the Attorney, including his own department, the Victorian Law Reform Commission and the Parliamentary Law Reform Committee. As a continuing body it can, and has, built up the expertise to deal with a narrower range of issues than is dealt with by more comprehensive law reform bodies; as a body with statutory independence, it may have more legitimacy than internal governmental agencies.

As discussed above, sentencing reform is sometimes the product of moral panics (Cohen, 2002) and scandals. These events provide the worst possible context for law reform, whether they relate to child sexual abuse, drug use, gang warfare, asylum seekers, child killers or inadequate sentencing. As Pratt has argued in this volume, penal populism can create a cycle of controversy, panic or alarm, political reaction, more controversy or alarm, ad hoc responses, legislative intervention, dismay at the failure of the (ill-considered) responses, more panic, more interventions and so on until some more rational or effective response is developed (or another moral panic supersedes the previous one). In the sometimes heated political environment in which debates about sentencing policy may take place, the Council can play a useful role in defusing issues by taking on conten-tious matters and considering them in a calmer atmosphere and over a longer period when some of the emotion produced by the original event has dissipated.

The Attorney has sought advice from the Council on six matters between 2004 and mid-2007: suspended sentences, sentence indication and sentence discounts, sentencing trends for homicide cases, continuing detention for high-risk offenders, maximum penalties for preparatory offences and maximum penalties for the offence of negligently causing serious injury. The first of these references was the result of public concern over a suspended sentence of imprisonment for rape[9] that resulted in a protest by several thousand people on the steps of Parliament House with calls for mandatory minimum sentences and the restriction or abolition of suspended sentences. This occurred almost immediately after the Council had started operating.

The 2002 Sentencing Review had examined the use of suspended sentences in Victoria (Freiberg, 2002, ch 4) and had recommended their abolition – a recommendation that the Attorney-General had rejected at the time. However, in August 2004, the public mood had changed, or at least the public mood as represented by some of the media, and the Attorney's reference requested advice on the current use of suspended sentences and whether "reported community concerns about their operation" indicated a need for reform, and if so, what those reforms might be. The Attorney expressed particular interest in the views of the community, including victims of crime, on this issue (Sentencing Advisory Council, 2006b, p 11), thus reflecting the original purpose of the Council as a mechanism for incorporating community views into the development of sentencing policy.

The Council's response involved extensive community and professional consultation, including meetings with victims' groups, which resulted in the publication of an Interim Report (Sentencing Advisory Council, 2005b). After extensive community debate on this report, the Council released Part I of a Final Report (Sentencing Advisory Council, 2006a) that dealt with restrictions on the use of suspended sentences but left open the question of wider reforms to the sentencing options currently available to the courts. The Part 1 recommendations were, to a large extent, enacted in the *Sentencing (Suspended Sentences) Act* 2006 (Vic).

The Council's second request from the Attorney was on sentence indication and specified sentence discounts. The issue of sentence indication had initially been referred to the 2002 Sentencing Review, but had ultimately been withdrawn from its consideration. The Attorney noted that there was substantial support for such processes and that they were seen as ways of improving criminal procedure, in particular for victims of sexual assault (Sentencing Advisory Council, 2007a).

Another request related to the highly contentious issue of continuing detention of offenders who have completed their sentence but who are considered to continue to pose a serious risk to the community if released. This issue emerged from public concern over the release, or pending release, of notorious offenders who had been characterised by some elements of the media as "fiends" and "monsters", and from the example set by other jurisdictions that had recently enacted similar legislation to deal with such cases (*Dangerous Prisoners (Sexual Offenders) Act* 2003 (Qld); *Crimes (Serious Sex Offenders) Act* 2006 (NSW); *Dangerous Sexual Offenders Act* 2006 (WA)). Although Victorian law already had provisions for incarcerating dangerous sexual and violent offenders indefinitely (*Sentencing Act* 1991 (Vic) s 18A) and for monitoring child-sex offenders following their release from prison (*Serious Sex Offenders Monitoring Act* 2005 (Vic)), the issue was whether further powers were needed in relation to such offenders. Once again, a request to the Council was seen as a mechanism by which highly contentious issues could be carefully considered over a longer period and in a more temperate environment (Sentencing Advisory Council, 2007b; Gelb, 2007).

Another reference before the Council related to maximum penalties for preparatory offences such as being armed with criminal intent, loitering with intent to commit an indictable offence and going equipped to steal. The project arose from concerns by Victoria Police about recent court rulings relating to these offences and about the perceived inadequacy of the sentences imposed. This reference was indicative of the fine line that the Council has to tread between providing advice as to substantive criminal law questions (that is, the nature and adequacy of these offences as preventive tools) and providing advice on specific sentencing issues (whether changing the maximum penalties would have a deterrent or incapacitative effect). In the case of preparatory offences, the Council recommended against any changes in the statutory maximum penalties (Sentencing Advisory Council, 2007c).

Conclusion

The Victorian Sentencing Advisory Council is an innovative organisation performing the functions of a specialised law reform commission, bureau of statistics, sentencing guidelines panel and public education body combined. It was designed for a particular polity, at a particular time to deal with both local and broader issues of sentencing policies and practice. It is a body that is able to see sentencing as a wider matter than simply the pronouncements of judicial officers in court. To that extent, it reflects a criminological, rather than legal, view of the sentencing process.

The Council is an experiment in the incorporation and institutionalisation of diverse voices in the development of sentencing policy, both through its constitution and its processes. Though such a body can never be truly representative, its representation is wider than many similar councils and its legitimacy, if it has some, derives from this diversity. It also derives from the perhaps vain attempt to ground sentencing policy in empirical evidence, research, thorough and considered deliberation of options and respectful consideration of professional and community views.

In operation for only three years, it is too early to evaluate the success of the Council in terms of its own goals and statutory purposes. If legitimacy and usefulness are to be measured by references to the Council made in the press, by formal requests arising from government, by the legislative implementation of its recommendations and by the proposed referral of contentious issues by both sides of politics, then the Council has succeeded in occupying a hitherto vacant space in the political and social discourse on sentencing.

Notes

1   Chair, Sentencing Advisory Council. Some of the material in this chapter is drawn from the Sentencing Advisory Council's Annual Reports and the Council's website. The views expressed in this chapter are personal and do not purport to represent the views of the other members of the Council.

2   A Chief Executive Officer, a criminologist, four legal officers, two statistical officers, a community engagement officer, a publications officer and two administrative support staff.

3   Though the Council is statutorily independent of government in the sense that Council members are appointed by the Governor-in-Council for fixed terms, Secretariat staff members are appointed under public service conditions and the Chief Executive Officer is responsible to the Director of Court Services, a senior executive officer in the Department of Justice. Funding is provided by that Department.

4   See also *Ngui & Tiong* [2000] VSCA 78.

5   *Wong & Leung* [1999] HCA 64; *Makarian* (2005) 79 ALJR 1048.

6   For further information, see the SAC website: Sentencing Statistics.

7   *Bangard* [2006] VSCA 313; *Fevaleaki* [2006] VSCA 212; *Ioane* [2006] VSCA 84; *Ross* [2006] VSCA 223.

8   All these pages can be accessed at the Council's website: <www.sentencingcouncil. vic.gov.au>.

9   *Sims* [2004] VSCA 129.

References

Cohen, S (2002). *Folk Devil and Moral Panics*. 3rd ed, London: Routledge.

Fox, R (1993). Victoria Turns to the Right in Sentencing Reform: The *Sentencing Amendment Act* 1993 (Vic). *Criminal Law Journal* 17(6): 394.

Fox, R and Freiberg, A (1999). *Sentencing: State and Federal Law in Victoria*. 2nd ed, Melbourne: Oxford University Press.

Freiberg, A (2001). Affective vs Effective Justice: Instrumentalism and Emotionalism in Criminal Justice. *Punishment and Society* 3: 265.

Freiberg, A (2002). *Pathways to Justice: Sentencing Review*. Melbourne: Department of Justice.

Freiberg, A (2003). The Four Pillars of Justice, Review essay on *Penal Populism and Public Opinion*, Roberts, JV, Stalans, LJ, Indermaur, D and Hough, M. New York: Oxford University Press; *Australian and New Zealand Journal of Criminology* 36: 223.

Gelb, K (2006). *Myths and Misconceptions: Public Opinion versus Public Judgment about Sentencing*. Melbourne: Sentencing Advisory Council.

Gelb, K (2007). *Recidivism of Sex Offenders: Research Paper*. Melbourne: Sentencing Advisory Council.

Houlihan, L and Ross, N (2004). Lack of Voice Angers Victims. *Herald Sun*, 4 August.

Pratt, J (2000). Emotive and Ostentatious Punishment. *Punishment and Society* 2(4): 417.

Pratt, J (2002). *Punishment and Civilisation*. London: Sage Publications.

Ross, N (2004). Crime Victims Left Standing in the Wings. *Herald Sun*, 3 August.

Sentencing Advisory Council (2005a). *Maximum Penalties for Repeat Drink Driving*. Melbourne: Sentencing Advisory Council.

Sentencing Advisory Council (2005b). *Suspended Sentences: Interim Report*. Melbourne: Sentencing Advisory Council.

Sentencing Advisory Council (2005c). *Annual Report 2004-05*. Melbourne: Sentencing Advisory Council.

Sentencing Advisory Council (2006a). *Suspended Sentences: Final Report Part 1*. Melbourne: Sentencing Advisory Council.

Sentencing Advisory Council (2006b). *Annual Report 2005-06*. Melbourne: Sentencing Advisory Council.

Sentencing Advisory Council (2007a). *Sentence Indication and Sentence Discounts: Discussion Paper*. Melbourne: Sentencing Advisory Council.

Sentencing Advisory Council (2007b). *High Risk Offenders: Post-Sentence Supervision and Detention, Discussion and Options Paper*. Melbourne: Sentencing Advisory Council.

Sentencing Advisory Council (2007c). *Review of Maximum Penalties for Preparatory Offences*. Melbourne: Sentencing Advisory Council.

Silvester, J (2004). Policeman's Widow becomes Voice for Victims. *The Age*, 27 August.

Stannard, J (2002). *The Cathartic Function of the Sentencing Process*. Unpublished Paper delivered at the Sentencing and Society, 2nd International Conference, Strathclyde University, Glasgow, Scotland

Strong, G (2004). Anger Pours Out at Rally Backing Tougher Sentences. *The Age*, 9 August.

Victorian Community Council Against Violence (1996). *Community Knowledge and Perceptions of Sentencing in Victoria: A Report on the Findings of the Consultation*. Melbourne: VCCAV.

Victorian Sentencing Committee (1988). *Report: Sentencing*. Melbourne.

VLRC (Victorian Law Reform Commission) (2004). *Defences to Homicide*. Melbourne: VLRC.

Wilkinson, G (2004). Fightback: Victims of Crime Take a Stand. *Herald Sun*, 20 August.

12

A perspective on the work of the Victorian Sentencing Advisory Council and its potential to promote respect and equality for women

Thérèse McCarthy[1]

Introduction

In most justice systems in the developed world, police, courts and correctional services have had almost two decades of experience in contending with a vocal and sophisticated group of advocates for survivors of gender-based violence. Justice systems across the globe are being asked to collaborate in an effort to clarify the role of law and justice in the elimination of this violence. One last bastion of this system, relatively untouched by gender-based violence activism, is the critically important policy site of sentencing. Here, the struggle for harsher or more lenient sentences plays with monotony in the background of what could be a far more informed, just and fair discussion focused on the role of sentencing, of punishment, of rehabilitation and of denunciation in the prevention and elimination of gender-based violence. Before us now is the challenge to forge sentencing policy that eradicates violence-supportive attitudes, racism and xenophobia in relation to rape and other gendered violence.

This is one aspiration, one sense of possibility for advocates of survivors of gender-based violence participating in the work of the Victorian Sentencing Advisory Council. Formally established in 2003 but commencing operations in mid-2004, the Council comprises individuals with specialist expertise and a commitment to wide-ranging debate on sentencing policy. The Council was established at the same time as significant work was being undertaken by the Victorian Law Reform Commission (VLRC) in relation to sexual offences (VLRC, 2004). In July 2004 the Victorian Court of Appeal confirmed a decision of the County Court to wholly suspend a sentence for a convicted sex offender, which produced vigorous public debate about the perceived leniency of the sentence.[2] Soon after, the VLRC released its report on defences to murder (including a recommendation that the discriminatory defence of provocation be abolished), as well as a report on domestic and family violence law (VLRC, 2006). There is thus a considerable opportunity for the Sentencing Advisory Council to examine the role of sentencing in the process of the elimination of violence.

At the global level, the 2002 World Health Organisation's Report on Violence and Health and the 2006 United Nations Secretary-General's Study on Violence Against Women each make a case for all members of the community, institutions of government and business to contribute to the effort of eliminating violence against women and children. The Secretary-General's study identifies the need for a coordinated and systemic approach to violence prevention that comprises: legislation; activities of the criminal justice sector; economic and social policy; and awareness-raising across the wider services and education systems. Importantly, both studies link prevention measures with more general efforts to secure women's substantive equality. In her 2006 report to the General Assembly, the Special Rapporteur on violence against women focused on the concept of "due diligence", or the "accountability" obligation, which appears in the Declaration on the Elimination of Violence against Women (United Nations, 1993) and which provides that states shall "exercise due diligence to prevent, investigate and, in accordance with national legislation, *punish acts* of violence against women, whether those acts are perpetrated by the State or by private persons" (Yakin, 2006, emphasis added).

Against this background, and in the Australian context, this chapter will discuss the potential for reducing sex discrimination in sentencing through accurate understandings of the aetiology and nature of gender-based violence. Through a critical reflection on some of the current debates and their history, this chapter will propose that potential gains are possible through open engagement between gender-based violence advocates, the judiciary and the community, and that the Victorian Sentencing Advisory Council provides one such mechanism for doing so. The purpose of this chapter is also to explore the potential role of sentencing policy in the prevention of gender-based violence.

This chapter will also distinguish a feminist, gender-based violence prevention approach from that of penal populists. Ultimately, it proposes that significant gains are now achievable through the institution of the Sentencing Advisory Council. The Council provides a means whereby penal populism can be challenged at the same time that sentencing practice can be more actively attentive to gender discrimination in its practice, ultimately contributing to the prevention effort. To this end, it is possible to pursue the goal of "ending impunity" (consistent with the global call identified in the United Nations Secretary-General's study). However, the aim is not to replace impunity with more punishment and retribution. Rather, the work of the Sentencing Advisory Council in community engagement and education can contribute to both informing sentencing policy and altering community attitudes and responses to gender-based violence. The chapter describes the Council's work through a case study of a reference by the Victorian Attorney-General to review suspended sentences.

Ultimately, I take the view that the Sentencing Advisory Council's existence has created new possibilities for reform and dialogue that presage non-discriminatory, inclusive and relevant sentencing policy that takes account of individuals and the interests of the wider community, formerly excluded, in ways that could not and have not been contemplated in the past.

Attempts to use the power of the law to end impunity for gender-based violence

Vast resources of states are dedicated to responding to the consequences of gender-based and other forms of violence. These resources can be measured in the long-term mental health consequences for victim/survivors of gendered violence, the cost of foregone talent/work potential of women and children who never reach this potential, unwanted pregnancy, disability and the spread of HIV/AIDS. One Victorian study found that intimate partner violence contributes 9 per cent to the total burden of disease in Victorian women aged 15-44 and 3 per cent in all women. This violence has also been found to be the leading contributor to death, disability and illness in Victorian women aged 15-44, being responsible for more of the disease burden than many well-known risk factors such as high blood pressure, smoking and obesity (VicHealth, 2004). The United Nations Secretary-General denounced violence against women as one of the "most shameful human rights violations" (Annan, 1999; United Nations, 2006), and the World Health Organisation has now spearheaded an international program to measure the nature and impact of violence on individuals and communities. These ground-breaking reports have each demanded that our focus must shift from only responding to the injuries and harms caused by gender-based violence to a focus on prevention. The United Nations Secretary-General's study uses the term "ending impunity" which strongly suggests that sentencing needs to be considered as part of this global effort to stop violence (United Nations, 2006). Nowhere in this literature is "ending impunity" explained. Leadership in integrating sentencing into a violence *prevention* approach has been slow. It is therefore timely to ask: what is the role of sentencing in preventing as well as responding to gender-based violence?

Much has been done to improve responses to women who have reported gender-based violence. Throughout the western world, women subjected to violence have increasingly had access to crisis services, emergency health services, social support and legal advice funded mainly through the state. Gender-based violence is now widely recognised as a violation of human rights, based on fundamental power imbalances between women and men (World Health Organisation, 2005; United Nations, 2006). In 1987 in Victoria, Australia, Centres Against Sexual Assault (CASAs) were first established to take up the challenge of providing this support, information and advocacy to women and children who had been victims of sexual assault. These centres, along with community legal centres, created a structure through which the collective voices of women and children could be mediated as a means of informing and changing the hegemonic systems of law and medicine that affect their recovery from violence. If one is concerned about the recovery of women and children who have been subjected to sexual assault, it is impossible to ignore the role of the criminal justice system because of its damaging effects and its potential to contribute to the prevention of such violence through denunciation and deterrence. When speaking about the therapeutic function of the criminal justice system after rape, renowned North American trauma psychiatrist Judith Herman said: "if one set out intentionally to design a system for provoking symptoms of traumatic stress it would look very much like a court of law" (Herman, 2005, p 574).

Funded advocacy inevitably led to active involvement in the reform of policing (through the development of the first Victorian Police Code of Practice responding to Victims of Sexual Assault in 1991), to the changes to the Victorian *Crimes Act* 1958 (1991 and 2006), to challenges to the Criminal Injury Compensation system and to the culture and approach taken by the Office of the Public Prosecutor to the management of sexual offences.

By establishing the CASAs, the State ensured that there was a formal mechanism to improve the legal process. Some examples of the law reform projects of gender-based violence activists around the globe over the past two decades include an end to the immunity for rape in marriage and a challenge to the doctrine of provocation as a defence to murder.

Despite a large body of feminist literature regarding the failures of the criminal justice system in controlling men's violence against women,[3] the efforts of support services for victims have been dedicated to highlighting the fact that survivors of sexual assault have always met with particular impediments when contemplating whether they will report to the police. These include fear of the process of going to court and seeing the offender. Sentencing is also a factor in reporting, as many "complainants" are aware that the likelihood of their complaint leading to a sentencing decision is slim. The purpose of engagement in law reform was to improve reporting and prosecution of sex offences, because this is the desire of many women. The most recent data collected by the Australian Bureau of Statistics show that rates of reporting sexual assault in Australia have increased marginally. Nineteen per cent of women who experienced sexual assault in the past 12 months reported the incident to the police in 2005, compared with 15 per cent in 1996 (Australian Bureau of Statistics, 2006). However, the VLRC's 2004 study of attrition rates shows that a relatively low proportion of sexual offences result in prosecution. It reported that fewer than one in six reports to police of rape and fewer than one in seven reports of incest or sexual penetration of a child proceeded to prosecution (VLRC, 2004).

Rates of conviction were also found to be lower than for other criminal offences (VLRC, 2004). In sum, it would appear that rates of reporting, rates of prosecution and rates of conviction have not been overly affected by law reform efforts designed to increase community confidence in the justice system and to end impunity for gender-based violence. Most sex offenders still have no contact with the justice system, and the under-reporting and under-exposure of the justice system to the scale of the harms suffered by women and children makes sentencing policy in this area extremely challenging. For women and children who do not report, sentencing policy has little symbolic relevance other than when they read about a sentence in the media and form a view about the level of justice or impunity served by the penalty. Sentencing practice is viewed in the distant horizon with only symbolic relevance to a kind of obscure but unreachable idea of justice.

However, law reform activity to improve the operation of the system and to reflect more accurate definitions and statements about the social phenomenon of rape has always been an ethical obligation of support and advocacy services. The data provided by the Australian Bureau of Statistics (above) and the VLRC each provide one measure of the levels of confidence in the police and the courts. However, a survey of community attitudes to violence against women undertaken by VicHealth in 2006, indicated that 65 per cent of respondents agreed that the legal system treats rape victims badly; however, this is less than in 1995 when 77 per cent agreed with this statement. Ten per cent neither agreed nor disagreed or were unsure (VicHealth, 2006, p 62). This slight improvement in the level of confidence in the police and courts is encouraging. But the low level of reporting remains a challenge for both feminist services and the criminal justice system.

The success of rape law reformers to date can also be measured in amendments to the processes of reporting and changes to the criminal trial focused on improving the experience of victim/survivors of the justice process. Alternative methods for victim/witnesses to give their evidence (through closed circuit television or behind a screen) and restrictions on the accused's ability to examine the victim on her prior sexual history have each been the focus of reformers.

Interest in the symbolic and the educative power of the law expressed through changes to the definition of consent reflect the potential of the law to communicate non-violence supportive attitudes toward sexual activity. For example, it is now virtually impossible to argue that an unconscious woman could consent to sexual activity.[4] Victoria's criminal law now prescribes judges' directions to juries to educate them about the role of fear in sexual violence – fear that might obviate the victim's physical struggle (so as to give rise to evidence of injury) or physical resistance.[5] Of critical importance, Parliament clarified the law regarding the responsibilities of men in sexual engagement to the effect that "the fact that a person did not say or do anything to indicate free agreement to a sexual act at the time at which the act took place is enough to show that the act took place without that person's free agreement".[6]

As a counsellor and advocate working at a Centre Against Sexual Assault in Melbourne, I participated in the 1991 Victorian law reforms to the *Crimes Act* and criminal injuries compensation legislation. Counsellor-advocates worked alongside police and forensic medical practitioners to develop a Victorian Police Code of Practice to guide police responses to victims of sexual assault at the time of reporting and throughout subsequent processes. Each of these measures was designed to reduce the attrition rates in reporting or progress of complaints of sexual assault through the justice system.

Much later, we took every opportunity to participate in judicial education, and the education of prosecutors and others across the human services sector. These efforts were not simply in pursuit of symbolic goals, but rather were inspired by a belief that the goals of the *Declaration on the Elimination of Violence Against Women* resolved by the United Nations General Assembly in 1993 could be realised in Australia.

As each woman must decide for herself as to whether she can withstand the tests of her credibility and behaviour in court, the question is raised as to what information is relevant to reporting decisions? Almost as a corollary to decisions made by individual men about whether to plead guilty, individual women are more likely to sift through their socially entrenched catalogue of self-blaming mantras (or "she asked for it" mantras in the case of the accused), rather than such relevant data as the VLRC's most recent study that found that only around 14.5 per cent of cases, or less than one in seven reports, reported to and recorded by police ultimately proceeded to prosecution. Would it also be relevant to know that of the 86.4 per cent that went to trial, 44.9 per cent were convicted of at least one offence (VLRC, 2004)?

Most women and children did not report rape in 1991 and, according to the most recent data from the Australian Bureau of Statistics, this situation has not varied to any great extent. In this process of decision-making, sentencing is a very relevant factor. Women often state that this is an important reason not to report the incident to the police.

Many of my colleagues who participated in the first round of law reforms in 1991, now have daughters. They still express no confidence in the system. They are still affected by their work and are outraged by the sentencing stories told in the media because of their lack of denunciation and general deterrence. They have opinions about sentencing, mostly expressed in the form of questioning why any-one would report rape; even if people do report the incident, their hope of seeing any justice is extremely limited. Importantly, and in contrast to the law and order advocates, these colleagues simply call for an end to the impunity.

Sentencing law – the power of the law to play a part in the prevention of gender-based violence

In recognition of the continuing problems in the criminal justice system, a set of guiding principles was inserted into the *Crimes Act* 1958 (Vic) by the *Crimes (Sexual Offences) Act* 2006 (Vic). These require "courts to have regard to the fact that there is a high incidence of sexual violence within society; and sexual offences are significantly under reported; and a significant number of sexual offences are committed against women, children and other vulnerable persons including persons with a cognitive impairment".[7] Also mentioned are the facts that "offenders are commonly known to their victims and sexual offences often occur where there is unlikely to be any signs of an offence having occurred".[8] These principles have guided the interpretation of the laws of rape from December 2006, and also contribute an educative element to the deliberations of those who apply it.

A combination of these principles guiding statutory interpretation, and the requirement that judges direct juries as to the approach they should take to assessing consent, reflect a commitment by Parliament to eradicate violence-supportive attitudes in rape law. The opportunity to carry this logic over to sentencing policy has thus been created. Such engagement with these principles in the law of sentencing might produce no change in sentencing trends in terms of tariffs (for example, maximum penalties), but has the potential to change significantly sentencing comments to reflect an intolerance of violence.

In the course of engaging with the law and challenging institutionalised sexism within the criminal justice system in the 1980s and 1990s, comparatively little attention was given by participants in law reform to the sentencing of sex offenders, and it is this engagement that is now possible through the work of the Sentencing Advisory Council.

Jody Clay-Warner and Callie Harbin Burt, who considered the limited effect of sexual assault law reform in North America, suggest that a strong motivation for such rape law reform is "symbolic goals", with groups "explicitly focused upon the measurable, instrumental outcomes but also on the ability of the law to inform society about the gravity of sexual assaults" (Clay-Warner and Harbin Burt, 2005). This concept of symbolism is well encapsulated by the principles of "denunciation" and "deterrence". These principles, roundly embraced in the *Sentencing Act* 1991 (Vic) (s 5(2)(a) and (d)), affirm an interest in the wider potential of sentencing to communicate to the community an abhorrence of gender-based violence. However, these two principles sit in tense opposition at times to the principles of individual deterrence and punishment. Yet in her ground-breaking work on justice from a victim's perspective, Judith Herman argues that justice, for those whom she interviewed and who had experienced sexual and domestic violence, is "neither restorative nor retributive in the conventional sense" (Herman, 2005, p 597):

> [T]heir vision of justice combined retributive and restorative elements in the service of healing a damaged relationship, not between the victim and the offender but between the victim and his or her community. The retributive element of the survivor's vision was the most apparent in their virtually unanimous wish to see the offenders exposed and disgraced. Their aims, however, were not primarily punitive. The main purpose of exposure was not to get even by inflicting pain. Rather, they sought vindication from the community as a rebuke to the offenders' display of contempt for their rights and dignity.

Rather than a vindictive desire for revenge, Herman seems to be suggesting that, were an abhorrence of gender-based violence communicated through sentencing and the justice system, perhaps the goals of individual victims might be met. It is this veiled suggestion that perhaps foreshadows the real possibilities of sentencing in the prevention endeavour. For example, courts have the institutional power to communicate a message that sexual violence is not consistent with the values of a society that supports gender equality and abhors violence against women and children. Moreover, a court that challenges attitudes that trivialise violence and its impacts would not tolerate violence-supportive attitudes in legal argument or in mitigation. Attributing blame to the victim in a plea might not be allowed (for example, remarks about dress or consent on an earlier occasion), just as justifying rape or providing excuses that diminish men's responsibility would be frowned upon. Could a system be devised where a court seeks to convey, on behalf of the community, "a rebuke to the offenders' display of contempt for victims' rights and dignity"?[9] While some would argue that this is the current approach to sentencing, it is evident from case examples, such as the suspended sentence given to a sex offender,[10] that the community did not feel that this objective had been served.

Clearly, this approach suggests that the criminal justice system still has much to offer to both individuals and the wider community and thus proposes continuous pursuit of reform to this end. Alternative forms of justice, such as restorative justice,[11] are not discussed as they are beyond the scope of this chapter.

Violence prevention, sentencing policy and law and order

In this law reforming context, on behalf of a group of committed counsellors and advocates, I was on a panel at a criminology conference in the mid-1990s that addressed sentencing policy. When it came to my turn, I posed the question of what a feminist judge would do with a convicted sex offender. How do the principles of sentencing apply in the context of such an enormous social phenomenon involving about one in four female children before the age of 16? How should the principles of rehabilitation, deterrence and punishment apply when we know so little about recidivism and when most victims of sexual assault march away in droves from the criminal justice system?

These rhetorical questions were not well received by legal practitioners in the audience. Searching for a way forward, it is easy to offend against very real foundational doctrine of sentencing policy – and appear to engage in "penal populism". The antipathy of this audience seemed to suggest that those of us interested in the prevention of sexual violence, and the role of sentencing in contributing to that agenda, were not distinguished from the law and order proponents of "prison as the only panacea" to offending, the penal populists. Sadly, a gender-based violence prevention message was being confused with unreflective support for imprisonment. A further "crime" was a charge that gender-based violence activists do not understand the gravity with which the denial of a person's liberty should be regarded within a civilised and democratic society.

A discomfort with law and order approaches and annoyance at being conflated with such approaches has led to some of those advocating for an end to gender-based violence to engage in sentencing policy and to insist on key distinctions being drawn. As the "victim-rights" movement and a victimology discipline have emerged, it is undeniable that these social movements have shared some important concerns about the functioning of the justice system. A loss of public confidence due to an apparent failure of courts to "protect" victims of crime/gender-based violence from further social and psychological harms through the processes of justice is also a shared concern. There is also occasionally, but not always, a common perception of the inadequacy of individual penalties to reflect the harms suffered as a consequence of the crime itself, because they appear to fail the lowest standards of denunciation and deterrence. Prima facie, a suspended sentence for an adult convicted of sex offence is one such example.

While there are some shared concerns between gender-based violence advocates and the broader victim-rights movement, there are also some key distinctions. For example, gender-based violence services are concerned with human rights and civil liberties that demand acknowledgement of human dignity, equality and freedom from discrimination. Gender-based violence services would also challenge the sexist nature of the operation of the criminal justice system and its particular violation of women in the course of the justice process. Attempts to change violence-supportive attitudes in the community and to encourage men to negotiate sexual activity with women need clear and unequivocal messages at the point of sentencing that are consistent and that communicate abhorrence of the violence itself. Sentencing tariffs in this respect might be less important than sentencing comments. Sentencing principles, such as those outlined in the Victorian *Sentencing Act* 1991, are entirely consistent with this ethic. However, rather than an engagement with the role of sentencing in prevention or addressing the role of individual victims in sentencing (or whether there should be such a role or what it legitimately might be), a law and order approach has seen some problematic law "reform" such as the introduction of victim impact statements and a further category of "serious sex offender". The risks of victim impact statements are manifest. For example, they expose women subjected to gendered harms to cross-examination and, by implication, seek to differentiate between various women ("prostitutes or nuns") rather than to raise awareness of gendered harms to individuals or their communities (such as children, families, friendship networks). The category of "serious sex offender", in turn, is problematic as it communicates, at least symbolically, that other sex offenders are not as serious.

These are not easy messages to communicate to those in a justice system under frequent attack. It is impossible to disregard the role of the media in this situation over these past two decades. Is it possible to suggest that the media have generated this loss in public trust and confidence, or at least contributed to it? As Karen Gelb has argued, public opinion on crime and justice issues, and on sentencing in particular, is far more nuanced and complex than (such crime) surveys show (Gelb, 2006; this volume). Similarly, it is possible to argue that the role of the media in generating that public opinion is also more nuanced. Perhaps it is possible to suggest that, in the absence of institutional mechanisms such as the Sentencing Advisory Council, the media mediate the relationship between the justice system and the community, sometimes more effectively than others.

It is arguable whether courts can generate public confidence merely by continuing to do their work. The pressure of the media, of politicians and their moral panics, of the increasing divisions between rich and poor, and the increased understanding of the very particular and gendered crimes of domestic violence and sexual assault, mean that states must find new ways to generate dialogue between courts and communities. Over the past decade, a suite of initiatives have assisted this process. Drug courts, family violence courts, the VLRC and now the Sentencing Advisory Council play significant and changing roles in the bolstering of public confidence in a dynamic and changing justice system.

The Sentencing Advisory Council – mediating the interests of offenders, victims and the community

The desire for more effective penal policy occurs within a political context; in it, a sentencing body provides a mechanism for mediation between these interests. When the Sentencing Advisory Council was first established, we debated how we would express our purpose. After much discussion, we decided that the aim of the Council is to "bridge the gap between the community, the courts and government by informing, advising and educating on sentencing issues".

What characterises the work of this Council is the consensus among Council members that there be informed debate. The Council, as is clear from its composition, is a reflection of the community. Just as the community struggles with the ethics of sentencing, the Council grapples with the detail of sentencing policy and practice, and it aims to inform and lead the public debate. The Council also attempts to engage the community in a debate about sentencing policy that is characterised by compassion and mercy, in the full knowledge that if it fails to manage these messages then the media will do it instead.

Members of the Sentencing Advisory Council are conscious that most members of the community have a view about sentencing, not all of it well-informed, some of it reactionary, but also some of it based on very real experiences of the criminal justice process culminating in a sentence. There is a consciousness that the Council can have a positive effect on the workings of the justice system and, one hopes, at the same time, contribute towards improvements in the public's perception of, and confidence in, the justice system.

Organised and informed public involvement in these debates is now possible as the public is already demonstrably and increasingly involved in the justice system, through their participation as victims, witnesses, family, friends and colleagues of those who use the system and who read and watch the media. A commitment through the work of the Council must be to make that involvement as meaningful and informed as possible.

The breadth of the work over the three years of the Council's operation is also important. The Council not only contributes to sentencing policy; its community education role is also crucial to its work. Mismanagement of sentencing reform can result in loss of trust and confidence in the justice system. Alienation from the justice system can be as much of a driver of penal populism as the media and politicians. A loss of public trust and confidence should be of interest, as the relationship between penal policy and crime rates is complicated. For example, any accuracy in measuring gender-based violence is frustrated by the significant number of women and children who have no confidence in the justice system and who vote with their feet by not reporting to police.

The Council fiercely protects its independence. The difficult process of arriving at a result in the suspended sentences reference shows an early example of the Council's consideration of the views of a variety of stakeholders, while ultimately arriving at its own conclusion.

Suspended sentences for "serious" sexual offenders: a test case

In August 2004 the Attorney-General wrote to the Council requesting the Council's advice on suspended sentences. This reference followed considerable media and community debate about suspended sentences after a convicted sex offender was given a suspended sentence.[12] Community interest in the subject was substantial and ongoing, with the main concern being that sentences ought to mean what they say. A demonstration was held on the steps of Parliament where speakers called for an end to the fiction of prison when the offender remained free, which appeared to the community as nonsensical.

The facts of the case seem relevant. It involved a 38-year-old man who committed a burglary, two counts of rape and one indecent assault upon a woman who was sleeping in her ground floor apartment. His "disinhibition" due to drugs and alcohol, combined with an early plea of guilty, "great remorse", admissions to police and no "relevant" priors all gave rise to a decision at first instance that the total effective sentence be two years and nine months' imprisonment, wholly suspended. This sentence was upheld by a majority in the Court of Appeal.

The Scope of the Council's inquiry was to examine the following:

1. Whether reported community concerns are indicative of a need for reform of any aspect of suspended sentences.
2. The current use of suspended sentences including:
   · the frequency with which they are used;
   · the offences for which they are used; and
   · the length of sentences and their breach rates.

3.   Whether the operation of suspended sentences can be improved in any way; for example,
    ·   whether suspended sentences should be available in relation to all offences; and/or
    ·   whether suspended sentences should be subject to any conditions (for example, conditional upon treatment orders).

The Attorney expressed particular interest in the views of the community, including victims of crime, on these issues.

This was the Council's first reference and it represented a substantial challenge to mediate the various interests in the debate. There were special challenges to addressing properly the issue of the sentencing of sex offenders. The Council released an issues paper on suspended sentences in March 2005, followed by a discussion paper in April 2005. Community and stakeholder input was also solicited through a series of public meetings, and meetings with drug and alcohol services, Centres Against Sexual Assault and victim of crime organisations.

Charged with the need to consult with the widest range of community members, the Council conducted six community forums (one in metropolitan Melbourne and five regional locations: Ballarat, Geelong, Wodonga, Warragul and Shepparton). Between 20 and 60 community members attended each forum with participants discussing suspended sentences and options for reform. Several specialist roundtables were also held with legal practitioners who work with offenders with a mental illness/cognitive impairment, offenders with drug and alcohol issues and young offenders.

It is arguable that the very process of these discussions and consultations is a measure of some achievement: to establish meaningful communication between survivor advocates and sentencing policy-makers is a useful starting point. The institutional involvement of the Centres Against Sexual Assault allowed the Council to mediate between a human rights approach and penal populism, thus for example supporting a justice response that treats a young person on a first offence differently from the rapist of a woman in her own home. Harms arising from property crime are distinguished from crimes against the person; issues of safety and prevention can be discussed in the context of the aggregated experiences of women and children that is a product of 20 years of organisational experience across the CASAs. Such an approach readily accords with the United Nations' conception of the application of a due diligence standard that calls for an end to this impunity (United Nations, 2006). However, this approach has also had the potential to take forward the goal of ending this impunity without further progression of penal populism.

In its interim report, the Sentencing Advisory Council recommended the abolition of suspended sentences as part of broader reforms to sentencing in Victoria. After further consultation, the Council released the first part of its final report (May 2006), which recommends a transition phase in the implementation of a new range of orders and the phasing out of suspended sentences.

The outcome of the suspended sentences review provides an example of the reforming possibilities of the Council. The Sentencing Advisory Council's recommendations were accepted by the government, and the *Sentencing (Suspended Sentences) Act* 2006 (Vic) has among its purposes a list of factors to which a sentencing court must have regard in considering whether to suspend a sentence of imprisonment. The Act also created a presumption against a wholly suspended sentence of imprisonment being imposed for a serious offence. The Act inserted s 27(1A) into the *Sentencing Act* 1991 which outlines the factors that a court must have regard to before suspending a sentence, including:

> (a)   the need, considering the nature of the offence, its impact on any victim of the offence and any injury, loss or damage resulting directly from the offence, to ensure that the sentence –
> > (i)   adequately manifests the *denunciation* by the court of the type of conduct in which the offender engaged; and
> > (ii)   adequately *deters* the offender or other persons from committing offences of the same or a similar character; and
> > (iii)   reflects the gravity of the offence ... (emphasis added)

Future challenges

In her 2006 report to the General Assembly, the Special Rapporteur on violence against women described the duty of states to take positive action to prevent and protect women from violence, to punish perpetrators of violence and to compensate victims. Further, she applied an obligation to exercise due diligence to the root causes of violence, thereby expanding the scope of state responsibility to non-state actors. By extending this standard of accountability to the area of violence prevention, she has opened the door to a more comprehensive challenge to the public/ private divide under which violence against women in the private sphere has largely gone unpunished. Moreover, she has highlighted the need for policy-makers around the globe to examine sentencing policy for its potential to contribute to wider social goals of respectful, responsible and equal relationships between men and women. As the concept of due diligence gains a foothold in each nation, international non-government organisations and the United Nations increasingly encourage us to see the challenge of violence prevention as part of the obligation of states.

As the human rights approach to violence obliges states to undertake prevention activity, contemporary leadership in relation to prevention has come from the World Health Organisation, at the insistence of women advocates within the global community (World Health Organisation, 2002; Heise and Ellsberg, 1999; Watts and Zimmerman, 2002). Calls for the law to be involved in this effort to end impunity and to take a part in prevention of gender-based violence are yet to be comprehensively answered. The capacity for sentencing policy to satisfy a violence prevention standard while not trampling on other human rights is now fully realisable.

In Victoria this means challenging sex discrimination in sentencing as well as examining how the different cultural and linguistic groups, Indigenous Victorians and, increasingly, people living in poverty are sentenced. This project will be advanced by the Council's commitment to continuous improvement and engagement with all stakeholders, and the development of new ways to hear the voices of those who traditionally do not participate in such dialogues yet who are affected by them.

The Sentencing Advisory Council must be vigilant in its performance. This is particularly important in the area of community engagement on the topics of safety and security in an environment fuelled by fear of crime and fear of terrorism. The Council will also need to look to an understanding of those who are over-represented, or who face particular disadvantage in the justice system, because alienation from community and courts plays a role in a criminal level of disrespect for people and property, while gender inequalities and discrimination contribute to the prevalence of gender-based violence.

The Council has an important institutional function in relation to violence prevention with which it now grapples in the context of community calls for indefinite sentences for "serious" sex offenders. As the Council contemplates the challenges of media interest in a particular and very small cohort of the sex offender population, it must steer a steady course in relation to the larger population of perpetrators of gender-based violence, mindful of the potential to prevent the abuse of power within existing relationships such as father-daughter, husband-wife and employer-employee relationships.

The Sentencing Advisory Council can also demonstrate, by its intolerance of injustice and discrimination, that violence supportive attitudes have no place in sentencing. The causes of violence are complex; attitudes to violence are not the only contributing factor. However, as a recent study on community attitudes to violence against women suggested, "the influence of attitudes on community and institutional responses are particularly important, since these in turn contribute to the development of broader social norms that either sustain or sanction violence" (VicHealth, 2006).

There is much that remains to be done in preventing the spread of violence in the community. In many respects, the global project to end violence has only just begun. Leadership on the issue must come from all levels in the community, including those active in the realm of sentencing policy and practice. When renowned human rights activist Nelson Mandela launched the world report on violence and health in 2002, he provided sage advice to institutional structures such as the Sentencing Advisory Council to take our work forward into the future when he said (Mandela, 2002):

> Safety and security don't just happen: they are the result of collective consensus and public investment. We owe our children – the most vulnerable citizens of any society – a life free from violence and fear. In order to ensure this, we must become tireless in our efforts not only to attain peace, justice and prosperity for countries but also for communities and members of the same family. We must address the roots of violence. Only then will we transform the past century's legacy from a crushing burden to a cautionary lesson.

Notes

1   The author was appointed to the Council because of her broad experience in community issues affecting courts. This material is drawn from some of the Council's work on suspended sentences, however, the views expressed in this paper are personal and do not purport to represent the views of the other members of the Council.

2   *DPP v Sims* [2004] VSCA 129.

3   See, for example, the discussion in Daly and Stubbs (2006).

4   *Crimes Act* 1958 (Vic) s 36(d).
5   *Crimes (Sexual Offences) Act* 2006 (Vic) Part 2 s 4(a).
6   *Crimes Act* 1958 (Vic) s 37(1)(a).
7   *Crimes Act* 1958 (Vic) s 37B.
8   *Crimes Act* 1958 (Vic) s 37B (d) and (e).
9   Derived from the range of violence-supportive attitudes in Taylor and Mouzos (2006).
10   *DPP v Sims* [2004] VSCA 129.
11   See, for example, the discussion in Daly and Stubbs (2006).
12   *DPP v Sims* [2004] VSCA 129.

References

Australian Bureau of Statistics (2006). *Personal Safety Australia, 2005*, Catalogue 4906.0.

Clay-Warner, J and Harbin Burt, C (2005). Rape Reporting After Reforms: Have times really changed? *Violence Against Women* 11(2): p 171.

Commission on Human Rights (1994). *Adopted Resolution 1994/45*. 4 March.

Daly, K and Stubbs, J (2006). Feminist Engagement with Restorative Justice. *Theoretical Criminology* 10(1): 9.

Gelb, K (2006). *Myths and Misconceptions: Public Opinion versus Public Judgment about Sentencing.* Melbourne: Sentencing Advisory Council.

Heise, L, Ellsberg, M and Gottemoeller, M (1999). Population Reports: Ending Violence against Women [0]Center for Communication Programs. Johns Hopkins University, <http://www. infoforhealth.org/pr/l11/violence.pdf>.

Herman, J (2005). Justice from a Victim's Perspective. *Violence Against Women* 11(5): p 571-602.

Mandela, N (2002), *World Report on Violence and Health*, World Health Organisation, 11(5): 571.

Taylor, N and Mouzos, J (2006). *Community Attitudes to Violence Against Women Survey: A Full Technical Report.* Canberra: Australian Institute of Criminology.

United Nations (1993). *Declaration on the Elimination of Violence Against Women. UN Resolution 48/104 (444).* Proceedings of the 85th Plenary Meeting, United Nations General Assembly.

United Nations (2006). *Secretary-General's Study on Violence Against Women. Background Documentation for 61st Session of the General Assembly*, <http://www.un.org/ womenwatch.daw/vaw/violenceagainstwomenstudydoc.pdf>.

VicHealth (2004). *The Health Costs of Violence: Measuring the Burden of Diseases Caused by Intimate Partner Violence: A Summary of Findings.* Melbourne: Victorian Health Promotion Foundation.

VicHealth (2006). *Two Steps Forward, One Step Back: Community Attitudes to Violence Against Women: Progress and Challenges in Creating Safe, Respectful and Healthy Environments for Victorian Women.* Melbourne: Victorian Health Promotion Foundation.

VLRC (Victorian Law Reform Commission) (2003). *Sexual Offences: Interim Report.* Melbourne: VLRC.

VLRC (2004). *Sexual Offences: Law and Procedure: Final Report.* Melbourne: VLRC.

VLRC (2006). *Review of Family Violence Laws: Report.* Melbourne: VLRC.

Watts and Zimmerman (2002). Violence against Women: Global Scope and Magnitude. *The Lancet* 359: 1232.

World Health Organisation (2002). *World Report on Violence and Health.* World Health Organisation.

Yakin, E (2006). *Economic and Social Council: Integration of the Human Rights of Women and the Gender Perspective: Violence Against Women: the Due Diligence Standard as a Tool for the Elimination of Violence Against Women.* Report of the Special Rapporteur on Violence Against Women, its Causes and Consequences. UN Economic and Social Council.

13

Sentencing reform in New Zealand: a proposal to establish a sentencing council

Warren Young

Introduction

In February 2006 the New Zealand Law Commission was asked by the government to consider whether improvements could be made to New Zealand's sentencing and parole structures. More specifically, we were asked to consider whether New Zealand should establish a Sentencing Council to give more guidance to judges as to the appropriate quantum of punishment, and whether there should be changes to parole to ensure a closer relationship between the length of the prison sentence imposed by the court and the time that a prisoner actually serves.

This work was conducted within the context of a broader government project to examine ways in which responses to crime by the criminal justice system might be made more effective. This broader project included an examination of the structure and implementation of community-based sentences; issues relating to bail and custodial remand; options for more effective crime prevention programs; and options for expanding the array of rehabilitative and reintegrative programs for offenders.

The Commission's Report *Sentencing Guidelines and Parole Reform* was published in August 2006 and recommended the establishment of a Sentencing Council to draft sentencing guidelines (New Zealand Law Commission, 2006). It also recommended that prisoners should serve at least two-thirds of their sentence before being eligible for parole.

The government announced at the time of the Commission's report that it accepted the recommendations in their entirety and would introduce legislation to give effect to them. That was an unusual experience for the Law Commission, whose reports have often languished for months or years before they receive government attention. The legislation, which includes a number of significant changes to the structure and hierarchy of community-based sentences, was introduced into Parliament in the form of the Criminal Justice Reform Bill in November 2006, and in July 2007 was enacted as the *Sentencing Council Act* 2007 and the *Sentencing Amendment Act* 2007.

This chapter outlines the background to the Commission's recommendations and the context within which they were developed; the problems that the Commission perceives with the current sentencing regime; the nature of the Commission's reforms; and the reasons why the Commission believes that they will address those problems.

Background

In common with other western jurisdictions, sentencing has become a fertile area of legislative endeavour in New Zealand over the past couple of decades. The reasons for this are discussed by John Pratt in his chapter elsewhere in this volume. Suffice it to say here that the law and order lobby has become more vocal and strident and political pressure to respond has steadily increased. The most tangible manifestation of that was a question posed under the *Citizens Initiated Referendum Act* 1993 (NZ) and asked in conjunction with the 1999 general election:

> Should there be a reform of the criminal justice system placing greater emphasis on the needs of victims, providing restitution and compensation for them and imposing minimum sentences and hard labour for all serious violent offences?

Perhaps not surprisingly, given the multi-faceted nature of the question, 92 per cent of voters in the general election responded positively, which was widely regarded as an expression of the public view that the sentencing of serious and violent offenders needed to be tougher. The new Labour government, elected in 1999, set about responding to that referendum with some urgency. The result was the enactment of the *Sentencing Act* 2002 (NZ), the *Parole Act* 2002 (NZ) and the *Victims' Rights Act* 2002 (NZ).

Notwithstanding the political imperative to be seen to be responding to the referendum result, the *Sentencing Act* 2002 (NZ) in most respects actually took a cautious and fairly traditional approach to sentencing reform. It responded to calls for harsher sentencing by increasing the minimum terms for murder and widening eligibility for preventive detention (the indeterminate sentence available for repeat violent and sexual offenders). It also inserted a requirement that courts are to impose the maximum penalty for the offence if the offending is within the most serious cases of its type, and a penalty near to the maximum if the offending is near to the most serious, unless circumstances relating to the offender make that inappropriate. Arguably, these latter provisions simply codified the common law, but they were a clear statutory expression of the view that all maximum penalties were to be given effect. To the extent that judges might not have been adhering to that view, therefore, the provisions might have been expected to have some impact in practice. However, apart from these provisions, which have now been repealed by the *Sentencing Amendment Act* 2007, the legislation gave little or no guidance to judges as to the levels at which the quantum of punishment should be set; that was left to the discretion of the judiciary in the traditional way.

In one respect, the legislation did represent a significant departure from earlier statutory approaches. For the first time, it attempted to lay down in a fairly comprehensive narrative form the purposes and principles of sentencing. It thus specified the purpose or purposes for which a sentence may be imposed (s 7); it specified the general principles to be applied by the courts (s 8); it provided a non-exhaustive list of the aggravating and mitigating factors that are to be taken into account (s 9); it introduced a ladder or hierarchy of sentences (ss 11 to 18); it created a strong presumption in favour of reparation (s 12); and it provided guidance as to the purposes for which, and the circumstances in which, community-based sentences are to be used (ss 46 and 56). While some of these narrative statements chart new territory, most are simply codifying long-standing principles that would already have been very familiar to judges and counsel in the criminal courts. Their codification did have the value of drawing together caselaw that was previously scattered throughout various reported and unreported judgments and was therefore fairly inaccessible. However, this was not intended to effect a major change to current sentencing practice. Its principal significance lay in the fact that it implicitly asserted that the legislature has primary responsibility for determining the overall purposes and principles of sentencing.

The effect of the Sentencing Act 2002

As measured by per capita prison population rates, New Zealand has always been a relatively punitive jurisdiction. Sentencing trends since 2002 have merely reinforced that reputation. Prison population growth has accelerated in the past decade, from 4530 in 1996 to more than 7700 now. That is an increase of more than 40 per cent and an increase of approximately 25 per cent since the Sentencing and Parole Acts came into force at the end of June 2002, when the prison population stood at 5800. If neither sentencing policy nor practice changes, it is predicted that the prison population will continue to grow, reaching just short of 9000 by 2011.

Disentangling the various drivers of the prison population is always a complicated and challenging task, and it is beyond the scope of this chapter to provide a full analysis of the reasons for these trends over the past decade. However, the prison population growth in the past few years, contrary to popular belief, cannot be attributed directly to the 2002 legislative changes. Not only did significant growth occur before those changes, but in the assessment of the Law Commission there is nothing in the 2002 legislation that would directly account for the subsequent shifts in sentencing patterns. Indeed, the key changes that were made at the upper end of sentencing have only just begun to have an impact on the system.

At the risk of oversimplifying a complex picture, it seems plausible to suggest that one of the primary drivers of the growth in the prison population has been that judicial sentencing patterns have shifted in response to the prevailing political and public mood. That mood has been developing in New Zealand for well over a decade now, observable in the years leading up to the 1999 referendum, the referendum result, the passage of the 2002 legislation and the political and public debates surrounding it, and so on. On this analysis, the legislation has done no more than offer a focal point for debate and an outlet for judges to respond. Quite simply, sentences have been talked up. As a result, sentences have become tougher on average in almost all offence categories, with the proportion of cases resulting in custodial sentences increasing and custodial sentences themselves getting longer. Many would say that judges have responded rightly, because that seemed to be what the public and the politicians wanted. However, what may arguably have started as rhetoric is now having a major impact on the prison population and on the system's ability to manage it. At the same time, of course, it is imposing major fiscal and social costs.

Problems with the current sentencing structure

It is against that background that I turn to assess the problems perceived by the Commission with the current sentencing structure in New Zealand. These problems broadly fall into six categories: the lack of legislative input; the inadequacies of judicial guidance; inconsistency; lack of transparency; unpredictability; and the failure to give proper consideration to issues of cost-effectiveness.

The lack of legislative input

Under the current structure, there is no effective mechanism whereby Parliament can alter sentence levels and thereby effectively determine the overall quantum of punishment. If it wishes to try, it has recourse only to the blunt tool of amending maximum penalties (intended to be reserved for the worst hypothetical class of case of its type) in the hope that this will have some unspecified trickle-down effect on sentencing in the ordinary run of case. There is something a little odd about a system that requires Parliament, if it wishes to increase the starting point of five years' imprisonment for rape cases, to increase the maximum penalty from 14 years to 20 years, in the hope that the five-year starting point may then be adjusted upwards to some degree. Yet this is precisely what occurred in New Zealand in 1993. Furthermore, the lack of legislative input into appropriate levels of punishment results in what Andrew Ashworth (2005, p 57) has rightly described as a "democratic deficit": a central area of social policy is in essence determined not by elected representatives who are accountable for their decisions at the ballot box but by unelected judges who must of necessity distance themselves from the political and public debate that swirls around that policy.

The inadequacies of judicial guidance

In the absence of effective legislative input into the appropriate quantum of punishment, the principal mechanism for directing the exercise of judicial discretion in sentencing under the current structure is appellate review. In particular, over the past 20 years in New Zealand the Court of Appeal has developed the practice of issuing guidance for the benefit of lower courts in the form of "guideline judgments" for discrete offence categories. More generally, appellate review provides a source of precedent that may be drawn on by counsel and judges in determining the appropriate sentence in subsequent cases.

However, judicial guidance, whether through guideline judgments or otherwise, has some significant limitations:

- It is issued by the higher courts (typically the Court of Appeal) and therefore lacks the input of the District Court judiciary (who are responsible for the vast bulk of sentencing) and the wider range of perspective, experience and expertise that would be required to inform sentencing policy development properly.

- The Court of Appeal does not have the resources to undertake systematic research, nor to investigate policy matters such as the effectiveness of different sentencing options and the wider impact of sentencing policy. Although greater research is undertaken, and more time is spent in the delivery of guideline judgments than other types of appellate guidance, they are still largely dependent on the quality of information provided by counsel appearing in the particular case that is being used as the vehicle for each judgment.

- Because appellate guidance is provided within the context of an individual case in which the parties to the appeal are awaiting the outcome, it is subject to time constraints. This means that, even if adequate resources were available, the sort of research that might be desirable in developing a policy as to sentencing levels cannot feasibly be undertaken.

- Because guidance is delivered in the context of particular cases coming before the appellate courts, it tends to yield an unbalanced set of precedents. Serious crimes and severe sentences predominate in such appeals; consequently guideline judgments rarely focus on offences at the lower end of the spectrum of seriousness. Hence guidance as to the custody threshold for routine offences, such as common assault or repeated driving with excess blood alcohol, is difficult to find. The result is that comprehensive guidance that ensures a coherent sentencing policy across the full range of offences, or even those that result in imprisonment, cannot readily be pursued through the vehicle of guideline judgments, or more generally through appellate guidance.

Lack of consistency

Partly as a result of the incomplete nature of appellate guidance, there is a great deal of anecdotal evidence about the degree of sentencing inconsistency between judges and courts. This was confirmed by some empirical research commissioned by the Law Commission in the course of its work on this project (Taylor Duignan Barry, 2006). That research undertook a national comparison across court districts of imprisonment practices in relation to offence categories with sufficiently large numbers to enable a robust analysis. It demonstrated substantial variations in practice that were unlikely to be explicable on the basis of differences in offence and offender variables. It clearly indicated that some courts are systematically more severe than others, at least in relation to the percentage of convicted offenders who are imprisoned.

Sentencing is an inherently imprecise undertaking that requires a significant number of variables to be weighed up and assessed. Some variation from judge to judge and from court to court is therefore to be expected. However, it is simply unjust that offenders appearing before one judge or court should receive systematically more severe or more lenient sentences than equivalent offenders appearing before another judge or court. That is precisely what the existing structure, with its emphasis on individualised justice, allows to occur. Individualised justice, it seems, has become an excuse for inconsistent justice.

Lack of transparency

Because policy as to sentence severity levels, to the extent that it exists, is developed by appellate courts in the context of decisions in individual cases, it tends to be non-transparent and relatively inaccessible. It is thus not the subject of any informed political or public debate. The result is that public acquaintance with the reality of sentencing levels is minimal. Media coverage does little to address this; indeed, one might credibly argue that it is one of the primary causes of public misinformation. The law and order debate is thus conducted on the basis of ignorance, misunderstanding and a focus on atypical cases.

Unpredictability

The absence of a systematic and transparent mechanism for setting sentence severity levels makes the system inherently unpredictable, and thus creates substantial difficulties for the executive in managing its penal resources. In order to determine the number of prison beds needed, governments must of necessity attempt to predict the number of people who will be received into prison and the length of time they will spend there over a planning period of five years or so. That prediction is based on assumptions about the number of defendants being remanded in pre-trial custody and the length of remand time; the number of convicted offenders receiving imprisonment; the average length of prison sentences imposed; and the proportion of the sentences that will be served. These assumptions must be made in the absence of any reliable information about the policies that are likely to be adopted by either the judiciary or the Parole Board.

It is not surprising, therefore, that forecasts have often been woefully inaccurate (as has happened in New Zealand over the past five years) and that governments in various jurisdictions have been confronted with prison overcrowding crises.

Lack of consideration of issues of cost effectiveness

Under the present structure, sentence severity levels are determined without any explicit consideration or weighing up of relative costs and benefits. Given that the determination of these levels is in the hands of the judiciary, this is only to be expected: even if it were appropriate for judges to undertake such an exercise in the context of an individual case (which is debatable), they do not have the information to enable them to do so. However, the inevitable result is that punishment is somehow regarded as a "free good"; it is the only budget item on the government's agenda that is set without reference to cost effectiveness and that is not determined by reference to competing demands. Other elements of expenditure within the criminal justice system (such as policing, crime prevention and access to legal services) are not similarly exempt.

When the Commission was consulting on its draft proposals, the view was strongly put by some that, in the punishment context, it would be inappropriate to take resources into account. It was argued that punishment was a matter of justice and that justice should not be constrained by cost. However, the argument that "justice" should determine punishment levels without reference to expenditure assumes that there is a notional "right" sentence that can be intuitively identified without reference to considerations of cost effectiveness. That is patently not so, in relation to sentence levels generally as opposed to punishment in individual cases. Although advocates of tougher sentencing often behave as if there were no choices to be made in this area, the reality is that there must be, either explicitly or by default. If punishment levels are set at a level that absorbs all additional funding available within the justice sector, then there will necessarily be less expenditure available for policing, crime prevention, access to legal services, rehabilitative and reintegrative programs for offenders and so on. Choices about expenditure within the justice sector (and for that matter between the justice sector and other areas of government) ought to be identified explicitly and properly debated; they should not simply occur as an inexorable consequence of the sentence levels that happen to be selected by the judiciary without those considerations in mind. It makes no sense to ration how much justice society may buy at the front end, but have an open cheque book at the back.

Reform options and the Commission's proposals

In order to address these deficiencies in the current sentencing structure, the Commission formed the view that a more systematic and transparent mechanism for providing sentencing guidance to the judiciary in the individual case is required.

The Commission considered whether this could be achieved by the provision of more, and more detailed, legislative guidance. However, past attempts by the legislature to provide numerical guidance as to sentencing levels, both in New Zealand and overseas, have invariably proved problematic. Section 104 of the *Sentencing Act* 2002 (NZ), which establishes a presumptive 17-year minimum term for murder in specified aggravating circumstances and is the only numerical guidance provided in the legislation, is a case in point. By virtue of the nature of the crime, many murders meet the requirements of at least one of the aggravating factors and therefore attract the minimum term. The problem is that they are often combined with mitigating factors that might otherwise be expected to result in a reduction in the length of time served. In order to give effect to the legislative direction, while at the same time making proper allowance for these mitigating factors, judges have imposed a big clump of sentences at just over the 17-year threshold. The distribution of sentences is thus not spread in a way that would truly reflect the varying levels of culpability. In short, neither legislation nor the legislative process is suited to providing detailed and nuanced numerical guidance that can be modified systematically and rationally in a timely way.

Some of the limitations of the current structure could be overcome by empowering the Court of Appeal (either on its own initiative or at the request of some other party) to issue guidance without waiting for a suitable case to come before it, and by providing it with sufficient resources and access to external expertise to enable it to do so. That would provide the opportunity for better researched and informed guideline judgments across the full range of offence types, without the need for the court to await an appropriate case.

However, the Commission identified two weaknesses with this option. The first is that the Court of Appeal is a body that is select in its membership and thus perspective: better-resourced and proactive guidance would not address the "democratic deficit" problem, nor would it facilitate the engagement of the lower court judiciary who are responsible for most of the sentencing. In theory, this could be addressed to some extent if the court were to undertake a consultative approach to the setting of guidelines. However, the reality is that judges are probably not well placed to consult with the full range of stakeholders that would be required to ensure robust and publicly acceptable guidelines.

This leads to the second weakness: the issue of whether sentencing guidance is an adjunct to the sentencing function, or a key policy function in relation to which there needs to be a great deal more democratic participation by way of accepted consultation practices and, ultimately, a degree of parliamentary owner-ship. Because of the Commission's unequivocal view that sentencing guidance is fundamentally a policy issue, it did not consider it a viable option to leave that guidance solely in the hands of the higher court judiciary.

Instead, the Commission reached the view that a Sentencing Council should be established as an independent statutory body with two broad tasks: drafting numerical and narrative sentencing guidelines; and undertaking related infor-mation and policy advice functions. That body is now in the process of being established and should be fully operational by mid-2008.

The guidelines issued in New Zealand are intended to differ, both in structure and operation, from the "grid systems" that have been employed for this purpose in the United States. Instead, they will in all likelihood be similar to the approach of the Court of Appeal to its guideline judgments and to the approach that has been taken by the English Sentencing Guidelines Council to its work (on whose experience we extensively drew in developing our own proposals). Sentencing guidelines will be developed for each offence type (for example, grievous assaults or burglary) that routinely comes before the courts and results in significant num-bers of prison sentences. They will have a numerical element by providing sentence ranges and will also provide a brief commentary to provide a context for those ranges. At the lower end of the spectrum, the guidelines are likely to concentrate on the factors that are relevant to the custody threshold (the "in/out" decision). The Council will also draft guidelines that are purely narrative in form, covering such matters as aggravating and mitigating factors, the sentencing dis-count for a guilty plea, sentencing for multiple offences, the impact of restorative justice processes on the application of the guidelines, and so on.

The guidelines will have statutory force: sentencing judges will be required to adhere to them unless they are satisfied that it would be "contrary to the interests of justice" to do so, and it is intended that there will be a guideline as to when departure from the guidelines will be justified.

The proposed Sentencing Council will differ in several respects from the Sentencing Guidelines Council established in England and Wales in 2003. First, a majority of the English Council is drawn from the judiciary. In contrast, the New Zealand Council will have an equal number of judicial and non-judicial members. There will be five judicial members – four appointed by their Heads of Bench in consultation with the Chief Justice, and the Chair of the Parole Board ex officio – and five non-judicial members appointed by the Governor-General on the recom-mendation of Parliament. The non-judicial members will be appointed on the basis of their expertise in one or more of the following areas: criminal justice matters; policing; the assessment of risk of reoffending; the reintegration of offenders into society; the promotion of the welfare of the victims of crime; the effect of the criminal justice system on Maori and people from minority cultures; community issues affecting the courts and the corrections system; and public policy.

The Commission recognises that judges are at the coalface of sentencing decisions and must have a significant input into the development of sentencing guidelines. Otherwise the guidelines may well be rendered unworkable for two reasons: they might not be fit for the purpose, because they are not sufficiently tailored to the range of circumstances that confront judges on a daily basis; and they may not have the confidence of the judiciary that is likely to flow from significant judicial input. On the other hand, since the Council's responsibility for developing guidelines gives it a significant policy function, it would not be desirable for it to be, or be perceived to be, a body that is wholly or chiefly judicial. That would fundamentally undermine another of the Council's objectives: to rectify the "democratic deficit". Hence the equal proportion of non-judicial membership on the Council.

However, in saying this we do not envisage that the Council will be a "representative" body. To purport to achieve "representation" of the diverse views of a disparate community by five non-judicial members would be a fiction: the best that those five members can achieve is to offer five views that represent a greater diversity of experience, interests and values than is likely to be provided by the judiciary acting alone. Nor do we consider it necessary to ensure representativeness, as eliciting the range of stakeholder views is precisely the purpose of the public consultation and parliamentary approval process that is required for draft guidelines under the new legislation. In short, we consider both non-judicial membership and extensive public consultation to be necessary, but not sufficient, conditions for the success of a Sentencing Council. Ultimately the purpose of both endeavours is the same – to achieve the community confidence that derives from a sense of enfranchisement – but there are also subtle differences.

The second key distinction between the English Sentencing Guidelines Council and the New Zealand reforms is that, whereas the English Council is developing its guidelines incrementally and somewhat slowly, it is intended that the New Zealand Council will develop a comprehensive set of initial guidelines (described in the legislation as the "inaugural guidelines") that will be subject to public consultation and approval as a package. The Commission does not believe that an incremental approach would achieve the purposes for which guidelines are proposed. Apart from anything else, it would not enable their impact on penal resources to be accurately predicted, and it would take some time for them to achieve sufficient coverage for them to have a meaningful impact. Moreover, the English approach, under which a draft or final guideline in relation to each offence type is issued into the public arena by the Advisory Panel or the Council on no less than four separate occasions, invites repeated scrutiny of individual offence guidelines, with the inevitable media tendency to search for aspects that seem to reflect leniency. In contrast, the Commission is of the view that a package of guidelines that are presented and debated as a whole will mitigate this risk.

Thirdly, the proposed legislation requires that, when the Council produces draft guidelines for public consultation, they should be accompanied by a statement of their forecasted impact on the prison population. This will enable the public debate as to the sentence severity levels reflected in the guidelines to take into account not only what benefits they are likely to produce but also how much they will cost. This, we believe, carries a significant potential to shift the nature of the law and order debate. If submitters advocate sentence severity levels that are harsher than those contained in the draft guidelines, and if the impact of that over the medium term planning period would be an extra $1 billion in expenditure, they will need to justify their views in those terms and engage in a debate as to whether that expenditure is better spent on prisons or on policing, crime prevention, hip replacement operations or more funding for the education system. For the first time there will be at least some prospect that political debates will be conducted, and political choices made, on a properly informed basis. The Commission predicts (and evidence from the United States suggests) that in time this will produce a more rational penal response and that a reduction in the per capita prison population may result. However, that will be a matter for political choice.

Finally, the English Council is wholly autonomous: although it has a statutory obligation to consult with the list of specified persons or bodies, and in practice also consults with the Lord Chancellor, the Home Secretary and the Home Affairs Select Committee, its guidelines do not require the approval of any external body; they come into force when they are issued. In particular, there is no parliamentary ratification of the guidelines. In contrast, the Commission believes that if its goal of changing the nature of the law and order debate is to be achieved, there must be some political ownership of the guidelines that result from the Council's work. The legislation therefore requires that the guidelines issued by the Council should be tabled in Parliament, referred to the appropriate select committee for consideration, and automatically come into force after a specified period of time (30 sitting days in the case of the inaugural guidelines and 15 sitting days thereafter) unless they are disallowed by way of a negative resolution of Parliament.

Although the Commission's proposals have been largely welcomed, there has been some criticism that the establishment of a Sentencing Council will undermine judicial independence. There are a number of different strands to this criticism.

First, the view has been expressed by some, although significantly not by the judiciary themselves, that it is the responsibility of the judiciary to determine sentencing severity levels. The fact that the guidelines may be rejected by Parliament has therefore been attacked as undermining one of the fundamental planks of the constitutional separation of powers in Westminster democracies. This is an argument without substance. It is clear that Parliament has always been able to set sentencing policy (including sentence severity levels) in any way that it thinks fit. From time to time this has included the introduction of mandatory and semi-mandatory penalties that remove judicial discretion altogether, of which the most notable example is the mandatory life sentence for murder. Judicial independence requires that judges should be able to pass sentence in each case without fear or favour, affection or ill will; in other words judges should decide individual cases impartially without interference from or control by any other branch of government. However, it does not follow that it is exclusively for judges to determine the details of the overarching framework. If the legislature is constitutionally able to prescribe maximum, mandatory or mandatory minimum penalties, it is equally constitutionally able to dictate the nature or range of penalties that ought to be applied in the ordinary run of cases. The fact that it has traditionally not done so has been a matter of political preference, not constitutional principle.

Secondly, it has been argued that it is inappropriate for judges to participate on the Sentencing Council, because it will be required to take into account social policy considerations. The suggestion is that social policy is a matter for Parliament and the executive, not the judiciary. On the face of it, such a suggestion is nonsensical: it would be fanciful to argue that judges have no role in the development of social policy, as that is precisely what they do all the time when they develop the common law through judicial decisions. The real concern seems to be a rather narrower one: that the Council will be required to take into account considerations of cost effectiveness and that fiscal considerations ought not to be the concern of the judiciary. However, in the Commission's view it is (or at least ought to be) a fundamental prerequisite to the proper determination of sentencing severity levels that the cost effectiveness of those levels are taken into account, regardless of whether the levels are set by the judiciary or some other body. Moreover, while the Council will be required to provide an assessment of the impact of its proposed guidelines on the prison population, that is merely for the purpose of ensuring that public debate and comment about the proposed guidelines occur on an informed basis with knowledge of the cost and other implications of the levels that have been proposed. There is no suggestion that the Council will be required to set guidelines within prison capacity constraints already determined by the government.

Finally, perhaps the most significant concern is that a comprehensive system of guidelines will unduly fetter judicial discretion, stifle judicial innovation and ultimately result in injustice in the individual case. Oddly, this has never been a criticism of guideline judgments promulgated by the Court of Appeal, at least in New Zealand. It is true that guideline judgments have focused on the most serious offences and have therefore been concerned with fixing the length of a prison sentence rather than guiding the choice of sentence at the lower end of seriousness. However, the principle is still the same; if guidance can be given without causing injustice at the top end of seriousness, it can equally be given at the lower end of seriousness. The challenge is to create a system of guidelines that allows sufficient flexibility to enable judges to take relevant differences between the cases into account, so that dissimilar cases are not treated in the same way. That is a question of how the guidelines are drafted, not whether they should exist at all. The right balance needs to be struck between prescriptiveness and flexibility. On the one hand, the guidelines need to be sufficiently prescriptive to enhance consistency and transparency and the ability to manage penal resources. On the other hand, they need to be sufficiently flexible to enable judges to cater for the variety of circumstances that they confront in individual cases and to experiment with sentencing innovations.

Conclusion

The premise of the establishment of a Sentencing Council is that the quantum of punishment is fundamentally a matter of public policy. As such, it ought to be determined by a process that is based on a much wider range of perspectives and that takes into account a much wider range of considerations than is possible under the traditional structure that relies simply upon the exercise of judicial discretion.

In New Zealand the failure to provide such a process has arguably led to a real sense of disenfranchisement and a perhaps misguided belief that the judiciary who have been responsible for determining sentence severity are out of touch with the public mood. One manifestation of this has been the impetus that gathered behind the 1999 referendum and the overwhelming public response to it.

The dubious merits of that response were matched only by the dubious merits of the question. However, both the process and the outcome were in a sense inevitable: a microcosm of the ambiguity and misinformation that has for many years dogged public sentencing debates that are conducted in a vacuum, without a structure to allow all relevant considerations to be aired.

The referendum and its aftermath, however, did perform one invaluable function: nothing could have better illustrated the need for a different forum and method of conducting and giving effect to the debate about sentencing levels. The Sentencing Council will meet that need.

References

Ashworth, A (2005). *Sentencing and Criminal Justice*. 4th ed, Cambridge: Cambridge University Press.

New Zealand Law Commission (2006). *Sentencing Guidelines and Parole Reform* Report 94. Wellington, New Zealand.

Taylor Duignan Barry (2006). *Variations in District Court Sentencing: Regional Analysis*. Unpublished Report, <www.lawcom.govt.nz>.

14

A sentencing council in South Africa

Stephan Terblanche

Introduction

The South African Law (Reform) Commission investigated the country's sentencing practices towards the end of the previous century. Its findings and recommendations, as well as a draft Sentencing Framework Bill, are contained in its *Report: Sentencing (A New Sentencing Framework)*, published in December 2000 ("the Report"). The Report proposes many radical changes in sentencing laws and practice in South Africa.

Two proposals in the Report lie at the core of all the recommendations. The first is that the basic principles of sentencing should be established in legislation. These basic principles are explained in the Report and are contained in the draft legislation. The other core proposal is that some type of sentencing guidelines commission be established in South Africa. The Report refers to this body as the "Sentencing Council" and this is the term that will be used in this chapter. The main function of the Sentencing Council would be the creation of national sentencing guidelines, but many other tasks are also envisaged.

This chapter focuses on the following six issues:

1. The Law Commission's research method is set out, in order to explain the amount of consultation that accompanied its production.

2. The deficiencies in the South African sentencing system are listed, as found by the Law Commission. This is followed by a brief opinion whether these shortcomings remain, or whether they have been superseded by other problems.

3. The Law Commission's main proposals for changing the current sentencing system are discussed.

4. The role of the Sentencing Council within the changed system is addressed in some detail.

5. An attempt is made to explain why these proposals were thought to provide the best cure for the current deficiencies.

6. Finally, an assessment is made of whether the stated proposals remain the best solution to the problems facing sentencing in South Africa.

The Law Commission's research method

The South African Law Reform Commission is a permanent commission and a creature of statute. The Commission follows a fairly consistent research method, employing various forms of public consultation, especially when the topic arouses as much public interest as sentencing inevitably does.

Initially, a group of knowledgeable people with an interest in sentencing was appointed as a project committee, chaired by Professor Dirk van Zyl Smit. This committee was charged with oversight of research and the compilation of various papers and reports. The project committee continued the work started by another committee, appointed by the Minister of Justice in 1996, which, with Judge Leonora Van den Heever as chairperson, had already produced an issue paper dealing mainly with mandatory minimum sentences and restorative justice (South African Law Commission, 1997). The project committee published a discussion paper early in 2000 that was widely disseminated and backed up by a number of workshops throughout the country.[1] During these workshops the members of the committee explained where the report came from and highlighted the core issues and recommendations, after which those present had the opportunity for feedback and to ask further questions. During the final phase, the issues were hammered out during a workshop involving several international and local sentencing experts. The international experts included people such as Arie Freiberg (then from the University of Melbourne), Hans-Jörg Albrecht (from the Max Planck Institute for Foreign and International Criminal Law, Freiburg, Germany), Rod Morgan (then from the University of Bristol, United Kingdom) and James Jacobs (from New York University). After this workshop the final report was drafted and eventually published.

What should be clear is that the drafting and consultation process was a lengthy one. It would not have been easy, within the South African context, to have had a more inclusive process or to have included more expert knowledge in the process. In short, the Report deserves to be taken seriously.

The deficiencies of the current sentencing system

In 2000 the Law Commission's discussion paper identified a number of short-comings within the existing sentencing system. It is notable that the Commission did not really *find* these shortcomings to exist, but merely stated that they "have been identified" (by others) and that they persistently arise as criticism against the existing system. The Commission only went as far as accepting that there was substance to this criticism. The list of shortcomings included the following:

1. Offenders were not treated equally, but were discriminated against on grounds of race and social status. This allegation is difficult to refute or to substantiate within the South African sentencing system, as it gives the sentencer a wide discretion, with few guidelines, to determine an appropriate sentence.

2. Certain offences are not punished sufficiently severely. This complaint was especially aimed at certain types of sexual offences.

3. On the other hand, less serious offences resulted in imprisonment too easily, when more imaginative alternatives could have been employed with better results.

4. Prisoners were released from prison too soon.

Whether these four points represent the most pressing shortcomings of the sentencing system is as open to argument today as it was in 2000. Certainly inconsistency in sentences imposed for similar crimes remains a major problem. The same is true with respect to the lack of sufficient standards to ensure proportionality between offences and the resultant sentences (this is the basic problem behind shortcoming 2, and partly behind shortcoming 3 as well). As far as the release of prisoners is concerned, any early release is likely to be problematic for the public, especially when it is not accompanied by sufficient information and education. Whether it really is a pressing shortcoming of the *sentencing system* is debatable.

It would be rather easy to extend this list quite dramatically, but one would soon start raising questions of detail.

The Law Commission's main proposals

Introduction

The Law Commission found that an ideal sentencing system should promote consistency in sentencing, should allow for victim participation and restorative initiatives and should take into account the capacity of the state to enforce such sentences in the long term (Report, para 7 of Executive Summary). In its view, these criteria could best be achieved through a legislative statement of sentencing goals (in the broadest sense of the word), combined with a functioning sentencing council to provide sentencing guidelines and collect sentencing data.

Statement of sentencing goals

The principles of sentencing are briefly explained in the Report and then set out in the draft legislation. The general principles have a clear retributive bias. Clause 2 of the Sentencing Framework Bill declares the purpose of sentencing as being "to punish convicted offenders for the offences of which they have been convicted". Sentences will have to be proportionate to the seriousness of the offence, not in the abstract, but relative to other offences. The seriousness of the offence is further refined in the following terms (cl 3(2)): "The seriousness of the offence committed is determined by the degree of harmfulness or risked harmfulness of the offence and the degree of culpability of the offender for the offence committed".

Based on these primary principles, every sentencer should attempt to find an optimal combination of restorative justice, the protection of society and a crime-free life for the offender (cl 3(3)). Relevant previous convictions may moderately increase this proportionate sentence. These basic principles are to be used for the determination of all sentences, whether or not sentencing guidelines have been set for the particular offence.

These statements of principles conform to most modern sentencing goal statements and comply with constitutional requirements as well.

The motivation for the establishment of the Sentencing Council

Why should sentencing guidelines be provided by a sentencing guidelines body, rather than by the legislature, the judiciary or the executive, or another of the bodies that is currently available? The basic answer is that neither the courts nor the legislature have the capacity to do so. To begin with, both suffer from the problem that they are not in a position to have "the holistic view of national sentencing requirements that a comprehensive system of guidelines should take into account". And when it comes to the problem of disparity in sentencing, the courts simply have not been able to ensure consistency, despite a long history of appellate review of sentences. By 2000 it was still considered a core principle that the sentencing court should be left with as wide a discretion to determine an appropriate sentence as possible (see also Report, para 2.6(b)). Appellate review was, therefore, an unlikely source of the solution to the problem of disparity. In 1997 the legislature tried its hand at prescribing mandatory minimum sentences through the *Criminal Law Amendment Act* 105 of 1997. Now, almost 10 years after its implementation, many of the more serious offences should still be sentenced in accordance with its terms. Typically of legislation, it provides a crude system, badly suited for the sentencing of individual cases.

In the end, the Commission came to the conclusion that only a body of knowledgeable people, specifically appointed for this purpose, would be able to develop guidelines to drive sentences to more consistent outcomes. The role of the legislature would be limited to setting realistic sentencing goals in legislation. The judiciary would use the guidelines as a point of departure for the imposition of just but consistent sentences.

Specifics regarding the Sentencing Council

Membership of the Sentencing Council

The membership of the Sentencing Council is recommended to be the following (Sentencing Framework Bill cl 6):

1. Two judges, appointed on recommendation by the Judicial Services Commission (the body normally recommending the appointment of judges to the President);
2. Two magistrates, appointed on recommendation by the Magistrates' Commission;
3. The National Director of Public Prosecutions or his nominee;
4. A member of the Department of Correctional Services, appointed after consultation with the Commissioner of Correction Services;
5. A sentencing expert, not in the full-time employment of the State; and
6. The director of the Council.

These members will be appointed by the Minister of Justice, for five years at a time, after which they can be reappointed. The proposed legislation also permits the Minister to remove a member on grounds of misconduct, incapacity or incompetence (cl 7(5)).

In the interest of manageability, membership of the Council is limited. So many people, organisations and institutions have a legitimate claim to be involved with sentencing that it would result in an unacceptably unwieldy body if all of them had to be included (Report, para 3.2.1). It was recommended that only the core of the sentencing system should be represented in the Council itself. Other interested parties would be accommodated through a process of consultation. In particular, this includes the following:

- the National Commissioner of Police;
- the organised legal profession;
- the judiciary;
- the Commissioner of Correctional Services;
- the Director-General of Welfare and Population Development;
- the Director-General of Justice; and
- any person or organisation with special expertise relevant to the establishment or reviewing of sentencing guidelines.

The choice to select mostly members from the judiciary for the Council is necessarily somewhat controversial. There are arguments for and against this recommendation, but the Law Commission argued that this would ensure the independence of the Council and the sentencing process, and would be the most pragmatic solution (Report, para 2.10).

Functions of the Sentencing Council

The proposed functions of the Sentencing Council are contained in clause 7 of the Bill. The main function will be the establishment of sentencing guidelines. The Council is tasked to take the initiative in this respect, both with regard to the establishment of guidelines and their review. If certain cabinet ministers or Parliament request the Council to establish or review a guideline, the Council must do so. Any other person may request that the Council establish or review a guideline, but in this case the Council has the discretion to respond or not. Other functions of the Council are to set the monetary values of unit fines, to develop community penalties or other penalties, and to create judicial training programs. It will also have to do research and to produce various publications.

Sentencing guidelines

The Report does not define a "sentencing guideline". From the context it appears that "guideline" should be understood in terms of its usual meaning, which would leave a wide range of formats of guidelines from which the Sentencing Council could choose. In a previous contribution, I attempted to give a sense of possible guideline formats that might be relevant to the South African context (Terblanche, 2003, pp 858-82). It is important to keep an open mind in this respect. It is not as if the South African Council will have to produce a sentencing grid or matrix in the American fashion, or any list of aggravating and mitigating factors with numbers attached. It might well be that the English way of setting out guidelines in the same format as its guideline judgments would be a more acceptable approach to take in South Africa. It is always possible that the Council might come up with a new format of guidelines that is not employed anywhere else at the moment. However, the Report proposes that guidelines should allow for variations of up to 30 per cent, indicating that the guidelines should somehow involve numbers.

Whatever form the guidelines take, they will have to comply with the general principles of sentencing, as set out in the draft Bill.

The importance of the capacity of the system

The Law Commission repeatedly stressed that the sentencing guidelines have to take the capacity of the system into account. For example, when explaining the different needs of the various arms of government, it mentions that the executive is always confronted with budgetary restrictions, but must at the same time meet constitutional requirements in executing the sentences (Report, para 1.5). More explicitly, it states that "the ideal [sentencing] system should ... produce sentencing outcomes that are within the capacity of the State to enforce in the long term".

How do the guidelines become "law"?

One of the perennial difficulties with sentencing guidelines is how they should come into force. This question also concerned the Law Commission. In the end it decided not to give too much attention to this issue. However, the draft legislation states that the guidelines must be published by notice in the *Government Gazette* (cl 11(1)). This is the vehicle for all levels of official legislation and notices to become law. The date on which such guidelines will become operational should be specified in the notice.

In the interests of the independence of the Council, it is important that Parliament should not be the body to legislate the guidelines. Parliament is simply too cumbersome for this purpose and too politically driven. Legislation often tends to create imbalances in the whole sentencing scheme, as it tends to focus on certain issues at the expense of the whole (Report, para 2.6(a)). By publishing the guidelines in the *Gazette*, advanced notice is given of a sentencing guideline; it would therefore be possible for anybody to point towards any fatal flaws inherent in a proposed guideline before it actually comes into force.

Determining the value of fine units

In terms of the recommendations, the sentencing guidelines should not be limited to imprisonment, but should include fines and community sentences as well. The Law Commission left the Sentencing Council with a rather onerous task as far as fines are concerned. The report accepted that a unit fine system is inherently more just than the current fixed amount system and that sentencing guidelines based on the seriousness of the offences could hardly include fines without a unit fine system. At the same time, it found that it would be impractical in South Africa to require the accurate establishment of every offender's income (Report, para 3.3.27):

> Instead, it recommends that the Sentencing Council create broad means categories to which fine units of a specified value will be related. Sentencers will then have to follow a simple two-step process in setting fines. First, they will have to determine the number of fine units that are appropriate to the offence in terms of the general principles relating to the seriousness of the offence. Thereafter they will have to determine the means category into which the offender falls. The actual fine is set by multiplying the number of fine units with the

value of the units set for the relevant means category. In practice, sentencers can be provided with tables to assist them in making these simple calculations.

Policy recommendations on development of community penalties

The making of recommendations regarding the development of community penalties is another of the Council's proposed functions. The community penalties are basically correctional supervision (a kind of intensive probation) and community service. This duty is not described in more detail in the Report, but it could include an investigation and the making of recommendations if a particular penalty appears not to be utilised, or if the community appears to be unhappy about the operation of a specific penalty, or if further kinds of community penalties are proposed.

Doing research and various publishing duties

There is a dearth of data on current sentencing practices in South Africa and this has been a problem for all sentencing researchers for a long time. It will not be possible for the Sentencing Council to perform its functions without such data (Report, p 48). It will probably have to do its own research on current sentencing practises and the publication of that data will be a valuable source of information on sentencing in general.

The proposed role of public opinion

It is not the intention that the Sentencing Council should set sentencing guidelines in a vacuum or divorced from public opinion (Report, para 2.12). However, the Law Commission's recommendations did not really deal with the question of how public opinion is to be gauged. It was happy that public opinion could be expressed through the various institutions that could compel the Council into establishing or revising guidelines, and through the fact that the general public is entitled to approach the Council towards the same purpose. The Law Commission stressed (in para 2.13) that:

> A new sentencing framework requires not only a new partnership amongst the different arms of government. It requires also a new partnership between the State and the public in general and victims of crime in particular. The key to this partnership is improved provision for victim involvement in the sentencing process and recognition of victim concerns in the type of substantive sentences that are handed down.

The Council will have to consult widely in order to maximise the acceptance of its guidelines. Apart from regularly publishing the full set of sentencing guidelines, it is also envisaged that the Council report on the efficacy and cost effectiveness of the various sentencing options.

Beyond this, however, the proposals are largely silent as to the role of public opinion in the functioning of the Council. It might be that these aspects will have to be attended to more closely once the Council becomes a reality.

The role of education and information provision and guideline judgments

The issue of judicial training has been discussed for some time in South Africa. In the past, judicial officers received little practical training; they still rely heavily on the experience they gain during their years in practice. It appears to be generally accepted that judicial training is a shortcoming in need of correction, but there is still not much agreement as to the form or provider of this training. Some argue that any training other than by other judges would breach their judicial independence.

It is well documented in international experience that the revamp of any part of a legal system is unlikely to be successful if not accompanied by effective training of the bulk of judicial officers. There is no apparent reason why this would be any different if sentencing guidelines or any other reform were implemented in South Africa. The new framework will be a radical departure from current practice. As a result, the training of judicial officers in the use of sentencing guidelines would be yet another function of the Sentencing Council (Report, para 3.2.4). If it is not done, sentencers are likely to find a way around changing their sentencing practices and revert to what they have been doing all along.

Why these proposals were considered to provide the best cure

According to the information available to the Law Commission, a properly functioning body of knowledgeable people, working towards establishing a range of sentencing guidelines covering the whole spectrum of offences, had the best chance to bring about an acceptable level of consistency in sentencing. As these guidelines would (eventually) cover the whole spectrum of offences, it would ensure that there is proportionality in the guidelines, ranging from the most severe sentence for the most serious offences, through offences of lesser seriousness and sentences of intermediate severity, down the scale to the least severe sentences for lesser offences. Throughout, the Report envisages dividing the offences into as many subcategories as would be needed to ensure such proportionality for the majority of offences. In terms of this proposal, both the first shortcoming (inconsistent sentences) and the second (insufficient punishment for serious offences) would be addressed. By not limiting the sentencing guidelines to imprisonment, the third shortcoming is also attended to. These principles are supported by related functions, such as the training of judicial officers and the maintenance of sentencing data.

Should this still be the position?

The Sentencing Council as proposed for South Africa is not unique. Similar institutions can be found in the western world and their experiences show that sentencing guidelines can be made to work reasonably effectively. However, as Michael Tonry (1991, p 314) observed: "There have been many more failed sentencing commissions than successful ones".

One needs to remain realistic about the extent to which they can transform sentencing practices in the countries of their deployment. It is clear that budgetary problems can severely hamper the workings and continued existence of such a commission; within the South African context this will be a very real problem.

My main concern with the Law Commission's proposals is that, increasingly, they appear simply to be a few bridges too far. A number of the proposals, especially those involving the general principles of sentencing, are tried and tested in many parts of the world. They need little additional research, if any. But other issues need further research and elaboration. For example, the setting of "sentencing guidelines" is a core aspect of the recommendations, but it is not explained in terms of any exactness. Without a specific proposed format it will be almost impossible to provide convincing proof that these guidelines will actually achieve greater consistency than the current system. It is also possible that the current proposals are not sufficiently sensitive to the fact that sentencing is not the exclusive prerogative of the judiciary.[2] The current proposals might work well if the Council performs perfectly and if all its members completely subscribe to the ideals of the Sentencing Framework Bill. But perfection should not be required for the functioning of any aspect of the criminal justice system.[3]

Perhaps the Law Reform Commission might be requested to reconsider the complete set of proposals in the Report and, without revisiting the whole issue and repeating the whole exercise, to set priorities to the current proposals. Then, by tackling the issues one or two steps at a time, it might be possible to achieve more meaningful change in time than by taking one massive jump and leaving everybody else behind.

Notes

1   For details of the consultative process, see Report, paras 1.42 to 1.46.
2   Compare this with *S v Dodo* 2001 (1) SACR 594 (CC) at [25].
3   For further notes of caution, see Dixon, 2001, pp 168-78.

References

Dixon, B (2001). From Cafeteria to à la Carte: the Law Commission's New Sentencing Framework. *South African Journal of Criminal Justice* 14: 168.

South African Law Commission (2000). Discussion Paper 91: *Sentencing (a New Sentencing Framework)* (all South African Law (Reform) Commission investigations can be accessed at <www.doj.gov.za/salrc/index.htm>).

South African Law Commission (1997). Issue Paper 11: *Sentencing: Mandatory Minimum Sentences.*

South African Law Commission (2000). Project 82: *Report: Sentencing (a New Sentencing Framework).*

Terblanche, SS (2003). Sentencing Guidelines for South Africa: Lessons from Elsewhere. *South African Law Journal* 120: 858.

Tonry, M (1991). The Politics and Process of Sentencing Commissions. *Crime and Delinquency* 37: 307.

15

A federal sentencing council for Australia

Australian Law Reform Commission

Introduction

In June 2006, the Australian Law Reform Commission (ALRC) released a report on the sentencing of federal offenders. As part of its examination of measures that might promote better and more consistent sentencing, the ALRC considered the potential benefits and disadvantages of establishing a federal sentencing council.

In its report, the ALRC concludes that three of the primary functions of sentencing councils – research, advice and rule-making – are currently performed by other Australian agencies, will be performed by other agencies if the recommendations in the Report are implemented, or (in the case of rule-making) are not appropriate in the federal criminal justice system.

This chapter reproduces the extracts of the ALRC's report *Same Crime, Same Time: Sentencing of Federal Offenders* (ALRC, 2006) that examine the viability of a federal sentencing council for Australia.

Establishment of a federal sentencing council

Background

A third measure that may promote better sentencing decisions is the establishment of a sentencing commission or council to advise on matters related to sentencing. In recent years, governments have established a number of such bodies. The objectives of these bodies usually include the promotion of consistency in sentencing, but their constitutions and functions vary greatly.

At present, there is no sentencing commission or advisory council at the federal level in Australia; however, both New South Wales and Victoria have established sentencing councils at the State level.[1] Broadly speaking, these councils are constituted by persons with experience in community issues affecting courts, senior academics, members of support or advocacy groups for victims of crime (or persons who have expertise in matters associated with victims of crime), at least one prosecution lawyer and one defence lawyer, and others with experience in the operation of the criminal justice system.[2]

The functions of the State sentencing councils include advising the government – or stating their views to the courts – on guideline judgments; advising and consulting with the government in relation to offences suitable for standard non-parole periods and their proposed length; conducting research and disseminating information on sentencing matters to the government, the judiciary and other interested persons; and consulting with government departments, other interested persons or bodies and the general public on sentencing matters.[3]

Although the State sentencing councils have only advisory, research and consultative functions, similar bodies in overseas jurisdictions have rule-making powers and a more direct impact on individual cases. For example, the main function of sentencing councils in the United Kingdom and a number of jurisdictions in the United States is the development and promulgation of sentencing guidelines.[4]

ALRC 44 recommended the establishment of a sentencing council within the Australian Institute of Criminology (AIC) (ALRC, 1988, paras [275], [277], [282]). It was envisaged that the major function of the sentencing council would be to provide judicial officers with comprehensive information in order to promote consistency in the sentencing of federal offenders. In addition, the proposed sentencing council was to: advise the Attorney-General on the need for particular programs relating to punishment and sentencing; monitor sentencing practices; provide information on a systematic basis to the public through its own publications and through the mass media; and provide education programs to judicial officers. The proposed sentencing council was also to review maximum prison terms and to provide advice on new non-custodial sentencing options, and the impact of punishment on young offenders.

Issues and problems

A significant number of stakeholders supported the establishment of a federal sentencing council.[5] There was some disagreement about the tasks such a body should perform – ranging from research alone,[6] to research and the provision of advice,[7] to a broader role including oversight of the federal sentencing system, preparation of guidelines and consideration of mitigating and aggravating factors.[8] Although there was some judicial interest in the establishment of such a council, there was also concern that its functions may be seen as interfering with the independence of judicial officers.[9]

One stakeholder expressed the view that a sentencing council could play an important role in responding to public opinion and helping to correct public misconceptions about sentencing. It was acknowledged that a number of functions that a federal sentencing council could perform can be discharged by existing bodies such as the AIC. However, it was submitted that there is clear benefit in having an organisation dedicated exclusively to monitoring and guiding the sentencing process, and that the impact of a sentencing council on the sentencing process at the federal and State level may be considerable. It was suggested that the recommended national sentencing database is an example of a task that could be assigned to a sentencing council.[10]

Commentators have expressed support for sentencing councils on the basis that, being one step removed from political processes, councils can provide more objective information to legislators and courts on how the sentencing process should develop. It is also said that councils can promote the development of sentencing principles (Findlay, Odgers and Yeo, 2005, pp 282, 283, 285), recommend changes to make sentencing more socially defensible and scientifically based (Bagaric and Edney, 2004, p 126), and ensure that the media receives accurate information about sentencing policy and practices (Findlay, Odgers and

Yeo, 2005, pp 282, 283, 285). One commentator observed that the broad-based membership of both the New South Wales and the Victorian sentencing councils allows greater community input into the sentencing process. He argued that councils can play a role in gauging as well as creating public opinion, and that this may address public concerns about judges being seen as out of touch with community expectations on sentencing (Abadee, 2006, pp 3, 5).

Arguments against sentencing councils are that: they displace Parliament in determining an appropriate sentencing framework; their advice to courts on sentencing guidelines and principles is an unacceptable interference with the role of the courts and has the potential to interfere with the exercise of judicial discretion;[11] they may place the courts under moral pressure to assimilate the council's views and to determine sentences according to statistical norms rather than individual circumstances;[12] and they represent unnecessary bureaucracy (Silverii, 2003, p 20).

ALRC's views

In the ALRC's view, the functions discharged by State sentencing councils in Australia are to be commended. Better sentencing decisions and sound evidence-based policies can be promoted by disseminating sentencing statistics, analysing sentencing trends and conducting broad community consultation.

However, these functions do not necessarily require the establishment of a new body at the federal level. In general it is undesirable to establish new government agencies unless there is a compelling case to do so, particularly where new functions can be performed effectively by existing agencies. In order to justify the establishment of a federal sentencing council it would be necessary to show that the functions to be performed by the council were necessary at the federal level and were not being, or could not be, performed by other bodies. The ALRC has come to the view that three of the primary functions of sentencing councils – research, advice and rule-making – are currently being performed by other bodies, will be performed by other bodies if the recommendations in this Report are implemented, or (in the case of rule-making) are not appropriate in the federal criminal justice system (ALRC, 2005, para [19.30]).

In relation to the research function, the ALRC has recommended that the Australian government continue to support the establishment of a national sentencing database to provide detailed information on the sentencing of federal offenders to judicial officers, prosecutors, defence lawyers and others (see Rec 21–1). In addition, the AIC already conducts research and statistical analysis in order to provide advice to the Australian government and other key stakeholders (such as law enforcement agencies and community organisations) to support the formulation of evidence-based policy in the field of criminal justice.

In relation to the advice function, the Office for the Management of Federal Offenders (OMFO),[13] once established, will be responsible for overseeing federal offenders, liaising with the States and Territories, and providing advice to the Australian government in relation to federal offenders and relevant aspects of the federal criminal justice system (Rec 22–4). The OMFO will not have the independence from government that a sentencing council would have. However, given the number of federal offenders and the fact that most other functions of a sentencing council are being or will be taken up by other bodies if the recommendations in this Report are implemented, the ALRC has concluded that the establishment of a stand alone federal sentencing council is not warranted at this time.

In relation to the consultative function, the ALRC has made no specific recommendations in this Report on community input into the federal sentencing process. However, there is no impediment to the OMFO or other areas of the Attorney-General's Department engaging in community consultation to inform the policy development process. For example, the terms of reference for the Australian government's *Review of Criminal Penalties in Commonwealth Legislation* require the Department to seek to understand community expectations about penalising criminal offences (Attorney-General's Department, 2006). The Minister for Justice and Customs, Senator the Hon Chris Ellison, has said that the government is keen to hear the views of the community on this matter and will be seeking public comment in response to an issues paper (Ellison, 2006).

In relation to the rule-making function, provision of advice on guideline judgments and factors that aggravate and mitigate sentence will not be necessary if the relevant recommendations in this Report are implemented (see Chapters 6 and 21).

Notes

1   A sentencing council was proposed in Queensland but the Penalties and Sentences (Sentencing Advisory Council) Amendment Bill 2005 (Qld) failed to pass through the Queensland Parliament: Queensland, *Parliamentary Debates*, Legislative Assembly, 29 September 2005, 3046. The establishment of a sentencing advisory council in Tasmania has been raised in the Tasmania Law Reform Institute's issues paper on sentencing (Warner, 2002, p 133).

2   *Sentencing Act* 1991 (Vic) s 108F. New South Wales has an express requirement that the Sentencing Commission be chaired by a retired judicial officer, and that the Commission include persons with expertise or experience in law enforcement: *Crimes (Sentencing Procedure) Act* 1999 (NSW) s 100I, Sch 1A cl 2.

3   *Crimes (Sentencing Procedure) Act* 1999 (NSW) s 100J; *Sentencing Act* 1991 (Vic) s 108C(1). Not all the stated functions are performed by each sentencing council.

4   See, for example, *Criminal Justice Act* 2003 (UK) s 170 (Sentencing Guidelines Council); *Sentencing Reform Act of* 1984 28 USC (US) s 994; (United States Sentencing Commission); *Minnesota Statutes* 2004 s 244.09(5), (7), (11) (Minnesota Sentencing Guidelines Commission).

5   J Roberts, *Submission SFO 67*, 16 January 2006; Attorney General B Debus, *Submission SFO 65*, 9 January 2006; Sisters Inside Inc, *Submission SFO 40*, 28 April 2005; WT, *Submission SFO 23*, 11 April 2005; Australian Taxation Office, *Submission SFO 18*, 8 April 2005; BN, *Submission SFO 17*, 8 April 2005; A Freiberg, *Submission SFO 12*, 4 April 2005; LD, *Submission SFO 9*, 10 March 2005.

6   JC, *Submission SFO 25*, 13 April 2005.

7   Sisters Inside Inc, *Submission SFO 40*, 28 April 2005.

8   A Freiberg, *Submission SFO 12*, 4 April 2005; A Freiberg, *Consultation*, Melbourne, 30 March 2005.

9   Deputy Chief Magistrate E Woods, *Consultation*, Perth, 18 April 2005.

10   J Roberts, *Submission SFO 67*, 16 January 2006.

11   Queensland, *Parliamentary Debates*, Legislative Assembly, 29 September 2005, 3031-2 (L Lavarch – Minister for Justice and Attorney-General).

12   Queensland, *Parliamentary Debates*, Legislative Assembly, 29 September 2005, 3034 (K Shine).

13   The establishment of the OMFO is recommended in Ch 22: Rec 22–3.

References

Abadee, A (2006). The Role of Sentencing Advisory Councils. Paper presented at Sentencing: Principles, Perspectives & Possibilities, Canberra, 12 February.

ALRC (Australian Law Reform Commission) (1988). *Sentencing.* Report No 44. Sydney: Australian Law Reform Commission.

ALRC (2005). *Sentencing of Federal Offenders*, DP 70. Sydney: Australian Law Reform Commission.

ALRC (2006). *Same Crime, Same Time: Sentencing of Federal Offenders.* Publication No 103. Sydney: Australian Law Reform Commission. Copyright Commonwealth of Australia, reproduced by permission.

Attorney-General's Department (2006). *Terms of Reference – Review of Criminal Penalties in Commonwealth Legislation*, <www.ag.gov.au/penalties>.

Bagaric, M and Edney, R (2004). The Sentencing Advisory Commission and the Hope of Smarter Sentencing. *Current Issues in Criminal Justice* 16: 125.

Ellison, C (2006). *Review of Criminal Penalties in Commonwealth Legislation.* Minister for Justice and Customs, Press Release, 23 February.

Findlay, M, Odgers, S and Yeo, S (2005). *Australian Criminal Justice.* 3rd ed.

Silverii, J (2003). Concern over Government Sentencing Reform. *Law Institute Journal* 77(5): 20.

Warner, K (2002). *Sentencing – Issues Paper No 2.* Hobart: Tasmania Law Reform Institute.

16

Institutional mechanisms for incorporating the public

Neil Hutton

Sentencing policy

The development of sentencing policy has become problematic over the past 30 years or so in most western democracies. There are a number of different but related aspects to this. There is a perception that the public has steadily diminishing confidence in judges as sentencers: survey evidence from a number of jurisdictions suggests that the public sees judges as out of touch with community sentiments and their sentencing as overly lenient. Over the same period, prison populations in these same jurisdictions have risen steadily. In the United States this has sometimes been deliberately engineered by politicians through legislation and the manipulation of sentencing guidelines, but in other jurisdictions, for example in the United Kingdom, sentencing appears to have become more punitive because judges, exercising their discretion, have sent more people to prison for longer. Anthony Bottoms (1995) has coined the phrase "populist punitiveness" to characterise this transformation, whereby law and order is at the top of the political agenda and political parties feel obliged to "talk tough" for electoral purposes.

There is, however, another side to this story. Research using techniques such as focus groups and deliberative polling shows that the public is not as punitive as survey data suggest. When people are given a case to deal with, are provided with background information about criminal justice and are allowed to engage in dialogue with each other, they are less punitive, more constructive and more rational in their approach to sentencing (Hutton, 2005). Under the conditions of a deliberative poll – with accurate information, open debate and expert facilitation – it appears to be possible to stimulate rational debate about penal policy amongst the public.

The trouble is that it is not possible to reproduce these conditions at a national level. At this level, debate takes place through the mass media; the volume of information available is overwhelming and perplexing, and political representatives have to try to win our votes. Indermaur and Hough (2002) have made a number of suggestions as to how we can try to change public attitudes, largely through the provision and dissemination of information about sentencing and punishment, as a way of improving public knowledge and understanding. These are worthy aims, but the issue is not just about changing attitudes or providing better information; it is about the wider problem of the growing disenchantment with democratic politics.

Political disenchantment

Penal policy is only a small part of the political field, although one to which politicians have become hyper-sensitive. Concerns about the decline in public engagement in politics go beyond penal issues to encompass all areas of policy. Stoker (2006) argues that people have become cynical and disillusioned with politics. Mass representative democracy has been one of the greatest achievements of the past century, but it is now perceived to be failing. Part of the reason for this, according to Stoker, is that people have lost sight of some of the main characteristics of politics. It rarely delivers what it promises; it is untidy; and it is never final. The processes of compromise and reconciliation that characterise political activity mean that it is "designed to disappoint". The values of the market economy and the fusing of reporting and commentary in the media have led to unrealistic expectations being placed on politics. Politics is represented as constantly failing to deliver and the result is a culture of cynicism. Penal policy is almost a paradigmatic example of this. Although sentencing policy can at best have a tiny impact on crime, the assumption underpinning most public discourse is that tougher punishment is the answer to the problem of crime. It is perhaps not surprising that cynicism develops as impossible targets are not achieved.

Stoker's solution to disenchantment is to develop a "politics for amateurs". He argues that people want their voices to be heard and want influence, but that they do not necessarily want to become more actively engaged or involved in the political process. He is therefore critical of those who want to develop a more deliberative politics and focuses instead on proposals to revive representative democracy. These proposals go well beyond the scope of this chapter. However, following Stoker's manifesto, I argue in what follows that the development of a new generation of sentencing institutions offers at least some potential for the development of a more rational approach to penal policy. These institutions can help the judiciary to explain their decisions and thus improve accountability; they can provide politicians with some shelter from the emotionally charged media discourses of crime and punishment; they can enable the judiciary to participate in policy-making alongside other criminal justice experts and knowledgeable members of the public; they can provide more effective information about sentencing; and they can engage with the general public more directly.

Multi-level governance

Over the past 25 years or so, governments across the English speaking world have developed new approaches to the governance of public affairs. There has been a shift away from a directive and paternalistic state to the vision of a state that enables public and private organisations to collaborate (Bevir, 2005). This can be seen in all areas of public policy, including health and education.

In criminal justice there has been a significant shift of responsibility from the state to various agencies, which has contributed to the development of partnerships between public organisations and the voluntary sector. This has been seen in the fields of community policing (Rosenbaum, 1994), crime prevention (Crawford, 1999), community safety and restorative justice (Bazemore, 2000; Braithwaite, 2002; Matthews and Pitts, 2001). Garland (2001) has argued that this characterises an attempt by the state to shift the responsibility for crime control away from conventional state institutions and at least partly on to communities. Governments realised that high levels of crime were here to stay and that there was little that state institutions, "issuing sovereign commands to obedient subjects" (Garland, 2001, p 205), could do to change this. Effective government required harnessing the power, knowledge and organisational capacity of communities. This applied not just to criminal justice but to almost all areas of government activity, such as education, health care, welfare and economic development. In fact, the shift of responsibility to communities occurred relatively recently in the field of crime control and even more recently with respect to the sub-field of sentencing.

The development of sentencing institutions that sit somewhere between legislatures and the courts began in the United States in the early 1980s with the development of State sentencing commissions. England and Wales introduced a Sentencing Advisory Panel in 1999 and a Sentencing Guidelines Council in 2003. In the early years of the 21st century, other western jurisdictions have introduced or proposed a range of sentencing institutions which, although distinctive, share common features. They sit somewhere between Parliament, the executive and the judiciary and although their power, remit and degree of independence vary widely, the significant point is that authority over sentencing is distributed among a number of institutions.

This chapter reviews the development of institutions that incorporate the public in the development of sentencing policy. I only deal with a selected range of western English-speaking jurisdictions, partly because they share certain features in common and partly because of my own ignorance of continental European and other jurisdictions.[1] The chapter concentrates on the various forms of sentencing commission and council that have been adopted (or proposed in some cases) in England and Wales, Scotland, Australia, New Zealand, South Africa and the United States and that have been reviewed in the preceding chapters of this volume. In what follows, three main issues are addressed. The first concerns the political legitimacy of sentencing. How can sentencing institutions contribute to the distribution of authority and sharing of power over sentencing policy amongst legislators, executives, judges and other criminal justice agencies? The second related issue concerns the incorporation of the public into the development of sentencing policy. To what extent is sentencing a "legal" decision and how, if at all, can sentencing institutions be used to enable the public to contribute to the development of sentencing policy? In particular how, if at all, can sentencing institutions confront the challenges posed by the dramatic politicisation of crime and punishment that has developed over the past 30 years? The third issue concerns the contribution that sentencing institutions can make to the development of a rational and efficient approach to sentencing policy.

The distribution of authority over sentencing

What exactly is sentencing policy, where is it to be found and who has the authority to make sentencing policy? These are large political questions concerning the relationships between legislatures, judges, sentencing commissions/councils and the public more broadly. The term "sentencing policy" suggests a more coherent project than is usually found in practice. Sentencing policy may be found in the following sorts of places: legislation, sentencing guidelines, guideline judgments from a court, reported sentencing decisions of first instance cases, decisions of appeal courts, sentencing textbooks and encyclopaedias, research studies of sentencing practices, decisions of parole boards, political speeches and so on. Sentencing policy in any jurisdiction is rarely coherent and is in a constant state of flux.

Sentencing decisions do not just take place in courts. Many actors play a part in sentencing, including legislators, prosecutors, judges, parole board members and officials from a range of executive agencies such as prisons, probation and social work (Chanenson, 2005). There is a common misconception that judges have sole authority over sentencing decisions; this is never the case even in those jurisdictions where judges exercise very wide discretion. Sentencing always takes place within a legally authorised structure. Judges make sentencing decisions within a regulatory legal framework, although in many jurisdictions, prosecutors, parole officials or others will have made decisions about a case before the sentencing decision of the judge.

Judges exercise varying degrees of discretion. At one extreme, the United States Federal Guidelines permit judges virtually no discretion; at the other, a jurisdiction like Scotland, with no tradition of sentencing reform, allows judges very wide discretion. In between these extremes there exists considerable variation. All State guidelines systems in the United States (with the single exception of the Federal Sentencing Guidelines of the United States Sentencing Commission) leave varying degrees of space for the exercise of discretion by judges. The development of sentencing policy thus involves multiple actors and takes place in many settings. In the language of some political scientists, these actors might be described as the stakeholders in sentencing (Bevir, 2005).

There is also diversity in the distribution of authority over sentencing (Reitz, 1998). Not only is there the widespread misunderstanding that judges are the only actors who *do* have authority over sentencing decisions; there is also the view that judges are the only actors who *should* have this authority (the latter is a view often held by judges themselves).

The Sentencing Report from the Review of the Model Penal Code in the United States provides one example of how authority over sentencing has been distributed in one jurisdiction (Reitz, 1998). Under the 1962 Penal Code, the legislation provided for a maximum penalty of 10 years' imprisonment for a second degree felony such as aggravated assault. The judge could select a sentence of between one and three years, which was a minimum term of imprisonment. That is, the legislature fixed the first 12 months of the sentence and the court could fix up to 24 months on top of this. Once the offender was in prison the Parole Board had the power to decide on a date of release. This date could stretch beyond the initial period of the sentence passed by the court, up to a total incarceration period of 10 years. In addition, prison officials had the power to deduct time from the sentence and could award up to 40 per cent good time credits. In other words, both the Parole Board and prison authorities had the power to decide when a prisoner would be released. This demonstrates that authority over the time actually served in prison was not held solely by judges but was shared by the legislature, the court, the Parole Board and prison authorities. In considering how the public has been or might be incorporated into sentencing decisions, it is therefore important to bear in mind the framework of authority over sentencing, how any public involvement fits into this framework and what impact on sentencing outcomes public incorporation might have. Despite this distribution of authority, ultimately it is the legislatures that can have the final say over sentencing policy and can pass legislation which other agencies and individuals are required to implement.

Strengths and weaknesses of the distribution of authority

One main advantage of a wide distribution of authority over sentencing is that there are several checks on the power of any single institution. This may be a good thing where the liberty of a citizen is being removed or curtailed. On the other hand, the involvement of a multiplicity of agencies can lead to a lack of clarity, consistency and accountability. There is plenty of evidence that the public is ill-informed about sentencing and the "truth in sentencing" movement is further evidence of the demand for a simpler and more straightforward relationship between the decision of a judge and the length of time an offender will serve in custody. Despite reforms of sentencing conducted by sentencing commissions in the United States, sentencing remains in many jurisdictions a complex process with authority vested in a range of institutions. The public debate in England over the sentence passed on a violent sex offender, Craig Sweeney, is an example of the confusion that can exist, even in a case where, at least to a lawyer, the decision is both clear and defensible. The judge passed a life sentence on the offender who had a previous related serious conviction. The judge had to indicate the earliest point at which this life sentence could be reviewed by the Parole Board. After considering the seriousness of the offence and the personal circumstances of the offender, the judge indicated a term and then deducted one-third in recognition of the plea of guilty that had been tendered. This left the minimum time to be served before review at five years. This was widely mis-reported as the maximum period of time the offender would serve, and the parents of the victim were given wide media coverage as they expressed their outrage at this (misunderstood) sentence (see Home Office, 2006).

Symbolic function of sentencing

Another advantage of the distribution of authority over sentencing is that it makes it easier for sentencing to serve a range of often mutually contradictory purposes or functions. One of these is the symbolic function of reproducing the boundaries of moral tolerance in a society (Durkheim, 1933). It may be socially useful to have a severe maximum penalty enacted in legislation for a violent offence. It may also be useful for judges to impose a severe sentence in court. This allows the public expression of outrage at the commission of a serious offence (Pettit, 2002). On the other hand, it may also be socially useful and desirable that courts very seldom use maximum penalties and usually sentence well beneath that maximum, and also that legislation provides that prisoners can be released into the community having served a particular proportion of the custodial sentence imposed in court. Where the authority of sentencing is distributed over a number of different institutions, it is easier to manage these contradictions. However, where certainty of sentencing is given priority, and where there is a public demand that authority over the administration of the sentence become more centralised this becomes more difficult. For example, where authority is more concentrated with the sentencing judge or with a legislature, there may be a tendency for sentencing to become more severe and for prison populations to increase. This may occur as public demands for severity may be perceived to override contradictory demands for more rational administration of punishment or for the exercise of parsimony or restraint in the allocation of punishment.

Institutions such as sentencing councils enable authority over sentencing to be more widely distributed between the different branches of government and the other stakeholders who participate in the institution. At the same time, they can also help to resolve potential confusion as they offer a more effective means of communication with the public about sentencing and penal policy than that which is available to the courts or to political representatives.

The relationship between sentencing institutions and legislatures

The conventional democratic expression of the "public voice" in sentencing policy has been heard through the legislature. In the United States and in many European jurisdictions the executive has to work hard to persuade the legislative authority to pass a Bill. In England and Wales the executive typically has an easier task (Tonry, 2003). Legislation provides powers for sentencers and sentencing commissions/councils and sets outer limits for their use, such as the setting of statutory maximum penalties, mandatory minimum sentences and "three strikes" provisions. However, within these limits sentencing practice has been characterised by the exercise of considerable discretion.

Governments typically respond to a perceived public demand for changes in sentencing by introducing legislation that is debated and passed through the legislature. This approach to the regulation of sentencing has a number of weaknesses. Where mandatory minimum penalties are imposed, this can diminish the authority of judges, sentencing commissions and parole boards. Legislatures have neither the time, the attention span nor the expertise to deliver any fine tuning of punishments or sentencing systems. Politicians are more vulnerable to perceived shifts in public opinion, particularly following a shocking case. All of these factors can generate sentencing policy that is inconsistent, excessively severe, unpredictable and disconnected from any evidence about its effects. The introduction of sentencing institutions can provide relief from the immediate demands of electoral politics.

In general, United States commissions tend to have a significant degree of authority over the development of sentencing guidelines, although there is considerable variation.[2] The Minnesota Commission (the first, established in 1980) began with the assumption that the guidelines produced by the commission would become effective unless the legislature voted otherwise, although in later years the legislature took back some of this delegated power (Frase, this volume). By contrast, in Washington State the legislature has dominated the processes of revising guidelines (Frase, 2005; Barkow, 2005).

The Sentencing Guidelines Council in England and Wales has the authority to produce guidelines that do not have to be ratified by Parliament. The proposed sentencing councils in New Zealand and South Africa would have the power to implement guidelines. In New Zealand the legislature could either accept or reject the comprehensive set of guidelines but would not have the power to change individual guidelines. In South Africa the key proposals recommend that "the different arms of government enter into a new partnership" (South African Law Commission, 2000, p xxi). The proposed sentencing council would publish sentencing guidelines in the *Government Gazette*, but they would not be legislated through Parliament (Terblanche, this volume). The Australian councils do not have powers to make guidelines; nor does the proposed Advisory Panel on Sentencing in Scotland, although this body has the power to propose guidelines to the Appeal Court. In these latter jurisdictions the power to develop guidelines, if it exists, resides with the judiciary.

There is considerable variation in the power over sentencing policy granted to sentencing institutions by legislatures. This can best be explained by local cultural, political and social conditions. Where sentencing institutions have the power to develop a comprehensive system of guidelines such as most of the United States commissions and the proposed New Zealand council, the issue of the initiation of business for the institution is less relevant. However, in those jurisdictions where the institution has only an advisory capacity or develops guidelines in an ad hoc iterative process, this issue is more central. In England and Wales, the Sentencing Guidelines Council can take the initiative itself and it can have matters referred by the executive or by the Sentencing Advisory Panel (which can also initiate its own business) as can the Victorian Council. In South Africa, the proposed Commission can generate its own business and can have matters referred by the executive and by members of the public (although it is not obliged to act on these). The proposed Scottish Panel can initiate its own business or have business referred to it by the Appeal Court, the Scottish Ministers or the Lord Advocate.

The "independence" of a sentencing institution from its political masters is rarely absolute. A representative from the executive, with observer status, attends the Sentencing Guidelines Council for England and Wales, which is otherwise a judicial body with considerable political independence. This practice has been recommended in the proposals for a New Zealand Sentencing Council and also in the recommendations for an Advisory Panel on Sentencing in Scotland (APSS). The stated aim of this recommendation from the Sentencing Commission for Scotland was "to facilitate communication between the executive and the APSS". The proposed South African Council would not include a representative from the executive, but the Council would be obliged to consult with the executive.

Barkow (2005) has argued that it is useful for independent sentencing institutions to have good lines of communication with the executive. There would be little point in a commission producing proposals that were so politically controversial that they stood no chance of being acceptable to the executive. Barkow reminds us that ultimately the executive could pass legislation that could nullify politically unacceptable sentencing guidelines. It therefore makes sense pragmatically that an independent commission should have good lines of communication with the executive. At the same time, the independence of the institution allows a range of parties to participate in the development of sentencing policy.

Public opinion and public participation in sentencing institutions

The demand for increased public participation in the development of sentencing policy comes at least in part from a perception of public dissatisfaction with existing policy.

The past 15 years have seen sharp rises in prison populations across many, if not all, western jurisdictions. The "populist punitiveness" thesis (Bottoms, 1995) attempts to explain this phenomenon in terms of the response of politicians to perceived popular demands for increased penal severity as reflected in survey research and as represented in tabloid headlines. Law and order has risen to the top of the political agenda and political parties have tried to ensure that they cannot be portrayed by their rivals as being "soft" on crime. This has been particularly marked in majoritarian democracies such as the United States and the United Kingdom (Green, 2006) where law and order has become a major focus of political debate between two adversarial political parties.

There has been considerable debate about how the methodologies chosen to measure public opinion and attitudes can themselves influence what they are supposed to be measuring (Hutton, 2005). An approach combining a range of methods is likely to provide the most accurate representation of public opinion (Green, 2006).

Recent research into public knowledge and attitudes to punishment and sentencing has cast doubt on the argument that the public is becoming ever more punitive. The use of focus groups and deliberative polling methodologies to gather information about public attitudes shows that when provided with information and given an opportunity to engage in dialogue with each other and with experts, people's views on punishment are more moderate and more rational than survey data suggest (Roberts and Hough, 2002; Matthews, 2005). There is also support for this argument from a variety of recent public consultation exercises conducted in the United Kingdom, such as the Halliday Report (Home Office, 2001), the Coulsfield Report for the Esmée Fairbairn Foundation's *Rethinking Crime and Punishment* program, research commissioned by the Scottish Parliament Justice Committee (Anderson et al, 2002) and research commissioned by the Sentencing Advisory Panel in England and Wales into public attitudes to house burglary, which informed the guideline judgment issued in 2002 (McInerney and Keating).

The implication from this body of work is that there would be considerable public support, at least in the United Kingdom, for a more rational approach to penal policy-making. It is also worth noting that, alongside the dramatic rises in prison populations, there have simultaneously been more "liberal" penal developments including restorative justice, therapeutic justice and risk/needs assessment (Hutchinson, 2006). This provides further evidence for the existence of a public constituency that supports a more rational, evidence-based approach to penal policy and practice. The political challenge is to find a means of involving the public in penal policy-making in a forum that creates space for rational debate away from the harsh spotlight of tabloid journalism and electoral politics.

Judges recognise the need to take some account of public opinion in their sentencing decision-making. They also recognise that the legitimacy of the courts depends on the confidence of the public. In those jurisdictions where judges are not elected, they have been appointed to pass sentence on behalf of the public as a matter of trust. United Kingdom survey research has consistently shown declining confidence in judges and the courts for a number of years (Roberts and Hough, 2005), but judges and courts have been slow to address this issue. Of course, judges are not in a good position to do so. Judges cannot respond to media criticism of their decisions in individual cases. Nor does the discourse of individualised sentencing allow judges to talk about consistency and explain how the sentence in a particular case relates to sentencing for similar cases (Hutton, 2006).

Politicians appear to pay considerable attention to public opinion as represented in the mass media, with scant regard to whether or not it is an accurate representation of public views. One of the main tasks given to some sentencing councils has been public communication as a means of informing public opinion (Indermaur and Hough, 2002). This is explicitly part of the remit of the Victorian Sentencing Advisory Council.

David Green (2006) makes a number of useful proposals for fostering the conditions to generate informed public judgment (rather than shallow "public opinion"). These include extending the use of deliberative polling and reforming political and journalistic cultures. Sentencing institutions may have a small role to play in fostering the conditions for public judgment that Green argues are desirable. These institutions are politically independent and are thus to at least some extent sheltered from the immediate demands of the contemporary political and media world. They also offer the judiciary an institutional opportunity to participate with the public in the debate over sentencing and penal policy, something that their judicial office does not normally permit. These institutions may also be able to perform other functions that will foster more rational public judgment. They may be able to consult with the public using deliberative polls or focus groups and they may be able to collect and disseminate information on sentencing patterns, sentencing effectiveness, the use of parole and early release and so on. None of these guarantees a more rational approach to penal policy. As Barkow notes, politicians can always "get tough" if they judge that the electoral climate requires it. However, sentencing institutions at least offer an opportunity for the development of a more rational approach to penal policy.

As well, guideline judgments may have the capacity to improve public confidence, and in some jurisdictions this has been a justification for their introduction, but there is little evidence about their impact on public confidence. In England and Wales, for example, there is no information on the extent to which guidelines are followed because there is no monitoring. However, the ability to explain a sentence by reference to a guideline, whether it adheres to the guideline or departs from the guideline, does offer judges an opportunity to give an account of their sentencing decisions, which is not available where guidelines do not exist.

What does public participation mean?

Which sections of the community are included in "the public"? Commissioners are usually appointed by the executive branch and are therefore independent, in so far as they are not directly elected. In the United States elected representatives are always in a minority and there is always a balance between the two main parties. The membership of most of the State sentencing commissions in the United States (there are 31 commissions: Frase, 2005) is set out in statute and usually includes judges, prosecutors, defence lawyers, corrections officials, members of the public who may or may not be representatives of victims' organisations and sometimes legislators. The incorporation of the public into the development of sentencing policy in United States commissions seems now to be entirely uncontroversial, although far from universal. While there is considerable diversity in the details of the powers, remits and budgets of these commissions, there appears to be a general acceptance of the need to include representation from the public. This appears to be mostly from those with expertise in some area of criminal justice practice or from members of the public who represent an interest group, very often a victims' organisation.

In the proposals for the New Zealand Council, there is a clear intention to ensure that sections of the community beyond the judiciary have an important part to play in the development of sentencing policy. Non-judicial members will be in a majority on the Council. The "lay" involvement in the Council is to come from those with relevant expertise. Public involvement is not by elected representatives or by self-selecting volunteers, but by non-judicial experts.

One of the main aims of both the NSW Council and the Victorian Council is to enable wider public views to be taken into account in the development of sentencing policy in the hope that public acceptance, understanding and confidence in sentencing will be improved. It is hoped that this will also contribute to enhanced accountability and transparency in sentencing practice.

The chair of the NSW Sentencing Council has argued that "it is of considerable importance that some body exists to not only gauge informed public opinion but to also participate in its creation"(Abadee, 2006, p 5). The reference to *informed* opinion and the role of a sentencing council in its creation is interesting. This suggests that Abadee has a concern about the potential influence of ill-informed public opinion on sentencing policy, and recognises the need for a public institution that has a responsibility for public education about sentencing issues. Both Australian Councils have public representation, and there is a statutory obligation to include representatives of victims' organisations.

The Sentencing Guidelines Council in England and Wales is in effect a judicial body with no representation from the public. The Sentencing Advisory Panel, on the other hand, does have significant representation from members of the public with expertise in various aspects of criminal justice. The proposed Advisory Panel on Sentencing for Scotland includes representatives of the public with criminal justice expertise. The South African Council includes representatives from the prosecution and correctional authorities and a "sentencing expert".

As is clear from the discussions of sentencing institutions in this book, most of these bodies appoint people with expertise and/or experience in criminal justice.

Membership of sentencing institutions is rarely drawn from the general public and in this sense is very different from most jury systems.

Why is this? One explanation may be that the development of sentencing policy and/or sentencing guidelines is seen as a complex technical task requiring specific knowledge, skills and expertise. Expertise is seen as more important than "representativeness". It is important that people have the knowledge, experience and skills to contribute to good quality decision-making about sentencing policy. In most institutions, for example in Victoria, members are explicitly appointed as individuals and not as representatives of particular organisations or interests.

For some, this will promulgate the perceived "democratic deficit" in sentencing. Indermaur (this volume) argues that, despite their claims, sentencing institutions do not effectively incorporate public views. In no sense do the public members of these institutions "represent" the wider public. The inclusion of representatives from special interest groups does not resolve this difficulty. Even where the sentencing institution consults the public more widely, there is little evidence that public views expressed in consultation exercises have any significant impact on the development of policy. This is not so much a criticism of sentencing institutions themselves as a broader criticism of the way in which democratic institutions work, or do not work, to involve the public in making decisions about public policy.

Stoker (2006) argues that there has been a decline in levels of public participation in politics and that a culture of disillusionment and cynicism has developed. He reviews research evidence showing that people do not want to become more actively engaged in politics, although they do want to be consulted and have the opportunity to express their views. Stoker's solution to political cynicism is not to try to engineer a deeper level of participation from the public but rather to try to use political institutions to engage people in a "lighter way" which he describes as "politics for amateurs". "Amateurs" do things because they are interested or care rather than for financial reward. Amateurs may also be characterised as "unskilled" but there is a difference between amateurs with some levels of skill, knowledge and competence and those who do not have these qualities. In the field of sentencing policy, judges, civil servants and politicians might be characterised as "professionals", but in the residual category of "amateurs" there is a big difference between the skills and competences of an experienced prison governor or senior criminal justice social worker or the director of a criminal justice charity, and someone who works in a shop and has no experience of criminal justice. This is not to say that the views of unskilled amateurs are not relevant or important, just that some amateurs have different skills to offer the policy-making process.

Sentencing institutions tend to be populated with skilled amateurs, with expertise. The practical work of a sentencing institution involves tasks such as digesting large amounts of information, making judgments, contributing to informed debate, reaching compromises with others and so on. Not everyone has these skills but the work of an institution would be very hard if it was populated by people who did not have them. The criteria for appointing lay people, or amateurs, to a sentencing institution should concern the capacities required to contribute to good quality decision-making in such a body.

In addition to enabling different sorts of amateurs to participate in their work, sentencing institutions should also engage directly with the public using a range of methods including deliberative polling, focus groups and surveys. The Sentencing Advisory Panel in England and Wales already does some work of this nature. Sentencing institutions should also be involved in engagement by providing information, education and training. A good example is the outreach work done in schools and communities by the Victorian Sentencing Advisory Council with their "You be the Judge" program.

The incorporation of the public into the development of sentencing policy is therefore best achieved through the development of a sentencing institution which has a degree of independence from the other branches of government (legislature, executive and judiciary). It should involve both "professionals" and "skilled amateurs" and should also engage more widely with the public using a wide range of methods. Indermaur is probably right to argue that none of the sentencing institutions developed so far has achieved all of these desiderata. However, institutions are products of their political, social and cultural circumstances. Even if one were to set out the ideal arrangements for a sentencing institution, these are unlikely ever to be fully realised in practice.

Sentencing institutions, judicial discretion and public participation

While it might be politically desirable to involve the public in the development of sentencing policy, does the public have the necessary skills? Is sentencing a task for legal professionals or do "amateurs" have something to contribute? Before considering these questions, it is useful to focus on the nature of the sentencing decision itself. What does judicial discretion in sentencing mean and is it incompatible with the provision of sentencing guidelines?

There is a widespread misunderstanding about the extent to which sentencing commission guidelines affect judicial discretion in the United States. In seven States guidelines are voluntary and not subject to appeal, although in some of these jurisdictions judges are required to give reasons for departures. In some of these jurisdictions compliance rates tend to be high (for example, 79 per cent compliance in Virginia). In those States where guidelines are "legally binding", there remains considerable variation. In practice, in most of these States review by the appeal court is "highly deferential" and even in jurisdictions like Minnesota where a considerable body of substantive appellate caselaw has developed, judges still retain considerable discretion (Frase, 2005). There is also considerable variation among commissions over the decisions each system seeks to regulate including parole release, the use of intermediate sanctions (community sanctions) and the revocation of probation or supervised release.

Frase (2005) argues that all commissions share the goals of eliminating unwarranted disparities in sentencing and promoting more rational sentencing policy formation, "decision-making that is at least partially insulated from short term political pressures" (Frase, 2005, p 1202). Again, however, the authority of the Commission over sentencing varies. In Minnesota offenders receive good time credit of up to one-third of their guideline prison term, but in many States the sentence reduction for good conduct cannot exceed 15 per cent.

Despite the many important differences between State guidelines systems, Frase (2005) argues that there are also some pervasive similarities shared by most commissions (which are also, he argues, probably desirable features for any would-be successful sentencing commission). These include: recognition that sentencing must reflect a range of purposes, theories and functions that will change over time; agreement that guidelines need to be developed, implemented, monitored and revised by a permanent, broadly based and independent sentencing commission; extensive use of resource impact assessments; the need to keep guidelines simple; and the value of distributing sentencing authority between various institutions and actors (Reitz, 1998).

The New Zealand Law Commission argues that judges should cease to exercise a monopoly over the quantum of punishment. The current system produces what Ashworth has described as a "democratic deficit" (Ashworth, 2005, p 57). It does not allow for the range of "perspective, expertise and experience that is required for a robust sentencing policy that is acceptable to the community". It is not desirable that judges are required to be the sole judge of the public and political mood, because it places them in the political spotlight for their decisions in individual cases. In the same vein, the Commission proposes that the Chair of the New Zealand Sentencing Council should not be a judge because the Chair would be required to promote and defend the policies of the Council and this is not an appropriate function for a judge.

The New Zealand proposals thus recognise that there is a distinction to be drawn between sentencing decisions in individual cases and broad statements of sentencing policy. Judges alone should make sentencing decisions in individual cases. This is conceived as the independent, impartial exercise of judgment. However, this judicial task is to be carried out within a sentencing policy framework that is to be designed by a Council with judicial members, but also with members drawn from those with a wider range of relevant experience. Parliament would retain the power to pass legislation governing sentencing, but the fine detail of sentencing policy would be delegated to a body independent from the executive branch, with individual sentencing decisions made by judges within the framework set by the Council.

This chapter began by acknowledging the popular misconception that sentencing is a task performed exclusively by judges with the further assumption that most judges are legally qualified. Leaving aside for a moment the very significant role played by lay judges (magistrates in England to take one example), there is a perception that passing sentence is a "legal" decision. From this perspective, to involve the "public" in this decision-making or in the development of the policy that is perceived to underpin the individual sentencing decisions, is to add a distinctive quality to the decision-making, a quality that is distinctively non-legal. So one debate concerns the extent to which sentencing is a "legal" decision and to what extent members of the public without a legal qualification or training can legitimately participate in sentencing. This debate tends to assume that lawyers are experts and the public is non-expert. However, when one looks at the composition of sentencing commissions and councils, at the members of the public who have been incorporated into the sentencing policy-making process, one finds that most of these people are experts though usually not legally qualified experts. They almost always possess considerable expertise either in criminal justice or in a closely related area of public life. In this case the relevant distinction is between legal expertise and other sorts of expertise. The distinction is also between elected representatives, non-legal experts appointed by elected representatives, and legally qualified persons similarly appointed. It is very rare to find the "ordinary" dis-interested member of the public being invited to participate in the making of sentencing policy (Barkow and O'Neill, 2006; Barkow, 2005).

To what extent is sentencing a "legal" decision?

All jurisdictions have rules that govern the sentencing decision. In those juris-dictions where there are sentencing guidelines, there are rules that prescribe whether the guidelines are voluntary or prescriptive, whether judges can depart from the guidelines and, if they do, under what circumstances. In non-guideline jurisdictions, legislation typically provides sentencers with powers and defines maximum and sometimes minimum penalties, and otherwise leaves judges to exercise fairly extensive discretion in sentencing a particular case. Ashworth (2005) identifies four groups of factors that may enter the sentencer's thought processes when using discretion to make a sentencing decision in a particular case:

1. Views on the facts of the case.
2. Views on the principles of sentencing (the seriousness of the offence, the relative weight of aggravating and mitigating factors, the aims and effectiveness of different types of sentence).
3. Views on crime and punishment (the aims of sentencing, the causes of crime, the effects of sentencing).
4. Characteristics of sentencers (age, class, race, gender, religion, political beliefs and so on).

Taking the fourth point first, there is considerable evidence that the views and attitudes that people hold about crime and punishment are related to their social class background, level of education and, to a lesser extent, their age. Judges in most jurisdictions come from an educated middle class background and tend to be middle aged or older; to that extent, they represent a fairly homogeneous group. This is only a problem for those who would argue that judges should somehow be more representative of the community. A counter argument is that judges should be professionals able to distance themselves from their prejudices and make rational and disinterested judgments. This is a question of what makes good quality sentencing decisions.

Moving to the other three points, it is arguable that anyone may have views about these issues. Those with experience of criminal justice may have developed their views from a different knowledge base from those with only second-hand knowledge of the system. Indeed, this expertise may be a valuable contribution to the development of sentencing policy. However, the point is that legal training does not provide an objective set of "views" about the aims of punishment or the assessment of seriousness. In other words, there is nothing distinctively "legal" about sentencing decisions once the discretionary stage of the decision is reached. This is not to deny that sentencers develop a "professional frame of reference" (Hutton, 2006) as part of their working practice that helps to develop a degree of consistency in sentencing. However, this is developed through their professional practice; it does not derive from any more precise manipulation of legal rules or principles. There is no reason why lay persons may not develop similar practices and there is evidence that lay magistrates in England and Scotland do exactly this.

In other words, there is nothing distinctively "legal" about applying views about punishment, sentencing, seriousness and blameworthiness to reach "just" sentencing decisions. There is therefore no reason why lay people should not be able to make sensible sentencing decisions or to contribute to the formulation of sentencing policy. This does not mean that there are no skills required to do the job. Making sentencing decisions requires balancing the desire for consistency with sensitivity to the facts of each case, and it requires the ability to assess the relevance of large amounts of information and to make delicate judgments about seriousness, culpability and the relative weights to be attached to aggravating and mitigating factors. Both legally qualified and lay judges are likely to be assisted in these difficult tasks by the provision of a system of sentencing guidelines that allows discretion to be exercised within a structure that provides an element of consistency. This issue is recognised by the New Zealand Law Commission whose report conceives of sentencing as two separate, but related, tasks: the production of broad sentencing guidelines is a task for an independent council, in which the public has a role to play alongside judges; the choice of sentence in an individual case is a task for a judge.

Sentencing institutions, legitimation and the management of correctional resources

Barkow and O'Neill (2006) have asked why legislators in many State jurisdictions in the United States have delegated power to sentencing commissions to make sentencing policy. Delegation is usually done to shift responsibility for a policy area away from the executive in areas where the executive wants to avoid choosing between powerful interest groups. The government can take credit for success and allocate blame for failure to the delegated agency. Garland has argued that this shift of responsibility for criminal justice policy-making has been a characteristic of governments in the United Kingdom and the United States over the past 30 years. However, Barkow argues that, when it comes to sentencing policy, all the powerful interest groups are on the same side – they all favour tougher punishment. The only groups arguing against this are politically marginal, such as prisoners' groups or liberal intellectuals. Why then is sentencing policy delegated to commissions when the risks of failure are low? One argument is that the executive places a value on expertise and believes that a specialised body with the capacity to collect and analyse large quantities of data and to make detailed and sophisticated policy choices can provide a more effective policy. Barkow and O'Neill suggest that this argument is limited in its explanatory force. Sentencing is not seen by the public as the province of experts and, indeed, legislators frequently pass sentencing legislation without the benefit of advice from either the general public or experts.

When the political climate rewards punitive legislation, why delegate the task? Barkow and O'Neill's research identifies a range of political and economic factors that help to answer this question. One reason might be to avoid the long-term financial costs of tougher sentencing policies in terms of increased expenditure on prisons and corrections. Commissions can also provide an attractive means of limiting judicial discretion, particularly where judges exercise wide discretion. This might also be the case in a jurisdiction where judges retain high status and exercise considerable political power (such as Scotland and Victoria in Australia). Barkow and O'Neill expected to find that commissions would be used less frequently where judges were elected rather than appointed and were therefore likely to be influenced by the same electoral demands that apply to legislators. However, their research found the opposite: a stronger correlation between elected judges and sentencing institutions than between appointed judges and these institutions. This difference, they argue, is likely to be explained by legislative concerns with costs, which were the driving force behind the development of sentencing institutions. As elected judges would be as likely to drive up sentences as elected politicians, resort to a commission may be a way of trying to control costs. It is perhaps no coincidence that those jurisdictions that either have developed sentencing institutions or have proposed these institutions are those in majoritarian democracies where law and order has become a major focus of party political contest between two dominant parties.[3] They may represent an attempt by politicians both to deflect attention away from the government and an attempt to seek an alternative institutional approach to sentencing policy that can put a brake on corrections budgets.

All United States jurisdictions that have permanent sentencing commissions conduct assessments of the impact of guidelines on prison populations. These assessments are made possible by the more predictable nature of guidelines-based sentencing and by the staff and resources available in a State sentencing commission. Only the proposed New Zealand council has followed this approach. The Australian institutions have no formal remit to consider the cost or effectiveness of sentences. The proposed South African Commission has these powers as does the Sentencing Guidelines Council in England and Wales although it is difficult to see how the impact of sentencing guidelines on correctional budgets can be accurately forecast unless there is a comprehensive system of guidelines. United States commissions routinely model the impact of guidelines, indeed this has arguably been one of the most politically significant functions of these commissions. Similarly, only in the United States is there routine monitoring of adherence or departure from guidelines. No other sentencing institution appears to carry out this function. This is a point worth further discussion. If the introduction of commissions and guidelines is seen as the introduction of managerialism into criminal justice, then it is perhaps notable that the evaluation/monitoring/ performance measurement that is a crucial part of most other areas of public sector management has not been transferred to sentencing institutions, at least not outside the United States. This raises the issue of how to measure the effectiveness of sentencing institutions.

Effectiveness of sentencing institutions

While from a theoretical perspective there might be good arguments to support the development of sentencing institutions as a means of getting around the problems of populism and political disenchantment by trying to develop a more rational approach to penal policy, how do we know whether they are effective? If we continue to measure public attitudes to sentencing and punishment using traditional survey methods, it is unlikely that the development of sentencing institutions will have much impact, at least in the short to medium term (Hutton, 2005). Attitudes to sentencing and punishment are complex and have deep roots. They are not likely to be radically changed by a relatively modest institutional change.

Where sentencing institutions are able to develop a comprehensive set of sentencing guidelines and have the resources and political will to monitor adherence to these, as has occurred in some United States jurisdictions, then some measures of impact can be calculated. Analysis of sentencing under the Minnesota Guidelines suggests that the prison population of that State has risen much more slowly than might have been expected were the guidelines not there. This is not the case for other States, where politicians have been able to exercise their influence to use the guidelines to increase levels of punishment. In other jurisdictions, such as England and Wales, rising prison populations have been generated by judges sending more people to prison for longer.

Sentencing institutions do not have a particularly strong record in generating rational penal policy. Ultimately, the value of sentencing institutions depends more on a belief in the capacity of human societies to develop new institutional ways of doing politics to replace those methods that no longer work. The construction of a new process might be at least as important as the outcome.

Conclusion

This chapter has argued that for those who are concerned about the rising prison populations across western jurisdictions, and who would like to see the development of a more rational sentencing policy, the recently developed and proposed sentencing institutions offer an opportunity. They offer judges a forum in which they can contribute to the development of policy, something for which they have no current institutional arrangements in most jurisdictions. They offer politicians an element of protection from febrile law and order politics, particularly in majoritarian democracies, and a tool to control rising correctional costs. They offer experienced criminal justice practitioners, penal reformers and academics the opportunity to work with the judiciary to develop more rational policies. They offer an opportunity to provide information to the public, to educate the public and to engage with the public in ways that are very difficult for courts and politicians to do by themselves.

The problems of public disillusionment with politics and the growth of populist policy-making are shared across western jurisdictions and have deep cultural roots. They will not be easily solved. However, the increased interest in building new sentencing institutions is evidence that there are at least some grounds for hope that more rational approaches to penal policy can be developed.

Notes

1   For details of the sentencing commission work in Belgium, see van zyl Smit (2004). For a discussion in English of the development of sentencing guidance in the Netherlands, largely through the prosecution service, see Terblanche (2003).

2   The recent cases of Blakeley and Booker in the United States have challenged the legality of sentencing guidelines. For a recent overview of this, see Berman (2005).

3   Cavadino and Dignan (2006) characterise the same jurisdictions as "neo-liberal" in their typology. They argue that neo-liberal states are more punitive and provide some tentative explanations for this. They acknowledge that their analysis shares much in common with that of Downes and Hansen (2006) and Beckett and Western (2001).

References

Abadee, AR (2006). *The Role of Sentencing Advisory Councils*. Paper presented to the National Judicial College of Australia's National Sentencing Conference, Canberra.

Anderson, S, Ingram, D and Hutton, H (2002). *Public attitudes towards sentencing and alternatives to imprisonment*. Scottish Parliament Paper 488 session 1 2002. Edinburgh: HMSO. <http://www.scottish.parliament.uk/official_report/cttee/just1-02/j1r02-pats-01.htm>.

Ashworth, A (2005). *Sentencing and Criminal Justice*. 4th ed, Cambridge: Cambridge University Press.

Barkow, RE (2005). Administering Crime. *UCLA Law Review*: 52.

Barkow, RE and O'Neill, KM (2006). Delegating Punitive Power: The Political Economy of Sentencing Commission and Guideline Formation. *Texas Law Review*. 84(7): 1973.

Bazemore, G (2000). Community Justice and a vision of collective efficacy; the case of restorative conferencing. In J Horney (ed), *Policies, Processes and decisions of the Criminal Justice System* 3: 225 Washington, DC: National Institute of Justice.

Beckett, K and Western, B (2001). Governing Social Marginality: Welfare, Incarceration, and the Transformation of State Policy. *Punishment and Society* 3: 43.

Berman, D (2005). *Reconceptualising Sentencing*. University of Chicago Legal Forum, <http:// ssrn.com/abstract=801206>.

Bevir, M (2005). *New Labour: A Critique*. London: Routledge.

Bottoms, A (1995). The Philosophy and Politics of Punishment and Sentencing. In C Clarkson and R Morgan (eds), *The Politics of Sentencing Reform*. Oxford: Clarendon Press.

Braithwaite, J (2002). *Restorative Justice and Responsive Regulation*. Oxford: Oxford University Press.

Cavadino, M and Dignan, J (2006). Penal Policy and Political Economy. *Criminology and Criminal Justice* 6(4): 435.

Chanenson, SL (2005). Guidance from Above and Beyond. *Stanford Law Review*: 58.

Crawford, A (1999). *The Local Governance of Crime: Appeals to Community and Partnerships*. Oxford: Oxford University Press.

Downes, D and Hansen, K (2006). Welfare and Punishment in Comparative Context. In S Armstrong and L McAra (eds), *Perspectives on Punishment: The Contours of Control*. Oxford: Oxford University Press.

Durkheim, E (1933). *The Division of Labour in Society*. London: MacMillan.

Frase, RS (2005) Sentencing Guidelines: Diversity, Consensus and Unresolved Policy Issues. *Columbia Law Review* 105: 1190.

Garland, D (2001) *The Culture of Control*. Oxford: Oxford University Press.

Green, D (2006) Public Opinion Versus Public Judgment about Crime: Correcting the Comedy of Errors. *British Journal of Criminology* 46(1): 131.

Home Office (2006). *Making Sentencing Clearer*, <www.noms.homeoffice.gov.uk/news-publications-events/publications/consultations/Making_sentencing_clearer_consul>.

Hutchinson, S (2006). Countering Catastrophic Criminology: Reform, punishment and the modern liberal compromise. *Punishment and Society* 8(4): 443.

Hutton, N (2005). Beyond Populist Punitiveness. *Punishment & Society* 7(3): 243.

Hutton, N (2006). Sentencing as a Social Practice. In S Armstrong and L McAra (eds), *Perspectives on Punishment: The Contours of Control.* Oxford: Oxford University Press.

Indermaur D and Hough, M (2002). Strategies for Changing Public Attitudes to Punishment. In JV Roberts and M Hough (eds), *Changing Attitudes to Punishment. Public Opinion, Crime and Justice* Cullompton: Willan.

Matthews, R (2005). The Myth of Punitiveness. *Theoretical Criminology* 9(2): 175.

Matthews, R and Pitts, J (eds) (2001). *Crime, Disorder and Community Safety: A New Agenda?* Routledge.

Pettit, P (2002). Is Criminal Justice Politically Feasible? *Buffalo Law Review* 5: 427.

Reitz, KR (1998). Modelling Discretion in American Sentencing Systems. *Law and Policy* 20: 389.

Roberts, JV and Hough, M (eds) (2002). *Changing Attitudes to Punishment: Public Opinion, Crime and Justice.* Cullompton: Willan.

Roberts, JV and Hough, M (2005). *Understanding Public Attitudes to Criminal Justice.* UK: Open University Press.

Rosenbaum, DP (1994). *The Challenge of Community Policing: Testing the Promises.* Thousand Oaks CA: Sage Publications.

South African Law Commission (2000). *Report on a New Sentencing Framework.* Pretoria, South Africa.

Stoker, G (2006). *Why Politics Matters: Making Democracy Work.* Basingstoke: Palgrave MacMillan.

Terblanche, SS (2003). Sentencing Guidelines for South Africa; Lessons from Elsewhere. *South African Law Journal* 120: 858.

Tonry, M (2003). Evidence, Elections and Ideology in the Making of Criminal Justice Policy. In M Tonry (ed), *Confronting Crime: Crime Control Policy under New Labour.* Cullompton: Willan.

Van zyl Smit, D (2004). De Blik van een buitenstaander op de voorstellen tot hervorming van de straftoemeting in Belgie. *Fatik* 101: 5.

17

Does it matter? Reflections on the effectiveness of institutionalised public participation in the development of sentencing policy

Rob Allen and Mike Hough

Introduction

The contributions to this volume make it clear that there is a significant trend towards increasing public participation in sentencing policy in many countries in the world. Handled well, this should lead to greater public trust in justice. Mishandled, public opinion can exercise a dire impact on penal policy. The aim of this chapter is to assess how best to achieve positive and constructive community engagement in penal policy. We take it as axiomatic that "community engagement" is a two-way process, involving on the one hand, the provision of information and education, and on the other, a genuine responsiveness to what people think about justice. How this is best done involves not only substantive decisions about the right balance to strike in informing and responding, but also the building of the right institutional framework to allow for effective community engagement.

In considering these questions, we draw heavily on England and Wales as a case study. This is not because we have solved the main problems of community engagement, but because, quite clearly, we have not. The recent history of penal policy in that country – over the 12-month period from January 2006 – provides some clear lessons on how *not* to engage with the public on issues relating to penal policy. One might argue that very special circumstances applied at the time. The Labour administration was suffering badly in the polls, in the aftermath of the Iraq War. Tony Blair was serving out his last term as Prime Minister, struggling both to regain public confidence and to recover the prospect of some sort of political "legacy". In hindsight it may look like an atypical year. From our viewpoint, and at the time of writing, it represents in exaggerated form the sort of risks that democratic governments often run of losing the initiative over penal policy. We hope that, despite our domestic preoccupations, some of the reflections may have a wider resonance for readers from other countries.

We start by outlining the place that public opinion holds among the various drivers of sentencing policy. We then describe a series of events in England and Wales in 2006 that had the effect of locking the Labour government into an ever tougher stance on sentencing. In essence, these were all forms of failure in the criminal justice system that in other circumstances would have posed much less significant political difficulty. However, the fact that they happened to occur within a few months of each other – and at a particular stage in the life of the government – had far reaching consequences both for public confidence and sentencing policy.

We conclude by looking at what, if anything, might have made a difference to the way in which those events have shaped policy developments, drawing out wider lessons. In particular, we address the question of whether mechanisms such as sentencing councils can act as a brake on penal populism. They will turn out to be of real value if they prove able to interrupt the way that governments privilege perceived public opinion about the desirability of ever harsher sentences over other considerations, including the effect of measures in reducing and preventing crime. We also give some attention to alternatives, or complementary initiatives that could be adopted by sentencing councils, such as the Rethinking Crime and Punishment initiative that one of us led from 2001 to 2004.

Drivers of sentencing policy

The United Kingdom Cabinet Office White Paper "Modernising Government" defines policy-making as "the process by which governments translate their political vision into programmes and actions to deliver 'outcomes' – desired changes in the real world". For most of the second half of the 20th century, British penal policy in general evolved with very little regard to public opinion. Public opinion was something to be *managed*, but it was not regarded as something that should be a significant driver of policy. Since the early 1990s, however, there has been a radical shift towards a greater responsiveness to public opinion. Several factors are responsible.

In the first place, the authority of "expert opinion" and the legitimacy of professional judgment has waned, not just in penal policy but across the political landscape. This is a trend associated by sociologists such as Giddens (1990; 1991) with global patterns of development in "late modern" industrialised societies linked to declining levels of deference and greater democratisation in decision-making. Secondly – a linked phenomenon – the reform agendas of British public sector services by both Conservative and Labour governments over this period have emphasised the need for greater responsiveness to the public as both pay-masters and consumers of public services. Thirdly, penal policy itself has become increasingly politicised. While this process of politicisation has been evolving over a much longer period,[1] it was in 1992 that, as shadow Home Secretary, Tony Blair famously mounted a credible challenge to the Conservatives as the party of "law and order" by promising a new Labour government that would be "tough on crime, tough on the causes of crime". Since then, both parties have taken care to ensure that their penal policies resonate with public opinion, at least as it is con-structed in, and reflected by, the popular press.

Fourthly, there has been a growing political recognition of the centrality of public confidence in the criminal justice system; there are important linkages between compliance with the law and confidence in the fairness and effectiveness of the system (see Tyler and Huo, 2003). The authority of the police in particular, but also that of the other agencies of justice, requires institutional legitimacy, and government needs to be sure that public confidence in justice is not ebbing. Since 1998, the government has established "key performance indicators" and targets relating to confidence in justice. More recently, there has been a variety of government initiatives to promote community engagement in the justice system through, for example, "community justice centres" and efforts to make community penalties more visible to the public and responsive to the needs of local people.

There are, of course, other drivers of penal policy that have continued to play an important role and may push sentencing policy in a rather different direction to penal populism.

For one thing, although political parties may nowadays attach more weight to the electoral advantage of crime policies than to the principles that underlie them or their effectiveness, such considerations have not entirely trumped core political values. Traditionally, Labour's values include social justice and the idea of community in which "we live in a spirit of solidarity, tolerance and respect". Notwithstanding the repositioning towards "tough on crime" in the mid-1990s, such values might suggest a leaning towards a more sparing use of imprisonment than those of the Conservative party historically associated with discipline and the rule of law (Allen, 2003).

Aside from political philosophy, there is the question of how comfortably the principles or effects of penal policy sit alongside broader governmental objectives such as tackling social exclusion or promoting human rights. From its inception, New Labour has proclaimed an overarching commitment to combating social exclusion and, given what is known about the personal and social circumstances of offenders, it did not take long for the Social Exclusion Unit – the government department set up to develop policy in this field – to turn its attention to prison (Social Exclusion Unit, 2001). The broad thrust of its report on "Reducing re-offending by ex-prisoners" was accepted by the Prime Minister in 2002. The report identified a "growing consensus that we are sending some people to prison who should not be there" and concluded that "there is a considerable risk that a prison sentence might actually make the factors associated with re-offending worse".

On human rights, the *Human Rights Act* 1998 (UK) requires ministers to state that any legislative provisions are in their view compatible with rights under the European Convention on Human Rights. It is debatable how far human rights considerations have acted as a constraint on penal policy-making, although they have played an important part in shaping particular legislative provisions, particularly in relation to terrorism. Over many years, a steady stream of rulings from Strasbourg has forced governments to amend the law, or at least consider doing so, on a range of issues. At the time of writing, a consultation is underway about the voting rights of convicted prisoners in the United Kingdom following a ruling by the European court (Department for Constitutional Affairs, 2007).

In respect of sentencing, decisions of the European Court of Human Rights (ECHR) have played an important role in clarifying how indeterminate sentences should be implemented. We discuss below how one such ruling, relating to the minimum period of detention to be served by offenders sentenced to discretionary life sentences, contributed to the media and political row in the case of Craig Sweeney, an offender convicted of paedophile offences. The tension between the demands of the ECHR and government has been most vividly illustrated by a statement made by Tony Blair, the then Prime Minister, at the height of the furore about foreign prisoners that in his view all foreign prisoners should be deported regardless of the dangers they face in their home nation – a clear reference to the European Court ruling that prevents this (and that the government has subsequently vowed to work to overturn).

Other drivers of policy include, of course, feasibility, cost and cost-effectiveness. Harsher sentencing policy inevitably produces a greater demand for prison places. As the review of the correctional services conducted by Patrick Carter recognised, "in the short term, the capacity of prison and probation is relatively fixed – it takes three to six years to build a prison and two years to train a probation officer" (Carter, 2003).

Despite the high costs of prison and guidance from the Treasury about appraisal and evaluation of policy options, criminal justice appears relatively immune to the sophisticated methods used to evaluate whether new drugs should be introduced or whether to build new roads. Carter recommended that decisions on changing the capacity and composition of prisons and probation need to be set against other interventions to reduce crime and improve public confidence. These investment decisions need to be informed, he argued, "by evidence of what works, when and for whom".

The substantial review of the sentencing framework undertaken by John Halliday (Home Office, 2001) does contain a section on costs and benefits but the review makes no attempt "to say what general level of severity of punishment would be appropriate". This, it argued, "is matter for political judgment" (Home Office, 2001, p 58).

And indeed, political judgment is the factor that seems to have been particularly significant in England and Wales over the past 10 years. There are at least two aspects to this. First is the personal attitudes and beliefs of Tony Blair in his period as Prime Minister; and, secondly, the media-driven need to respond to events.

It is generally held that on criminal policy, the Blair government epitomised penal populism.[2] With its repositioning in the early 1990s, New Labour set out to proof itself against the appearance of being soft on crime, which was judged to have contributed to two electoral defeats. The "tough on crime" mantra continued after Labour's electoral victory in 1997, and there has been a continued appeal to what the Prime Minister referred to in a leaked memo in July 2000 as "gut British instinct". His answer on that occasion – "We should think now of an initiative, for example, locking up street muggers. Something tough, with immediate bite which sends a message through the system" – appears to confirm this view of a government obsessed with the message rather than the substance of policy.

This is not, of course, a distinction that Blair would necessarily accept. When confronted in 2003 with the criticism that he likes to sound tough for the sake of it, he responded thus:

> I know, but is what we're trying to do right? When I say we need to get tough on anti-social behaviour, is that right? I think it is right. If you're an old lady and you're walking down to the shops, then you shouldn't have a gang of youths jostling you, pushing you around and abusing you. It absolutely disgusts me when people are treated with that type of disrespect. So that's why I am doing it. It's the vulnerable who suffer from crime.

When asked about his plans to remove the right to jury trial for certain crimes, he went on:

I'm not doing it for machismo, because I want to sound tough. I actually believe in it, I'm afraid. I believe in it very, very strongly. I think the criminal justice system is in many ways abused today by the guilty. I don't think there's any doubt at all that not nearly enough of the guilty are convicted in front of a court.

There is clearly a combination at work of personal prejudices and political strategy.

The second aspect relates to what is perceived by politicians as a need to respond quickly and decisively to significant day-to-day events that blow up in the media. This is not a new phenomenon. It was the *Dangerous Dogs Act* of 1991 that came to epitomise ill thought out "knee jerk" legislative response to particular tragic events. More relevant to sentencing was the speedy reversal of the key principles of the 1991 *Criminal Justice Act* within a few months of its implementation in October 1992 (Ashworth and Hough, 1996).

Case Study – England and Wales 2006

Sentencing policy in the early part of 2006 in England and Wales appeared reasonably settled. The 2003 *Criminal Justice Act*, given Royal Assent in November 2003, represented according to the government[3] "the most significant overhaul of the criminal justice system in a generation", comprising "end-to-end reforms to modernise and rebalance the system in favour of victims, witnesses and communities", helping to "tackle and reduce crime, from detection to the rehabilitation of offenders, by bringing more offenders to justice, making trials a search for the truth, and making punishments work more effectively".

The government described the Act as responding "to widespread calls for reform to update the criminal justice system and restore public confidence bringing forward a coherent, imaginative and balanced package of provisions". These provisions were based, the government claimed, on detailed recommendations made in a series of independent inquiries and reviews – from the Law Commission (the body responsible for legal reform), from Sir Robin Auld, a High Court Judge who had conducted an inquiry into the structure of the court system, and from a senior civil servant, John Halliday, whose review of the sentencing framework, "Making Punishment Work", had been published in 2001. The Auld and Halliday reviews (Auld, 2002; Home Office, 2001) had incorporated extensive public consultations, although the bulk of the 500 and 200 responses made to the two reviews respectively came from criminal justice professionals and from interest groups rather than from the general public.

As far as sentencing was concerned, the Act aimed to introduce clarity and consistency, setting out the purposes and principles of sentencing in statute for the first time and introducing a guidelines council. Specific measures included tougher sentences for murder, sexual and violent offences, persistent offenders, firearms offences and dangerous drivers who kill; and imaginative and robust alternatives to custody that could be tailored to individual offenders and be based on what is most effective in reducing reoffending. Most of these provisions were implemented in April 2005, a month ahead of a general election in which the government would have to defend its record of two terms in office.

Crime policy did indeed play a part in the May 2005 general election, with the Conservative party pledging to end Labour's early release from prison scheme and to provide 20,000 extra prison places as part of a policy of honesty in sentencing. The Labour manifesto contained no specific new pledges, concentrating rather on the powers it had recently legislated. After the election, Prime Minister Blair said that he had been struck during the campaign by public concern about crime and anti-social behaviour, vowing to "make this a particular priority for this government, how we bring back a proper sense of respect in our schools, in our communities, in our towns and our villages". Within a few weeks of their third election victory, the government introduced its Respect Action Plan (Home Office, 2005) but there was no expectation that further reform of sentencing would play much part in the third term.

If the sentencing framework appeared to be reasonably settled, this could not be said of the organisational arrangements for the prison and probation services responsible for the execution of sentences that it produces. From June 2004, both had become part of a merged National Offender Management Service (NOMS), a new body whose creation had been recommended in Patrick Carter's review of the Correctional Services that had reported to the government at the end of 2003. Without consultation, the government had almost immediately accepted what turned out to be highly controversial proposals. Legislation to give effect to perhaps the most controversial – the introduction of a market to deliver probation services – was introduced in early 2005 but made little progress before the election. After the election the government produced a consultation paper on restructuring probation, responses to which were almost entirely hostile.

Leaving aside these radical plans for reform of prisons and probation, sentencing policy looked at the start of 2006 to be fairly stable. The government's five-year strategy for protecting the public and reducing re-offending, published in February 2006, mainly concentrated on plans to implement what had already been legislated (Home Office, 2006). Within only five months, however, the government was publishing another document of a very different kind, the result of a hurriedly conducted but "thorough audit of the entire system". The immediate improvements that were put in place, it argued,

> [H]ave given us the breathing space needed for a fundamental examination of how the criminal justice system is working and, in particular, whether the rights of the accused and those of the victim and the community are correctly balanced. Our intention is to stimulate a wide ranging public debate on the way forward, on sentencing for example.

How come within a matter of months of "the most significant overhaul of the criminal justice system in a generation", the government found itself revisiting some of the basic questions of sentencing? The answer lies in the series of events that took place during the first part of 2006. These raised public and political concern about three distinct but overlapping subjects: the supervision of released prisoners in the community, the failure to deport foreign national prisoners and the adequacy of sentencing arrangements for the most serious offenders. Individually, the three concerns were about undoubtedly serious problems. However, the way that they emerged simultaneously lent each an added importance and significance.

Supervision in the community

On 28 February 2006, the Chief Inspector of Probation published a report on the circumstances in which a Chelsea banker had been murdered and his wife seriously wounded during a burglary. The dreadful crime had been committed by two offenders subject to supervision by the probation service (Bridges, 2006). The review had been commissioned by the Home Secretary in part because, in his words, "it is vital to public confidence in community orders and licenses that your findings and recommendations lead to lessons being learned by the responsible authorities and that any necessary changes are implemented as the top priority".

The report found "serious deficiencies" and a "collective failure" in the supervision of both the offenders. This was not the first such report: in 2005 a Youth Offending team and an electronic tagging company had been criticised for errors in the supervision of Peter Williams, found guilty of the murder of Nottingham jeweller Marian Bates. The report said the authorities failed to act quickly enough when Williams had repeatedly breached his curfew order and removed the electronic tag that was supposed to restrict his movements.

But the publicity generated by the Monckton report was increased by two further cases that came to prominence, both of which involved serious crimes committed by offenders on probation supervision. March saw the trial of Yusuf Bouhaddaou, a crack addict who had murdered teacher Robert Symons in his Chiswick home. Bouhaddaou had been released on licence from a five-and-a-half-year sentence five weeks before the murder and was under the supervision of the London Probation Service at the time he killed Mr Symons. To make matters worse, a further case attracted national attention only a week later. Six men were found guilty of the torture and brutal murder of Mary Ann Leneghan in Reading. At the trial it emerged that four of them had been subject to probation supervision.

All three cases received a great deal of media attention, and serious questions were asked about the system of early release from prison and supervision in the community. Home Secretary Charles Clarke acknowledged in a speech on 21 March that there was "a major problem of public protection ... There have been serious mistakes within our probation system and Parole Board system, which let out people who ought not to be free. I would say this is my number one priority". A newspaper reported him privately describing probation as "the dagger at the heart of the criminal justice system, undermining public confidence in criminal justice as a whole" (*Daily Telegraph*, 21 March 2006).

Little effort was made by the government to put the issue of offending under supervision into any kind of context. When Chief Inspector of Probation Andrew Bridges described the number of early-release prisoners re-offending as "tiny", his comments were criticised by the mother of a woman who was killed by a sex offender while on parole. Verna Bryant said "every week" someone seemed to re-offend during parole. In fact Bridges' figures suggested that serious re-offending took place twice a week but little sustained attempt was made to set the figure in the context of the 20,000 offenders under supervision on licence at any one time following release from prison. There was no attempt to confront the difficult reality that however perfectly implemented, community supervision of dangerous offenders would always pose some degree of risk and that, by definition, some risks would go badly wrong.[4]

The government's response was to propose more stringent supervision for ex-prisoners in the form of violent offender orders – restrictive orders similar to those applied to sex offenders. At the time of writing, little more detail has emerged about what these orders would involve.

This was not, however, the last case of this kind. May 2006 saw the publication of a report into Anthony Rice, who had been convicted of the murder of Naomi Bryant nine months previously, at a time when he was being supervised on a Life Licence by Hampshire Probation Area. The report again found a number of deficiencies, in the form of mistakes, misjudgments and miscommunications at various stages throughout the whole process of this case, that amounted to what the Probation Inspector called a cumulative failure. Moreover, his report argued that the human rights dimension was posing increasing levels of challenge to those charged with delivering effective public protection. This criticism fed into broader concerns about the *Human Rights Act* 1998 that had arisen following the second case.

Foreign prisoners

The second wave of concern began on 25 April when the Home Office admitted that more than 1000 foreign criminals were released from prison between 1999 and March 2006 without being considered for deportation. These were all cases where judges had recommended that they be deported, but not only had the Home Office not made the decision to deport them, they had simply been released at the end of their sentence.

This became a headline story, particularly when Home Secretary Clarke revealed that five of the released criminals who had been convicted of serious offences had committed new crimes since their release, including violent and drug offences. Mr Clarke insisted he would stay in his job to repair the situation, but when it emerged that it took him three weeks to tell the Prime Minister that serious criminals were among the prisoners not considered for deportation, his position became increasingly fragile. The opposition parties argued that the government had lost control of the situation and, after heavy losses in local government elections on 4 May, Clarke was sacked as Home Secretary after refusing the offer of another cabinet post. Defence Secretary John Reid was named as his successor.

The new Home Secretary quickly revised the number of serious offenders freed without being deported from 90 to at least 150, admitting that the final figure could end up being "several hundred" if armed robbers were included. Ten days later, Mr Reid revealed that one murderer was among the freed criminals still at large. He again changed the figure for the number of serious offenders on the list but was able to tell Parliament that 880 of the total 1023 cases had been considered for deportation, with an initial decision to deport made in almost three-quarters of cases.

However, the issue did not go away but became embedded in a series of rows about immigration that were stoked by a number of further events: a senior official telling a Parliamentary Committee he had not the "faintest idea" how many illegal immigrants there are in the United Kingdom; another admitting that National Insurance numbers have been given to people without checking their immigration status; allegedly corrupt immigration officers offering passports for sex; and even illegal immigrants employed in cleaning jobs at Home Office buildings.

The end of May saw the new Home Secretary telling Parliament that the Immigration Department (which took the blame for the administrative failings in respect of foreign prisoners) was not fit for purpose and that the whole department could be dysfunctional. Further rows emerged during this period: over the 700 prisoners who absconded from open prisons; over the Criminal Records Bureau (CRB) after it emerged that 2700 innocent people had been wrongly labelled criminals – with some being turned down for jobs as a result; and over asylum when it was disclosed that 223 foreign nationals arrested in counter-terrorism operations were allowed to remain in Britain as asylum seekers. It all added up to a picture of incompetence. It was little wonder that the Home Office's top civil servant, the Permanent Secretary, described the first part of 2006 as being like a "tropical storm" and the previous few weeks as a "hurricane", accepting that the controversies, including those over foreign criminals, had "inflicted immense damage" on his department.

Sentencing

On 11 June, under the headline "Lenient judges shamed in list", the *Sunday Times*, Britain's leading broadsheet Sunday newspaper, wrote a story about the increasing number of cases considered unduly lenient, which had gone up by one-third in the past four years. The figures, released under the *Freedom of Information Act*, showed that in 2005 389 sentences thought to be too lenient were sent to the Attorney General by prosecutors and the public, compared with 277 in 2001. In fact, fewer than one in three was then sent to the Court of Appeal, with 75 per cent of the 106 reviewed by the Court found to be "unduly lenient". Nonetheless, the Attorney General was quoted as saying he was particularly concerned about judges being lenient on sex offences against children which needed "to be dealt with very harshly indeed".

The next day the tabloid paper *The Sun* (like the *Times*, a title owned by Rupert Murdoch) launched a vitriolic campaign demanding "harsh punishment for judges who favour thugs and their own liberal consciences – while failing our society". Alongside photographs of the judges the paper found guilty of being "soft on killers, child sex beasts, rapists and other violent criminals" were demands that the men pictured here were put in the dock. *The Sun's* agenda was clear: "It is part of our campaign to have tough action – including sacking – taken against judges who hand down lenient sentences. We demand that bad judges be suspended or dismissed and lists of them, and others disciplined, be published".

The campaign made demands for toughening up specific aspects of the appeals process for unduly lenient sentences – abolishing automatic discounts on any longer term imposed, extending to three months the deadline to appeal against a sentence, and requiring judges to tell crime victims they have the right to appeal against a soft sentence.

In addition, to address their concern that "some of the sentences handed down for the crimes that most appal society are so inadequate that they undermine confidence in the criminal justice system and compound the anguish already felt by victims", *The Sun* called for elected public prosecutors and community judges.

The Sun did accept that the fault did not lie entirely with a judiciary who "must administer the law as laid down, sometimes bizarrely, by ministers".

Nobody, for instance, it went on, "understands why sentences are automatically halved for good conduct or slashed in return for a guilty plea".

As if to illustrate the point, the very same day a major row erupted about the sentencing of a particular case – more precisely, about what sentencing actually entails in practice. Craig Sweeney, a paedophile who had abducted and sexually abused a three-year-old girl, was sentenced to life imprisonment with the judge giving him an 18-year tariff. The outcry followed when it emerged that he would be eligible to be considered for parole in as little as five years. The minimum tariff was five years because in accordance with recently produced guidelines, the judge had reduced the tariff by a third to reflect the early admission of guilt; he had further reduced it by 11 months to reflect time already served on remand; and offenders serving discretionary life sentences are eligible to be considered for parole halfway through their sentence. The recorder of Cardiff, Judge John Griffith Williams QC, said he could be eligible for parole after five years, but added that an early release was "unlikely".

Nonetheless, the relatives described it as an insult and within hours Home Secretary John Reid criticised Sweeney's sentence for being "unduly lenient" and asked Attorney General Lord Goldsmith to consider referring the case to the Court of Appeal, claiming the tariff did not "reflect the seriousness of this crime".

In the controversy that developed over the following days, blame was distributed fairly widely. One minister criticised the judge for getting the sentence wrong but was forced to retract her criticism and apologise when her boss, the Lord Chancellor, located the problem with the law and not the judge. Lord Falconer warned of the need to be extremely careful that "we don't attack the judges on these issues where it is the system" and went on to suggest, "it's not one or other political party, it's 30 years of statutes that have led to this". This did not prevent the row taking on a party-political dimension. Conservative leader David Cameron claimed the government played a part in the reduction of Sweeney's sentence by a third, by introducing the Sentencing Guidelines Council in the first place. He also blamed Labour's *Criminal Justice Act* for the fact Sweeney would be eligible for parole after five years.

The Labour government was not slow to respond. Although the Attorney General decided that the Sweeney sentence was not unduly lenient (finding that, in setting the term, the judge acted within existing sentencing guidance and law), he made clear his view that judges should have more discretion over the discount they give for an early guilty plea, and that the way discounts apply when a case is referred to the Court of Appeal should be re-examined. "It is also plain", he opined, "that there is a need to re-examine the automatic 50 per cent reduction in fixing the minimum term".

By June 2006 the pressure on the Labour government over law and order was intense. Whether in response to this pressure or not, Blair made a major speech in which he argued for placing a far higher priority, in what is a conflict of rights, on the rights of those who keep the law rather than break it. For penal policy "the blunt reality is that, at least in the short and medium term, the measures proposed will mean an increase in prison places".

The Sun newspaper was able to claim a victory in its "crusade against lenient judges":

Sentencing guidelines will be changed so out-of-touch judges can get it right every time. Killers, paedophiles and rapists will be freed only by a unanimous parole board decision. The prison overcrowding crisis will be addressed. And the shocking release of foreign inmates without deportation will also be dealt with.

Detailed proposals along the lines predicted by *The Sun* were contained in the July report, "Rebalancing the criminal justice system in favour of the law-abiding majority". The government's review had revealed that they had "not yet convinced the public that the sentencing process is delivering what it must". The report promised 8000 new prison places and a range of tough measures. Proposals to address the issues that had emerged in the Sweeney case were contained in a further consultation paper, "Making Sentencing Clearer", published in October. The *Times*, under the headline "Top judges revolt over reform of sentencing", reported that responses from the senior judiciary rejected 14 out of the 16 proposals in the paper and reflected anger at "change for the sake of change".

The firestorm that engulfed the criminal justice system in 2006 burst back into flames in the early part of 2007 with a major row over a failure to record details of British criminals who had committed serious crimes abroad. At the time of writing it is unclear what will happen as a result, but what is clearly an unhappy period in criminal justice policy-making looks set to continue.

What could have made a difference?

While it is tempting to accept what happened in 2006 as an example of what Harold Macmillan described as "events, dear boy, events", it seems important to reflect on whether the way that government responded to those events was inevitable or whether alternative strategies might have been adopted. In particular, it is important to consider whether bodies such as the Sentencing Guidelines Council and the Sentencing Advisory Panel might have played a more prominent role. As we shall discuss, they actually had only limited visibility, and when they were visible they were regarded not as part of the solution, but as part of the problem.

The preconditions for a "penal firestorm"

In considering how jurisdictions might best protect themselves against the sort of events we have described in this chapter, a first step is to identify the factors that were accidentally assembled to trigger the process. First, it has to be recognised that the sequence of events happened a decade into the life of an administration that had initially attracted enormous electoral support, not least by wooing the traditionally conservative media. By 2006 – three years after the Iraq war – both the media and large segments of the population had fallen out of love with New Labour. The government could reasonably expect to "get a good kicking" in *some* policy arena.

What was it about penal policy that created just the right opportunity to deliver this kicking? In the first place, crime and punishment have long provided the staple that media news values require: crime stories are about people, and they involve conflict, violence, sex and shock; these stories come with the added bonus of a *dramatis personae* that includes out-of-touch judges, incompetent bureaucrats and ineffective politicians. Secondly, penal politics have become increasingly hotly contested, ever since New Labour stole the "law and order" clothes of the Conservative Party in 1992, with the promise to be "tough on crime, tough on the causes of crime". As the battle over penal politics has intensified, both the main political parties have been keen to portray themselves as the only possible choice for tackling such a grave and pressing problem. In other words, neither party has really been interested in correcting the media portrayal of a criminal justice system in a state of crisis.

Could the firestorm have been averted, or at least contained? While we have moments of deep pessimism about the impossibility of ever interrupting the sort of dynamic we have described, we think it essential to continue to try to do so. Fire-fighting of this sort almost by definition uses information as a resource. There are two sorts of task that need to be done. The first can be labelled broadly as community engagement and the second is brokering improved understanding of criminal justice problems among the key institutional players in penal policy.

Community engagement

One of the features of penal politics at the turn of the century is that the public is woefully ill-informed – or indeed misinformed – about crime and justice. People think that crime is rising, and have thought so consistently over the whole decade that it has been falling. People think that the courts are far too soft, and their views have not shifted significantly over a period in which we have almost doubled our use of imprisonment. Who can convincingly correct these deep-rooted misperceptions? The media have no interest in doing so. The government cannot command sufficient trust to deliver a credible message to the public. Opposition politicians certainly do not wish to support the government of the day in telling a good story about law and order. Clearly there is a need for an authoritative, trusted institution that can perform this function.

Can sentencing councils do so? To date, the Sentencing Guidelines Council has not aspired to take on this role in England and Wales – nor indeed has any statutory authority. The *Criminal Justice Act* 2003 (UK) specifies its sole responsibility as the provision of judicial guidelines. Nor does the Sentencing Advisory Panel adopt such a role. The Panel, which supports the work of the Council, takes account of public opinion in formulating its advice but does not take any responsebility for ensuring that the public is better informed about crime and justice. Neither body has acquired any significant public visibility as an authoritative and independent body that can be trusted to speak on matters relating to crime and punishment.

This is not intended as criticism of the performance of either body. However, it is worth considering whether these institutions should have their remit broadened and their resources extended, to give them the responsibility of improving public understanding of crime and justice. In our view, the Sentencing Guidelines Council could provide the nucleus for the institutional structures needed to achieve a real impact on public attitudes about crime and justice. One might also ask whether it has sufficient distance from the senior judiciary, and a sufficient balance between judicial, professional and lay members, to achieve a fully independent role.

Precisely how the Sentencing Guidelines Council should tackle a new responsibility for community engagement is a complex challenge. Clearly the main means of reaching the public remains the mass media, and even a well-resourced, fully independent and well-regarded council might not begin to dent the vested interests of some media sectors. On the other hand, not to make *any* attempt to do so is to our minds unthinkable. Whatever the case, new communication media, most obviously the internet, are providing opportunities for direct access to growing proportions of the public, and this could eventually provide a means for surmounting the baleful effects of the media on penal policy.

There are also practical things that sentencing councils can do to ensure that there is greater public understanding of sentencing. Most obviously, we need a less opaque system of labelling our sentences. Life sentences never meant "life" – even if they are beginning to do so for increasing numbers of prisoners. Offenders serve half the nominal sentence of all determinate sentences. Finding the best way of presenting sentences to the public is something that requires urgent attention.

If community engagement is not an appropriate function for a sentencing council, one might reasonably ask where such responsibilities should be placed. One model is to engineer a matrix of institutional partners to take on the work. The closest model that we can think of is "Rethinking Crime and Punishment" (RCP), a voluntary sector initiative set up by a charitable foundation in 2000 to raise the level of debate about prison and its alternatives in the United Kingdom (Esmée Fairbairn Foundation, 2004). The work has since inspired an identically named initiative in New Zealand that was established by Prison Fellowship.

The original RCP funded a wide range of activities relating to the use of prison, including research (for example, the work of Hough et al, 2003); inquiries such as a major commission on alternatives to prison (Coulsfield, 2004); awareness-raising campaigns and events; and public involvement exercises.

Projects of particular relevance to the question of understanding and confidence included: "Local Crime Community Sentence", in which probation staff and sentencers made presentations about sentencing to community groups; the Case Study project in which ex-offenders are trained to appear on local and regional media to explain the impact of sentences; "Making Justice Relevant", a campaign to educate trade unions, professional groups and the police about the realities of criminal justice; information packs such as "What you really need to know about Crime and Justice and What can I do?", a guide to getting involved, plus a Prisoners' Sunday Parish Pack; and a website[5] that provides a range of up-to-date information and explanation about the system.

The experience of the 60 projects funded by the initiative fed into a set of recommendations relating both to substantive criminal justice and social policy questions, and to increasing public understanding and involvement. RCP can be seen to have had some impact at both levels. Some of the key recommendations made by RCP are reflected in recent government commitments to look at expanding the capacity of residential rehabilitation for drug users (Blair, 2006), enhancing mental health treatment within prisons (Prime Minister's Strategy Unit, 2007), and further developing restorative justice provisions (Prime Minister's Strategy Unit, 2007). Also reflecting the work of RCP is the interest in increasing both the visibility of community penalties and the involvement of local people and organisations in the delivery of unpaid work, the largest single component of community-based alternatives to prison. Indeed, a practical follow up to RCP is exploring initiatives to give community groups a say over the type of unpaid work undertaken by offenders.

In terms of influencing the overall trajectory of sentencing policy, it is difficult to assess RCP's impact. One of the aims of RCP was to communicate to politicians and policy-makers the reality of public attitudes in this area and lay bare the "comedy of errors in which policy and practice is not based on a proper understanding of public opinion, and that the same opinion is not based on a proper understanding of policy and practice" (Allen 2002).

Notwithstanding the rather gloomy turn of events in 2006, the government's most recent criminal justice review published in March 2007 (Prime Minister's Strategy Unit, 2007) contains a more balanced approach than the rather frenetic documents that preceded it. But even at the height of the concern to protect the public and rebalance sentencing, there has been both a recognition that there are people in prison who should not be there and a desire to replace short prison sentences with community penalties. Despite strong support for this approach from the Lord Chief Justice, the courts have not responded in a way that has produced expected falls in short sentences. Some sentencers may have reacted against what they see as attempts to tailor judicial decision-making in order to ease over-crowding in the prison system; for others, it is likely that any messages about a sparing use of prison for less serious offenders is in large part drowned out by the overarching rhetoric of toughness. Nonetheless, we are encouraged by the government's assessment that, following the recent toughening in sentencing, it is now in a position where "it can aim to achieve stability in sentencing and a greater focus on rehabilitation" (Prime Minister's Strategy Unit, 2007). To an extent, this assessment reflects the tenor of the work of RCP.

Brokering improved relations between key players

Few would argue that there are comfortable four-way relations among the govern-ment, the judiciary, senior criminal justice managers and the media. Relations between politicians and the senior judiciary are at an all-time low. For example, at the height of the row over Sweeney, a judge told the *Times*:

> The Lord Chancellor has failed to defend judges; the Home Secretary is attacking sentences; and the Attorney-General is publishing material about lenient sentences. These are the criminal justice ministers with whom we are meant to be working. If you damage public confidence in judiciary in this way, by saying, in effect that judges are incompetent, the next step is vigilantism. It is very dangerous.

The Lord Chancellor agreed that "[w]e need to be very, very careful to ensure we work together to reach a solution". However, it is far from clear that the structures and willingness to attempt this exist. Sentencing councils could provide a forum for precisely that sort of process. Again, the ability of the Sentencing Guidelines Council to play such a facilitative role requires visibility, authority, resources and independence from all key players, and these conditions are not yet met in England and Wales. One clear need is to find a more effective means for engaging the voice of parliamentarians in the work of the Council.

Finally, sentencing councils might also provide help and support for beleaguered institutions within the criminal justice system. When courts or prisons or probation come under attack for poor performance, they often struggle to justify their position. The problem is one of credibility – "They would say that, wouldn't they?". The value of having an independent, authoritative institution that could speak on such matters – to the media, to politicians, to other criminal justice agencies – is obvious. Throughout the unfolding of events that we have described, both the judiciary and the probation service could have benefited from a council that could have persuasively explained, for example, that a *review* date for an indeterminate sentence is not a *release* date, and that no probation service, however perfect, could ever offer 100 per cent protection to the public from dangerous offenders after release from prison.

We are not simply advocating the establishment of an "arms length" spin-doctoring institution. To have credibility and authority, councils have to recognise and address problems when these are real. However, the recent history of penal politics in Britain is in large part a sorry tale of ignorance, misinformation and prejudice, and the need for some sort of effective counterbalancing body strikes us as unarguable.

Postscript

Since this chapter was written, sentencing policy has been subjected to significant structural change within government. On 9 May 2007, the Home Office was divided in two with responsibility for sentencing, prisons and probation moving to a new Ministry of Justice, which also continues to exercise the responsibilities previously exercised by the Department for Constitutional Affairs, including the administration of the courts and support for judges. While widely welcomed in principle, the change has led to concern among the senior judiciary that the resources demanded by the prisons could threaten the budget available for courts and for legal aid, and could put pressure on sentencers to make more sparing use of prison. By the end of May 2007, the prison population had reached a record 81,000.

There have also been major changes in government. Gordon Brown replaced Tony Blair as Prime Minister in July 2007. There are entirely new ministerial teams in both the Home Office and the Ministry of Justice. There is a commitment to less "spin" in government – and indeed signs of a less frenetic style of politics. It remains to be seen whether fresh political leadership can fundamentally change the direction of penal politics in the 21st century, or whether there are overwhelming structural pressures towards penal populism.

Notes

1   Downes and Morgan (1997) regard the 1970s as a watershed decade. However, neither the 1970s nor the 1980s saw the relentlessness of competition between politicians in "out-toughing" each other that emerged later.

2   A generous interpretation would be that populist policies in this arena were seen as a small price to pay for gaining and retaining the opportunity to make real gains in other more important areas of social policy – in other words, a case of "noble cause populism".

3   Home Office Press Release, November 2004.

4   We certainly do not wish to make light of the tragedies that followed incompetent probation supervision. But there is a political reluctance to accept that the supervision of offenders on release from prison can *never* control all risks.

5   <www.crimeinfo.org>.

References

Allen, R (2002). There Must be Some Way of Dealing with Kids: Young Offenders, Public Attitudes and Policy Change. *Youth Justice* 2(1): 3.

Allen, R (2003). Attitudes to Punishment: Values, Beliefs and Political Allegiance. *Criminal Justice Matters* No 52.

Ashworth, A and Hough, M (1996). Sentencing and the Climate of Opinion. *Criminal Law Review*: 761.

Blair, T (2006). Letter from the Prime Minister to the new Home Secretary, John Reid, <http:// www.homeoffice.gov.uk/about-us/news/pm-letter-home-sec-150506?version=2>.

Bridges, A (2006). *An Independent Review of a Serious Further Offence case: Damien Hanson & Elliot White*. London: HM Inspectorate of Probation.

Carter, P (2003). *Managing Offenders, Reducing Crime*. London: Prime Minister's Strategy Unit.

Coulsfield, Lord (2004). *Crime Courts and Confidence*. London: Esmée Fairbairn Foundation.

Department for Constitutional Affairs (2007). *Voting Rights of Convicted Prisoners Detained within the United Kingdom*. London: Department for Constitutional Affairs, <http://www. dca.gov.uk/consult/voting-rights/cp2906.pdf>.

Downes, D and Morgan, R (1997). No Turning Back: The Politics of Law and Order into the Millennium. In M Maguire, R Morgan and R Reiner (eds), *The Oxford Handbook of Criminology*. 4th ed, Oxford: Oxford University Press.

Esmée Fairbairn Foundation (2004). *Rethinking Crime and Punishment: The Report*. London: Esmée Fairbairn Foundation.

Giddens, A (1990). *The Consequences of Modernity*. Cambridge: Polity Press.

Giddens, A (1991). *Modernity and Self-identity*. Cambridge: Polity Press.

Home Office (2001). *Making Punishment Work: Report of a review of the sentencing framework for England and Wales* ("The Halliday Report"). London: Home Office.

Home Office (2005). *Respect Action Plan*. London: Home Office, <http://www.homeoffice. gov.uk/documents/respect-action-plan?view=Binary>.

Home Office (2006). *A 5-year Strategy for Protecting the Public and Reducing Re-Offending*. London: Home Office.

Hough, M et al (2003). *The Decision to Imprison*. London: Prison Reform Trust.

Prime Minister's Strategy Unit (2007). *Building on Progress: Security Crime and Justice*. London: HMSO.

Social Exclusion Unit (2001). *Reducing Re-Offending by ex Prisoners*. London: HMSO.

Tyler, TR and Huo, YJ (2003). *Trust in the Law: Encouraging Public Cooperation with the Police and Courts*. New York: Russell-Sage Foundation.

Index

advising the Attorney-General, 161-162
appellate guidance, New Zealand,
    182-183
Auld, Lord Justice, 20, 46, 61
Auld Report *see* Report of the Review
    of Criminal Courts of England
    and Wales
Australia, federal sentencing council *see*
    federal sentencing council, Australia
Australian Institute of Criminology
    survey, findings, 76
Australian Law Reform Commission,
    126
    federal sentencing council, Australia
        200-203
    Same Crime, Same Time: Sentencing
        of Federal Offenders report, 126-
        127, 200
Australian Survey of Social Attitudes,
    findings, 76-77

Canadian Sentencing Commission, 21
"capacity constraint", 91
capital punishment *see* death penalty
Centre Against Sexual Assault,
    167-168, 175
citizen juries *see* juries
community attitudes *see* public opinion
community-based sentences, 18, 33
community consultation
    see public consultation
community education
    see public education
community engagement
    see public involvement
community knowledge of
    sentencing, 77-79
community sentences
    see community-based sentences
community values and judicial
    practice, 16-17
conceptions of legitimacy, 24
consultation, 21, 45, 54, 80, 113,
    117-118, 122, 160-161
    see also focus groups

consultation papers, 113-14, 118, 121
councils, government and the
    public, 9-11
Court Administration Authority,
    South Australia, 22
Court of Appeal, English, 112-114,
    116-117, 119-120
Court of Appeal, New Zealand, 185, 189
courts
    crisis of confidence, 45-49, 54-56
    engendering confidence, 51
    gender-based violence, 168-170
    leniency, 69, 75
    New South Wales Sentencing
        Council, 128, 130, 134-136
    populist pressure, 12-24
    public confidence, 20, 22, 172-173
    public opinion, 15-17, 19-24, 26-27
    public sentencing preferences, 75-76
    public understanding, 47
    punishment, 88
    Sentencing Advisory Council,
        Victoria, 150-157, 159, 162
    sentencing and community
        expectations, 46
    suspended sentences, 176
    victims' rights and dignity, 171
Criminal Justice Act 2003 (UK), 228,
    233, 235
criminal justice rights, 34
criminal justice system
    adverse effects of, 151
    guiding principles, 170
    impact on offenders, 80
    imprisonment, 42
    institutionalized sexism in, 170
    jury system, 134
    lack of public understanding, 73-74
    legitimacy of, 12
    media, 13, 74
    men's violence against women, 168
    operation of, 9, 154, 157
    perceived leniency, 69, 72
    problems in, 170
    problems with,
        New Zealand, 11

public confidence, 5-6, 12, 14, 47,
  50, 225, 227-228, 230
public knowledge, 73-74, 157
public opinion, 69, 118, 153
public participation, 68-69, 103, 107
public understanding, 47, 160
punitive, 60
reform of, 32, 47, 72
relations between key players, 13
responses to the public, 20, 25
sentencing reform, 90
shifts in responsibility, 206-207, 219
transparency and accountability, 153
victims, 32, 49, 68, 151, 167
crisis of confidence, 45-62,
  Australia and New Zealand, 48-50
  courts, 45, 55-56
  England and Wales, 46-48
  media, 54, 56-57
  populism, 46, 48-49, 55, 56-61
  potential solutions, 59t
  public consultation, 47-49, 51, 58, 60
  responses to, 46-50
  social and political dimensions, 54-57
crisis of legitimacy
  see crisis of confidence
custodial sentencing, 141-146
custody rates see prison populations

death penalty, 19, 52, 97
deliberative polls
  see polls; public opinion research
democratisation of the news media, 3
democratisation of sentencing policy,
  58-60
development of sentencing policy,
  68-69,149, 158, 161-163
  effectiveness of
    institutionalised public
      participation, 224-238
  formal public participation, 68-69, 81
  institutional mechanisms for public
    involvement, 68, 205-221
  penal populism, 69
  public involvement, 6
  public opinion, 158
  review of, 149
  role of the public, 68
  distribution of authority
    over sentencing, 207-210

political legitimacy, 207
strengths and weaknesses, 209
drivers of sentencing policy and
  public opinion, 225-228
cost and cost effectiveness, 227
penal populism, 226-227

early release, 138-142, 145-146, 151
English sentencing guidelines, 112-123
  Court of Appeal, 112-114,
    116-117, 119-120
  Crime and Disorder Act 1998
    (UK), 112
  Criminal Justice Act 2003 (UK),
    113-114
  formulating guidelines and the role
    of the public, 116-119
  House of Commons Justice
    Committee, 121
  media influence, 121
  political context, 112, 119
  position of the judiciary, 119-120
  Sentencing Advisory Panel
    (UK), 112-122
  Sentencing Guidelines Council
    (UK), 112-122
European Court of Human Rights,
  226-227
evolving role of public opinion, 20-24
expert advice, 79-80

federal sentencing council, Australia,
  200-203
  Australian Law Reform Commission
    recommendations, 202
  establishment of, 200-201
  functions of, 201
  issues and problems, 201-202
feminist judges, 171
feminist services, 168
focus groups, 54, 69, 71-72, 77, 79-81,
  205, 212-213, 216
foreign prisoners, 231-232

gauging public opinion
  see measuring public opinion
gender-based violence, 165-172,
  174-177
  human rights, 167, 172

gender-based violence (*cont*)
   law reform, 168-171
   power of the law, 166-173
   prevention of, 166-167, 172, 176-177
   rehabilitation, 165, 171
   sentencing policy, 165-166
generating informed public judgment
   dissemination of information, 213
   proposals for, 213
globalisation, 35
   effects of, 3
guideline judgments, 112-114, 117, 120,
   129-131, 133, 135-136, 155-156,
   182-183, 186, 189
guilty pleas, 25, 78-79 117-118, 122,
   142

Halliday Report *see* Making Punishment
   Work: Report of a Review of the
   Sentencing Framework for England
   and Wales
Home Office Review of Sentencing
   Report *see* Making Punishment
   Work: Report of a Review of the
   Sentencing Framework for England
   and Wales
Human Rights Act 1998 (UK), 226
human rights and penal policy, 226

impact of public opinion on sentencing
   practice
   individual sentencing decisions, 15-16
   sentencing patterns, 16-17
   sentencing policies, 17-19
imprisonment, 56, 119-120, 151, 153
   see also prison populations
institutionalised public participation
   see public involvement

judges 149-151, 153, 155, 158-159,
   169-170
   access to previous High Court
      decisions, Scotland, 144
   conservatism of, 120
   development of sentencing guidelines,
      New Zealand, 186
   early release, 142
   guidelines and severity of
      sentencing, 120

guidelines, Minnesota, 86-88
guidelines, Scotland, 142
judicial discretion, 55, 62
judicial system, Minnesota, 85
jury directions, 169-170
lay judges, 26, 217, 219
media, 16, 23
public confidence, 213
public opinion, 15-17, 23-27, 135
Sentencing Advisory Council, 112, 115
sentencing authority, 208
sentencing decision within a
   regulatory framework, 208
Sentencing Guidelines Council
   (UK), 114, 118
sentencing guidelines, 119-120
sentencing, pre Guidelines,
   United States, 104
surveys of, 15, 26
United States Sentencing
   Commission, 103, 105, 107-108
judicial discretion, 55, 62, 155, 20, 233
   sentencing guidelines, 216-219
judicial guidance, New Zealand,
   180, 182, 185
judicial independence, 24
judicial officers *see* judiciary
judicial practice and community
   values, 17
judicial registry, 23
Judicial Studies Board, 149-150, 152
judiciary
   accountability, 14
   Advisory Panel on Sentencing in
      Scotland, 144
   balancing interest with the public,
      politicians, and media, 2
   community outreach, 25
   crisis in confidence, 55
   open engagement, 12
   public confidence, 6, 237
   public mood, New Zealand, 11, 189
   public sentencing preferences, 75-76
   sentencing guidelines, 119-120
   surveys, 15
   under increasing public attack, 2
juries, 26, 169
jurors *see* juries
jury system, 134
Justice for All White Paper, 46

lay judges, 217, 219
lay magistrates, 26
lay members, 138, 214-215
legitimation
    blame shifting or policy buffer, 12-13
levels of imprisonment
    see prison populations
"liberal" penal developments, 212
liberal reformers, 55, 58, 60

Making Punishment Work. Report of a
    Review of the Sentencing
    Framework for England and Wales,
    20, 21, 46, 228
Making Sentencing Clearer
    Consultation Paper, 47,
mandatory sentencing, 3, 6, 10, 23, 48,
    54-55
meaning of public participation, 214-216
measuring public opinion, 6-7, 51-54,
    69-81, 131, 145, 150, 152-154,
    158-159, 212
measuring public preferences see
    measuring public opinion
media
    changes in structure, 37
    court judgments, 46
    coverage of the Minnesota Sentencing
        Guideline Commission, 83-85,
        92-93, 95-97
    crisis in confidence, 54, 56-59
    democratisation of, 3, 37-38
    deregulation, 37-39
    judicial leniency, 6, 25, 233-234
    measure of public impact, 146
    misconceptions, 235
    misreporting, 3
    naming and shaming, 23, 232
    negative media coverage, 16-18, 23
    new information technology, 37
    penal populism, 36, 60
    power of scandal, 40-4
    public disenchantment with
        sentencing and sentencers, 27
    sentencing guideline system, 121, 123
    sentencing reform, 61
Minnesota Sentencing Guidelines
    Commission, 83-100
    defining "public", 84

dissemination of information,
    83, 93, 95
Dru Sjodin case, 96-97
evolution of the guidelines, 83, 87,
    92-93
formal roles of public members, 93-94
guideline development and public
    opinion, 89-90
legislative purposes of, 88-89
media coverage, 83-85, 92-93, 95-97
members, 90-94, 96, 99-100
political and social context, 85-86
prescriptive changes to sentencing
    policy, 90-91
public knowledge of sentencing
    issues, 83, 95
public opinion, 83-84, 89-90, 93,
    95-97, 99-100
role of the public in Commission
    meetings, 83, 92-95, 99,
scope and operation of, 84
sentencing laws, 86
Myths and Misconceptions: Public
    Opinion versus Public Judgment
    about Sentencing, 159

naming and shaming, 23, 232
    penalties, 34
national sentencing database, 202
    establishment of, 202
    research function of, 202
negative media coverage, 16, 18
New South Wales Law Reform
    Commission, 22
New South Wales Sentencing Council,
    22, 49, 126-146
    Crimes (Sentencing Procedure) Act
        1999, 126-127, 130-131, 133
    Crimes (Sentencing Procedure)
        Amendment (Standard Minimum
        Sentencing) Act 2002, 126
    Crimes and Courts Legislation
        Amendment Act 2006, 131
    establishment of, 126-127, 130
    functions and operations, 129-134
    members, 128-129
    public education, 130-131
    publications, 128-133, 135-136
    relationship with the courts, 134-135

New Zealand Law Commission, 22, 179
  Sentencing Guidelines and Parole
    Reform report , 179
  recommendations, 179
New Zealand, proposed sentencing
  council *see* proposed sentencing
  council, New Zealand

Office for the Management of
  Federal Offenders, 202
  establishment of, 202
  advice function of, 202
ontological insecurity, 3, 36

parole, 18, 21-22, 25, 31, 34, 39, 42,
    50, 52, 73, 86, 88-90, 97-98
  boards, 42, 55, 68
  policies, 50
penal authority, changes to, 3
"penal firestorm", preconditions for,
    234-235
penal policy in New Zealand, 39-42
penal politics, 234-235
penal populism, 23, 31-42, 46, 48-49,
    57, 59-60, 69, 82
  causes and effects of, 32-38
  drivers of sentencing policy, 225-227
  see also populism
policy buffers, 12-13, 24, 58, 82
policy process, role of Victorian
    public, 149-150
political disenchantment, 35, 38, 205-20
political judgment, 227
politics, public involvement and
    sentencing policy development,
    58-62
polls, 20, 23, 32, 52, 69, 108, 158
  deliberative, 53, 70-72, 205,
    212-213, 216
  media, 69-70
  representative, 72
populism, 55-57, 59, 61
  see also penal populism
populist pressure and courts, 23-24
"populist punitiveness", 3, 69, 205, 212
power of scandal, 39-42
  media, 41
  penal policy in New Zealand, 39-42

principles and purpose of sentencing,
    139-140, 180-181, 193, 228
prison and probation,
  reform, 229
  services, 229
prison conditions, 41-42
  overcrowding, New Zealand, 184
prison, high cost of, 227
prison populations
  controlling growth of, 99
  crisis of confidence, 55
  impact of shifts in sentencing patterns
    in New Zealand, 180, 181
  increases, 3-4, 32, 34, 93, 140
  low rates, 85-86
  media, 17
  monitoring rates of, 153
  monitoring the impact of sentencing
    guidelines on, United States, 220
  persons remanded in custody, 142
  private prisons, 151
  projections, 91, 98
  public opinion, 15-16
  reduction of, 42
  trends in, 157
probation, 230
proposed sentencing council,
    New Zealand, 49-50, 179-190
  functions of, 179
  members, 186
  New Zealand Law Commission
    recommendations, 179
proposed sentencing council,
    South Africa, 191-199
  determining the value of fine units,
    196-197
  development of community penalties,
    197
  education and information, 198
  functions, 195
  guideline judgments, 198
  members, 194-195
  motivation for the establishment
    of, 193-194
  research and publishing, 197
  role of the public opinion, 197
  sentencing guidelines, 195-196, 199
public attitudes
  see public opinion

public confidence, 5-7, 27, 127-129,
133, 135, 142-143
criminal justice system, 225,
227-228, 230
guideline judgments, 213
judges and courts, 205, 213
judiciary, 237
public consultation, 47-49, 51, 58, 60,
131-132, 135-136, 165, 173, 187,
203, 213
public debate
see public consultation
public discussion
see public consultation
public education, 25, 49-50, 54-56, 58,
130-131, 159-160, 163, 166, 174
public engagement see public
involvement
public influence on punishment
policies, 17
public involvement, 24-25, 45, 134, 174
in sentencing institutions, 212-216
institutionalised, 68-69,
sentencing policy, 50, 205-221
sentencing reform, 50-54
strategies for, 50-54
public judgment, 213
public mood, 31, 33, 42, 49
sentencing patterns in New
Zealand, 181
"public opinion",
meaning of the term, 31
public opinion
drivers of sentencing policy, 225-228
evolving role of, 20-24
ill-informed, 235
impact on sentencing law, 3
informed, 131-133, 135, 153, 158-
159, 212
proposed role of, South Africa, 197
punitive, 149
relationship between politics
and development of sentencing
policy, 158
research techniques, 205
sentencing institutions, 212
sentencing policy and practice, 15-27
shift toward greater responsiveness
to, 225
sociological significance of, 31

public opinion and policy development
case study, England and Wales,
228-234
public opinion research 15-19, 23-25,
31-33, 35, 42, 104-105, 107-108,
113, 117-118, 168, 173
see also measuring public opinion
public participation
see public involvement
public protection, 140-143
punishment
capital, 19, 97
courts, 88
crisis of confidence, 54-55
effective, 228
gender-based violence, 13
increases in, 108
interest groups, 219
media, 3, 17, 37, 206, 232, 234
misinformed public, 60
politicians, 221
principles of, 4, 171
public opinion, 16-17, 21, 32-34, 47,
57, 76, 78, 158, 205-206, 212, 221
purposes of, 89-9
quantum of, 179-180, 217
rational administration of, 210
recidivism, 171-172
Sentencing Commission for Scotland
recommendations, 141
severity of, 227
views on, 218-219
young offenders, 201
punishment policies, 17, 19, 21
victims, 16
punitive
criminal justice system, 60, 74
penal policy, 69, 73
public, 69, 73, 75, 79, 81-82, 149, 212
sentencing, 81, 205
sentencing policy, 69
punitive legislation and political
climate, 220
punitiveness, 76
levels of, 73, 75

rape see sexual offences
referendum, New Zealand, 32, 49-50,
57, 180, 189-190
government responses to, 180-181

referendum, New Zealand (*cont*)
  public response to, 189
  results of, 190
rehabilitation, 41, 78, 88-89
relationships
  between public opinion, politics
    and development of sentencing
    policy, 158
  between sentencing institutions and
    legislatures, 210-212
Report of the Review of Criminal Courts
  of England and Wales, 46, 61
research, undertaking, 157-158
Rethinking Crime and Punishment
  project, 46, 236-237
rising crime rates, 23
roundtable/focus group discussions
  see focus groups

Scottish Parliament, 20
Scottish Sentencing Commission *see*
  Sentencing Commission of Scotland
Sensible Sentencing Trust, 39
sentence lengths and media-driven
  public demands, 17
sentence reductions
  see sentencing discount
Sentencing Act 1991 (Vic), 149-150,
  153-155, 157-158, 162
sentencing advisory bodies, 45-49, 54,
  60-62, 126
  establishment of, 1-2, 7-8
  functions of, 8
  members, 22
Sentencing Advisory Council Victoria,
  49, 68, 79-82, 148-163
  as a mechanism for mediation, 173
  consultation strategy, 80-81
  creation of, 153-155
  functions of, 22, 153-162
  guiding principles of, 155
  members, 154
  potential to promote respect and
    equality for women, 165-177
  public opinion research
    methodology, 80-81
  recommendation for, 152-153
  terms of reference, 151, 157

Sentencing Advisory Panel (UK)
  Court of Appeal, 112
  creation of, 46, 112, 119
  Crime and Disorder Act 1998 (UK),
    112
  Criminal Justice Act 2003 (UK),
    113-114
  draft sentencing guidelines, 9
  functions of, 9
  guidelines, 114-115
  judiciary, 119
  members, 68, 112, 160, 214
  public engagement, 216, 235
  public opinion, 21-22, 68
Sentencing Commission of Scotland,
  69, 132, 138-146
  appointed membership, 138
  impact of, 145
  media, 145
  reports, 140-146
  recommendations, 139-146
  remit, 139
  working practices, 139-140
sentencing as a "legal" decision,
  218-219
sentencing commissions, United
  States, 1, 7-8, 69, 83-100,
  103-109, 120, 122
sentencing councils, 2, 126, 132
  emergence of, 2
  functions of, 2
  penal populism, 13-14
sentencing decisions
  impact of public opinion, 15, 19
  regulatory framework, 208-209
  Roe v Wade, 19
sentencing discounts, 25, 29,
  116-117, 122
sentencing grids, 86-87, 97-98, 107
Sentencing Guidelines Council (UK)
  creation of, 46,
  functions of, 9
  guidelines, 11, 113, 186-187
  judiciary, 119
  members, 8, 68, 115, 214
  public engagement, 235
  public opinion, 68
  relations between key players, 237
  sentencing, 233

sentencing guideline systems, 21,
83-100, 113, 118-120, 121
sentencing guidelines
adherence or departure from, 220
Advisory Panel on Sentencing,
Scotland, 144
authority to develop, 210-211
English, public and political context,
112-123
impact on correctional budgets, 220
impact on prison populations, 220
judges, 119-120
judicial body, 114
judicial discretion, 216-219
judicial input, New Zealand, 186-187
Judicial Studies Board, 149-150
New Zealand, 185-187
sentencing bodies, 1-2, 5-6, 8-11, 13
Sentencing Guidelines Council (UK),
46, 48, 68, 112-122, 186-187
South Africa, 195-196, 198
United States, 21, 83-100, 103-109
Victorian Sentencing Review, 150-151
sentencing institutions
development of, 207
effective sentencing policy, 219
judicial discretion and public
participation, 216-218
lay members, 214-215
legitimating and the management of
correctional resources, 219-220
measuring the effectiveness of,
220-221
new generation of, 206
public involvement, 235
public opinion and participation,
212-216
public understanding of
sentencing, 236
sentencing law
gender-based violence, 166-170
prevention of gender-based violence,
170-171
structure of, Minnesota, 84, 86, 93
sentencing patterns
impact of public opinion, 16-17
shifts in, New Zealand, 181
sentencing policy
accountable and transparent, 45,
58, 59

case study, England and Wales
democratisation of, 58
drivers of, 225-228
gender-based violence, 165-166
impact of public opinion, 17-19
public participation, 45-47, 50-54,
58-62, 205
see also development of
sentencing policy
sentencing policy and practice,
public opinion, 15-27
sentencing policy shifts, 18-19
sentencing reform, 10, 20, 45-46, 50,
54, 61, 85, 89-90, 103, 105
sentencing reform, England and Wales,
228-229, 233
sentencing reform, New Zealand,
179-190
background to, 180-181
options for, 185-189
public participation, 50-54
sentencing reform, South Africa,
191-199
sentencing structure, New Zealand
consistency of, lack of, 183
current problems, 182-185
inadequate judicial guidance, 182-183
issues of cost effectiveness, 184-185
legislative input, lack of, 182
numerical guidance,185
sentence severity levels,
unpredictability of, 184
transparency, lack of, 183-184
sentencing system, South Africa
early release, 192-193
imprisonment alternatives, 192
inconsistency in sentences, 193
levels of punishment, 192
treatment of offenders, 192
sentencing trends in New Zealand, 181
effects on prison population, 181
serious offenders, 162
sex offenders, 41, 87, 94, 96-98, 100,
162, 168, 170-171, 173, 175, 177
newspaper articles, 96
notification, 69
proposed sentencing grid, 87, 98
registration, 23, 98
sentencing, 95, 97-98

sexual offences, 165, 167-171, 174
South Africa, proposed sentencing
    council *see* proposed sentencing
    council, South Africa
South African Law (Reform)
    Commission
    research methods, 191-192
    Sentencing (A New Sentencing
    Framework) Report, 191
    Sentencing Framework Bill, 191,
    193-194, 199
    sentencing reform proposals, 191,
    193-199
statistical information, 156-157
submissions, 54, 80
supervision in the community, 230-231
surveying *see* surveys
surveys, 173, 216
    design of, 51-52
    judges, 5, 15-16, 75
    media, 173
    methods, 69-72, 81, 221
    offenders, 80, 160
    public confidence, 213
    public opinion, 21-23, 27, 32, 36,
    32-36, 46, 54, 56, 72-74, 75-79,
    150, 158, 212
    violence against women, 168
survivors *see* victims
suspended sentences, 154, 161
symbolic function of sentencing,
    209-210

"the new punitiveness" *see* penal
    populism

United States Sentencing Commission,
    21, 103-109, 152
    failures of, 103-05

Federal Sentencing Guidelines,
    103-108
    functions of, 103
    idea of, 103-05
    impact on judges, 107
    members, 104-106
    public opinion, 104-105, 107-108
    public participation, 103, 107, 109
    Sentencing Reform Act 1984, 21,
    103-108

victim and offender support
    services, 159
victim impact statements, 26, 68, 148-150
victim rights movement, 68, 148, 172
victims, 25-26, 148, 150-151, 155,
    157, 159, 161
    advocates, 80, 151, 165-166
    groups, 71, 77, 152, 154, 159-160
    input into sentencing, 25-26
    media, 37-38
    of crime, 34, 148, 154, 159-161
    of gender-based violence, 165-166
    of sexual assault, 162, 168-169
    representatives, 71, 148, 154, 160
victims' movement
    see victim rights movement
Victorian Association for the Care and
    Resettlement of Offenders, 80
Victorian Community Council
    Against Violence, 77-79, 150
Victorian Law Reform Commission, 151,
    157-158, 161, 165, 168-169, 173
Victorian Sentencing Advisory Council
    see Sentencing Advisory Council
    Victoria
Victorian Sentencing Committee,
    149, 155
Victorian Sentencing Review 2002,
    150-151